ELIZABETHANS

Also by Andrew Marr

Non-fiction
The Battle for Scotland
The Day Britain Died
My Trade: A Short History of Journalism
A History of Modern Britain
The Making of Modern Britain
The Diamond Queen
A History of the World
A Short Book about Drawing
We British: The Poetry of a People
A Short Book about Painting

Fiction
Head of State
Children of the Master

ELIZABETHANS

How Modern Britain Was Forged

ANDREW MARR

WILLIAM
COLLINS

William Collins
An imprint of HarperCollins*Publishers*
1 London Bridge Street
London SE1 9GF

WilliamCollinsBooks.com

First published in Great Britain in 2020 by William Collins

1

Extract from Jan Morris's *Conundrum* (Faber & Faber Ltd)
used with the kind permission of the publisher
Extract from 'Monster' by Robin Morgan from *Monster: Poems* (Random House and
Vintage Press, 1971). All rights reserved. Reprinted with permission of the author.

A catalogue record for this book is available from the British Library

ISBN 978-0-00-829840-1 (hardback)
ISBN 978-0-00-829841-8 (trade paperback)

Typeset in Adobe Garamond Pro by Palimpsest Book Production Ltd, Falkirk, Stirlingshire
Printed and bound in Great Britain by CPI Group (UK) Ltd, Croydon CR0 4YY

In memory of William Donald Marr, 1930–2020,
a wonderful father and a fine Elizabethan.

Contents

Introduction:

THE CROWN AND THE CORONA

On the evening of 5 April 2020, speaking at Windsor Castle and attended by a single BBC cameraman hidden behind protective clothing, Queen Elizabeth II gave the fourth televised address of her reign outside her annual Christmas messages. She was talking to the British about coronavirus, as deaths soared and most of her subjects chafed indoors under tight government restrictions. Her subject was patriotism. As she was speaking, her Prime Minister, Boris Johnson, was being taken to St Thomas's Hospital in London, where he would be placed briefly in intensive care, as his coronavirus symptoms worsened.

The Queen was too subtle to compare the coronavirus crisis directly with wartime conditions. Indeed, she emphasized the difference: 'This time we join with all nations across the globe in a common endeavour using the great advances of science and our instinctive compassion to heal.' However, the separation of family made necessary by social distancing and the general lockdown in homes made her, she said, think back to the broadcast she had made during the Second World War to the evacuee children.

The Queen repeated the government's key messages about staying at home and supporting the NHS – she had not spent her life as head of state for nothing – before making her central patriotic appeal.

> In the years to come everyone will be able to take pride in how they responded to this challenge. And those who come after us will say, the Britons of this generation were as strong as any; that the attributes of self-discipline, of quiet good-humoured resolve and of fellow feeling, still characterize this country. The pride in who we are is not part of our past. It defines our present and future.

This is without doubt how most British people would like to think of themselves. The Queen went on to mention specifically the then regular 8 p.m. Thursday applause for NHS and key workers, which would be 'remembered as an expression of our national spirit'.

'Our national spirit' is quite close to being the subject of this book. Exceptionalism – how different are we? – is the staple question of all national history. Yet, in modern circumstances and particularly during a global pandemic, it may be the wrong question.

Most developed human societies are moving in roughly the same direction when it comes to their economies, attitudes to fairness and rights, and their failures, particularly over the environment. There are renegade countries and dissenting civilizations, such as Hungary, Russia and China – far more so than when the 'end of history' was vaingloriously proclaimed after the collapse of the Soviet Union in 1991. But among liberal democracies today's Elizabethan Britain is broadly in the mainstream. After Brexit, it is still (much) more like other European cultures than unlike.

So let us turn to that Thursday applause, both origin and object. It should not be too much of a surprise that inspiration came not from a native Briton but from Annemarie Plas, a thirty-six-year-old Dutch software saleswoman and yoga teacher, who got the idea from friends in the Netherlands. Her message, sent by a variety of social media, read: 'Please join us on 26th March at 8pm for a big applause (from front doors, garden, balcony, windows, living rooms, etc) to show all the nurses, doctors, GPs, and carers our appreciation for their ongoing hard work and fight against the virus.'

All over Britain, huge numbers of people heeded her call. Soon, among those standing on their doorsteps or in their houses to clap were many members of the Queen's family, the Prime Minister and actors such as Daniel Craig. Television channels made a point of stopping normal programming to record it.

It was heartwarming and proper, and made most British people feel better. But it wasn't a specifically British thing. Locked-down individuals and families in virus-hit Lombardy, in southern Italy and in Spain had done similar things – as, of course, had the Dutch.

Then there are the identities of those who were being applauded. As the *New York Times* reported three days after the Queen's address, of the first eight doctors who died in Britain of coronavirus while treating it, all were immigrants here. Lists of those who had died began to appear in newspapers. One, in the *Daily Telegraph*, at around the time of the Queen's address, included the following names: Abdul Mabud Chowdhury, a fifty-three-year-old Muslim consultant virologist working in Romford Essex, who had recently warned the government about the lack of personal protection equipment in hospitals; Edmond Adedeji, sixty-two, working in Swindon; Fayez Ayache, seventy-six, who had migrated from Syria, working in Ipswich; Alice Kit Tak Ong, a seventy-year-old nurse from Hong Kong, working in the Royal Free Hospital in North London; Jitendra Rathod, fifty-eight, a heart surgeon working at the University Hospital of Wales in Cardiff; Alfa Saadu, from Nigeria, still working at sixty-eight in the Whittington Hospital North London; and Adil El Tayar, a sixty-three-year-old Sudanese doctor working in Middlesex. The *New York Times* listed the countries from which the first dead had come as being India, Nigeria, Pakistan, Sri Lanka and Sudan.

Again, anyone familiar with modern Britain would be unsurprised by that list. The British National Health Service has long relied on doctors and nurses who have migrated here from poorer countries. European medical staff, at the beginning of the epidemic, may well have gone back to their own health services to help; and sadly it is not a surprise that immigrant doctors were on the front line doing some of the most dangerous jobs when it struck. But had something similar happened in the early years of the Queen's reign, then the surnames of the dead doctors would have been more likely to read Wilkins, Smith, Walker, McDonald, Davies, Jones.

When we talk about the experience of the British in 2020, we're talking about a different people compared to when we talk about the experience of the British in, say, 1950. Contemporary Britain is unusual in European terms in its porousness to migration from non-European parts of the world, for obvious historical reasons. The reader may argue that the essence of modern Britishness is in neither surnames nor radically different behaviour, but in subtler matters: taste in food and drink, humour, propensity to queue or, in the Queen's words, self-discipline and quiet good-humoured resolve.

There is a lot in that. But it is easily overdone. As lockdowns took place first of all in Italy, France and Spain, the online jokes, cod videos and memes showed that Gallic, Iberian and Lombard humour weren't much different from British – and just as funny. They felt, reacted and joked just like us. They were as self-disciplined and grumbled just as much. They revered, and applauded, their doctors and nurses just as we did.

One area in which the British response to coronavirus did seem remarkable was when the government asked for volunteers to aid the NHS, deliver food and medicines to the most vulnerable and help keep basic services running. Within a few days 750,000 people had signed up to help, more than three times ministers' original target. Here, if anywhere, was a whiff of the exceptional. Yet all across France the 'solidaires' were doing much the same thing. In the United States, local volunteering networks had sprung up in Minnesota and spread a system of mutual aid from state to state. In Italy, when the government asked for volunteer doctors for the front line, more than 8,000 immediately signed up, while non-medical citizens volunteered to help in other ways through the Protezione Civile and by distributing food. Human nature is pretty much the same the world over. A border-ignoring pandemic seems to make it more so.

The year of the pandemic raised more interesting issues than whether countries were culturally very different. Across Britain, it brought people more together for a common purpose. For many of us it was the first time in which the demands of community and common purpose clearly outstripped the daily prodding for profit and self-advancement. People did start to look to their neighbours, buying and delivering food to the vulnerable, performing innumerable acts of kindness. More important than who the British were exactly in 2020 was perhaps how they thought about themselves and their country. This bigger picture did include some kind of revived patriotism, to which the Queen was speaking.

But there were other storm clouds ahead. The coronavirus lockdown seemed likely to provoke a major recession. As this book was completed during the lockdown, it is hard yet to be sure. Perhaps Britain will bounce back economically more quickly and more vigorously than the current economic consensus expects. But vast numbers of businesses suddenly found their income drying up; and a government spending spree to try to support them would eventually, everybody knew, have to be repaid. Inside the Treasury, the mood was bleak. Within a month of the lockdown, 2 million people had already lost their jobs. One former Bank of England adviser, David Blanchflower, predicted that unemployment could hit more than 6 million and the experience would be worse than the Great Depression of the 1930s.

Whether that proves to be the case or not, the year of coronavirus provoked questions about equality, fairness and all-in-it-togetherness. More of those on the front line who were infected came from minority communities. Then there was the division during the lockdown between those living in the gardenless apartments or tower blocks, observing Britain through windows only, and the more affluent with gardens or even second homes. There was a divide between the older, on whose behalf the lockdown was being implemented, and younger Britons losing their jobs, social lives and hopes for the future. There was a division between the naturally obedient, carefully observing government advice and reporting on errant neighbours, and the disobedient, disinclined to believe 'experts' and ready to believe conspiracy theories flying around online. Finally, there was the division between those who observed the epidemic from a distance – if infected, barely noticing the fact – and those who died, or whose relatives and loved ones did. The gap between those who experienced coronavirus essentially as a public-policy news story and those ripped in pieces by it – a misery scale running from inconvenience to screaming disaster – was the biggest inequality of all.

Many of those issues of class, fairness, conformity, immigration and culture are at the centre of this book. Alongside those, it investigates attitudes to work, gender, sexuality and 'abroad'. To do so, I have been looking at individual lives, the Elizabethans of the title. It has been a genuinely painful process of selection. There are many eminent Britons, from the trade unionist Jack Jones to the artist Barbara Hepworth or the newspaper editor Paul Dacre, who deserved space but haven't received it. Sometimes that is because they are very well known and have already been well described elsewhere or it is because they have featured in another book I have written. More often, it is simply because I found somebody different to do the same job in this particular history of attitudes. Inevitably, the selection is partial, random and personal, but I hope readers will find it an interesting and thought-provoking slant on contemporary Britain.

The book covers the period between the Coronation of Queen Elizabeth II and 2020, when she was ninety-four. The reign of a monarch is an unusual measurement of time. Even for historians, centuries, decades or individual years have become more popular. But when a monarch has been on the throne for a long time, as in the case of Queen Elizabeth II, then that measurement, a reign's-length, becomes more useful than quirky. The period from 1952 to today is, for most British people, at least as long as their adult consciousness of being alive. It's a lifetime's-worth. So to ask the questions – What were we like then? How different are we today? And how did *that* Britain become *this* Britain? – makes sense.

Most histories of this period focus heavily on the established systems of power, the well-known critical turning points – Suez, the arrival in power of Margaret Thatcher – and changes in consumer behaviour, from holidays to cars. This one is slightly different. I have called it *Elizabethans* for two reasons. First, it invites us to think of ourselves as people in history, just as much part of our period as the late Tudors were. Yes, we are the second-time-around Elizabethans, or the 'new Elizabethans', but we won't be new for very long. We will be, ourselves, part of history quite soon. Second, the plural is key: I want to tell the story of change through the histories of the individual people.

Why? Social change can seem an abstract concept, as if we all move together in a mass or block. Textbook sociology suggests that we become less religious together, we become more accepting of sexual minorities together and so on, a swooping, twisting, thickening murmuration of attitudinal starlings moving through human history. That's an unfair caricature, perhaps, but there's an element of truth in it. And yet every shift in thinking or behaviour is led, then shaped and then confirmed by individual lives, fundamentally solitary experiences. In short, the single bird turns first. Brave or reckless pioneers thrust ahead; other individuals may resist and fight back. Very often the pioneers make mistakes and are promptly outstripped and forgotten. But sometimes they are veering, only half consciously, in the direction the rest of the flock will then follow. Such people, often good, sometimes bad, are the subject of this book.

For instance, we live at a time when women are trying to negotiate lives in which they are both sexual actors and yet also in control of their own destinies. The 'It Girl' who appears on front covers and reality TV shows, and is knowingly complicit in her own Instagram brand, has become, for better or worse, a kind of role model. Where did *that* start? For me, it was right at the beginning of the Queen's reign with the story of that remarkable, knowing and very tough cookie Diana Dors. But if hers seems too self-congratulatory a story, what about somebody else, in many ways like her (and for a time her friend), Ruth Ellis, the last woman to be hanged in Britain? Together, they tell a story of some of the perils and opportunities for women in the 1950s.

Or take the great arguments about the shape of the economy and society in the 1970s, between socialists and Conservatives. These tend to be examined through the prism of general election results and the views of the dominant Westminster leaders – what Heath thought, what Wilson did. But unless you understand how Jimmy Reid, the charismatic communist who led the Upper Clyde Shipbuilders' work-in, or Jayaben Desai at Grunwick really thought and how they hoped things would turn out, then you are missing a crucial perspective.

What I have been trying to capture here is often subtle. We all understand the big, visible changes. Hats disappear. Airports become gigantic as millions fly on foreign holidays or take regular business trips abroad. The number of British people with brown or black skins increases fast. Churches empty. Mosques spring up. All of these things are a significant part of our story and must be recorded.

If we really want to know how we have changed as a people however, we should dig a little deeper. At some point in the late 1950s and early 1960s, for instance, the British seem to become cheekier, even rebellious. An insolent contempt for established authority begins to creep in. Why? Is it the hangover of irritation about uniformed dolts making bad decisions during the Second World War? That was certainly Spike Milligan's motivation. But was something else going on? That is worth looking at.

Then there is patriotism in itself. Back then, there did seem to be a clearer understanding of what it meant to be British. It had much to do with swankier, more preening institutions, with bigger flags and brighter brands – the monarchy, the armed forces, the still-present if subsiding Empire. But, under all that, we just felt unEuropean. We felt ourselves to be more private, less exhibitionist than the continentals. We were, and we proudly acknowledged it, more class-conscious. We read and judged one another via minuscule gradations of vowel sound and language, impenetrable to outsiders. Our television dramas and our popular novels are about little else. Compared to coarse Germanic guffaws or the regrettable lewdness of the French, we felt our sense of humour was finer, flint-dry. Our art, from Piper to Britten, was sparer and leaner. Our ritual year was shaped by a Church very different from continental Lutheranism or southern Catholicism. These things were true for the English middle classes: were they true, at all, for working-class Britons, for the Scots, for the Welsh and so on? And if they were not, was there really such a thing as 'the British people'?

These are hard questions, and I can't pretend in what follows to have convincingly answered all of them. If I have an end point, it is to ask what it means to be British today. Whom do we admire? Whom do we applaud? Whom do we especially dislike? And here one unmistakable, tousled, deeply divisive and noisy figure elbows his way as ever to the front of the queue. Fresh from his brief confrontation with mortality at St Thomas's Hospital, Boris Johnson grabs us by the lapels and demands to be inspected.

Here is a man born of intellectual and liberal-minded parents, whose early years tell us much about the Britain of the 1960s. At the time when we were, however reluctantly, accepting American leadership of the world, Boris Johnson was born in New York and spent some time being brought up in Connecticut while his father was working for the World Bank. For most of his adult life he kept an American passport and has publicly speculated about emigrating to the US. But his Americanism goes deeper than citizenship rights. His instinctive belief that everything will get better, a bouncy, untethered optimism, is a far more American than an English trait. Although Boris Johnson is no Donald Trump, Trump recognized a fellow spirit.

'Make America Great Again' is not so different from the 'unleash Britain' rhetoric of Prime Minister Johnson. Like Churchill, there is a hazily American tinge to Johnson. And yet, in his enthusiasm for classical literature, in his command of French and, as Mayor of London, in his embracing of modern European liberalism, Johnson could also seem a most unAmerican politician. His father Stanley came from an eminent diplomatic Turkish family – although he was born in Cornwall, his father was Osman Kemal, and he was registered at birth as Osman Ali Wilfred Kemal. In 1973, Stanley Johnson moved to the European Commission. Boris was then brought up in Brussels, mingling in the multinational educational soup of bureaucratic exiles. Later, he would make his name at the *Daily Telegraph* by amusingly if inaccurately lampooning EU directives and senior figures; but in 2016, as he agonized about what to do in the EU referendum, his family were convinced that his fundamental pro-European instinct would win out. Britain's ambiguous love–hate relationship with the continent is played out in Johnson's personality; it forms a major theme in this book.

Another theme will be British family life. Boris Johnson's mother was an artist, Charlotte Johnson Wahl, who came from a liberal English, American and Russian-Jewish family. When Johnson was young, she suffered a nervous breakdown. She divorced his father in 1979. Later she told a BBC interviewer she thought Johnson's oft-described childhood ambition to be 'World King' was a reaction to that experience, 'a wish to make himself unhurtable, invincible, somehow safe from the pains of life – the pains of your mother disappearing for eight months, the pains of your parents splitting up'. Conservative moralists who see infidelity and family break-up in the 1960s at the root of many current problems could pull up Johnson's childhood as an example.

He and his three siblings formed a tough, tight 'us against the world' team, albeit riven by personal rivalries. Johnson went to Eton on a scholarship, learning to make potentially threatening boys laugh and causing staff to despair at his reluctance to follow the rules. His housemaster wrote: 'I think he honestly believes it is churlish of us not to regard him as an exception, one who should be free of the network of obligation which binds everyone else.' Many acquaintances and colleagues would echo that.

Does it matter, in the wider scheme of things, that Boris Johnson was educated at Eton? In some ways, not very much. A great swathe of the British political class is privately educated in one way or another – and that even included Johnson's 2019 socialist opponent Jeremy Corbyn. And wherever he acquired it, Johnson certainly had the common touch. From his two elections as London Mayor through to the 2016 referendum and 2019 general election, his bluff directness meant many working-class voters simply didn't see him as an alien toff.

But on a wider perspective Johnson's Eton upbringing matters a lot. Despite all the social reforms in Britain during the post-war period, our retention of a deeply divided educational system stands out as marking the modern country. Around 7 per cent of British children are expensively educated in private schools. That is a relatively small number, but they then tend to sashay into plum jobs, partly through the social networks based on those schools. Politics, the Army, the civil service, the media, business and the City, all tell the same story.

As with so many of the political elite, Johnson then went on to Balliol College, Oxford (which will also feature later in this book) where he mingled with among others a predecessor as Prime Minister, David Cameron, and other Tory colleagues and rivals such as Michael Gove and Jeremy Hunt. Long ago, after the prime ministership of another Old Etonian, Harold Macmillan, the senior Tory politician R. A. Butler suggested that the party was run by a 'Magic Circle' of Eton friends, which visited much damage upon the party's democratic reputation. But in some ways Balliol College in particular and Oxford in general provide further tight circles of the clever and privileged. The notorious photograph of Boris Johnson and other members of the restaurant-smashing Bullingdon Club, including his rival and one-time boss David Cameron, had something of the same effect in the twenty-first century as the Magic Circle had in the 1960s. None of this defines Boris Johnson. But it tells us a lot about the sticky persistence of an exclusive class divide in modern Britain.

However, it is the final part of Boris Johnson's sentimental education that may be the most important. He became a journalist. Throughout the age of parliamentary democracy in Britain, journalism and politics have been deeply intertwined. Many of the great Victorian statesmen formed close friendships with newspaper editors. Some even wrote for the press and, although this was looked down on, by the time Winston Churchill embarked on his career at the very end of the nineteenth century, a bit of journalism on the side was becoming accepted as a way of subsidizing unpaid politics. Since then, journalism has grown in influence, almost beginning to rival the law as a background occupation. As an American columnist once reflected, in the old days journalists had waited at the gates to watch politicians going in to dine: 'Then we began to dine with them. And then we dined on them.'

In London, Michael Gove was a journalist before he went into politics. So was the Scottish Tory leader Ruth Davidson. Margaret Thatcher's Chancellor Nigel Lawson was a journalist. On the Labour side, this was likewise true of the shadow Chancellor Ed Balls and his wife, the powerful shadow minister Yvette Cooper, and many more. Boris Johnson, thanks to a personal connection, landed a job on *The Times* until he was caught making up a quote and sacked. He moved briskly on to the *Daily Telegraph*, first as a leader writer and then, crucially, as its Brussels correspondent, where from 1989 to 1994 he became a pungent and highly criticized opponent of the EU hierarchy.

From the 1990s to the first decades of the new century, Johnson's journalism made him famous. He used his deep reserves of education and native wit to make similes skip and metaphors turn cartwheels. He demonstrated a witty, salty, addictive and provocative style that made editors desperate for his copy – admittedly partly because he often filed so late. Johnson himself said his journalism gave him a 'weird' sense of power and influence inside the Conservative family. Margaret Thatcher was a fan. But he wasn't a journalist who stood instinctively with other journalists. He deeply angered many when a recording emerged in 1995 in which he agreed to pass the address of an investigative reporter to a friend of his, Darius Guppy, who wanted to have him beaten up for probing into his criminal behaviour. In due course, Johnson became an editor himself, of the *Spectator*. By then he had become a staple on popular TV news channels and chat shows, perfecting the cheerfully dishevelled appearance behind which he has always hidden his ambition.

In a broader account of modern Britain, does any of this matter? It does, because contemporary British journalism tells us much about the strengths and weaknesses of contemporary British culture. Its strengths – let's start with those – are inherently democratic and conversational. As we would expect from a culture which extols the liberal arts over science and engineering, British newspapers – and on rare occasions British broadcasting – produce some of the strongest and most vivid writing anywhere. Clever, voluble, fluent people trade controversies daily. Following Orwell, polemical writers from the left and from the right hone and sharpen their philosophical disagreements into headlines and phrases with the cutting power of Neolithic hand axes. Millions of British people feel more connected to political arguments because of the daily hard work and anti-bullshit thinking done by much maligned journalists.

But admiration of its raucous verbal forum, essential to popular democracy, is as far as it goes. British journalism is notoriously innumerate. It prioritizes the shock factor and polarized arguments over sophistication and nuance. The cheaper newspapers have a disgraceful history of bending the truth in order to score a political point, to indulge in prurience or even just to make a joke. Deadlines and speed of writing are admired over strict accuracy; presentation wins awards which footnotes never do. Too few journalists have any deep understanding of the sciences, medicine or engineering. Detailed inquiry reports and official documents, crammed with useful and enlightening information, languish unread. British journalism is, in short, a slapdash preparation for serious politics. And when Boris Johnson, remarking that 'They don't put up statues to journalists,' moved into politics, he brought some of that slapdash quality with him.

Again, perhaps, so what? His direct, provocative way with words and his clowning – though his schtick always seemed to this writer more that of an opinionated landlord in a chaotic popular pub than a circus act – brought him the chuckling adulation of the Conservative Party and millions of voters who never thought of themselves as natural Tories. 'Boris' won; and who can argue with winning?

Electorally, he had a lot in common with his political hero

Winston Churchill, still the dominant figure at the beginning of the Queen's reign. They both produced an instantly recognizable physical caricature – wild blonde hair or cigars, gurning or growling. Both used short, memorable phrases to define themselves. Both were adept at employing humour to defuse embarrassment and unbalance opponents. Both were adored by some but loathed by others. Both were compulsive and speedy writers of quotable prose. Both ended up known almost universally by their first names. What's not to like?

Historians will note that the great successes based on Boris Johnson's obvious strengths as a campaigner and national figure – the 2016 Leave campaign and the 2019 general election that completed it – were immediately followed by the coronavirus crisis, which demanded very different qualities both from Johnson and from the British state. This is being written in the middle of things, before the lockdown has ended. It is a bit like trying to produce the verdict on a rugby match (Johnson is a rugby fan) while the game is still going on, a greased ball shooting through slippery hands in heavy rainfall. Nevertheless, the statistics seemed to show that the countries coping best were ones whose political managers had instantly followed scientific advice and ignored populist hostility to new regulations and whose health systems were based on years of patient investment and on carefully accumulated and stored kits for testing and intensive-care ventilation. Britain was not one of these countries.

Johnson, in characteristic style, had begun with boosterish promises that all would be well, and assuring people that he for one would continue to shake hands. His initial instincts were all against forcing people to stay in their own homes, closing pubs and the rest of it. In 1911 Arnold Bennett published a short novel, *The Card*, whose hero, the rising politician and chancer 'Denry' Machin, is said to stand for 'the great cause of cheering us all up'. That's Boris Johnson. Yet nothing could be further from cheering than the news he was now bringing Britain. As things became graver, he became graver. After being admitted to the intensive care unit at St Thomas's Hospital, where his very survival hung in the balance all through one long day and night, he gave an eloquent and deeply moving tribute to the National Health Service.

There was no doubt now about just how serious coronavirus could be. But his beloved NHS was still struggling to acquire enough protective equipment. Johnson's government had been unable to conduct the kind of extensive testing programmes that had allowed South Korea, Germany and Denmark, for instance, to limit the viral spread and fatalities.

Was there something in all this, that spoke to the weaknesses of the British state and economy, and more generally of its political culture? The Elizabethans were being tested at home; but their government was being tested also by international comparison. Relative death rates are a clear, hard measure of individual national administrations' success in dealing with a common viral threat. As I say, this is a report being written in the thick of things. Elizabethan Britain may yet come out of this nightmare well. Ministers were not slow to reassure us that we had the very best scientists and health system in the world. But did we have the best industrial pharmaceutical capacity; the best levels of investment; the most robust preparation? Or had we become a little slack, not quite serious enough, even a little slapdash as a country?

In the early summer of 2020, what was perhaps most remarkable in politics was that the great division which had riven Britain apart even before the referendum of 2016 now seemed to belong to a different century. Under a common threat, the bitter tribal hostility between pro-Brexit Leavers, convinced that the country was regaining its glorious independence at last, and defeated, bitter Remainers, who saw in all of this only xenophobia, nostalgia and retreat, was fading as fast as old election posters left out in the sun. Boris Johnson had arrived in office determined, he said, to heal.

And he had many of the strengths a healer would need. When he emerged from hospital himself, he made a point of particularly thanking two nurses who had stood by his bed all night during the darkest time – Luis Pitarma, a senior staff nurse from Aveiro in Portugal, and Jenny McGee from Invercargill, New Zealand. The dependence of the NHS, like the rest of Britain, on migrants from the EU as well as from other countries around the world, hardly needed to be spelt out.

Many questions about the quality of modern Elizabethan life and politics, brought into sharp focus by coronavirus, lie behind what follows in this book. Here you will find scientists and inventors who often don't make it into general histories of the period; industrialists who messed things up or valiantly fought through; the shapers and makers of our modern cult of individualism, and those who battled them every inch of the way. William Langland, the great English medieval poet, described a vision he had in the Malvern Hills as showing 'a fair field full of folk'. This, I hope, is something similar.

Part One

ELIZABETHANS AT HOME

1

MOUNTAINS TO CLIMB

Tuesday 2 June 1953: Coronation Day, and with London *en fête* for the twenty-five-year-old Queen, there was only one story in town. Obvious – but untrue. *The Times* newspaper had a scoop of its own, though this was long before it would do anything so vulgar as to put it on the advertisement-crammed front page. A British team of climbers had conquered Everest and it alone had the story. Never mind that in this context 'British' meant a Tibetan and a New Zealander; like the Coronation, this was a moment of imperial pride. It was also a great moment for *The Times*. But why had that newspaper beaten all its rivals, not just in Britain but around the world? The answer tells us a lot about how we misremember the real character of this second Elizabethan age – the radical variousness, the unexpectedness, of the Queen's subjects.

This story starts on the previous Friday, 29 May 1953. Two men, hacking through the snow, made it to the top of the world's highest mountain. One was a tall Kiwi beekeeper with a huge, goofy smile. Edmund Hillary, despite strong pacifist instincts, had served during the war with the flying boats of the Royal New Zealand Air Force. He would go on to reach both the North and South Poles. Tenzing Norgay, who had been born in either Tibet or Nepal and who had lived a life of profound physical poverty as a mountain bearer, was a devout Buddhist who had survived several unsuccessful attempts on Mount Everest during the 1930s; he had originally been picked out by previous British expedition leaders partly for his brilliant and enthusing smile.

Reaching the summit of Mount Everest was, in the early 1950s, an extraordinary achievement. Modern technology and accumulated experience have made it much more common now. Then, it required tremendous physical endurance, mental determination and a great deal of raw courage – as well as a lot of luck. The 'race' to the top was a subject of fierce national competition. After a previous failed attempt, the British knew that a French team was next in line to try the following year and, if they failed, a Swiss team the year after that. So all Britain was keeping one eye on this particular attempt. Would they be aware of this crowning mountaineering achievement by the time the new monarch was crowned? Just behind the competition to reach the summit of Everest, there was a second race going on: who would get the news out first?

That was the responsibility of a relatively junior member of the team, waiting at base camp, nearly 18,000 feet up. James Morris was the correspondent of *The Times* of London and he was all too aware of the danger of being scooped. Had he sent the news openly, the information would certainly have been stolen and probably sold to his rivals by wireless operators working between Tibet and Britain. If he had sent it in an obvious code they would have been suspicious and might well have refused to pass it down the line to London. So Morris had agreed with his editors a fake message which contained hidden meanings. 'Snow conditions bad stop advanced base abandoned yesterday stop awaiting improvement' meant that the British team had reached the summit and that Edmund Hillary was the victorious climber. Morris wrote out his message and gave it to a runner – this is thought to be the last time a major news event relied on a physical runner – who in turn passed it down to the

Silk Road village of Namche Bazaar, from where it went by wireless to the British Embassy in Kathmandu. Although James Morris didn't know whether the message would make it through or if it had been properly understood in London, *The Times* had its story in time for a Coronation special.

Morris was on, if not cloud nine, then somewhere adjacent. As he wrote later:

> I think for sheer exuberance the best day of my life was my last on Everest . . . how brilliant I felt as, with a couple of Sherpa porters, I bounded down the glacial moraine towards the green below! I was brilliant with the success of my friends on the mountain, I was brilliant with my knowledge of the event, brilliant with muscular tautness, brilliant with conceit, brilliant with awareness of the subterfuge, amounting very nearly to dishonesty, by which I hoped to have deceived my competitors and scooped the world . . . I felt as though I had been crowned myself.

But as the slightly odd comment about 'muscular tautness' might imply, this former cavalry officer with the 9th Queen's Royal Lancers, and increasingly successful Welsh writer, had other things on his mind. He was thinking a lot about his strong male body. It was on Everest that he felt for the first time 'its full power, as one might realise for the first time the potential of a run-in car'. This wasn't, however, a reason for uncomplicated celebration. Ever since Morris was three or four years old, when he remembered sitting underneath his mother's piano while she was playing Sibelius, he had felt he had been born into the wrong body. He should have been a girl.

After years of private unhappiness, and despite a successful marriage and five children, Morris would make the transition from man to woman, first with drugs and then through perilous surgery in Morocco. James Morris, successful journalist, travel writer and historian, became Jan Morris, ditto. Although by that time, 1972,

Britain had around 150 transsexual people, Morris was the most prominent and more of a pioneer in attitudes to gender than he had ever been on the slope of the mountain.

Today 'trans' rights and gender fluidity are the most fashionable and recent aspects of Britain's fractious twenty-first-century culture wars. But this is not so new, and to think it is new is to misremember. Morris was not, by any means, the first Briton to change gender, as science made powerful yearnings physically possible. So far as we know, the first Briton to undergo male-to-female gender-reassignment surgery was a racing-car driver and former RAF Spitfire and Hawker Typhoon pilot. Robert Cowell's war had included some very close escapes before being finally shot down and imprisoned by the German Army in a camp so grim that the prisoners were reduced to eating cats before being liberated by the Soviet Union's Red Army.

Returning to motor racing after the war, Cowell became increasingly depressed and began to take oestrogen, realizing that his identity was fundamentally female. A young transgender doctor, Michael Dillon, who had made the transition from male to female himself, then performed an illegal castration operation on Cowell. Sir Harold Gillies, a famous plastic surgeon, and cousin of Sir Archibald McIndoe, whose 'Guinea Pig Club' was composed of burned and reconstructed RAF aircrew, finally carried out a full surgical operation, giving the war hero a vagina.

It is a curious fact that transsexual surgery, regarded today as being at the cutting-edge of gender liberation, owes so much to the horrors of the Battle of Britain and Second World War fighting generally. Gillies, like McIndoe, had made his name rebuilding the faces of damaged servicemen. In his case, they were mainly veterans of the First World War trenches. By the early 1950s the British certainly knew a great deal about what was then called 'sex change', not least because in 1954 Roberta Cowell sold her story to the hugely popular magazine *Picture Post*, which put her on the front cover, pouting and sultry as Marilyn Monroe.

Making the transition from one gender to another produces a ripple of effects, of course, spreading far beyond the individual concerned – to partners present, past and future, to friends, employees and colleagues, and ultimately to institutions circumscribed by their own rules. Roberta Cowell walked out on her wife (who had been an engineering student and had fallen in love with him before the transition), and in later life she never acknowledged her two daughters. Jan Morris maintained her membership of grand London clubs, whose doormen barely blinked, and won over almost all her friends and employers. These are normal human stories, to the extent that every experience is different in detail. It has been a social change made possible by technology – modern drugs and surgery. But it has been surrounded by ignorance and prurience on the one side and a certain amount of aggressive self-righteousness on the other.

What would the crowds awaiting the Queen in the centre of London have made of it all? Historians sometimes tell us that the Britain of the 1950s was repressed and ignorant compared to today. The shrewdest novelists tell different stories; but at any rate there is nothing so irritating as looking back at previous generations in a spirit of moralizing self-righteousness – what the historian E. P. Thompson called 'the enormous condescension of posterity'. People observing that Coronation in 1953 could not have known how science was about to reshape gender possibilities, any more than we know what is coming next for us.

Jan Morris later made the point that, in her case at least, transition was driven not by sexual urge but by something more profound. In her memoir *Conundrum* she said that she had realized that sex was not a division but a continuum,

> that almost nobody was altogether of one sex or another, and that the infinite subtlety of the shading from one extreme to the other was one of the most beautiful of nature's phenomena. Sex

7

was the biological pointer, but the gauge upon which it flickered was that very different device, gender. If sex was a matter of glands or valves, gender was psychological, cultural or in my own view spiritual.

Nuanced, reflective and fundamentally optimistic, Morris was able to survive darkly suicidal moments before confronting what she felt was the unavoidable decision of changing to become a woman. She was able to maintain a spectacularly successful and glamorous career, to stay in an emotionally intense and satisfying relationship with the woman she had originally married as a man, and to keep in touch with supportive and understanding children from that relationship. It is impossible to read her story and think that 'transgender' is a trivial or somehow flimsy issue, though it is hardly a majority issue in terms of numbers.

Morris described meeting fellow transgender people all of whom had just been operated on in the Casablanca clinic where she made the change. It reads like the gripping conclusion of a wartime adventure:

we were like prisoners, released momentarily from our cells for interrogation, meeting at last, colleagues known to us only by code or legend. We looked at each other at once as strangers and as allies, in curiosity and in innocence. And we had this in common too: that we were all gloriously happy. Just for those few days of our lives, if never before, if never again, we felt that we had achieved fulfilment, and were ourselves. Mutilated and crippled as we were, stumbling down the corridors trailing our bandages and clutching our nightclothes, we radiated happiness. Our faces might be tight with pain, or grotesque with splurged make-up, but they were shining with hope. To you we might have seemed like freaks or mad people . . . But for a week or two anyway we felt pure and true . . .

In the 2010s transgender rights became much argued about, from Parliament to the internet. Transition carries substantial legal and educational consequences. Nobody knows how many transgender people there are in Britain since no official statistics have been compiled. GIRES, an organization which tries to help transgender people, estimates the number as between 300,000 and 500,000. Whether this is an underestimate or an overestimate, their cause has been taken up by increasing numbers of young British people, often to the derision of their elders. The number of children being referred to the Tavistock Clinic's Gender Identity Development Service in London is said to be rising to around fifty a week. How has something once so rare become so popular? Is it because the culture is changing? Is it because drugs and surgery are so much easier to obtain?

By 2017 there were the beginnings of what seemed like a cultural war around this issue, a final extension of the permissive age, which Morris calls 'for all its excesses, a time of joyous liberation throughout the western world'. Perhaps a useful corrective is to think back to her story and remember that, whatever the statistical count, each of these stories is a unique and individual one, which depends upon the courage, sagacity and imagination of the person concerned. A great virtue of Jan Morris is that there is no self-pity in her account, however harrowing it may at times be. She never saw herself as a victim because she was always more interested in the great world than in herself.

That, perhaps, is a lesson for all of us. There is no such thing as a typical transgender story, any more than there was a typical cavalry officer standing at the base camp of Mount Everest in 1953. This is one small example of how, by digging back a little deeper into our national history through individual stories, we can recapture some of its lost freshness. Even our recent history was rarely as straightforward as it is often painted. This is, rightly understood, a cheerful truth.

There is a breezy historiography which, broadly speaking, sees the twentieth century in Britain as an erratic but unimpeded move from darkness into light. Once we were racist, misogynistic, homophobic, and we lived in a dim, gaslit pre-liberalism. In television terms, it's as if we have made the move from black-and-white into colour. And there is no doubt that aspects of post-war Britain were dingy. The food was meagre and tasteless, the cities were grimy, the clothes were unflattering, industrial and domestic smoke hung in the air.

We were a bit smelly. The literary critic Cyril Connolly, writing in the magazine *Horizon* in 1947, called London 'the saddest of great cities'. He went on to describe its 'miles of unpainted half-inhabited houses, its chopless chop-houses, its beerless pubs . . . under a sky permanently dull and lowering like a metal dish-cover'. A recent biography of the painter Lucian Freud reminds us that the Paddington area of London where he lived during roughly the same period was run by violent gangs, and so infested with rats that he bought a Luger pistol to keep them down. A calmer, cleaner, more law-abiding Britain it certainly wasn't. This was still the Britain of the school cane and the hangman, a Britain where homosexuals were hunted down in public toilets and publicly disgraced.

So much for the vast condescension of posterity. 'Everything is getting better.' But a moment of common-sense reflection tells us that the British of the early years of the Queen's reign must have lived their lives in full colour; that the young were brimming with youth; that every variety of sexual experimentation was vigorously attempted; and that, despite the Movietone News depictions of an endless grey winter, spring kept coming around more or less on time every April.

Was it a more prejudiced country? Certainly; but black American GIs in a segregated army had been warmly welcomed into a country whose ordinary bars, cinemas and restaurants were open to all colours. Gay men, to take another example, found many ways to live full lives, deploying private languages, discretion and a cultur-ally self-confident underworld of clubs and parties, a world now vanished. Britons may have more rights today, and be wealthier materially, but that does not make us necessarily happier, more fulfilled or more virtuous. We have a much greater understanding of our neighbouring cultures in Europe and others around the world; we consume more of their foods, books and films; but because we hover for far less time over dense, traditional texts we may also (whisper this) be shallower.

2

PROPER BEHAVIOUR

The monarchy inherited by Princess Elizabeth in 1952 was almost unimaginably different from the Britain over which she was still reigning in her nineties. Two years after the war, when still a young princess, Elizabeth had given a radio broadcast from South Africa in which she declared to the former Empire that 'my whole life, whether it be long or short, shall be devoted to . . . the service of our great imperial family to which we all belong'. That post-imperial system was still overwhelmingly white. 'We' did not properly include the vast mass of impoverished Asian and African workers, certainly not black women. Yet the Queen lived to see her grandson Harry marry a mixed-race, divorced American woman, in a service at Windsor Chapel addressed by a black American pastor and featuring a black South London choir. At roughly the same time, there was a move by Oxford students to tear down a statue of Cecil Rhodes, the imperialist pioneer who had helped create British South Africa.

How one Britain became the other is an intricate story. But at its heart are values – moral judgements, behaviour towards others, personal expectations from life. Often, historians instinctively distinguish between political and economic history on the one hand

– 'the serious stuff' – and lighter, brighter, apparently triter social history on the other. By starting with values, or 'right behaviour', we can see that the public sphere and the private sphere are not to be pulled apart. The Britain of 1952 was a society in which the vast majority of people felt they had a place. They might have resented that place or they might have biddably 'known' their place. Yet however much they may have chafed against their position in the social spectrum, people understood that certain norms of behaviour were expected – at work, in the family, in streets and in towns and villages. These covered everything from appropriate headwear to the need to keep the front doorstep spick and span, orderly queueing and daily formal greetings.

Of course, there are norms today as well; but they have changed and mean different things. In general, today's norms are more about blurring and ignoring difference than about reinforcing it. In 1952, it would have been rude, if common, to stare at somebody unusually dressed walking down the street: today, to *fail* to make eye contact with someone of a different culture, and smile at them, would be thought ruder still. In 1952, to wear a bowler hat showed that you were a member of the upper-middle classes. Today, to wear a bowler hat suggests bohemian and satirical tendencies. Today, to address somebody in a coffee shop or pub as 'Mr Jones' or 'Mrs Simpson' is likely to prompt a raised eyebrow – 'Are you trying to make fun of me?'

In 1952, to address a neighbour or shopkeeper by their first name only would be to make a daring assumption about intimacy. Today, to address someone simply by their second name – Jones or Simpson – would come across as insulting. In 1952, it would have been blandly unremarkable. Today, to turn up at work in stained jeans, with a T-shirt allowing you to display swirling arm-length tattoos, would say nothing of your social origins, although it might imply a high-value job in the tech sector or entertainment. In 1952, it would have signified that you were a filthy, jobless, unrespectable hobo. Or maybe a gypsy or a merchant seaman.

We still have our signifiers, but they crash across traditional barriers of class and employment. What was once literal has become sarcastic; and these are the norms for a more class-confused and culturally heterogeneous Britain.

This underlying sense of order in the Britain of 1952, against which many millions were already itching, was partly the result of the Second World War, which had mobilized and disciplined the British more comprehensively than ever before. A tiny little children's booklet produced in 1955 by the now defunct *News Chronicle* newspaper, *I-Spy People in Uniform*, is like a time capsule of a different society: Girl Guides are drawn in three sharply delineated varieties, as Sea, Air and Land Rangers; a sergeant of the Boys' Brigade is shown with white chevrons and a kepi-style cap; a bugler from the Church Lads' Brigade sports a tasselled and emblazoned uniform that wouldn't have disgraced a Napoleonic chasseur. Then there are pages of the various outfits and badges of the Women's Voluntary Service, the Civil Defence Corps and Red Cross Cadets, before we reach scores of uniforms for mainstream civilian jobs, from top-hatted bank messengers to water and gas employees.

Britain was a drilled and ordered place, and the war's direct consequences were still being felt – the continuation of rationing, a rolling mist of grey privation and the swagger-stick of National Service waving over almost all young men. Away from rural villages and suburbs, Britain was a factory-dominated industrial nation, millions of whose workers were subject to the alternative disciplines and solidarities of mass trade unionism. It was a country of clocking-on, bellowing foremen, compulsory branch meetings and the tyranny of the timesheet.

This was unusual in British history – we have rarely been a heavily organized and conspicuously law-abiding country – and it made Britain unusual in the world. Work was the most important thing. Britain was never more focused on manufacturing industry than in the 1950s and 1960s. As the historian David Edgerton has pointed out, 'The share of manufacturing workers in total employment peaked in the 1950s, the absolute number of workers in manufacturing in the 1960s. This was British manufacturing's moment; the moment too, of the industrial working class.'

The beginning of the 1950s saw 9.5 million people paying regular trade union dues (compared with around 6 million today, in a much larger workforce). Unions had their own clear hierarchies, and powerful, often socially conservative leaderships, whose writ ran in mines, dockyards, offices and engineering shops. Just as young men going into the Army would face bullying rituals, dramatic haircuts and parade-ground square-bashing designed to erode their individuality, so too, in thousands of factories, young apprentices would be subjected to initiation ceremonies designed to humiliate them and above all ensure that they knew their place.

A vivid sense of all this is conveyed by the former Labour politician Jack Ashley, who grew up in Widnes in Merseyside. As a child, he recalls, 'Respect for authority was a tangible factor in our lives. Mam was anxious about any contact with people such as priests, doctors or employers. For the priest's weekly "collection" visit, she always gave some money, no matter how impoverished we were. This was a practice I resented from a very early age.'

He then went on to work in a chemical factory owned by ICI and remembers the atmosphere for a fourteen-year-old beginning work in industrial Britain:

I began to capture the moods of industry which I came to know so intimately in the years ahead: bawdy banter, passionate arguments about football, dogmatic assertions about the job and the bosses, and an underlying sense of comradeship . . . The ribaldry caused me more embarrassment than it would any fourteen-year-old today. When the men had exhausted their standard repertoire of jokes about babies, busts and bottoms, left-handed

spanners, sky hooks and barrow-loads of steam, we settled down
to the humdrum work of the factory . . .

Later, he came across a classic foreman: 'A curt, sharp-spoken man,
he always wore a black suit and a dark cap. His word was law, and
I was surprised at the submissiveness of the men as he issued
instructions.'

Jack Ashley, this writer's father-in-law, is a good exemplar of many
working-class values in the immediate post-war period. He had
known genuine poverty, brought up with his sisters by his mother
in a dilapidated terraced council house, and he entered politics in
1946 as a teenage rebel councillor protesting against local Labour
Party housing policies. His was an Irish Catholic family and the
young Ashley, with a good singing voice, served as a choirboy. He
later turned against religion, but his values and passion for justice
seemed rooted in the Gospels.

It has often been argued that the 1950s were a golden age for
upward social mobility, as grammar school children from poor
backgrounds made it to the expanding universities. Ashley did not
go to a grammar school, but having left school at fourteen for the
chemical works became a crane driver: he got his chance thanks to
another ladder sometimes underplayed by historians – the trade
union movement, winning a scholarship to Ruskin College, Oxford,
where he got a diploma in economics in 1948, before he went to
Cambridge and started work again as a researcher for the National
Union of General and Municipal Workers.

Ashley had no visible lack of self-confidence about class origin:
from the first time he came across public schoolboys at Cambridge
and learned about mysteries such as homosexuality, he regarded the
'posh' as a mildly amusing form of eccentric fauna. As a young man
he had been fast with his fists but, rising to become president of
the Cambridge Union Society and travelling on debating tours to
the United States, he became fast with his tongue as well. After a

career as a producer and presenter with the BBC, he was elected Labour MP for Stoke-on-Trent South in 1966. Soon afterwards, as a result of an operation that went wrong, he became profoundly deaf.

Something in his hard, early years had given Ashley abnormal determination: against all expectations, he carried on in Parliament and learned to work effectively as a backbench MP. A lifelong admirer of Harold Wilson, and spoken of at times as a possible future Labour leader himself, Jack Ashley demonstrated through a wide range of campaigns, aided by his indomitable wife Pauline, that backbenchers could achieve as much as most ministers. He became Britain's foremost campaigner for disablement rights, as well as leading successful fights for compensation for Thalidomide victims and on behalf of victims of domestic violence and Army bullying. He was quietly but intensely patriotic, fascinated by military history and suspicious of all intellectual, ideological theories. He had been forged in a world which assumed everyone had a settled future. He simply thought that ridiculous.

The imposition of authority and hierarchy at industrial workplaces is often sidelined when compared to the effects of war and conscription; but in taming young men, and separating them from the female world, the parallel is obvious. Even in a much later television comedy, *Are You Being Served?*, set in a comparatively genteel department-store world, the social (and generational) hierarchies – departmental managers in stiff collars versus sarky, larky counter staff – are glaringly obvious. Another TV series from the same era – the early 1970s – *On the Buses*, shows the importance of work hierarchies in a very different setting: drivers and inspectors belong to different, mutually antagonistic worlds. If Britain today is a much more feminized society, this is not entirely the achievement of feminists; it is also a reflection of a fundamental shift in how people tend to spend their working days.

At the conclusion of a highly disciplined and hierarchical working week, Britons went to church. It was, compared to the country of the twenty-first century, a religious, churchgoing nation. Roughly speaking three times as many people were regularly attending Anglican services, for instance, as happens now – despite a vastly bigger population. In raw numbers, 1930 had been the high point for British church membership (an admittedly vague concept) with 10.3 million in regular attendance. But in the late 1950s the figure was almost as high, and in fact higher than church membership during the 1940s, perhaps reflecting a wish to bind and give thanks after the traumas of the war. Scotland, where the Scottish Presbyterian kirk had a strong grip, and Northern Ireland were particularly strong churchgoing societies.

Although the proportionate number of churchgoers across Britain continued to fall, it fell only gently during the late 1950s and early 1960s – perhaps thanks to a combination of the effect of the hugely popular Billy Graham Christian revivalist crusades, which each attracted more than 2 million followers, and the arrival of immigrant Irish Roman Catholics keen to attend Mass in their adoptive new home. The religious revival of the 1950s would have wider social effects. It was followed by a revived campaign against homosexuality, which in turn led to intense debates on the issue. These would lead to its decriminalization.

The big decline in church attendance came in the 1970s and afterwards. By 1990, the then Bishop of Southwark said that Britain had moved from a country 'where Christianity is culture, to one where Christianity is choice'. Ten years later the Archbishop of Canterbury called Britain a country in which 'a tacit atheism prevails'. It was an immense change, which perhaps we still do not understand. In 1950s Britain, churchgoing reinforced social conformity as powerfully as did factory working or National Service. Children attended Sunday school, where they were tutored in Bible stories and Christian morality. Their parents sat through sermons. Adulterers and the left-behind of broken marriages would be pointed out and embarrassed. Vicars, ministers and priests made regular visits to homes all over Britain, unannounced but expected. And whatever happened to overall churchgoing numbers, Christianity remained a powerful political and moral force throughout the Queen's reign.

Apart from passing references to the Festival of Light, such Christian moralism is rarely made much of by historians. This is because history is so often the history of institutions, and the deeper history, of what is going on inside people's heads, is hard to uncover. But we have the autobiographical testament of numerous political and social leaders to remind us of how important Christian values were in their lives. Of course, the very term 'Christian values' raises many questions. On the conservative side of the argument, its importance is perhaps better understood. The impact on Margaret Thatcher of her father's Methodism is accepted by all her biographers.

As a young woman, she was a preacher herself. She was a sophisticated enough Christian not to assume that the Bible required any particular line in voting. But for her the Bible always had political consequences. In a speech at St Lawrence Jewry in 1978 in the City of London, she argued that higher taxation was reaching its limits and that the time was soon coming when what the taxpayer was prepared to do would be less than what the individual had been willing to give 'from love of his neighbour. So do not be tempted to identify virtue with collectivism. I wonder whether the State services would have done as much for the man who fell among thieves as the Good Samaritan did for him?'

She had never thought that 'Christianity equipped me with a political philosophy,' but she thought it did equip her with standards by which political actions could be judged. Her Christianity emphasized the family rather than the collective; individual will; the virtues of hard work; private charity; and one's duty to look after one's own. It brought her into conflict with the Church of

England in 1985, after the publication of a report commissioned by Archbishop Robert Runcie, *Faith in the City*. This responded to inner-city tensions by calling for more public spending and declared that 'too much emphasis is being given to individualism, and not enough to collective obligation'. Criticizing the comfortable and well off, it argued that the exclusion of poor people was 'pervasive and not accidental'. According to her biographer Charles Moore, Mrs Thatcher underlined these words and drew two large question marks beside them, 'well aware that she stood accused'.

Hurt and offended by the Church's criticism, Mrs Thatcher tried to explain herself as a Christian three years later in her so-called 'Sermon on the Mound' to the General Assembly of the Church of Scotland. She argued that Christianity was not about social reform but about spiritual redemption. She quoted St Paul's adjuration, 'If a man will not work he shall not eat.' This infuriated some Scottish clerics; but what the row demonstrated, really, was that there were still very contrasting views of Christian ethics and that, as late as 1988, they mattered to both sides of the political argument. How important was it that the Good Samaritan was wealthy enough to have money in his pocket to help the man lying robbed and bleeding? Or was the instinct that sent him across the road to help his neighbour, unlike the wealthy and powerful Levite and Pharisee who had both passed by, the central part of the story?

Christianity encouraged some Conservative leaders to think harder about poorer and less powerful people, in a way that went well beyond market economics. With the exception of David Cameron, who said, quoting his then friend Boris Johnson, that his religious faith came and went like intermittent radio reception in the Chilterns (though he did so in the context of a speech robustly asserting Britain's Christian heritage), most Tory leaders have been overtly Christian. Harold Macmillan was religious, as, in a quiet way, were Alec Douglas-Home and Edward Heath. What did this mean in policy terms? It is probably fair to say that for twentieth-century British Christians the New Testament mattered much more than the Old; and that its kernel was Christ's Sermon on the Mount.

Thus politicians who were committed to limiting the size of the state and strongly believed in individual free will, exercised in the free market, also believed that they had obligations to all their fellow citizens. Much of the consensus evident in the so-called Butskellite social policies of the 1950s and 1960s – emphasizing high employment, the role of the trade unions, welfare spending and relatively lavish support for the National Health Service – was perhaps the result of a pervasive, slightly diluted New Testament ethic running through the Tory Party. Margaret Thatcher was in this, as in so much else, a partial exception to the rule.

The influence of Christianity is even more striking on the left of British public life. Harold Wilson said that the Labour Party owed more to Methodism than to Marx. When it came to mid-twentieth-century Labourism, he was absolutely right. He himself had been brought up, not quite as a Methodist, but as a Congregationalist (the man who followed him as Prime Minister, Jim Callaghan, was a Baptist) and was married in a chapel to the daughter of a church minister. In later life, he said that his religious views explained why he thought that high unemployment was immoral. The radical-egalitarian aspect of Christianity, the sense that everyone owes obligations to everyone else, and that everybody is equal in the sight of God, runs through modern politics as a constant, nervy source of virtuous disturbance.

Even atheists who went on to lead the Labour Party, such as Michael Foot and Neil Kinnock, had strong Christian noncon-formist connections – Foot's through his Plymouth family and Kinnock's through Welsh chapel culture. John Smith, who followed them, was a devout Christian. Among politicians we shall come to later, the effect of the New Testament on Tony Benn was profound and transforming. Tony Crosland was brought up in the strict

Plymouth Brethren tradition and, although he rebelled against its puritanism, 'thy brother's keeper' remained central to his political vision. Shirley Williams, another politician with a strongly ethical view of the role of politics in society, came from a devout Roman Catholic background.

Tony Blair, whose religiosity concerned his advisers throughout his political career ('We don't do God,' instructed his spokesman Alastair Campbell), converted to Roman Catholicism after he left office. He had been brought to a closer understanding of Christianity's political implications by an Australian priest while he was a student at Oxford, and later came under the influence of the Christian philosopher John Macmurray. In a speech to the Labour Party conference in 1995 he explained what religion meant for him: 'I am worth no more than anyone else, I am my brother's keeper, I will not walk by on the other side. We are not simply people set in isolation from one another, face to face with eternity, but members of the same family, same community, same human race. This is my socialism.'

His successor, Gordon Brown, was the son of a Church of Scotland minister and retained a close interest in the importance of the New Testament. In a book devoted entirely to the political use made of Christ's Good Samaritan parable, the writer Nick Spencer concluded of the Brown version, following the financial crisis of 2008, 'This was the Good Samaritan as justification for state intervention. The travelling Samaritan has become the multi-billion-pound British government, stepping across the treacherous financial road and binding the wounds of a damaged and vulnerable public with billions of pounds of taxpayers' money.'

So, is this something or nothing? If Christianity, indeed the same stories from the New Testament, can be used by Margaret Thatcher and Gordon Brown for almost opposite political conclusions, should we conclude that religious influence in British public life is meaningless? I am not arguing that, as a result of their faith, politicians were translated into junior members of the angelic horde – that they never fibbed or acted immorally. But it is possible for a way of thinking to be so widely distributed and so influential that we barely notice it.

In the case of Christianity in twentieth-century British life, its 'everywhereness' is the point. Millions of people who might not have been motivated by political philosophers had a moral imagination formed by the New Testament – by Sunday school, Bible class, church parades. This, consciously or otherwise, made them see the democratic system as more than a way of pursuing their own economic advantage. The Queen forthrightly referred to her religion in her Christmas messages, but for many millions of her subjects who didn't even go to church, Christianity was the ethical water in which they swam. For politicians of the centre-left, striving to make life more successful and tolerable for poorer fellow citizens, the impulse for their ideas did not come primarily from reading Friedrich Engels or *Das Kapital*, from Marcuse, Gramsci or Fanon, but from an early and immersive dunking in the four evangelists.

The Christianity of elective politicians is only the start. Consider the influence of Lord Soper, the prominent Methodist leader, on the Campaign for Nuclear Disarmament; of Bruce Kenrick, the founder of Shelter and also a minister in the United Reformed Church; of the Rev. George Macleod and his Iona community in Scotland; of the Quakers who helped found Oxfam. But even bearing all of them in mind, we only begin to scratch the surface of the impact of the New Testament on British social policy in modern times. As we shall see, the hugely popular *Eagle* boys' comic was a consciously Christian undertaking, created by a Southport vicar. Religious influence lingered long after church congregations had shrivelled. During the coronavirus crisis of 2020, the Archbishop of Canterbury Justin Welby and other Church of England priests delivered their services and sermons online. It seemed that ten times as many people were watching and listening as regularly attended physical churches, all of which were then closed.

In many ways, reading the novels of the period seems to show that respectability was as strong in the Britain of the early years of the Queen's reign as in the heyday of her predecessor Queen Victoria. Respectability, loathed or admired, is important in the early comedies of Kingsley Amis, as in the somewhat bleaker novels of his friend Philip Larkin. Jim Dixon, anti-hero of *Lucky Jim* (1953), a horny drunk, knows that his professional fate lies entirely in the hands of his professor and is constantly threatened by his own misbehaviour. He too had to worry about his equivalent of the factory foreman or the passing priest. Respectability mattered. In a famous attack in the *Sunday Times*, Somerset Maugham wrote of Amis's characters: 'They have no manners and are woefully unable to deal with any social predicament. Their idea of a celebration is to go to a public house and drink six beers. They are mean, malicious and envious . . . Charity, kindliness, generosity are qualities which they hold in contempt. They are scum.'

Britain of the 1950s was also an overwhelmingly white society, with only small numbers of immigrants from the Caribbean arriving in London and a few Midlands cities. The arrival of so many black American GIs ahead of the invasion of Europe had introduced many white British communities to their first dark-skinned neighbours. The overall reaction was mildly enthusiastic. There was considerable British hostility to the American 'color bar'.

But these were visitors. Visitors who were just passing through were easier to respond to than settlers. The docking of the *Empire Windrush* in 1948, bringing 492 West Indian immigrants to Tilbury and now celebrated as the real beginning of multicultural Britain, drew the following rebuke from eleven Labour MPs – Labour, not Conservative – to the then Prime Minister Clement Attlee: 'The British people fortunately enjoy a profound unity without uniformity in their way of life, and are blessed by the absence of a colour racial problem. An influx of coloured people domiciled here is likely to impair the harmony, strength and cohesion of our people and social life and cause discord and unhappiness among all concerned.'

There were smaller Chinese, African and Indian communities in the East End of London and some port cities. For the majority population, the Empire was still largely an abstraction – something people went across the seas to 'serve', not a policed global system whose unwinding would have big repercussions at home. Newspapers and political parties, except for small numbers on the far left, regarded the Empire as an almost unqualified good, an achievement British people should be proud of. Until 1958 (it was renamed by the then Prime Minister Harold Macmillan) Empire Day was celebrated every March, with decorous parades, speeches and church services. From the Prime Minister downwards, people spoke unselfconsciously about 'the British race', and regarded foreigners as humorous, dangerous or merely unfortunate. Blacked-up 'minstrel' entertainers featured on television; gollywogs were cuddled by small children and advertised by jam makers; newspaper cartoonists used racial stereotypes which would be unprintable today.

The British of 1952, in short, were a quietly religious, homogeneous, stratified, socially conservative, proud and comparatively closed-off country. Compared to today, they were much less connected with the European continent, socially, culturally and in terms of personal wealth. The middle classes didn't have boltholes in the Dordogne. The working classes had never been to Spain – unless they were part of a tiny minority who had been fighting for the International Brigades during the Spanish Civil War.

In this much more local world, people had less information at their fingertips. Perhaps, therefore, they concentrated harder on what they did know – memorized verses and songs, local nature lore and childhood stories, worn smooth and made familiar by repetition. Books, to be borrowed from libraries, and much more densely written newspapers provided a slower, more thoughtful way of spreading information and opinion. Television news, and radio news too, was calm and dry. Outside a few shadowed streets in a few city centres, where a few men lurked, pornography was little known.

If dim throbs of Elgar are by now hanging over these sentences, we must remember that ours was always, also, a contested country. Dissidents, whether sexual-minority groups or angry young men and women using new styles of clothing or music to cock a snook at their parents, were increasingly obvious as the wartime norms eroded. Communists and militant trade unionists – and, from the mid-1950s, anti-nuclear campaigners – were visible and much discussed. There was rising worry about inner-city gang violence.

Any would-be recorder of this period, therefore, is faced with a problem. Because the stories of the numerous rebels against an essentially conservative, stratified and rationed society tend to be colourful and specific – frankly, more exciting – there is a serious danger of forgetting the majority view. Oh, look! There is Sir Bertrand Russell sitting with his philosophical legs crossed as he protests against the Bomb. Look! There are some Teds in their dead-cool drainpipes and crêpe-soled shoes; and there's Lonnie Donegan twanging away at a skiffle club . . . And so, because our attention is stolen by the unusual and the vivid, the cavorting heralds of different futures, we fail to notice the calm majority – all the young people having serious conversations in Christian youth groups in the Midlands; the millions of Labour voters who admired stodgy, unprogressive mainstream leaders such as Herbert Morrison or Bessie Braddock; and all the households listening, not to the new rock 'n' roll, but to show tunes and swing bands.

Yes, everything was changing – but gently and piecemeal, in rivulets and plashing borders, not in one brightly coloured waterfall. Wartime disciplines slowly eased. For every would-be satirist who resented National Service, there were scores of youngish middle-aged men meticulously polishing their shoes, proudly maintaining shorn hairstyles and supping mild ale on a Friday night at the British

Legion. There's a common misconception that, having voted in a socialist government in 1945, the British were speeding towards the more open, liberal, rebellious country we became later.

But this is nonsense. There was no logical connection between the policies of the post-war Labour Party and the waves of liberalization which began a shift in values towards where we are today. The nationalization of the steel industry and the abolition of corporal punishment in prisons do not go hand in hand; nor do changes to the law on adultery and abortion have anything to do with a more progressive income tax policy; nor indeed does the end of hanging connect to a regime of trade union rights. The dominant figures of the left, from Clem Attlee to Ernie Bevin, were social conservatives – indeed, by today's standards, deeply reactionary.

Many other countries, from post-war France and Italy through to Britain's closest Commonwealth allies, Canada and Australia, stayed more conservative for longer. Nothing about British liberal reform was inevitable. Indeed, had there been a rolling political revolution after 1945, in which the Labour movement had gone much further than the creation of the National Health Service and limited nationalization and stayed in power for several decades, then Britain would probably have been a more socially conservative society than it has proved. The great sexual scandals of the middle part of the century and the rise in anti-establishment satire were products of Tory years, not of Labour ones. The angry young men of literature turned out to be men of the right, not of the left.

Yet somehow the left came to take ownership of social changes that went much wider than the agenda of earlier twentieth-century governments – the sexual revolution, the pushing back of the punitive state, the use and tolerance of drugs and an unmistakable decay in social and religious hierarchies. This was the achievement of a small number of individual politicians, of whom the most important were never Prime Minister themselves – Tony Crosland and Roy Jenkins.

They were reacting to a weariness in post-war Britain, and an anti-establishment frustration which has been a constant in British politics from the 1840s onwards. We have never been a particularly stable society. But a relatively small number of people saw their chance during the first part of the Queen's reign to push a shift in values and did so. Along with Margaret Thatcher, who saw herself to some extent as their nemesis, they were the most influential of Elizabethan weather-changers. And much of their thinking came from over the Atlantic.

3

A WORD ON AMERICANS

The most obvious division in British public life is between left and right. But the division between *social* conservatives and *social* liberals is just as important, and not the same. And in its influence on British social attitudes during Queen Elizabeth's reign, the impact of America cannot be overstated. Later, we will see how important the US-hating Enoch Powell would be when it came to the great argument over Britain and Europe. We will also see how fears over the violence and crudity of American culture grew in Britain during the 1950s and 1960s. But before all of that it's important to reflect on the vast admiration for America felt in the decades after the Second World War; and to recall that this was felt even more strongly on the liberal left than on the conservative right.

Take that influential woman Shirley Williams. The Labour, and later SDP, politician had a determined self-certainty which came from her intellectual and privileged upbringing. She was the daughter of the famous 1930s writer Vera Brittain, and was brought up in a Chelsea household where the Indian independence leader Jawaharlal Nehru and H. G. Wells were visitors. But her popularity as a politician came from her style, a breezy, no-nonsense rule-breaking informality that set her apart. A good example of it came in 1966 when she was appointed a minister in Harold Wilson's government, at the Home Office in charge of, among other things, pornography and prisons. There have been many prisons ministers. None of the others decided to have themselves incarcerated for a few nights as a prisoner to see what it was actually like.

Shirley Williams persuaded the authorities to send her to Holloway women's prison, her identity kept secret. This was a time when there was much newspaper comment about prison life being too easy and comfortable. In order to experience the lifestyle for herself – the smells and sensations, the food and the boredom – the Minister of State posed as a convicted prostitute:

> I did go through the business of being accepted into the prison, stripped and searched, given prison clothes, endlessly laundered and totally lifeless, and put in a stained and grubby cell. I had to explain to my cell-mates . . . what I was in for. I decided the hardest to check up on, was prostitution, so I told them I was 'on the game'. The 'game' extended to a wide spectrum of women, from the elegant mistresses of Mayfair to the cheap £5-a-go end of the business around mainline stations such as King's Cross and Victoria . . . I found the conversation highly enlightening.

This gave her a special authority back in Whitehall, and she became a particular expert on the poor quality of toilets and showers in female prisons.

So where did this airy readiness to ignore the normal way of doing things come from? The answer may simply be her temperament – by her own account, even as a young girl, Williams was tousled, impatient and unruly. But it's equally likely that she became a liberal rebel partly because she was educated not in Britain but, during the war, in America. Because her mother was a well-known pacifist and her book *Testament of Youth* was loathed by the Nazis,

Shirley Williams's parents were on a Gestapo blacklist to be elimi-
nated as soon as the Germans had invaded Britain.

Vera Brittain was determined to stay on and rally her fellow
pacifists: she decided, though, that her children should be sent to
the United States for safety. Brittain had done pre-war lecture tours
in the US. Friends she had met from Minnesota sent her a telegram
which simply read: 'Send us your children.' Williams and her brother
were dispatched across the Atlantic, despite the threat of U-boats,
to a farm outside Minneapolis. There they were exposed to a land
without obvious class divisions, and a culture far less formal than
contemporary Britain's. Williams later wrote that, in her three years
as an evacuee, 'I lived in a classless society, whose members shared
the same accent and the same values . . . the walls between the
social classes were porous . . . Money and talent would enable one
to traverse them. The absence of accent as a defining feature enabled
Americans to present themselves as whatever they wanted to be.'

This sunny world, without crabbed, confined divisions, would
greatly influence British liberals (though they seemed strangely blind
to America's extreme racial divide). It wasn't simply America's greater
material wealth – the domestic labour-saving gadgets, the lavish
food, the bigger cars – that impressed post-war visitors. It was also
the informality and democratic optimism that was so alluring. This
was primarily transmitted not in films or books, but person to
person and family by family.

Anglo-American relations were intimate as much as they were
official – evacuated children, billeted GIs and their brides, and
family friendships made between serving officers during the war,
which lasted well into the 1960s and beyond. Beyond all this, there
were the scholarships and the lecture tours which introduced ambitious young Britons to America – Jack Ashley had been one example.
British student bodies regularly sent their best debaters to argue
their way around the US during the 1950s and 1960s. The Rhodes
Scholarships founded in 1902, designed by the imperialist mining

magnate and politician Cecil Rhodes to bind together the Anglo-Saxon world through postgraduate study at Oxford University, were followed by similar programmes, taking Britons in the opposite direction.

In 1925 Edward Harkness, one of America's richest men through his family investments in Standard Oil, founded the Harkness Fellowships, bringing British students to study in the US. Among the post-war beneficiaries were a vast range of opinion-formers, including Alastair Hetherington who edited the *Guardian* from 1956 to 1975, Harold Evans, editor of the *Sunday Times*, the BBC broadcasters Alistair Cooke and Bridget Kendall; the writers Hugo Young, Jan Morris, David Lodge and Adrian Wooldridge; Geoff Mulgan, who ran policy for Tony Blair in Downing Street; Howard Davies, the Bank of England mandarin and Director of the London School of Economics; and Mark Damazer, Controller of BBC Radio Four – as well as innumerable politicians, composers, surgeons, scientists, historians and artists.

The Thouron Awards were established in 1960 to create a special relationship between Britain and the United States through exchanges between British universities and Pennsylvania University. Among its British beneficiaries was Norman Blackwell, another head of the Downing Street Policy Unit; Sir Paul Judge, who created the Judge Business School in Cambridge; Sir Mike Moritz, the California-based billionaire Welsh investor who supported education in Britain; Robert McCrum, the British journalist and author; and Sir Robert Cooper, one of the key British figures at the European Council on Foreign Relations. Bit by bit, name by name, personal life story by personal life story, the British and American elites were being quietly tied together in ways generally undiscussed by historians.

This was particularly true of politics. After the assassination of President Kennedy in 1963, the then Prime Minister, Sir Alec Douglas-Home, helped create Kennedy Scholarships, sending

Britons to Harvard and Massachusetts Institute of Technology in JFK's memory. The Trustees of the scheme read like a gazetteer of the modern British establishment with Kennedy Scholarships appealing strongly to the politically ambitious. Beneficiaries included Ed Balls, the Labour shadow Chancellor, who served in the Treasury under Gordon Brown; the former cabinet minister Yvette Cooper; the former Tory International Development Minister Alan Duncan; the former Labour Foreign Secretary David Miliband; the former Labour Environment and Culture Secretary Chris Smith; and William Waldegrave, cabinet minister under Margaret Thatcher; and influential journalists such as Stephanie Flanders, former economics editor of the BBC, Zanny Minton Beddoes, editor of *The Economist*, and Anatole Kaletsky, the columnist.

This knitting together of the elites goes both ways, of course. The Marshall Scholarships were created by the British Parliament in 1953 as a 'living gift' to the United States to say thank you for its generosity in the post-war Marshall Plan, which had helped rebuild Europe. Its beneficiaries have included members of the Supreme Court and US Congress, American cabinet members and no fewer than four winners of Pulitzer prizes. President Clinton was just one of the many American winners of a Rhodes Scholarship to Oxford. At a slightly lower level there are the more specialized programmes, such as the Lawrence Stern Fellowship, which brings British journalists to work for the *Washington Post* for one summer, and again, a vast number of prominent British broadcasters, newspaper editors and writers have benefited from that.

Now that's a long list. But it's here for a reason. It is easy to forget the importance of the life-changing effects of awards made to people at the most malleable periods of their lives. At a time when they are also ambitious and successful, the effects cascade over into society at large. We can spend a lot of time talking about the impact of Hollywood films, but changing the perspective of the future editors, politicians and judges can be more powerful still.

This is genuine 'soft power', pushing its long, well-manicured fingers through British life.

Decades before politics-obsessed young Britons became entranced by the liberal fantasy of the television series *The West Wing*, American democracy was tugging gently but persistently at the British class system. Many older Britons noticed, and didn't like it. They would point out the danger of exchanging a system based on caste and convention for one based crassly on money. In 1972, following the student demonstrations of the late 1960s, a British mimicry of American counterculture protest, Angus Maude, a Tory MP who would later serve in Mrs Thatcher's cabinet, complained that 'As we try to grapple with our major imports from America – violence, drug taking, student unrest, the hippy cult and pornography – our own permissive leftists have been hailing them as signs of progress.'

The truth was, American culture was simply too big and too magnetic to be resisted. Britain would be forced to 'copy and paste' ideas and fashions from the other side of the Atlantic. Pro- and anti-Americanism rose and fell among British liberals and conservatives, depending on the mood of the time. Tories found go-getting American business culture particularly appealing during the free-market boom of the post-war Eisenhower years, and then again during the Ronald Reagan period; the left, by contrast, was most pumped up by Kennedy's America; and much later by Obama's. Donald Trump's national optimism and use of social media was observed and copied by London. Throughout the Queen's reign, her country's leadership responded like a nervous and unpractised dance partner to new moves from across the Atlantic. And this was something that would not have surprised in the slightest the most vehement and emotional herald of Anglo-Saxon Atlanticist civilization, Queen Elizabeth's very first Prime Minister.

4

BETWEEN CATASTROPHE
AND GOLDEN AGE

The old man made the slow journey across wet and dismal London in the back of his car, weeping copiously. Winston Churchill had been busy preparing a major assault on Labour in the House of Commons over secret plans for war with communist China. All of that had been immediately forgotten when he had received the news he called simply 'the worst'. Churchill had known King George VI intimately throughout the war. So dominant is the Churchill cult these days, we tend to forget the King's role. But Churchill understood his importance and was shattered by his death. When reminded of the promise of the new young Queen Elizabeth II, he was, to start with, dismissive: 'She is only a child.'

Churchill, the old lion, was seventy-seven and little more than a year away from a major stroke. But he wasn't toothless. The story of his last administration is often told as a sad, withdrawing ebb – the hiss and rattle of impatient and jealous colleagues trying to nudge him into retirement; a few last great sea-gurgles, and clatterings of stones, as he warned of the dangerous new atomic age and tried to forge a better relationship with America, still committed as well to federal Europe; and then the slither of his great shadow into darkness.

This is a highly partial picture, however. As with the King's war, Churchill's old age has been unfairly remembered, thanks to the memoirs of the impatient younger men all around him. He might have been old, with his attention periodically wandering, but he had vast powers of recuperation and was intently interested in the modern world. This one-time cavalry officer under Queen Victoria, First World War Admiralty leader, staunch imperialist and global statesman of the 1940s, was able to see the beginning of the new reign with a perspective unlike anyone else's. The English, he came to believe, would again be Elizabethans – the Scots, of course, for the first time. As with Tudor England, the archipelago would be a magic island full of noises, crammed with invention and ambition, looking outwards to the world.

From the vantage point of the twenty-first century, Churchill's romanticism about Britain in 1952 is easy to mock. But despite the economic and physical hammering she had taken during the war, Britain was a potently interesting place. She boasted composers of the stature of William Walton and Vaughan Williams for her Coronation music. In the American-born poet T. S. Eliot and the philosopher Bertrand Russell, she had two recent winners of the Nobel Prize for Literature (Churchill himself would soon be a third). She had explorers and adventurers; cutting-edge scientists and inventors, responsible for everything from the hovercraft to the jet engine. British artists such as Stanley Spencer, Henry Moore, Jacob Epstein and Churchill's bugbear, Graham Sutherland, gave Britain the kind of serious role in art that she had rarely enjoyed in the previous century. In short, if the new Elizabeth's Britain wasn't quite the 'nest of singing birds' that Shakespearean England had been, it was a vigorous and striking cacophony of ideas, images and expressive ambitions.

Yet all around her were wild seas and fresh horrors. The Cold War was beginning. The scale and monstrosity of Stalin's dictatorship was only starting to become clear. The mushroom clouds of the nuclear age overshadowed all conventional diplomacy. From the hideous communal violence of India to uprisings in the Far East, the British Empire was coming bloodily apart. Five days after welcoming her to London, Churchill noted in the House of Commons that the new Queen was beginning her reign halfway through 'the terrible twentieth century'. He went on: 'Half of it is over and we have survived its fearful convulsions. We stand erect both as an island people and as the centre of a world-wide Commonwealth and Empire, after so much else in other lands has been shattered or fallen to the ground . . .' But what was coming next? That was the real question.

Churchill believed that the beginning of the Elizabethan era marked a moment when the British, still impoverished after the war, could look ahead with fresh ambition, and he wondered what would befall them. There would, he thought, be more material wealth. The first signs of a new consumer economy were already clear in the United States. New inventions, from atomic energy – thought then to imply almost free electricity – to jet airliners and the first computers, promised to reshape daily life. If there were terrors, there was also great promise.

Churchill told the Commons that Elizabeth 'comes to the throne at a time when a tormented mankind stands uncertainly poised between world catastrophe and a golden age'. He spent most of his waking hours worrying about the threat to peace, from divided Korea to divided Germany. But if the world's leaders could get themselves through this dangerous period and achieve a global armistice, Churchill suggested, 'an immense and undreamed-of prosperity with culture and leisure ever more widely spread can come . . . to the masses of the people in every land'. And, of course, he was largely right.

There is so much about the Britain of the 2020s which would utterly baffle the first of the new Elizabethans, looking at us from 1952. We have become a people who have forsaken factories; whose skies are now clear of choking smoke; who are as variegated in the colour of their skins as the world's population itself; whose mosques are crowded and whose churches are emptying; a people with only meagre armed forces to protect them; who spend much of their time staring at small glass screens on which images of all human culture can be seen; who are giving up the use of physical money; and whose children often browse pornography of an explicit nature that simply didn't exist in the 1950s. Churchill's 'immense and undreamed-of prosperity' has birthed an unexpected new Britain. But it has been made, not merely by anonymous historical forces, but by specific, identifiable individuals, leading the way and working together.

The British had two really big, overarching projects during the reign of Queen Elizabeth II. The first was to build the world's most successful – the most fair, the most equal and the most generous – welfare state. This was more the project of the left than of the right, though many Conservatives threw themselves into it with gusto and determination. The range of early supporters stretched from Winston Churchill to the likes of Jack Ashley. By the 1970s, however, this project was in crisis.

A collapse of industrial discipline which would have surprised Labour politicians of the immediate post-war period led to higher taxes and a sense of weary malaise, provoking a backlash among working-class voters as well as among the middle classes. There was a crisis of values, a widespread questioning of democratic socialism. In the decades since, although worship of the National Health Service has become a national religion, celebrated with fervour during the coronavirus crisis of 2020, that wider dream which gave it birth has been in retreat. Meanwhile, there has been a second great project.

This was to impress British influence on the new world, as a 'great power', even as the traditional Empire was wound up. This might be done through the Commonwealth or, some came to believe, through British membership of the European Union. This project too has failed. Despite thinking of themselves as one of the great change-making peoples in world history, the modern British proved unable to hold territory, win guerrilla wars or maintain moral authority far beyond their borders. Instead, those borders became porous, so that for many people they barely seemed to exist at all.

This, too, provoked a crisis of values: immigration and emigration changed the texture of the country and made it impossible for the modern British to believe there was a truly special 'British race', as their grandparents had imagined. Britain suffered a loss of national self-belief – and, with it, the single-mindedness, the brutality and the Machiavellian ruthlessness that would have been needed to impose British will on a more prosperous and fast-changing world. To make an empire requires a nation of imperialists. By the 1970s, certainly, the British were that no longer. Why not? One answer is that we simply became better educated about the rest of the world, and about the darker aspects of our own history. Nor did we have the muscle to impose ourselves – the huge Navy, the tanks and the fleets of bombers and missiles backed up by a potent world currency.

Modern Elizabethans, while displaying great ingenuity, and a certain amount of buccaneering commercial spirit, failed to produce the outstandingly energetic and highly productive economy that would have been needed to make Britain either a modern super-power or a lavishly funded and wealthy welfare society – the two big, ambitious projects.

During the reign of Queen Elizabeth II, the British made major advances in everything from aeronautics to the structure of DNA, computers, innovative substances such as graphene and much else besides. Although it is a pretty bizarre measurement, Britain easily beats any other European country in the number of Nobel prizes awarded to her citizens – and won far more during the 1950s and 1960s than before or since. What we apparently couldn't do, or do well enough, was to make things cheaply enough and well enough and consistently enough to earn ourselves the living we thought we deserved.

It's true that in financial services, insurance and other less tangible areas London (for the moment) still punches above her weight. But we have been cursed by that dullest of curses, low productivity. This is, of course, relative. Despite the Blitz, Britain had escaped the wholesale battering and expropriation of the war years: poorer and less developed rival economies, including some in Europe, were bound to catch up in the end, giving the appearance of British decline. In the 1950s Britain had the most manufacturing-centred economy of any country in the world except for Germany.

British governments poured money into research and development, as did private British companies. The historian David Edgerton says:

> The economic benchmark in the 1950s and 1960s in terms of income per head was the USA. It was roughly twice as productive per capita. In terms of rates of growth, the standard was not set by the USA but by France, Germany, Italy and Japan. They grew faster than the UK, but from a lower base of income per head. The fundamental process was that of convergence – with the poorer of these economies growing faster than the richer ones. Slow growth was for a country like the United Kingdom a sign not of weakness, but of wealth.

After a high-water mark of manufacturing in the 1970s, things began to decline, although by the 1980s the natural gift of North Sea oil and gas, and increasing agricultural efficiency, meant that Britain no longer needed to worry as much about manufactured imports as she had done. There are many stories of individual corporate failures, bad government investment decisions, goofy bosses and suicidally destructive shop stewards; but there has been more flagellation about economic failure than actual economic failure. The trouble is, we are a relatively small nation, with an inflated sense of ourselves, so we expect more in terms of wealth and a global prestige than is, perhaps, reasonable.

Here is the truth that grand old Winston Churchill, for all his perspective and wisdom could not confront: we are an ordinary country. We are a beautiful, diverse, law-abiding, hard-working and ingenious country, but we are an ordinary one – not New Jerusalem nor Greater Britain. Yet it seems we have never quite been able to believe it. That, really, was what eventually did for Tory dreams and Labour schemes. As somebody who loves Britain, the author does not find this depressing. Once we cast aside the illusions and forget the absurd ambitions, there is much in our recent history to celebrate, enjoy and learn from.

5

ON OUR UPPERS

So, in February 1952, what were the British arguing about among themselves when their new Queen touched down from Africa at London Airport – that modest new civil-engineering project plonked across some useful market gardens, now known as Heathrow? One sidelight on national talking points can be found by simply reading all the copies of *The Times* newspaper for that winter. It's a partial picture, naturally. There are few photographs, and no gossip, in what was a remorselessly factual upmarket news service; the voices of working-class people are almost completely absent, while for its staff all that really mattered was foreign affairs, politics and business.

And yet this dry paper is nonetheless juicily fascinating and unexpected. For one thing, just seven years after the end of the Second World War, Britain had not yet confronted the reality that her Empire was slipping away: *The Times* divided all its news pages into two categories – *home news*, on the one hand, and *imperial and foreign* on the other. Reading through both, the British still seem very much at war. A bloody conflict in Korea, the first hot war between the democracies and communism, staggers on. British tanks and troops are fighting 'terrorists' in Egypt, Africa and the

Far East. Later in the year, in October, Britain will become the third country in the world to test its own thermonuclear weapon.

War, war, war. As he folded his copy of the paper each morning, Churchill himself was obsessed about the danger of invasion by the Soviet Union. We think of Dad's Army as a phenomenon of the 1940s, but by 1952 some 30,000 men had been registered into the Home Guard as a protection against (Russian) 'raids, descents and sabotage'. Churchill's speeches described a new, still-unfamiliar world order, based on division between Soviet aggression and capitalist defence. Correctly, he believed that it would last for most of the century.

In the most famous of these speeches, at Fulton, Missouri in 1946, he laid out in uncompromising terms the basics of what would become the Cold War. On the one side, there was the Soviet Union, led by his old friend Joseph Stalin. The Soviets did not actively want war but did want 'the fruits of war and the indefinite expansion of their power and doctrines'. On the other side there was a new alliance between the people of the English-speaking Commonwealth and those of the United States. And of course an Iron Curtain now lay across Europe, 'from Stettin in the Baltic to Trieste in the Adriatic'. For a man who saw himself as a peacemaker, deeply worried about the coming nuclear age, this was a hard and aggressive speech. So much so that many of the leading American newspapers at the time recoiled from it in horror. *The Times* did not.

But how wise was Churchill, the dominant voice of 1950s Britain? Marilynne Robinson, the American Christian novelist and writer, gives the alternative view:

Has anyone really read the Iron Curtain speech lately and pondered how much of the worst policies for dealing with the Soviet Union in the post-war period are set out in it? And this is in 1946, when Russia had not yet had time to reckon its truly staggering losses? . . . After the Iron Curtain speech, angry crowds surrounded Churchill's hotel in New York. Stalin was not alone in considering the speech a declaration of war – in 1946, for heaven's sake, before the ashes of the last war were cool. In the speech Churchill proposed the British Empire as the de facto encirclement of the Soviet Union, urging Americans to sustain what Britain could not, for the advantage it would give us in a coming atomic conflict. From the side of wounded Russia, encirclement may have looked very much like an iron curtain. While Churchill did not foresee all the worst consequences of the Cold War, he did help to make them inevitable.

What this account of Churchill omits is how recently Britain had come close to invasion, and the effect of that on British thinking. However outlandish it seems today, in the early 1950s the possibility of a Russian invasion of the UK weighed deeply on policymakers in London. And the impact filtered, subtly, through British society. Churchill was talking to his ministers about organizing what would have been effectively a new British Army, 250,000 strong, into 500 'mobile columns' to answer an airborne attack by Soviet forces.

A high proportion of young British men spent eighteen months (or, after the declaration of the Korean War in 1950, two years) doing National Service in the Army, in the RAF or, more rarely, in the Navy. All men aged between seventeen and twenty-one were liable for call-up, though there were reserved occupations, such as coal mining, agricultural labouring and service in the merchant navy. In the average fortnight, 6,000 young men would be called up, given haircuts and put into uniform. A total of 2.3 million British men experienced National Service during the 1950s, and although its abolition was announced in 1957, it carried on until 1960 and the very last conscripted men were not returned to civilian life until 1963.

The cohort of young men who might otherwise have been at

their most rebellious were subjected to tough military discipline in wooden or prefab barracks. They were taught to obey orders, to look after their clothes and personal hygiene and to tolerate considerable boredom. Those who weren't going through this process were being disciplined in tough agricultural work or down coal mines. We have already seen the importance of manufacturing and religion in shaping social attitudes, but a drilled and more obedient country was first forged by National Service. It wasn't just the plan of Churchill's Conservatives. When people talk today about the great reforming Labour government of 1945, they tend to miss out the 1948 Act responsible for this last great blast of British militarism.

Enough, for the moment, of the men. One great issue for millions of British women was the impact of unregulated childbirth on family budgets. After the disruption of the war, when many marriages had been ruined and millions of children had grown up fatherless, there followed a time when rebuilding traditional families seemed a personal, and national, necessity.

The most dramatic years of the so-called 'baby boom' occurred immediately after the war, but there was an annual increase in births throughout the 1950s – an average of 839,000 a year, and then another increase during the 1960s, when the annual average rose again to 962,000. This happened even though British families had more opportunity to limit the number of babies. The birth rate had fallen markedly during the first half of the century, from twenty-eight live births per thousand to sixteen. Government statisticians believed that the major part of the fall was taking place in working-class families. The cause? Newly available contraception.

More mouths meant hungrier families. But if married women could keep the wolf from the door by using condoms and contraceptive caps, there were many others who couldn't. The war had brought a dramatic increase in single mothers. The National Council for the Unmarried Mother and Her Child (which continues in a different form today under the name Gingerbread) was dealing with ninety or so new cases a month in 1939: by the beginning of 1946 that had risen to 400, a total of more than 16,000 during the war years.

As a history of post-war single-parenthood explains:

In 1945, 25 per cent of all . . . cases concerned US servicemen. If these men denied paternity or had left the country, there was little hope . . . When the children were 'coloured' there was a particular problem, especially in the large areas of Britain unaccustomed to people of different skin colour. In 1945, the League of Coloured People reported to the [government] that it knew of 554 'illegitimate' children born to 'coloured' US servicemen . . .

Among those worried about this was Queen Mary, the Queen Mother, who wrote to the National Council via a lady in waiting. She did not blame the soldiers particularly: 'they are friendly, generous and have a great deal of money to spend; and there is no reason to believe that they are particularly ill behaved, though I fear there is very little doubt but that many English girls – often about 15 years of age – do run after these men (and their money!) most persistently . . .'

But, Queen Mary went on, rather contradicting her image as a starchy figure, 'This is not chiefly a question of morals . . . American men refuse to allow Negroes to associate with white girls, and they are ready (unpunished by their own authorities) to "beat up", first, the offending blacks, and subsequently the white girls who encouraged them.' Alarmed by the prospect of lynchings in Britain, Queen Mary suggested there should be no media coverage of the issue, and that English girls should be warned of the disastrous consequences that could follow if they became pregnant by black Americans.

But whether the fathers were black or white, many children grew up in the immediate aftermath of the war slowly realizing that they were not living with their biological parents. The rock musician Eric Clapton was born to a sixteen-year-old woman who had had an affair with a married Canadian serviceman. He went home. She too moved to Canada after the war, though with another man. This left Eric with his grandparents, whom he long assumed were his parents. It was, he wrote in his autobiography, a house full of secrets: 'But, bit by bit . . . I slowly began to put together a picture of what was going on and to understand that the secrets were usually to do with me. One day I heard one of my aunties ask, "Have you heard from his mum?" and the truth dawned on me that when [Uncle] Adrian jokingly called me a "little bastard" he was telling the truth.'

Illegitimate war children were common at the beginning of the Queen's reign; and illegitimate children continued to appear in large numbers throughout it. The 'moral 1950s' wasn't the fabrication of nostalgic historians or journalists. There was a desperation to get back to a kinder, more traditional, stable world, and for many British people that meant a return to an imagined Christian community. But it didn't restrain the sexual urge. And it didn't stop millions of women looking around and wondering whether there was a life of more fun, and less drudgery, to be had. That meant contraception, but it wasn't easy to get hold of. This was still the age of the backstreet abortionist, who had wearily seen it all, knocking on the back door with her bag full of knitting needles and vinegar. For many, giving birth and then passing on the inconvenient child was a safer, kinder and less terrifying option.

Many children born outside marriage lived perfectly happily with other members of their extended families, learning much later in life that 'Mother' was in fact a granny or aunt, and that brothers and sisters were, in biological fact, cousins. But large numbers of children were adopted, often informally or outside the law, through adverts in newspapers or even arrangements made in pubs or shopping queues. Pauline Prescott, then a hairdresser in Chester, who later married the future Deputy Prime Minister, had her first child in a Catholic home for unmarried mothers, St Bridget's House of Mercy. The baby boy was later adopted by a family living many miles away in Wolverhampton.

The Prescotts only made contact with him again when he was in his forties, after a long and honourable military career. The story is worth mentioning not because it is unusual, but because informal and formal adoptions were so very common, an inevitable result of a strictly pro-marriage culture. One more example: the mother of the novelist Ian McEwan had her first baby during the war, while her husband was serving overseas, and placed an ad in her local paper: 'Wanted, home for baby boy aged one month: complete surrender'. She handed the baby over to a couple at Reading Station. The boy, David Sharp, had a happy childhood and grew up to work as a bricklayer. He lived a few miles away from the famous novelist, without either knowing about the other's existence for half a century. It is an extraordinary story, but not as rare as we might think.

A careful study of the papers of the National Council by the historians Pat Thane and Tanya Evans challenges the notion that the mothers and children from 'illegitimate' marriages were generally harshly treated in the tougher ethical climate of the 1950s. It is true that there were moral panics in Parliament about the number of children being adopted by people other than their relatives – about a fifth of illegitimate children – and about the number of couples changing a surname by deed poll to hide the fact that they were not married. But the somewhat chaotic system of informal adoptions was reined in after the 1949 Adoption Act, which required all adoptions to be sanctioned by law, and everyone wanting to adopt a child to be properly assessed.

This meant that mothers lost their right to know the identities of the adopting families; and the children who were adopted in England and Wales had no right to know the names of their natural parents – until this law was finally amended again in 1978. It would cause a huge amount of pain and baffled misunderstanding for decades to come. Slowly, over the decades, attitudes changed and it became easier for unmarried mothers to live openly with their children. But in the meantime it seems that attitudes on the street were more kindly and more liberal than they were in the media and political establishment – where they could be icy. At one point, in a speech in 1959, the then Archbishop of Canterbury, Geoffrey Fisher, seriously proposed that adultery should be made a criminal offence. His argument was not pursued at Westminster – the Tory Prime Minister, Harold Macmillan, never took Fisher terribly seriously – and this probably marks the highest ambition of the post-war morality police.

When it came to contraception, the demand from ordinary British families suggested that things were already changing. In 1938, just before the war, there had been sixty or so birth-control clinics in Britain. By 1963 there were more than 400. In 1958, the Church of England – not the Roman Catholic Church – had at last accepted the importance of family planning, albeit only within the context of Christian marriage. By the beginning of the decade, contraceptive methods were spreading fast, with the IUD and the diaphragm preceding the pill in 1961.

Did this mean that people were increasingly seeing sex as a source of pleasure rather than simply procreation? Mass Observation, the pioneering sociological survey, conducted a poll in the late 1940s which found that only around a third of those questioned thought that a good sex life was essential to happiness. The same poll, twenty years later, found that 67 per cent thought sex was very important. People may have tried harder to limit the size of their families because they were worried about poverty in the austerity years; but having done so and having discovered contraception, they promptly revealed that it had cheering side-effects.

Even at this early stage, it's possible to see that the drilled and disciplined masculine Britain of National Service and the engineering workshops was giving way to a subtle but important power shift that started in the home. Contemporary observers thought so, anyway. The Polish-born sociologist Ferdynand Zweig said in his study *The Worker in an Affluent Society*, published in 1961 and based upon interviews with working-class Britons he had conducted in 1958–9, that there had been what he called:

> a process of softening in the worker . . . I would venture to call it his feminization. The worker's world was formerly known for its masculinity. Now he has mellowed considerably. The women around him imbue him with feminine values. He accepts his wife as his companion on more or less equal terms, especially when she goes out to work and earns her own living. All this means that the worker is moving away from his mates.

In 1957 Michael Young and Peter Willmott conducted a major survey of working-class families in Bethnal Green, East London, and in Essex, published that year as *Family and Kinship in East London*. They too found male authority and exploitation in decline: 'the old style of working-class family is fast disappearing. The husband portrayed by previous social investigation is no longer true to life. In place of the old comes a new kind of companionship between man and woman, reflecting the rise in status of the young wife and children which is one of the great transformations of our time.'

These assessments are fascinating and correct a too-simplistic view of the era. But this is also a class issue. Sociologists are better-educated, university people, peering down on their teeming subjects like biologists staring through a microscope. In the 1950s, as it happens, the majority of British people classified themselves as working class. They were still governed, as well as investigated, however, by aliens.

6

UPPER CLASS IN THE 1950S

Whitaker's Almanack, a book Sir Winston Churchill considered indispensable, contains a vivid portrait of just how class divided Britain was during the Queen's early reign. It carefully lists the orders of peers, the bishops, the greater clubs, the higher rankings of the civil service and the military high command, forming a meticulous social taxonomy of the hierarchy. And of course, in outer form, some of it still exists. London's clubland, from White's and the Carlton to the Reform and the Garrick, continues to fascinate foreign observers in the twenty-first century. Furtive-looking chaps in weary tweeds, named after the lesser counties of England, potter in and out for lunch; filmmakers use the grand staircases they potter up as sets; some of the richest clubs are still doing fine. They still smell of boiled beef and they still serve potted shrimps.

In 1952 it was all on a different scale. There were no fewer than 107 proper, grand, listed London clubs, including many long vanished. Who now remembers the comfort and glory of the Bath Club in Brook Street, or the Challoner (Roman Catholics only) in Pont Street, or the Eccentric in Ryder Street, or the Goat in New Bond Street, or that fine establishment, the Ladies' Empire Club in Grosvenor Street, or that succulently named gathering, the

Sesame, Imperial and Pioneer, also in Grosvenor Street, or the Oriental in Hanover Square, or even the Royal Toxophilite in Albion Mews (for archers, obviously)? And on, and on, and on. Nor was London the only city where the well-off and well-connected met daily to flock, nibble and murmur. In the early 1950s Birmingham boasted eight gentlemen's clubs. Liverpool had ten ornate, exclusive clubs. So did both Edinburgh and Glasgow, for the city's stockbrokers, bankers, accountants and councillors.

We must be careful not to confuse archaic names and a grandiloquent style with fundamental social change. It could be argued that the growth of private clubs in modern London, where rich City employees can mingle with the children of Russian oligarchs and riff-raff from television or the cinema, are pretty much the same phenomenon as the old clubs of the grandees. The designer clothes are very different from the Savile Row suits; the hair is longer and fewer buttons are done up; the cocktails are stronger and the wine, perhaps, is no worse. It's just that the nature of the elite has changed; in modern London, the influential, rich and connected can still hang out together well away from the prying eyes of ordinary folk. The real difference may be that in the 1950s the members of these clubs were part of a homogeneous English aristocracy – men and women who had gone to the same schools, had the same attitude to nation and Empire and shared the same private language.

From Moscow to São Paulo, Beijing to Chicago, the elites hang together. But in the lost Britain of the mid-twentieth century there was a tight solidarity of basic assumptions that we don't find today. Unironic, full-throated enthusiasm for the monarchy and a rather myopic view of British history ran through the old ruling order like golden threads, rejected by only a few weirdo socialists and faddists. The best novelists, Evelyn Waugh and Anthony Powell, knew this world well. As the 1952 *Almanack* reminds us, Britain's class structure also reflected a more Christian nation. It still observed twenty-eight 'red-letter days' when scarlet robes had to be worn by senior judges; and these mingled religious festivals (11 June, the festival of St Barnabas; 25 January, the Festival of the Conversion of St Paul) with royal birthdays (21 April, 'Princess Elizabeth's birthday').

But if one lifts one's eyes from the taxonomy, it was pretty clear that taxation had devastated much of the traditional British aristocracy in the decade after the war. Of all the grand London houses, only Londonderry House and those owned by the royal family were left. The Duke of Wellington's Apsley House at Hyde Park Corner, where the annual commemorative Waterloo dinners were held, had been handed over as a national museum in 1947, though the dukes of Wellington were allowed to carry on living there in a few back rooms. Almost all the rest of the grand houses had been sold to be redeveloped as offices or hotels.

With land prices still depressed, grand-sounding families were scuttling and giving up: this was the great age of pulling down country mansions, too. In his history of *The Decline and Fall of the British Aristocracy*, the historian David Cannadine gave a sonorous roll-call of destruction: 'Panshanger, Normanhurst, Lowther Castle, Rufford Abbey and Ravensworth Castle were only the most famous victims. Between 1945 and 1955, four hundred country houses were demolished, more than at any other period of modern British history. Indeed, by 1955, the peak year, they were disappearing at the rate of one every five days . . .' If you had the cash it was a good time to buy Old Masters. But of course not many people did.

Yet on the surface, despite the impact of socialist taxation, Britain still *felt* mildly feudal. This was certainly reflected in the culture. In Ealing comedies, in West End plays and in novels, both crime and comic, the country-house setting remained a standard one. And if many of the old houses had been abandoned, demolished or converted into golf or spa hotels, their occupants had certainly not departed the national stage. The British peerage was headed by an impressive battlefleet of 26 dukes, 39 marquesses, 210 earls and 121 viscounts.

Many would eventually be forced to find new ways of surviving. Cannadine, writing in 1990, revealed that the ninth Earl of Buckinghamshire, who had died in 1983, had ended his career as a municipal gardener in Southend. He continued:

> The present Earl of Breadalbane lives in a bed sitting room in Finchley while the Earl of Effingham – a cousin of the Duke of Norfolk – lives in the Cromwell Road . . . Earl Nelson is a police constable. Lord Northesk is a jewel salesman in the Isle of Man. The Countess of Mar is a saleswoman for British Telecom. Lord Simon Conyngham is an assistant in a delicatessen. Lord Teviot is a bus conductor. Lord Kingsale, the premier baron of Ireland, is a silage-pit builder in the west country . . .

In 1952, these horrors lay far ahead. The press was still greatly excited by the doings of a real-life, flesh-and-blood duke or baroness. Morning coats and top hats were worn even by socialist politicians. Up until 1958, when the practice was abolished by the new Queen, aristocratic young girls known as debutantes, sheathed in dresses of white, ivory or pink silk and garlanded with ropes of pearls, would be presented at court, curtsying and walking backwards as they bashfully sized up potential male admirers. This marked the start of the English social 'Season', to be followed by other highlights including Cheltenham races, the Chelsea flower show, the Badminton horse trials, the Epsom Derby and the Henley Royal Regatta – each of them an opportunity for flamboyant social display by the upper classes, a lengthy mating dance that kept milliners, florists and wine merchants in excellent humour.

To what extent was it all nostalgia for a pre-war world? There is no doubt that from the novels of Agatha Christie and Dorothy L. Sayers through to the 'society' pages of the newspapers, Britons were reacting to the disorientating new post-war world with its unfamiliar global order by burrowing snugly into the rituals and traditions of the first part of the century. But this post-war social conservatism, which would soon be so exuberantly challenged, was itself an aberration. There never has been a placid social or historic norm. The 1920s had been a turbulent decade, and the 1930s even more so. To the extent that the British of the 1950s were harking back to what seemed stable, ordered and reassuring, they were misremembering. And the same is true of those who hark back to the stable, comforting 1950s today. Underneath, the country is always changing fast. It just rarely seems to feel like it now.

7

NANCY, AND HOW TO
SPEAK PROPER

During the 1950s and early 1960s, class anxiety seems to have been at a high level. Consumerism and the break-up of the old industrial order meant that rebel working-class culture, which would soon take its most vivid form, was flowering. Yet the sense of a class-divided nation, in which those in charge spoke differently, remained very strong. Today, listening back to middle-class voices in films and broadcasts of the period, they sound like the Queen. (Rather, as she used to be: even the Queen in old age sounds less cut-glass regal than she did as a young woman.) In the 1950s, working-class people who wanted to 'get on' flocked to elocution teachers. More than trad jazz or skiffle bands, the confident plosives and icy sibilance of 10,000 neighbourhood elocution lessons should really be the sonic background to this period in British history.

Working-class icons were not exempt. In Liverpool, the young John Lennon, being brought up by his indomitable aunt, was taught from an early age not to speak the working-class 'Scouse'. His chaotic father returned, pleased to find a small boy who spoke 'like a gentleman' and who gravely enquired of him, 'Shall I call you Pater?' Down in Leicester, John Orton, who would later grow up to be the shock playwright and smasher of bourgeois convention Joe Orton, managed to escape from the Saffron Lane council estate by getting himself elocution lessons from a local lady.

Want to get on – in politics, retail, banking? First and foremost, water down the local tang. Ambitious for the stage or television? Elocution lessons for *you* then. The need to 'speak proper' not 'common' was fostered by the new mass influencers. In the days before the independent broadcasting companies, BBC 'received pronunciation' was squirted into millions of kitchens and workplaces, where it must often have sounded quite alien. Working-class poets such as the Glaswegian Tom Leonard, and Liz Berry from the Black Country, have recorded the powerfully undermining effect on working-class self-confidence.

By the early 1960s, actors, politicians and other public figures rarely had strong local accents, though comedians seem to have been a permitted exception. History's richly variegated and pungent archipelago of different speech patterns, phrases and words was starting to sound more like a modern British monoculture. This would change as a culturally rebellious working class fought their way to the front of the stage, but in the 1950s speech anxiety was impossible to dodge.

But class anxiety was not restricted to poorer Britons. One of the great, if ridiculous, talking points of the mid-1950s originated with a lunch in Paris, at which an earnest if witty professor of linguistics at Birmingham University, Alan Ross, was introduced to the wicked, hugely popular upper-crust novelist the Honourable Nancy Mitford.

Quite bizarrely, Ross had been asked to write an academic paper on British upper-class usage for a Finnish scholarly journal. Lacking conventional sources, he had rifled through one of Mitford's earlier novels as a guide for what was, and was not, acceptable usage for aristocratic Britons. (Academic rigour has intensified since then, not always with happy results.) Mitford, a successful writer and the daughter of an impecunious peer, was living in Paris, where she was pursuing a love affair with Gaston Palewski, one of General de Gaulle's leading supporters.

Despite living a glamorous life based at her chic townhouse in the centre of the city, Mitford was chronically worried about cash. With an instinct for the soft underbelly of the British psyche, she immediately saw the market potential in selling to her neurotic countrymen her explanation of what was – and what was not – acceptable aristocratic language. She asked Ross to send her a copy of his article. She loved it, writing to a friend in London that it was 'dreadfully funny throughout because written in a serious scientific style . . . He is a great new character in my life and a card if ever there was one.' Many pound signs flashed before her immaculately made-up eyes. She wrote to her bookseller chum in London, Heywood Hill, that her 'crazy friend Prof Ross's essay . . . is a natural for the Christmas market'.

Although he was initially reluctant to be dragged into a confected jape, Ross eventually allowed his piece to appear in the highbrow magazine *Encounter*. Mitford proved to be right. The magazine sold out. She then wrote her own essay to go with Ross's, on 'the English aristocracy'. With further contributions by Evelyn Waugh among others, and a fine satirical poem by John Betjeman, in 1956 Hamish Hamilton published it all in one slim volume, which may still be the most influential, if satirical, study in modern times of the British upper orders, *Noblesse Oblige*.

Professor Ross had briskly, ruthlessly divided words and accents into those acceptable for gentlemen, and presumably ladies – 'U' – and the mistakes made by lesser people, 'non-U'. He had a very clear notion of class, beginning his essay with the forthright sentence: 'Today, in 1956, the English class-system is essentially tripartite – there exist an upper, a middle, and a lower class.' However, he went on, after a period of socialism and war, 'It is solely by language that the upper class is clearly marked off from the others . . . Today, a member of the upper class is, for instance, not necessarily better educated, cleaner, or richer than someone not of this class.' Ross argued that, nevertheless, U or 'gentlemanly' people were different in their tastes and behaviour. They had an aversion to telephones, cinema and the wireless. 'Again, when drunk, gentlemen often become amorous or maudlin or vomit in public, but they never become truculent.'

To mark off real members of the upper class, the professor explained, certain pronunciations could be immediately spotted: 'In Berkeley, Berkshire, clerk, Derby, U-speakers rhyme the first syllable with dark (or bar), non-U speakers with mirk (or burr).' All of this transfixed a generation of Britons brought up on the importance of class distinctions. Help! More rules! Sent down from above, too. Where did they themselves stand? Innumerable conversations started, along the lines of 'Aunt Anne, say *Berkshire* for us will you, dear?' But if subtle distinctions of accent – and the essay is full of them – weren't enough, Ross also provided a long list of words and phrases used by proper gentlemen, as distinct from unctuous middle-class parvenus.

Here is a brief and necessarily incomplete summary, with posh U usage, followed by common non-U in brackets: have a bath (take a bath); bicycle (cycle); lunch (dinner); dinner (evening meal); sick (ill); rich (wealthy); hall (lounge); lavatory-paper (toilet-paper); looking-glass (mirror); writing-paper (note-paper); pudding (sweet); wireless (radio) . . . All of this was alarming enough to people who suddenly realized that talking about cycles and mirrors marked them out as being drearily middle-class; but Ross pushed ruthlessly on to explain that many apparently ordinary innocuous expressions, marked out their users as pathetically common: '*Pleased to meet you!* This is a very frequent non-U response to the greeting, *How d'you do?* U-speakers normally just repeat the greeting; to reply to the greeting (e.g. with *Quite well, thank you*) is non-U.' Suddenly new verbal landmines were being set and primed all across the land.

Nor did Alan Ross have much good news for those who had not been born into the upper orders: 'In England today,' he wrote,

> the question, 'Can a non-U speaker become a U-speaker?' is one noticeably of paramount importance for many Englishmen (and some of their wives). The answer is that an adult can never attain complete success. Moreover, it must be remembered that, in these matters, U-speakers have ears to hear, so that one single pronunciation, word, or phrase will suffice to brand an apparent U-speaker as originally non-U (for U-speakers, themselves, never make 'mistakes').

It is hard to imagine a more terrifying salvo aimed at the status anxiety of the British middle classes and, as Mitford had happily predicted, the Ross essay provoked a furore. It even rebounded a little on its authors: Mitford cattily complained of Ross himself, 'poor duck speaks of table napkins'; and she herself had to go back through her earlier novels obliterating mirrors, striking out mantelpieces, tearing up note-paper and censoring other solecisms.

Nancy Mitford's own essay on the British aristocracy began with all the breezy self-confidence of Alan Ross, before making an altogether more ambiguous argument about the current state of the upper orders. She was quite clear that the English aristocracy (she had little time for the Scots, or even the word Scottish, which she claimed was non-U; the hideous and incorrect 'Scotch' was her preferred form) 'is the only real aristocracy left in the world today. It has real political power through the House of Lords and a real social position through the Queen. An aristocracy in a republic is like a chicken whose head has been cut off: it may run about in a lively way, but in fact it is dead.'

She then roundly mocked modern British aristocrats for being indolently uninterested in making money, and so being forced to sell land, paintings and property in order to enjoy the easy lifestyle they expected for themselves. Although she must have known of the slaughter of the great country houses described by David Cannadine, Mitford produced her own list of grand homes whose owners had, either by dodging taxes or by letting in the public for a fee, stayed put. Most people, she said, took for granted that the aristocracy was utterly impoverished, 'a view carefully fostered by the Lords themselves'. Only a violent crime, which brought police and reporters into a country house, revealed that the world in which manservants waited on single women at dinner still existed.

> There are still many enormous fortunes in the English aristocracy, into which income tax and death duties have made no appreciable inroads. Arundel, Petworth, Hatfield, Woburn, Hardwicke, Blenheim, Haddon, Drumlanrig, Alnwick, Stratfield Saye, Harewood, Knole, Knowsley, Wilton, Holkham, Glamis, Cullen, Cliveden, Highclere, Althorp, Mentmore – all vast houses – are still inhabited by Lords who have inherited them, or by members of their families.

How had the peerage achieved this? Mitford argued robustly that they had done so by avoiding death duties, by handing the estates on to heirs. The duty did not have to be paid if the original peer then managed to live on for another five years: 'one agreeable result of this rule is that old Lords are cherished as never before. Their heirs will do anything to keep them alive.' But the aristocracy were also keen to flog off anything they could – farmland, outbuildings, Caravaggios – and charge outrageous sums for commoners to come and visit their homes.

This was all much too close to the bone for her fond but critical friend Evelyn Waugh. In his *Noblesse Oblige* essay he tartly reminded Mitford that she was twelve years old when her father succeeded to his peerage: 'at that age, an indelible impression was made; Hons were unique and Lords were rich.' Waugh accused her of revolutionary socialism – not, in his book, a compliment.

Clearly, a lot of this was what Nancy Mitford called 'a tease' and it had the desired effect. In September 1955, she wrote to another London friend about the response to the original *Encounter* article – 'such wonderful . . . mail – furious baronets, furious Scotchmen, furious friends saying how vulgar I am . . .' Eventually, as the mid-twentieth-century equivalent of a Twitter storm swirled around them, both Mitford and Waugh grew disgusted with the subject and referred to *Noblesse Oblige* as 'the book of shame'.

Across the British media, the controversy continued to gambol and frisk for years to come. An almost throwaway line in Waugh's own essay provided the next class-watchers with a new shorthand, MIF, for milk-in-first. Waugh wrote:

> All nannies and many governesses, when pouring out tea, put the milk in first. (It is said by tea-fanciers to produce a richer mixture.) Sharp children notice that this is not normally done in the drawing room. We have a friend you may remember, far from conventional in other ways, who makes it her touchstone. 'Rather MIF, darling,' she says in condemnation.

So now the mundane and humble business of making a cup of tea became yet another tiny battleground.

Waugh rejected the extreme vision of Britain as a class-divided society, substituting instead the more realistic idea that, status-conscious as it still was, everybody was alert to those below them in some obscure pecking order: 'everyone draws a line of demarcation immediately below his own heels'. There was relatively little horizontal stratification, he thought: 'There is instead precedence, a single, wholly imaginary line . . . extending from Windsor to Wormwood Scrubs, of separate individuals each justly and precisely graded. In the matter of talking together, eating together, sleeping together this mysterious line makes little difference, but every Englishman is sharply aware of its existence . . .'

Waugh was by far the greater novelist but Nancy Mitford, affectionately satirizing the retreating aristocracy and gentry, was enormously popular in the first part of the Queen's reign. Was she, therefore, in fact just an old-fashioned snob? Her biographer Selina Hastings thought not, but with reservations: 'She was not a snob in the sense of looking up to someone solely because he had money or rank; but Nancy was never a member of the public . . . She believed that everyone should know his place, and in language was to be found one of the most crucial lines of demarcation.'

Everyone should know his – or her – place. That was the real, old way of thinking behind the U and non-U kerfuffle, and behind 'milk in first'. David Hill, sent out as a young boy in the mid-1950s to start a new life in Australia, remembered Britain, even as the welfare state began to change things as a country in which 'most Britons lived and died poor, in a land of appalling class rigidity and social inequality where there was virtually no prospect of social mobility'. Speech inflections, from East End costermongers to south-coast baronets, policed this Britain. And it is often when things are breaking down that the policing becomes heaviest. British drama of the period (Terence Rattigan), British comedy of the period (Joyce Grenfell and Alastair Sim) and many of the novels of the period, such as those of Anthony Powell, suggest that widespread sensitivity to subtle class hierarchies was real. And as Nancy Mitford made clear in her essay, the class system depended then – as it does now – on the monarchy, with the Queen as apex.

8

BRITISH SHINTO

On 6 August 1957, outside Television House, then the head-quarters of ITN in London's Kingsway, a tallish, urbane man, briefcase in one hand, was assaulted. John Grigg, the second Lord Altrincham, received a forceful, full-hand slap across the side of his face. It was strong enough nearly to knock him over, though he was able to recover and clamber, with an unconvincing smile, into a waiting taxi. His assailant was Phil Burbidge, a well-known and active member of the League of Empire Loyalists – of whom more later.

Burbidge was quickly led away by two policemen and charged. The following day, when he was fined 20 shillings, he told the court that he was defending the honour of the Queen: 'Due to the scur-rilous attack by Lord Altrincham I felt it was up to a decent Briton to show resentment.' He added that the fine was the best investment he had ever made. The Chief Metropolitan Magistrate, Sir Laurence Dunne, who had fined him for breach of the peace, seemed to agree, remarking that '95 per cent of the population of this country were disgusted' by Grigg.

What was Grigg's offence? He wasn't an obvious candidate to infuriate patriotic Middle Britain, although by this time he was being attacked by almost every newspaper and commentator in the country. This Old Etonian and former Guards officer had served during the war with distinction. He was the son of an imperialist Conservative politician who had also been military secretary to the Prince of Wales and, indeed, a member of Churchill's wartime government. But now Grigg, the owner of a small-circulation monthly, the *National and English Review*, had broken the ultimate taboo and used it to launch a personal attack on the Queen.

He had argued that in her speeches she came across as too upper-class and British, and that she should strive to be more 'classless'. Her style of speaking was 'a pain in the neck . . . Like her mother, she appears to be unable to string even a few sentences together without a written text . . . The personality conveyed by the utterances which are put into her mouth is that of a priggish schoolgirl, captain of the hockey team, a prefect, and a recent candidate for Confirmation.' He hadn't thought it would be much noticed; and hadn't bothered to increase the print run of his review.

Instead, all hell broke loose. Grigg's attack echoed around the world. It was picked up and discussed in the United States, which the Queen was about to visit. There the author and early television celebrity Malcolm Muggeridge, published a second attack on the 'Royal soap opera' which implied that Britain no longer needed a monarchy at all. There were plenty of people who agreed with both Grigg and Muggeridge in the mid-1950s, but criticism of the royal family directly was well beyond the pale.

It was the middle of the summer 'silly season' when the press had little else to write about, and a tirade of abuse fell on the heads of both men. The pile-in included the Prime Minister of Australia, the Archbishop of Canterbury, the main newspaper columnists and even an irate Italian aristocrat who challenged Grigg to a duel. Grigg, who eventually accepted the challenge but suggested they fight with rolled umbrellas, always insisted that he was himself a monarchist and had meant the criticism to help the Queen modernize.

Intriguingly, she may well have agreed. Martin Charteris, then her assistant private secretary, had a quiet meeting with Grigg to discuss the matter. After it, in December of the same year, the Queen made her first televised Christmas broadcast, during which she said she hoped television would make her message more personal and direct, though she also warned against 'unthinking people who carelessly throw away ageless ideals as if they were old and outworn machinery'. Some thirty years later, meeting at Eton (where else?), Charteris told Grigg that by helping to change the atmosphere at court 'You did a great service to the monarchy and I'm glad to say so publicly.'

Grigg reflected much later in the *Spectator* magazine that the real reason why there had been such a sensation was that the article:

contained direct criticism of the Queen (as well as considerable praise), at a time when the general treatment of her in the media ranged from gushy adulation to Shinto-style worship. This most unhealthy climate had prevailed since her accession and had been intensified by the secular religiosity of the Coronation in 1953. It was completely out of keeping with the traditional British attitude to the monarchy, which has always combined strong loyalty to the institution with a readiness to judge individual members of the royal family, favourably or unfavourably, on their merits.

British public opinion is hard to fathom properly, in part because the media was intensely nervous about reflecting any possible support for the criticisms: the reason Grigg was leaving the head-quarters of ITN on the day he was assaulted was that he had just been interviewed there by Robin Day. The BBC had blacked out the entire controversy – in effect pretending that it hadn't happened, so horrific was the thought of comparing the Queen to a schoolgirl. But Grigg argued that opinion polls, letters to newspapers and letters he received himself showed that most people at least understood his position and also felt that the Royal Household was out of date.

If so, this is another powerful piece of evidence to suggest that the 1950s were nothing like 'the 1950s'. The Grigg episode is usually cited by historians to point out how different things were in the middle of the twentieth century. But consider the ferocious response to tweets criticizing Meghan Markle in 2018 when she was still engaged to Prince Harry. Direct attacks on the royals still produce the kind of Pavlovian response they did then. By the end of the Queen's reign, there is no evidence whatever that old-fashioned, stuffy monarchism had in fact gone out of fashion at all.

Progressive thinkers of the 1950s often argued that Britain was on the verge of a major democratic overhaul, and that this might need to include the monarchy itself. They have been proved wrong. A decade after the Grigg episode, Tony Benn tried much more seriously to shake up the court as part of a project that was self-consciously republican in its aim. There was a serious tussle about removing the Queen's head from postage stamps, but Harold Wilson's instinctive working-class monarchism ensured that the Benn project went absolutely nowhere. It may be discreet. It may be rarely discussed. But British Shintoism is alive and well.

9

DIANA AND RUTH

For the vast majority of the 49 million British people in the early 1950s, post-war daily life was physically harder than it is today. It has become a commonplace to say that there was a yearning for fun, colour and excitement in the early years of the Queen's reign, after the long, grey austerity years and the war itself. It is a commonplace because – basically – it's true. But the greyness was not uniformly distributed. For the wealthiest Britons, as we shall see, the post-war years quite quickly brought a return to continental travel and more interesting food. Further down the social pecking-order, things remained a lot more meagre for a lot longer. And the group who had the worst time were working-class women.

Men had returned from the war, traumatized and angry, to be accommodated into families which had learned to live relatively happily without them. Women who had had clerical or factory work were encouraged to give it up so that there was 'something for the men'. And this is the era just before labour-saving household appliances became common – when clothes were still often washed by red, calloused hands over porcelain sinks with wooden scrubbing brushes and dried in backyards with mangles; when doorsteps and stone floors were cleaned by hand, and when food shopping involved a long walk, a heavy basket and a sore back on the way home. Entertainment, before television became common, was limited to the wireless, comic strips in the newspapers and a weekly walk to the pictures. For the most impatient and ambitious women, who wanted something more – a more colourful and unpredictable life – this meant there could be dangerous choices ahead. The story of two friends reminds us why.

Among the films which had been playing in Britain in the winter before the Queen's accession was an embarrassingly duff comedy from the Rank Organisation called (titter ye not) *Lady Godiva Rides Again*. Filmed in Folkestone, Kent, it was a fantasy about a young provincial English girl who wins a local beauty pageant and then plays Lady Godiva, going on to fame and fortune. It might deserve to be entirely forgotten except for a curious coincidence, a real-life one more interesting than anything in the script. This is a true 1950s story about working-class women, power, manipulation, success – and failure.

Among the film's cast were three people who would all go on to become famous – in one case, notorious. The first was born Diana Fluck in Swindon; she had changed her name because, as she later said, 'what would happen if they put my name up in lights . . . and one of the bulbs burst?' She had chosen the name Diana Dors, and very soon was being touted as Britain's answer to Marilyn Monroe and Jayne Mansfield. The second was the young Joan Collins, in her first screen role. And the third, who became a friend of Diana Dors during this filming, was Ruth Ellis. She was the last woman to be hanged in Britain.

Dors and Ellis shared quite a lot that would help them to bond on the film set. Both had been born to working-class women having trouble with rackety men during the Depression in provincial towns. Though not quite the same age, they had much in common. Diana was born in 1931. Her father, a veteran of the First World War, was a railway clerk who played the piano in local pubs, although since her mother was having an affair with the lodger she was never quite sure whose daughter she was. Swindon was not the most exciting spot in the world in the 1930s and Diana's mother, Mary Fluck, enjoyed the most common imaginative escape route of the time, taking her daughter from a very young age to weekly films. Diana also attended a private school run by two spinsters, saying later, 'I loathed them and their stuffy little school.'

Not surprisingly, the young Diana dreamed as a child of becoming an actress, writing when she was nine years old in a school essay, 'I am going to be a film star, with a swimming pool and a cream telephone.' It's the cream telephone that tells you everything. Diana's relationship with the man who might have been her father was cold. She matured early and, aged thirteen but pretending to be seventeen, entered a local beauty contest, winning third prize. By the close of the Second World War, still a young teenager, she was entertaining American soldiers in camp concerts (the word camp is, at this early stage in Dors's career, used in a strictly military sense). By her mid-teens Diana Fluck had had numerous boyfriends, including the future writer Desmond Morris. She was also allowing herself to be photographed semi-nude for 'French postcards'. Aged fifteen, she enrolled at the London Academy of Dramatic Art and was appearing in plays and post-war British films remarkably soon.

Ruth Ellis was almost exactly five years older, but otherwise her early story is strikingly similar. She was born in Rhyl, North Wales to a French-Belgian mother, also in an unhappy marriage – and also to a jobbing musician. Arthur Hornby was always in the picture houses, but in his case playing the piano before the advent of the 'talkies' put him out of a job. He may have abused his daughters. The marriage was unhappy, and Ruth's mother carried her children off to Basingstoke and to Reading, until the family was reunited in London during the war. Ruth took longer than Diana to get into the glamour business, working in factories and as a waitress, though with a personal motto Dors would have approved: 'a short life and a gay one'.

While Diana was entertaining the soldiers, Ruth was a cinema usherette and a 'photographer's assistant'. Aged seventeen, she met and became pregnant by a Canadian soldier who turned out to be already married. Like Diana Dors, who had had a brief fling with an American soldier, Ruth Ellis was soon also enticed into nude photography. Not long after her first child was born, she saw an advert: 'Wanted. Model for camera club. Nude but artistic poses. No experience required . . .' With her dyed-blonde hair and good looks, she got the job and was quickly drawn into a very specific post-war world of Mayfair gambling and prostitution clubs. This was run under the dangerous and baleful eye of one of the major crime figures of the period, Morris Conley – named by the *People* newspaper as 'Britain's biggest vice boss and the chief source of the tainted money that nourishes the evils of London night life'.

Already, although their backgrounds and trajectories were similar, there were subtle but important differences between Diana and Ruth. Dors had more real talent as an actress and was appearing in her first films while still a teenager. She was hanging out with violent and predatory men in the hard-drinking so-called 'Chelsea set', but she had an obvious career escape route. Ruth Ellis did not. Her job as a 'hostess' involved sitting in one of Conley's clubs and having drinks with clients; sex was negotiated separately but Ruth was probably making around five or six times more money each week than she could have made in a factory. At one of the clubs she met her next husband, George Ellis, an alcoholic dentist who beat her up badly and made her pregnant for the second time. In fact, she was four months pregnant when she appeared in *Lady Godiva Rides Again*.

As her biographer Victoria Blake put it, there was already a pattern of unstable relationships between this working-class girl and dangerous men. It was a world of 'unpredictability, jealousy and violence, and a weak, alcoholic partner from a middle-class background who both tantalised and dashed her hopes of social respectability'. This man, David Blakely, was another outwardly smooth middle-class type with a serious drink problem and delusions of grandeur – in his case that he would be a successful racing-car driver. It was at one of the Conley clubs that he met Ruth Ellis and, despite her taking an instant dislike to him, began a relationship.

Soon, as Blakely pursued his dreams of building a racing car, he was sponging off Ellis. The two of them were living in a drunken, erratic West London milieu, dominated by traumatized former servicemen and young, would-be-theatrical women on the make. Backstreet abortions, furious public arguments and a perennial shortage of cash were the norm. A composed Ellis later told the court about Blakely at her trial: 'I realised that he didn't get any money. It would be spent on his racing car: but I did not mind this. I estimate that excluding rent, I was spending between £200 and £250 a year on David . . . He started becoming violent. He was constantly trying to belittle me . . .'

The comparisons with Diana Dors's husband, Dennis Hamilton, are close. Hamilton was also a violent, drunken sponger, a middle-class boy who was drifting through the alcoholic haze of post-war West London. Diana's biographer describes him as 'an out-and-out louse: a thug, gigolo and serial philanderer who treated even his friends and most especially his girlfriends despicably, while always seeming to get away with it'. Like Ruth Ellis, Diana Dors had a weakness for aggressive and dangerous men. Her marriage to Hamilton, who frequently interfered in her career, usually with disastrous results, went on for years; her friends often noticed bruises from his beatings. Just like Blakely, Hamilton had delusions of importance and grandeur. His arrogance cost Diana a full-fledged Hollywood career: after insulting the film bosses who had lured her out to California as the 'British Marilyn Monroe', Hamilton was at the centre of a drunken scuffle at a poolside party that led to the pair of them being drummed out of America.

But – and this is the key point – Dors was tough enough to ditch Hamilton. The conundrum about Diana Dors is how much she was exploited, and how much she was an exploiter – of the growing and increasingly frank British interest in sex. Hamilton, who had met her on the set of *Lady Godiva Rides Again* and married her within weeks, promoted her as a sex star. He took and sold nude pictures of her and – according to rumour at the time – hired her out to producers and other actors who wanted to experience her in bed. Hamilton, eventually rejected by Dors, died shortly after their return to the UK, in 1956, from tertiary syphilis.

Diana Dors flew high above him, continuing to make films, cut records and appear on stage and television, always exploiting her sexual allure. In 1960 she sold her memoirs, full of outrageously fruity stories, to the *News of the World* for the then unthinkable sum of £36,000. Towards the end of the age of 1950s austerity she outraged MPs by driving around in a powder-blue Cadillac and being filmed going down the Grand Canal in Venice wearing only a specially made mink bikini . . . though in keeping with the ethos of 'make do and mend' it later turned out that the bikini was in fact sewn together from rabbit fur.

The journalist who got the best sense of the real Diana Dors was the *Guardian*'s Nancy Banks-Smith. She wrote in April 1999: 'Certainly I remember Diana Dors. She was sitting on a wall looking like Jessica Rabbit and swinging her entertaining legs. At the other end was a humorous smile, like someone who has seen the joke first.' Damon Wise, who authored a biography of her, absolutely agreed:

She was way ahead of her time. There are elements of Diana, Princess of Wales, about her, and there are elements of the Sex Pistols about her. She created the idea of glamour as an illusion of wealth and success. She was her own Malcolm McLaren, her own press manipulator, and she lived her life in the full glare of publicity at a time when nobody did that kind of thing. She was the kind of woman the Archbishop of Canterbury called a 'wayward hussy' but she was also the kind of person the British public mourns like a royal when she died.

Trevor Hopkins, the producer who made an ITV biopic about her, said later: 'when I see all of these young British actresses trying to make it in Hollywood, and all the It girls trading their looks for tabloid pages, I see the mould Diana Dors created'. In the end, she was in charge. She was a change-maker and a pioneer.

But if Diana had indeed seen the joke first, she also understood what might happen to those who made slightly worse choices. After Ruth Ellis had been hanged, Diana Dors starred in a 1956 film *Yield to the Night* in which she plays Mary Hilton, a woman who shoots dead another woman she believes was responsible for her lover's suicide and is eventually led to the gallows. The film was based on a book by Joan Henry, but the story and film were heavily influenced by the Ellis story. Like Ellis, Hilton never denied that she had committed murder – and, like Ellis, she might have got away with it on the continent where the defence of 'crime of passion' was possible. As happened to Ruth Ellis in real life, Diana Dors's film character Mary is visited by her mother before she is hanged. Afterwards she sobs: 'She doesn't care about me. She never did. She always said I'd come to a bad end. Now she just wants to gloat at me because she was right. I didn't ask to be born!' *Yield to the Night*, Diana's most substantial, least glamorous piece of film work, suggests that just a little extra misfortune, a certain lack of steel, can have catastrophic consequences.

So how did Diana herself triumph, rather than trip? The truth is that she was a big enough star, and rich enough early enough, to be partially protected even from Hamilton. She also had a self-protectively ruthless streak. She was perfectly able to manipulate men and had a series of second-fiddle partners after she got rid of Hamilton. Although Ellis is often portrayed as being cold, perhaps she just wasn't quite as cold, as tough, as Dors – not quite as good an earner, nor as self-protective, or cynical. The two girls who had met and made friends on that cheesy film set in the early 1950s seemed on the face of it so very similar – two cheerful, determined, bottle-blondes from provincial towns, using their physical charms to escape the drudgery and boredom that was the lot of so many working-class women at the time. Yet there were small variations of temperament and talent that, for Diana and Ruth, would mean the difference between life and death.

This is also a story about booze. The British have always been big drinkers. Read accounts of Soho life or Fleet Street journalism in the period and the amount of alcohol being put away is astonishing. The flare-ups and the beatings between Hamilton and Dors generally happened late at night when both of them had been drinking heavily. In 1953, Dors ended up in court after Hamilton, following an all-night bottle party in Blackpool, took her with him and broke into a friend's house and stole the contents of his cocktail cabinet. Dors and Hamilton ran drink-fuelled sex parties and orgies in their houses, with two-way mirrors and, later on, cine cameras.

In Ruth Ellis's short life, the drinking and the rows happened in public, in clubs and bars rather than private houses. One of Ruth's fellow barmaids, who watched the relationship between Ellis and Blakely at first hand, explained that in the final six months they were both drinking 'a very great deal of spirits. Ruth Ellis would start drinking at 3 p.m. and go on to the small hours of the morning. She drank mainly gin and ginger and Pernod, sometimes champagne . . . I used to give her water instead without her knowledge. I estimate that she would regularly drink half to a bottle of gin a day besides Pernod.' In this woozy atmosphere, Ruth Ellis then met her final lover, Desmond Cussen, director of a family tobacco business and, like Blakely, part of the post-war motor-racing world.

A generous three-way triangle was formed and eventually, in one of the most notorious crime episodes of the 1950s, Cussen gave Ruth his revolver, taught her how to use it and helped her track down Blakely. And so, outside the Magdala pub in Hampstead, Ruth Ellis confronted her violent lover (who had recently punched her in the stomach, causing a miscarriage) and shot him repeatedly, emptying the six-chambered gun at point-blank range. As Blakely lay in a pool of blood she waited, quite calmly, for the police to arrive, telling them to take the gun and arrest her. She never made any attempt to deny the murder and would remain courteous and helpful throughout the grisly period that followed, of imprisonment, trial and finally execution at Holloway prison in London.

Placid, politely grateful to the guards and composed, she became the last woman in British history to be hanged, on 13 July 1955. There had been a fierce legal battle, centred on the extent of Cussen's involvement and provocation. He had, after all, driven her to the pub, and he had cleaned, oiled and prepared the gun, as well as giving it to her and showing her how to use it. Yet Ellis made no attempt to use this as part of a defence until far too late in the process. She had told the court, condemning herself at a crucial moment in her trial, 'It is obvious that when I shot [Blakely] I intended to kill him.' The night before the execution, she told her lawyer that she was 'still feeling all right' and that the staff in the prison had been 'simply wonderful'. After a tot of brandy, she was hanged by Albert Pierrepoint, who later told her sister that she had been 'as good as gold' and had 'died as brave as any man, and she never spoke a single word.'

Ruth Ellis's calmness and passivity helped stoke a ferocious public argument about hanging. The leading paper of the time, the *Daily Mirror*, conducted a poll, finding its readers two-to-one in favour of ending capital punishment. The *Mirror*'s popular columnist

William Connor wrote that the day of her death had been a fine day for fishing, or lolling in the sunshine, not for hanging: 'in this case I have been reviled as being a sucker for a pretty face. Well, I am a sucker for all human faces because I hope I'm a sucker for all humanity, good or bad. But I prefer them not to be lolling because of a judicially broken neck.'

Looking at the life stories of Ruth Ellis and Diana Dors, it's clear that the dividing line between them was paper thin. The hangman Pierrepoint had visited Dors on one of her film sets. She could move in just as dangerous and criminal an underworld as Ellis. She was friendly with and mildly supportive of the East London gangsters the Kray twins, for instance. Both women had to cope with violent and controlling men. Both had illegal abortions. Both had children out of wedlock. Neither was a saint. Diana Dors continued to run voyeuristic sex parties until shortly before her death, and her final husband, Alan Lake, was getting into trouble with the police as late as 1980 for knife fights and drinking.

Had Ellis been just slightly better as an actress and stayed a little less long in the worst of the West End clubs, it is not impossible to imagine her having a career almost as successful as that of Diana Dors rather than ending up as a hanged murderess. And yet the two have almost opposite reputations, the cold killer and the national icon. Two days before Diana died, of cancer in May 1984, even the sharp-taloned Jean Rook of the *Daily Express* told her that the nation was praying for her: 'You're our solid "Golden Oldie", the very best of unbeatable British. We love you and are proud of you for what you have been for 52 years. Our own! Bounce back, soon!'

Ruth Ellis never bounced back, but her legacy was more important. The hanging of Ruth Ellis contributed hugely to the campaign for the end of capital punishment. Thanks in large part to the efforts of the backbencher Sydney Silverman, working under the approving eye of Roy Jenkins, the death penalty was suspended for an experimental period of five years in 1965 and then, in December 1969, was abolished. It is almost always in this context that Ruth Ellis is remembered. But it was also a story about the ambitions of post-war working-class women, and the dangerous choices they made when they aspired to the short-cut route – the 'glamorous' route – out of drudgery and poverty. If Ruth Ellis is the classic example of a woman making bad choices, largely about violent and drunken men whom she allowed to control her, then her co-star Diana Dors shows how, even in the 1950s, it was possible to make slightly different choices and emerge triumphant.

Their stories were about class as well as about changing values. During the 1950s, particularly when power, alcohol and sex were shaken together, some remarkable pioneer travellers were crossing class boundaries in new ways. Another friend of Diana Dors, and of Ruth Ellis, was Stephen Ward, the mysterious man at the centre of the Profumo scandal. Ward was pro-Soviet, pro-hooker and a friend of one of Moscow's leading spies in London, the baby-faced Yevgeny Ivanov. In 1963, Ward entangled John Profumo, the Secretary of State for War (the euphemistic title Secretary of State for Defence had not yet been invented), with Ivanov, via the show-girls and models Christine Keeler and Mandy Rice-Davies.

10

THE BALLAD OF
STEPHEN WARD

From disguised princes in medieval stories visiting smoky cottages to the Tudors' upwardly mobile bureaucrats or Restoration rakes and whores interlacing frantic fingers in London parks, British society has always included bold migrants across the fiercely policed barriers of class division. But by the middle of the twentieth century a mixture of working-class self-confidence, rising up, and the dilapidated condition of the tax-ravaged upper classes, starting to look down, meant that social mixing was happening on a new scale.

This is why the Profumo scandal of 1963 remains such a reliable staple of modern British history. But the most interesting figure in it is not Christine Keeler or Rice-Davies; not Profumo himself, not even Ivanov. It is the shadowy man Stephen Ward around whom the rest of the cast of politicians, spies, call girls and super-rich aristos swirled. We will never properly know his side of what happened, because he committed suicide while standing trial for living off immoral earnings. The phrase about him that recurs endlessly, in books and on the internet, is 'socialite osteopath', or sometimes 'osteopath and artist'. That barely scratches the surface. With his weak face, large and hypnotic eyes and lank hair, he stares out of press photographs as if he's yearning to be loved or yearning at the very least to be understood.

There was a doomy masochism about Ward. He was the son of a quiet vicar and a flamboyant Irishwoman who was sent off to a boarding school, where he was unjustly accused of hitting another boy and thrashed in front of the rest of the school – even though 'everybody knew' he had done nothing. This was an incident which seems to have stayed with him throughout his life. Ward himself felt that this was, in essence, also the story of his involvement in the Profumo affair, calling it 'a political revenge trial . . . Someone had to be sacrificed and that someone was me.' The great contemporary critic Ken Tynan entirely agreed: 'Society created him, used him, ruthlessly destroyed him, and then closed ranks around his body.'

This is a story also about sexuality and – that slippery, loaded word – decency. Lord Denning, the judge employed by the then Prime Minister Harold Macmillan to report on the affair, bluntly described Ward as 'a really wicked chap . . . the most evil man I ever met'. Mervyn Griffith-Jones, the prosecution barrister, described him as 'this filthy fellow' who had slithered up 'from the very depths of lechery and depravity'. And listening agog to racy tales of 'swingers' (a word brightly redolent of 1963 but in fact in use in England since the 1540s) and sadomasochism, the jury was easily persuaded. One juror tracked down by the authors Phillip Knightley and Caroline Kennedy, told them:

> most of us had already made up our minds when we heard about all the perversions and sex. You have got to remember that we weren't as liberal-minded as we are today. It was all very disgusting to us. But some of us find it odd because Stephen Ward didn't look like what he was supposed to have done. It was all a bit beyond our comprehension, these two-way mirrors and whippings and things . . .

So who was this ambiguous, lecherous, shadowy martyr? The first thing is that Stephen Ward was not simply an 'osteopath'. He had a proper, full medical degree from a university in Missouri, where modern osteopathy was born. A genuinely talented healer, he had studied osteopathy before and during the war, when his patients included many British soldiers but also Mahatma Gandhi. The second thing to say is that he was not simply a 'socialite': he was one of the best-connected men in London in the late 1950s and early 1960s. As an osteopath and an amateur artist, he was friendly with the Duke of Edinburgh, Princess Margaret, the Duchess of Kent and other members of the royal family.

His political friends included not just John Profumo, the War Minister, but also Winston Churchill, Harold Macmillan, Anthony Eden and the Labour leader Hugh Gaitskell. Ward knew and treated a wide range of the richest people in Britain, including the pluto-cratic Astors. Among his show-business friends were Frank Sinatra, Douglas Fairbanks Jr, Ava Gardner, Sir Malcolm Sargent, Sir Thomas Beecham, Sophia Loren, Kenneth More, Jack Hawkins and Peter Sellers. He was thick with most of the powerful figures in British newspapers, and well known to important artists of the period, key London ambassadors and members of the European royal set. To call him a socialite is like calling Turner a chap who messed around with watercolour.

Once the scandal broke in 1963, most of these people dropped him, or pretended they'd never known him. The drawings he had made of the Duke of Edinburgh and other royals were mysteriously bought off the walls before his first West End exhibition opened, we must assume on behalf of the royal family. But before all that, while he was on the up and fashionable, Stephen Ward was almost ludicrously well plugged in. He had magical fingers.

So what about his seedy side? Ward's biographers believe that he himself did not have a strong sex drive, but rather that he got a kick out of bringing on vulnerable girls. He liked to educate them in the ways of the world, polishing and helping them, and then to introduce them to powerful men. He used them to weave a web of influence. Following George Bernard Shaw's character, who educated Eliza Doolittle in *Pygmalion*, friends called it Ward's 'Henry Higgins syndrome'. So he was able to introduce Lord Astor, Profumo and the spy Yevgeny Ivanov to women with whom they then had affairs.

The distinction between 'young and promiscuous women' and sex workers, and between 'making introductions' and living off the earnings of prostitution, can be narrow. The blurring of this line would destroy Stephen Ward. Yet any suggestion that he was a sainted victim is also ludicrous. At different times of his life he certainly enjoyed sex, and he certainly knew many prostitutes. Just as he revelled in mixing with the rich and famous, so he got a kick from mixing with West Indian drug dealers, gangsters and prostitutes in the poorer parts of West London. Prince Philip one day, the jazz singer 'Lucky Gordon' the next. In Britain's mid-century class system, Ward was both balloonist and deep-sea diver. He travelled vertically.

And that was the nub of the issue because, for goggle-eyed newspaper readers, what was most striking about the Profumo scandal was that it mashed together the grandest and most pompous men with cheeky, sassy young working-class women like Christine Keeler and Mandy Rice-Davies. It showed up the former and it raised up the latter. While stodgy, socially conservative middle-class readers trudged about their daily business, the upper classes and the wilder fringes of the working classes were, it appeared, behaving just as 'badly' as each other. Perhaps there was nothing new in this: in Queen Victoria's time, Lord Randolph Churchill famously said that 'the aristocracy and the working class are united in the indissoluble bonds of a common immorality'.

Rather like the Gloucestershire racecourse during the Cheltenham Gold Cup, the world of the Profumo affair was one in which the middle classes and their values were virtually absent. The nobs and the disreputable kids were having far too much fun and it *simply wasn't fair*. Peers of the realm had urges, it appeared, just as earthy – and often dirtier – than anyone cavorting in a drug-addled Notting Hill club. Sex was coming out into the open. (Seven years later Rupert Murdoch's *Sun* newspaper would print its first topless Page 3 girl.)

It now seems, however, that the scandal was, in truth, more serious than was widely understood at the time. Politically, Ward meant well. He had been working with MI5, and doing his naive, deluded best to bring the Americans and the Russians together during the most dangerous period of the Cold War. In October 1962, at the height of the Cuban missile crisis, Ward's friend the Russian naval attaché Ivanov, who was working for Soviet military intelligence, suggested on behalf of the Kremlin that Britain host a summit in London between President Kennedy and the Soviet Premier Khrushchev. The then Foreign Secretary Alec Douglas-Home felt that this was an attempt to drive a wedge between Britain and the United States and didn't like the idea; and it was, in any case, overtaken by events as the crisis played out.

There was a more malign and dangerous side to Ivanov's activities. In his history of Soviet intelligence, the historian Jonathan Haslam relates how Ivanov, introduced by Ward, got invitations to Jack Profumo's London home, overlooking Regent's Park. There, allowed to wander at will by Profumo's wife, the actress Valerie Hobson, Ivanov used a Minox camera to photograph key Western secrets, including details of experimental high-altitude hypersonic aircraft, as well as contingency plans for Western battle groups after the Berlin Wall went up in August 1961. Haslam writes: 'Had a conflict between NATO and the Warsaw Pact broken out at that moment, Soviet knowledge of these plans would have enabled them to inflict severe damage on Western conventional forces that held the line in Berlin.' Also revealed were the top-secret plans for the deployment of tactical nuclear weapons in Europe: 'These were matters of considerable importance for NATO during a period of heightened international tension . . .'

Thus the Profumo affair, which in theory centred on whether or not the War Minister had lied to Parliament (he had) and the sexual shenanigans at Lord Astor's grand country house Cliveden, went to the heart of Western security. This may explain, in what now looks like a rigged trial, the government's desperation to have Stephen Ward convicted for living off the earnings of prostitutes and sent somewhere 'safe', where he could name no more names. By safe, the security services, the political elite and the judiciary meant prison. Ward, swallowing handfuls of pills, chose to make an abrupt exit to somewhere even more secure.

Ivanov, in his ghost-written memoirs, was briskly dismissive of any suggestion that Stephen Ward was himself an agent:

> Frankly, a less suitable candidate for intelligence work would have been difficult to imagine. Ward was simply a loose cannon careering wildly across the deck of contemporary intelligence, demolishing the carefully assembled plots and counter-plots of each side indiscriminately. Far from being the 'thoroughly filthy fellow' or the 'wicked, wicked creature' painted . . . at his trial . . . Ward was merely a tremendously insecure fantasist, eager to please both sides for his own self-glorification.

However, in those same unreliable and highly entertaining memoirs, Ivanov reveals just how open to spies London in the early 1960s had become. This self-described Russian 'fox in the henhouse' recounts a detailed argument with Winston Churchill, for instance, and conversations with the Duke of Edinburgh and Princess Margaret.

And he, at least, understood the true tragedy of Stephen Ward – that this was a scandal of class and belonging, as much as one of sex. Ward, said Ivanov, worked for nobody and lived by his own rules, constantly trying to create a reputation for himself in medicine and in art:

> but his every attempt met a wall of rejection, at school, where he was ordered to keep silent about a crime committed in his presence; in the army, where his superiors used his medical skills but did not admit this officially; and in his family life . . . His tragic life was a protest against a society which he loved but which rejected him again and again. He climbed to considerable heights in his life, but there were also a number of falls. His main problem was that he could not find a foothold . . .

It took a Russian spy to see the thing clearly.

The Profumo scandal would help destroy Harold Macmillan's government. It revealed the crumbling morality of the establishment, and the ruthless willingness of powerful men to exploit young women, a constant from the beginning of written history right through to the early decades of the twenty-first century. All the ingredients for the scandal were there beforehand: Ward was simply the catalyst which made them blow up. At the time the British were sold a false account, which went no further than the misleading of Parliament and romps by a swimming pool. Jack Profumo went on to redeem himself with good works in London's East End.

Stephen Ward died the victim of corrupted and perjured evidence and a vindictive prosecution. The central role of Britain's secret services remained hidden. So did the genuine and serious loss of secret information to the Soviet Union. So, almost certainly, did the identity of many of Ward's close friends: today parts of the official archive remain closed, even to professional historians. The final part of this famous affair that has not, perhaps, received its full due is the racial aspect: part of the problem with Ward, in the eyes of the British establishment of the time, was that he was mixing with West Indians in a particularly volatile part of London.

11

PUNISHMENT BY ACQUITTAL

The Mangrove Restaurant in All Saints Road, in Notting Hill, West London, dished up rich, spicy food of the kind its owner, Frank Crichlow, remembered his mother serving when he was brought up in Trinidad. Frank was a large, bearded, genial figure whose regular customers included a wide selection of bohemian London life. He served Black Power radicals, literary voyeurs and the hipper celebrities of the age. Among his customers from 1968 to the early 1970s, he could count the rock legends Jimi Hendrix and Bob Marley, the singer-activist Nina Simone, Diana Ross and the Supremes, Sammy Davis Jr, the actress Vanessa Redgrave, the novelist Colin MacInnes and the Caribbean Marxist intellectual and cricket fanatic C. L. R. James. It was an acquaintanceship list almost as varied as Stephen Ward's. And indeed, among the occasional visitors to the Mangrove were many of the fringe players in the Profumo drama, including Christine Keeler . . . and Ward himself.

London is the crucible of multiracial Elizabethan Britain. What was about to happen in Notting Hill was a story that could only have happened in the capital. But it's important to remember that racial issues affected many other urban centres, from the Nottingham riots of 1958 when more than a thousand people fought using razors, knives and bottles, to the Bristol bus boycott of 1963, when black citizens fought for four months to overturn racial segregation which barred them from working on the city's transport system. In each case, these are truly stories of the end of Empire. The Bristol boycott was led by Paul Stephenson, whose father was West African and his mother British, who had served in the RAF and later became that city's first black social worker.

The Bristol story had national repercussions. It is widely thought that the bus boycott led to Britain's first race relations legislation, relatively puny though that was, in 1965. This, in turn, was strengthened with the 1968 Race Relations Act, which made it illegal 'to refuse housing, employment, or public services to a person on the grounds of colour, race, ethnic or national origins' and created the Community Relations Commission to promote 'harmonious community relations'. One of the targets of Enoch Powell's so-called 'rivers of blood' speech, the 1968 Act also provides the background to the big legal struggle that was about to erupt in London.

The Metropolitan Police hated the Mangrove. Was it because it was flying the flag for successful black business in the heart of West London? Was it because, as Crichlow suspected, they disapproved of the mingling of black men and white radicals? At any rate, in the eighteen months from January 1969, there were no fewer than a dozen major police raids, overtly in search of illegal drugs. None were ever found yet drawing a blank never seemed to diminish police enthusiasm for another raid, another go. Slowly, bit by bit, Crichlow came to believe he was the victim of police harassment. His anger grew.

Frank Crichlow had arrived in Britain as one of the early migrants from Trinidad, in the same month as the Coronation. When he first settled in West London, he felt lonely and uneasy. There were very few other black people around, and the locals were far from friendly. Working out of digs in Paddington he was employed by

British Rail before starting a moderately successful Caribbean band, a four-piece good enough to be broadcast on radio and television. But he wasn't good enough, or at least enthusiastic enough, to stick at it. With the money he had raised, he then decided to start a café, the El Rio, in Notting Hill. John Profumo and Christine Keeler were among his customers.

By the summer of 1970, when he had been repeatedly raided for non-existent drugs and had his licence revoked for technical infringements, this relatively diffident, even shy man who was in fact strongly opposed to drugs, had had enough. With the help of a recently formed group, copying their more famous US counterparts, the British Black Panthers (who had been able to acquire a headquarters in Britain when the art critic John Berger donated to them half his winnings for the Booker Prize for best novel), Crichlow organized a protest march around a handful of local police stations. It was always going to be angry and noisy, but it wasn't supposed to be a very big deal.

The banners attacking the 'pigs' were aggressive enough and there were ragged chants of 'black power', but those who took part estimated that only about 150 people were involved. The police responded with massed rows of constables in military formation, using snatch squads to haul out protesters and fling them into the backs of vans. The Mangrove demonstration was tiny compared to the major protests of the day against the Vietnam War, the industrial disputes of the time or indeed the urban riots of the late 1980s and early 1990s. But it attracted a barrage of prosecutions for riot, affray and physical assault on police officers. Nine black activists, seven men and two women, faced a variety of charges at Paddington Magistrates' Court, where some of the police charges of incitement were immediately dismissed.

There then followed one of the longest trials in British legal history, at the Old Bailey. Two of the nine, Darcus Howe and Althea Jones-LeCointe, decided to defend themselves and demanded to be tried by an all-black jury. The legally trained Darcus Howe called in aid Magna Carta's insistence on the right to judgment by a jury of one's peers. In the decades that followed, Howe would go on to be one of the most familiar and consistent critics of British racism. In the past, he argued now, Welsh defendants had been allowed a Welsh jury, Italians a half-Italian one, and so on. He got nowhere; but then the defendants successfully challenged potential juror after potential juror until they got two black ones. The trial went on for fifty-five days in 1971, with a constant small Black Power demonstration outside, as the prosecution did their best to persuade the court that the Mangrove Restaurant was 'a haunt of criminals, prostitutes and ponces'.

In the end, it seemed, the Mangrove was indeed just a restaurant: all the defendants were acquitted. By then, the judge had horrified both the Met Police and the Home Office by saying in his summing up that the case had 'regrettably shown evidence of racial hatred on both sides'. The implication of institutional racism within the police in London, which would become central to the Stephen Lawrence murder case in the 1990s, was something that the Met tried to have withdrawn. The judge, having reflected deeply, refused. Much later, in 1998, in his inquiry into the Lawrence affair, another judge, Sir William Macpherson, concluded that the Metropolitan Police had been 'institutionally racist'. If the Mangrove Nine affair had been – as it seemed – a trial of strength between the British Elizabethan state and its black subjects, then the subjects had won.

Frank Crichlow himself returned to Notting Hill and his restaurant, and set up the Mangrove Community Association to help drug users and alcoholics. Thanks in part to the socialist expatriate American Claudia Jones, who said she was trying to 'wash the taste out of our mouths' after the racist Notting Hill riots of 1958, West London was beginning to experience its annual carnivals. These have been compared to the ancient Bartholomew Fairs, a joyful popular celebration of misrule which continued into the nineteenth century. By the time the Mangrove Nine trial was finally over, the Notting Hill carnival was beginning to assume its modern form, with massed steel bands and exuberantly costumed dancers. The Mangrove became one of its hubs. Crichlow was one of its leading supporters.

The police continued to stalk him. Despite being hostile to marijuana, he was charged with drug offences in 1979 – and again cleared. Nine years later police officers smashed open the front of the Mangrove with sledgehammers in yet another drugs raid. This time Crichlow was charged with possession of heroin and cannabis, though he always insisted these were planted. He was – yet again – acquitted. Crichlow took action against the police for false imprisonment and malicious prosecution, finally winning damages of £50,000 in 1993. He died in 2010 of prostate cancer, and is remembered as one of the fathers of the Notting Hill black community, a pioneer in the fight for black rights. Subject for much of his life to 'punishment by acquittal' he was always gentle, always modest, always determined.

We have looked at class and morality, as they ensnared Ruth Ellis but not Diana Dors. We have looked at the toxic effects of shaking up sex and a crumbling establishment, leading to a rigged, unjust trial; and seen how the challenges of multiracial culture eventually provoked another, more influential trial. The first part of the Queen's reign had seemed a disastrous period for the old establishment. But sadly, and quietly, one establishment is always being replaced by another. Away from the headlines, at just the same time, a new moral order was forming itself.

12

THE DAVID AND JONATHAN OF PERMISSIVE BRITAIN

Often, pre-war homosexual affairs at Oxford and Cambridge were not merely private events. They affected the course of poetry, diplomacy and politics. The gay circles that intersected with student communist politics produced the infamous 'Cambridge spies'. The secrecy of gay men in the age of criminalization, with their secret assignations and private language, may have laid them open to blackmail, but it certainly helped them become good espionage agents. Later, David Cornwell, writing as John le Carré, persuaded modern Elizabethans that, despite the obscure heroism of his protagonist George Smiley, there was something deep, dark and rotten at the heart of the security state; and that this had been rooted in the fascism-haunted 1930s, before it spilled over into post-war crises. History books and popular films, following a similar agenda, probed the gay student friendships whose actors later did so much work for Moscow.

But there was a less well-known pre-war gay relationship – at Oxford not Cambridge this time – which would deeply affect the Elizabethan age in another way. It had nothing to do with spying, or indeed communism. This story was about mainstream domestic politics and social change. For this brief and passionate affair drew together two of the most important reformers in post-war British politics. It was a friendship and a rivalry which lasted a lifetime. Both debonair, thrusting, louche Tony Crosland and quicksilver, sardonic Roy Jenkins could, in very slightly different circumstances, have been famous British prime ministers. Neither made it. But between them they can claim to have reshaped the country more effectively than many of those who did, including their theoretical leaders Harold Wilson and James Callaghan.

As a young man, Tony Crosland had been irresistibly glamorous. Abrasive and brilliant, with the face of a corrupted choirboy, he was brought up in the strict and puritanical Exclusive Brethren sect, before fighting in the war with the Royal Welch Fusiliers. As a paratrooper in Italy, he had observed one of the most shameful moments for the British Army in its entire history. In 1945 many tens of thousands of disarmed German, Russian, Ukrainian and Cossack prisoners were passed over to the Soviet Army. They were then executed or sent to communist concentration camps. Crosland was well aware of what was happening, writing in his diary: 'all one saw was a lot of simple uncomprehending men being shepherded off under guard to a black and hopeless future: in the case of the officers, going to certain death. However, it all went off with only a single hitch . . .'

This traumatic experience hardened him against the Marxism that had attracted so many of his generation and pushed him instead towards a belief in social democracy. He was a tough-minded twenty-eight-year-old when he returned to Oxford in 1946 and threw himself into democratic socialist politics. The then Labour Chancellor of the Exchequer, Hugh Dalton, who had an eye for attractive young left-wing men, brought Crosland into his circle. By then, Crosland himself had seduced another socialist undergraduate.

Roy Jenkins was the son of a Welsh trade unionist who had served the National Union of Mineworkers. Jenkins left Oxford during the war to work in the British Army as an intelligence officer. He, like Crosland, would become central to the social democratic project of the more leftish Elizabethans. Politically, they were two of a kind. Jenkins remembered first coming across the older man: 'Tony was immensely good-looking and elegant. He wore a long camel-hair overcoat, and drove a powerful MG sports car known as the Red Menace. I found him rather intimidating, until he came to my rooms on some minor Labour Club business and remained talking for nearly two hours. Thereafter, I saw him nearly every day.'

The biographer John Campbell later confirmed, using love letters, that Jenkins had been seduced at least once by Crosland. From early on, Crosland realized that this lisping, apparently shy Welshman, who was already training himself to speak like a member of the upper classes, had an almost insatiable ambition, a well-disguised steely inner core and a determination to exercise power. Crosland would go on to write the book that provided the basic text for Labour thinking about society for decades to come; Jenkins would make himself the pivotal figure in a cascade of social reforms that followed it.

The two spent the rest of their lives eyeing each other, ambitious rivals whose friendship would endure to the end. Both were absolutely central to the shift in laws and values that would mark the middle years of the Queen's reign. They were both, through most of their adult lives, uncompromisingly and enthusiastically heterosexual; but they remained close allies for decades. Intellectuals, war veterans, deep drinkers and promiscuous lovers, they were the David and Jonathan of the permissive society. Yet we have some important things to blame them for: together they may have made Britain more civilized, but they didn't make it much more open or more equal. And that was down to the story of British schooling – Crosland's greatest cause, and biggest failure.

13

SCHOOLING: THE FIRST DEFEAT OF SOCIALISM

There is a common, easy and misleading story told about Britain after the Second World War – in brief, that a conservative country was turned decisively in a progressive direction by Clement Attlee's 1945 government. It's essentially the sentimental story told in Britain's Olympic Games extravaganza in 2012. In East London for the edification of the rest of the world, NHS nurses danced and Britons of all colours joined hands. And yes, after the war, a single nationalized health system was securely established, and under both Labour and the Tories there was a huge expansion in social housing, and an underpinning of welfare payments became available for the first time. For Elizabethans of today, the newly built 1940s hospital has become second only to the Spitfire in our national iconography. Yet other, similar societies – the French, the Germans, the Scandinavians – also run excellent health services, in some cases better than ours. Britain's system of almost comprehensive welfare payments came in half a century after the Germans had thought of it first.

The bigger truth is that Conservative England fought back very successfully after the war against the drive to turn Britain into a socialist country. The Labour Party dreamed of a new Britain, with genuine equality and much less of a gap between the classes. Nye Bevan's National Health Service extended care to millions who had fallen through the cracks in the old, private, pre-war system – but this was achieved only after socialist ministers had been beaten back by the private doctors' determination to keep their fees. Today, private health is dug in deeply across the NHS. As Bevan famously admitted of the private doctors, 'I stuffed their mouths with gold.'

The biggest Labour failure, however, was over schooling. If people can buy advancement, through better teaching and a vast web of social contacts, then a truly meritocratic society is impossible. And Labour Britain, in this respect, failed.

Throughout the modern period Britain has maintained a class-divided education system, which kept millions of people under-equipped for a modern economy, and a small number of the elite equally ill-prepared for the harsh choices Britain faced. The historian Correlli Barnett has argued that, as a result of schooling designed to produce gregarious, smooth colonial governors, Britain's ruling class was composed 'of essay-writers rather than problem solvers . . . an elite aloof from the ferocious struggle for survival going on in the world's marketplace; more at home in a club or senior common room than a factory'.

But away from the medieval and false-medieval quadrangles and chapels of the grandest schools, millions of other Britons were not being prepared either – with hard science, with maths or with the manual facility and knowledge that a world shaped by new engineering and design desperately required.

This was a gargantuan mistake, and one which explains many of our disappointments. A better educational system would have produced a richer country, better able to meet its ambitions abroad and its hopes for a more generous society at home. The failures of modern educational reform are often pinned on Tony Crosland in particular. But Labour in general focused its reform agenda on the existing state school system, virtually ignoring private schools. In terms of raw numbers of children affected, this might have made sense, but it failed to take seriously the problem of a self-perpetuating elite and left the apex of power in many ways unchanged.

Why did this happen? It is a genuine conundrum. During the key periods, the later 1940s and then the 1960s and 1970s, Labour was, after all, an unambiguously working-class movement. Its annual conferences were dominated by working-class trade unionists who had mostly been educated at secondary school and had no knowledge of the private system. With a few exceptions, its biggest, boldest figures were state educated and came from relatively poor backgrounds. Clement Attlee himself, of course, was an exception, who looked back all his life with affection on his years at Haileybury public school. But Nye Bevan, Ernie Bevin, Herbert Morrison, Jim Callaghan, George Brown and Frank Cousins were, all of them, in origin about as proletarian as it is possible to be.

The intellectuals, such as Richard Crossman (Winchester) and Tony Benn (Westminster), were privately educated but strongly hostile to it. And most of the rest of the key figures had come up through the grammar school system – Harold Wilson (Royd's Hall, Huddersfield), Denis Healey (Bradford Grammar), Roy Jenkins (Abersychan County Grammar), Barbara Castle (Bradford Girls' Grammar). Granted, Crosland himself had been privately educated at Highgate School, but he was independent-minded. Why did these variously educated, and not by origin elite, people never consider seriously reforming the top layer of the British education system, which was providing most of the key civil servants and the senior military officers, as well as staffing most British boardrooms?

The writer Robert Verkaik proposes that an unhappy love affair was part of the problem. Ellen Wilkinson, the Manchester-born working-class suffragist, socialist and Jarrow Marcher, had been appointed by Clement Attlee to reform British education after 1945.

Taking on the public schools was part of her original mission. However, writes Verkaik, it was not to be:

> Wilkinson became embroiled in the doomed plot of Herbert Morrison, with whom she had begun an affair, to overthrow Attlee and replace him as Labour leader. She worked tirelessly to achieve her lover's dream while Morrison, grandfather of New Labour politician Peter Mandelson, refused to publicly acknowledge their relationship. Two years later in 1947, convinced that she and Morrison had no future, she took her own life with an overdose of barbiturates. Morrison didn't even attend her funeral.

It's a sad story. But there is a little more to it than that. Labour politicians were themselves surrounded, boxed in as it were, by the assumptions and authority of the big private schools. Many of them had moved upwards via Oxford or Cambridge universities, at a time in their lives when this was by far their biggest achievement. There they were introduced to, and made friends with, the public school networks. Later, at Westminster, they would join a House of Commons heavily dominated by privately educated people and, if in office, would work in civil service rooms staffed by privately educated bureaucrats. The Eton and Harrow match, the Oxford and Cambridge boat race and the arch jokes about over-educated Wykehamists were in the rarefied air all about them. This is the reverse of a conspiracy theory. Everything was in the open. But, perhaps, to protest against all of this and try to extirpate it would have felt a little bit like trying to abolish the British weather.

Tony Crosland was, it could be said, the man charged with at least freshening the climate. Paradoxically his real influence in the Labour Party had come about because, although he was an MP at the very beginning of the Queen's reign, he lost his parliamentary seat in the 1955 election. After this, with time on his hands, he settled down to write a book he called, with insouciant self-confidence, *The Future of Socialism*. Published by Cape in 1956, it did indeed have a seismic effect on Labour thinking for decades to come. It laid out a genuinely different, more open British alternative to the top-down state socialism being imposed on so many other countries. This would be smiling socialism, socialism that liked a drink and some decent food, a socialism that was never too angry. But if there was to be genuine democratic feeling in this new world, its engine room, the schools, would have to change.

At the apex of Britain's schooling system at the beginning of the twentieth century had been a network of only a dozen or so private boarding schools, some dating back hundreds of years, others added by Victorians and founded to provide the British Empire with a governing class – to forge administrators, infantry officers and politicians. All these single-sex schools, generally with a strong games ethos, tended to prioritize the classics over the sciences, and to produce young men who believed they had a God-given right to be obeyed by the majority of their fellow subjects.

Providing many of the young officers who were slaughtered in the First World War trenches, the schools had emerged in the inter-war years with a kind of bleak moral authority based on long and epic rolls of honour, painted or inscribed in gold leaf on oak or carved in granite in innumerable school chapels. They were designed to look and feel ageless, part of the natural order, or at least as if they had been standing since the monasteries; but in truth, by the new Queen's reign, many were in severe financial trouble.

The Second World War had changed the atmosphere around them. Appeasement had been widely blamed on posh pro-Nazis, hanging around with the German Ambassador Ribbentrop at Mayfair parties and country-house weekends. By 1939–40, the sluggish nature of British preparations for war appeared to suggest that the ruling class was out of touch with modern technology. The popular David Low cartoon series featuring Colonel Blimp ('Gad

Sir . . .'), sweating through his moustaches in a West End Turkish bath, was one small example of the falling status of the Public School Chap.

Early wartime disasters, such as the Norway campaign and the defeat of the British Army in France, produced further mutinously radical mutterings. T. C. Worsley, a master at Wellington College, pertinently asked: 'If the public schools are national assets because of their leadership training qualities, what are we to think of those qualities when we surveyed the mess into which the leadership has brought us?' Meanwhile on the left, there was a widespread, albeit hopelessly mistaken, belief that Soviet communism was a much more ruthlessly efficient mechanism in time of war than class-divided British capitalism.

Alongside the public schools were the ancient grammar schools, often going back to genuinely medieval civic foundations. These siphoned off middle-class and bright working-class children through scholarships but were otherwise fee-paying. Finally, there were local-authority elementary schools catering for the working classes up to the age of fourteen and run either by local authorities or by the Churches. The writer Nick Timmins sums up the situation halfway through the century: 'the vast majority of children left school at 14 with no formal qualifications, exam passes or failures, of any kind . . . Overall it was calculated that one in 150 of the children in elementary school (in other words the working-class children) reached University, compared to one in twenty for secondary schools and one in eight for the public schools.'

The war rubbed Britain's nose up against these realities. When inner-city children were evacuated to the country, rural Conservative Britain had a chance to look – up close and personal – at the results of British education for working-class children in Glasgow, Birmingham and London, and didn't like what it saw. So, when Winston Churchill called upon the bright and wily former appeaser R. A. Butler, always known as Rab, to look again at the whole system of British education, the time seemed ripe for wholesale change. Churchill, a product of Harrow School, who had hated much of his time in its cold classrooms, nevertheless initially warned Butler not to mess with the private schools. But by February 1942 he had changed his mind, telling the Labour MP and junior Education Minister James Chuter Ede, that he wanted 60 to 70 per cent of places in public schools in Britain to be filled by bursaries.

This wasn't, in Churchill's view, an attack on the ruling class. It would be a way of strengthening the ruling class by bringing greater talent into it. Churchill said, according to Chuter Ede, that the new places must be brought in not by examinations alone but on the recommendations of local councils in the counties and cities – the local establishments, if you like: 'We must reinforce the ruling-class . . . We must not choose by the mere accident of birth and wealth but by the accident – for it is equally accident – of ability.' The British would become a meritocratic people.

Butler had hoped to incorporate the public schools into the state sector, but he became diverted by a more immediate fight with the Churches. The Church of England controlled around 9,000 schools in 1940, while the Roman Catholic Church controlled another 1,200. Neither they nor the free Churches that also ran schools wanted to surrender any influence to a secular government; yet they all needed extra funding for decrepit buildings and poor facilities. After a long series of wheedling meetings and outright confrontations with Church leaders Butler eventually won his argument. His Education Act increased state control while allowing the Church of England and its rivals to retain some schools with extra subsidies.

This 1944 Act introduced a sharp division between primary schools and secondary schools at age eleven, and a three-way system of secondary schools – the most academic being grammar schools, followed by secondary moderns and secondary technical schools. This created the overall structure and climate in which most Elizabethans were educated, and which Crosland would inherit.

But what the Act did not do in any serious way was to move against the grand private schools. This was not because of Butler's instincts: he was no great fan of them, despite being educated at one himself. He told an Eton housemaster: 'I do not personally think that the whole of the public school system is necessarily the best form of education, particularly when there is too much worship of games and the herd spirit.' Yet in the end he flinched from another confrontation, pushing the issue to an independent committee of inquiry run by a Scottish Tory judge, which eventually recommended very little change. Butler's biographer, Anthony Howard, regarded this as his greatest failure: 'The time was ripe, the public mood was propitious, the opportunity was there. And yet he contrived to throw it all away.' The most that emerged was a small number of bursaries from a small number of councils granting entry into a small number of schools, or as Howard put it: 'a smattering of council-financed schoolboys totally overwhelmed by a vast array of traditional public schoolboys'.

It has been a long-lasting failure. In 2016, the Sutton Trust educational charity published its regular survey of the effect of private education. It found that, although just 7 per cent of the population attended independent fee-paying schools, 71 per cent of top military officers, for instance, were educated privately. And the pattern continued: 74 per cent of top judges working in the high court and appeals court were privately educated, 61 per cent of top doctors, a third of MPs and half the cabinet (a much higher proportion than in Harold Wilson's governments). A 2019 report found a similar picture in sport. For example, 43 per cent of men playing international cricket for England were privately educated, as well as one in three Olympic medallists. Hacks could hardly point the finger: more than half of leading print journalists were also privately educated (and, in broadcasting, many more, including – full disclosure – the current author).

By refusing to confront the obvious fact that the British elites were educated separately, the 1944 Act, even though it encouraged bright and motivated working-class children to rise through the grammar schools (or, according to its critics, 'creamed off' the same pupils from other state schools), placed a heavy iron lid on social mobility. It was also responsible for one other huge failure, curiously little discussed either then or later.

Butler had envisaged a third tier of schools, technical schools, for children whose abilities 'lie markedly in the field of applied science or applied art . . . to prepare boys and girls for taking up certain crafts – engineering, agriculture and the like'. Had such schools spread across Britain in the 1940s and 1950s, the Elizabethans would have been much better prepared for the business and industrial challenges ahead. In a contemporary economy affected by designers such as James Dyson and Jonathan Ive, sculptors such as Anish Kapoor and Antony Gormley and hi-tech companies as various as East London financial start-ups and the McLaren racing team, the case for good technical schools might seem blindingly obvious.

But under the British system industrial training was kept well apart from 'education'. Worse still, by handing over the authority for this third system to local councils, but without ever giving them the necessary funding, it simply never happened. Britain's technical school system, unlike Germany's, exists only in ghost form, and in the footnotes of political histories. Backward-looking British industrial boardrooms, where they didn't want to pay for more technical education, and working-class schools dominated by the Churches, which managed to divert Butler away from more radical reform, ruined the national education system. Labour in 1945 would inherit class-divided and anti-business schools – which they then utterly failed to reform.

Back, then, to Tony Crosland, who in 1956 with *The Future of Socialism* had made himself the expansive and garrulous prophet of Labour's dreams for a changed Britain. His was a genuinely influential philosophy, not least on his old friend Roy Jenkins, and he made education one of his centrepiece arguments. He argued that although Britain, with its welfare system, National Health Service, full employment policies and nationalized industries, was no longer a properly 'capitalist' society, there was a vast amount of the equality agenda still to be achieved. Therefore, as Crosland put it, 'The socialist seeks a distribution of rewards, status, and privileges . . . to minimise social resentment, to secure justice between individuals, and to equalise opportunities; and he seeks to weaken the existing deep-seated class stratification, with its concomitant feelings of envy and inferiority, and its barriers to uninhibited mingling between the classes.' ('He', you notice: we are still in the mid-1950s.)

To do this, Crosland suggested the scheme very much like Churchill's in 1942. He wanted a democratized entry into the private school system – not the abolition of Eton, Harrow or Winchester but the forcible requirement for more bursaries and places at them for working-class children. 'A democracy cannot forbid people to fund schools and charge for going to them,' he said. But most of the pupils attending them must be non-fee-payers. Eventually, he thought, the state system would be so successful that the grandest and poshest schools would simply wither away: 'Once the state system is strong enough to compete, if parents want to send their children to some inferior fee-paying school for purely snobbish reasons, that's their affair.' For heroic self-delusion, that takes some beating.

His friend Roy Jenkins, in a personal essay for the 1959 general election entitled *The Labour Case*, argued against abolition in ways the schools themselves would have been delighted with:

> If the public schools were actually closed down (which has never been seriously suggested) there would be a substantial loss of school places, involving the squeezing into the already over-crowded State sector of the displaced children. And the loss would be qualitative as well as quantitative. Some of the best education

attainable in Britain today would be destroyed. Even if the public schools were not closed, however, but were fully absorbed into the State system, the abolition of fee-paying would still have some educational disadvantages. Unorthodoxy and experiment have a useful place on the periphery of any educational system. They are less likely to flourish within the sector controlled by local authorities . . .

After a long series of delays, in 1965 the Labour Party finally announced a Public Schools Commission, which would look into the whole matter under the chairmanship of Sir John Newsom, an educationist from Hertfordshire. It proposed the semi-nationalization of the boarding schools, under a Boarding Schools Corporation. Local education authorities would subsidize state pupils, using a means test, while some of the more ornate ancient traditions of the public schools, from the system of organized bullying called fagging to the military cadet forces and 'eccentric or archaic' dress that 'flaunts class difference' would all be abolished. What? Normal life for rich children?

It was a radical plan. But it was not followed by radical action. Even the majority recommendation to take away the tax advantages which independent schools had traditionally enjoyed fell by the wayside. Robert Verkaik again: 'Some ministers had misgivings about the final cost; others believed a massive overhaul of the education system was bound to count against them at the polls. Many of Labour's privately educated ministers were also far from committed to the comprehensive cause.' Then, when Edward Heath won the 1970 general election, any prospect of reform of Britain's public schools vanished almost overnight: his new Education Secretary Margaret Thatcher ditched the Public Schools Commission as one of her first acts.

So there was no general assault on the public schools during the decades when the Labour Party was at its most powerful. Perhaps its leaders simply underestimated the social connections that would continue to persuade the British upper classes to send their children to these schools for the rest of the Queen's reign – where they now mingle with the children of the Russian, Arab and Chinese elites – and what that would mean more widely for British society. The top schools' influence grew stronger, not less – partly because the royal family sent the next generation of their children to Eton.

By the time David Cameron, an Old Etonian, became Prime Minister in 2010, his inner circle contained so many people from Eton and other grand schools that it was being compared to the cabinets of Harold Macmillan in the 1950s. His Education Secretary and then friend Michael Gove attacked Cameron openly for what he said remained a major barrier to equality in Britain: 'more boys from Eton go to Oxford and Cambridge than boys eligible for free school meals'. The power of networks flung out from a small number of schools was indeed proof of the biggest failure of the post-war social-democratic project.

Instead of taking on directly the system that had schooled so many of his friends, Crosland turned his attention to the division inside the state system, headed by the very same grammar schools which had allowed so many working-class children a ladder up. Grammar schools were certainly numerically more important than private schools. At their height in 1964, there were 1,298 grammars in England alone, educating some 25.5 per cent of all pupils. (The figure today is about 5 per cent.) The divisive 'winners and losers' eleven-plus exam system had scarred the lives of many more, separating friends and siblings into 'sheep and goats'. Yet the culture of Britain would be broadened and improved by the sheer number who did squeeze through the narrow gate to these more academic schools. For whatever reason, Tony Crosland saw it as his mission not to take on the powerful private schools but to force local authorities to close down grammar schools or turn them into comprehensives. In a celebrated and notorious scene, recorded by his wife and future biographer, Susan Crosland, he felt the urge to explain to her what his new plan was:

> 'Good evening. You had better come in the study.'
>
> I put my novel aside and got smartly out of our bed, wondering what had caused this latest vexation.
>
> 'If it's the last thing I do, I'm going to destroy every fucking grammar school in England,' he said. 'And Wales. And Northern Ireland.'
>
> 'Why not Scotland?' I asked out of pure curiosity.
>
> 'Because their schools come under the Secretary of State for Scotland.' He began to laugh at his inability to destroy their grammar schools.

The project horrified conservative England, which resisted with quiet savagery. Crosland's first measure was 'Circular 10/65' (for 1965) which used the Department of Education's financial muscle to get recalcitrant local authorities into an armlock, more or less obliging them to convert their grammar schools into comprehensives. The following year, Circular 10/66 warned local authorities that there would be no funding for the new schools they desperately needed unless they were comprehensive. The writing seemed to be on the wall.

But in the shires of Tory England councillors fought to preserve their ancient grammar schools; and when the Tories were returned to power in 1970 the new Education Secretary Margaret Thatcher issued her own directive, allowing local education authorities to go their own way. Then came the second Harold Wilson government and battle was joined again. Legislation in 1975 forced the remaining selective 'direct-grant' grammar schools to choose between losing all their money from central government and agreeing to become comprehensives under local authority control. In the cash-strapped Britain of the mid-1970s, the only other option, of going independent, would be a huge financial risk. Many succumbed; but the fight went on. There are today more than 160 selective state-funded grammar schools left in England, as well as nearly 70 more in Northern Ireland. Crosland tried. But Crosland failed.

Labour was unable to wrench the education system in Britain towards the left, or towards technical education. Crosland left a complicated, messy sprawl of different schools that would be changed most dramatically during Margaret Thatcher's time by Kenneth Baker in his 1987–8 Great Education Reform Bill or 'Gerbil', which began to allow state schools to opt out of the control of local education authorities. The football continues to be kicked from one end of the muddy pitch to the other, with no goals being scored.

But Tony Crosland matters for another big reason. It was he above all who persuaded Elizabethan socialists that their vision of reform must go much wider and deeper than mere economics. He was a man of florid gusto himself. Such a heavy drinker that Attlee nervously kept him out of office for a while, Crosland was an enthusiastic womanizer and culturally curious.

He had, one could say, a continental rather than a Protestant island sensibility. He wrote in his book that Britain needed not only higher exports and better old-age pensions, but:

> more open-air cafés, brighter and gayer streets at night, later closing hours for public houses, more local repertory theatres, better and more hospitable hoteliers and restaurant owners, brighter and cleaner eating houses, more riverside cafés, more pleasure gardens on the Battersea model, more murals and pictures in public places, better designs for furniture and pottery and women's clothes, statues in the centre of new housing estates, better designed new street lamps and telephone kiosks and so on *ad infinitum*.

The social-democratic project of the post-war years was never simply about the nationalization of industries – the better welfare society that was promised was meant to bring in a more colourful, richer and liberated life for everybody. But these things come from the surplus, the spume and the foam of a successful, thrusting economy. Crosland later admitted that he had failed to understand how badly his project would be handicapped by persistently low growth and poor productivity. It is striking that so much of what he demanded – the cafés, the brighter streets, the longer opening hours, the better clothing and better design – all came about anyway through conventional market capitalism. But that list is also noteworthy for the social reforms it left out.

It was Roy Jenkins, David not Jonathan, who led the way on the 'civilization' agenda and made himself probably the most influential centre-left figure of all the Elizabethans. Jenkins was Home Secretary for less than two years in 1965–7 during Harold Wilson's first administration, but he brought in (often using backbench MPs to spearhead the changes) measures such as the effective abolition in Britain of both capital punishment and theatre censorship, the ending of corporal punishment in prisons, the decriminalization of homosexuality, the relaxing of divorce law and the liberalization of abortion law. This amounted to what he called 'the civilized society' and brought down on his head the wrath of alarmed Conservatives from Margaret Thatcher to Mary Whitehouse.

So what did 'civilized' mean? Roy Jenkins's time at the Home Office coincided with the sudden, thudding eruption and psychedelic swirl of the Swinging Sixties – from the Beatles' *Rubber Soul* all the way through to *Sgt Pepper's Lonely Hearts Club Band*. The pill had been introduced in Britain on the National Health Service in 1961, though in the first six years it was prescribed for married women only. In 1966, *Time* magazine extolled the 'narrow, three-block-long Carnaby Street, which is crammed with a cluster of the "gear" boutiques where the girls and boys buy each other clothing'.

LSD, or acid, was being more widely 'dropped' or taken – the suggestive comedian Frankie Howerd, for instance, was an unlikely tripper, having been given it by his psychoanalyst – until it was finally banned by the British government in 1966.

None of this feels very Roy Jenkins, who looked like a pink boiled egg in horn-rimmed glasses. He was a man whose musical tastes ran more to Elgar and Haydn than Lennon and McCartney, who was likelier to indulge in first-growth clarets than in lysergic acid – a man of tweed jackets, cashmere jerseys and cavalry twill trousers rather than tightly fitting Carnaby Street chic. He was clever, charming, intensely hard-working and lovable, but his notion of civilization was more about restraining the state from interfering in the lives of the cultured and affluent than it was about improving daily life in crime-ridden housing estates, still less confronting the unfairnesses of a class-divided country.

Class is the big political subject he talked about least. And if he did, he sounded posh. Surveying audio recordings and film of the 1960s, it is striking to note the prevalence of cut-glass accents: Roy Jenkins removed the sound of the South Wales valleys from his tongue and palate by the time he reached Oxford. He was a veritable balloonist of upward mobility. As a member of the cabinet, then of the European Commission, and then a founder of the centrist Social Democratic Party (SDP), and Chancellor of Oxford University Jenkins seemed almost a caricature of a certain kind of British toff. With his impeccable suits, richly rose-coloured Humpty Dumpty face and affected-sounding drawl, he appeared to have been assembled by hand in the senior common room of the grandest Oxbridge colleges.

He came from a family of rebellious Welsh miners and it had been a long journey. His father, Arthur Jenkins, was (unfairly, many felt at the time) arrested for riotous assembly during the general strike of 1926 and sentenced to nine months in prison. Granted, Arthur Jenkins rose through the trade union movement to become a councillor and ultimately an MP himself. This was a classic self-improving family and, although Roy went to a local school, it was settled from early on that he was to go to Oxford. He went to Balliol College. Among his fellow undergraduates there were the slightly older Denis Healey, later Labour Chancellor, and Edward Heath, who became Prime Minister. Already, little more than a teenager, Jenkins had joined the elite. Balliol was a tightly woven cat's cradle of political and social connections and perhaps the Jenkins seen on the public stage later in his life was created there.

This was meritocracy in action. But the public success of a small number of highly driven and exceptionally intelligent men, who had been the beneficiaries of a pressure-cooker education, isn't a satisfying answer to the national problem. From Butler to Crosland, a more equal Britain, where anybody with the determination and talent could rise, had been a dream, not an achieved reform. When Tony Crosland and Roy Jenkins first set eyes on each other, they both saw another charismatic and idealistic man, well capable of leading the country. Together they changed Elizabethan Britain in many ways, and mostly for the better. But on the most basic social reform of all, they did surprisingly little. And even when it came to their liberal social reforms, they didn't have it all their own way. For the 1960s was also an era of rebel conservatives.

14

THE REBEL CONSERVATIVE

Mary Whitehouse's first experience of the BBC was a happy one. She was a passionate monarchist, and as an evangelical Christian schoolteacher she broadcast a message to the new Queen just ahead of her Coronation in 1953 on *Woman's Hour*, during which she described herself as 'a loyal subject and housewife'. Although she had submitted the script off her own bat, she found the prospect of broadcasting frightening. When the BBC's acceptance telegram arrived in her house, 'I collapsed on the bottom stair, shaking like a leaf . . . I had never thought of what it would mean actually to do the broadcast!'

She would soon become an adept broadcaster and no friend to those running the BBC. Whitehouse would spend much of her adult life campaigning against bad language, violence and irreligious ideas – or, as she put it more pithily, 'filth' – whenever it emanated from Broadcasting House. And, in the future, she would recruit the Queen as one of her many supporters.

The overall cultural story of the 1960s and 1970s is usually portrayed as the victory of frankness and liberalism (good) over censorship and repression (bad). But there were millions of Elizabethans who felt very differently, and who fought back against the huge cultural changes washing over the country; and Mrs

Whitehouse was their Midlands Joan of Arc. This is a story about class – not 'working' but that bedrock of non-metropolitan England, 'lower-middle'. Mary Whitehouse came from a struggling business-man's family, and got her first leg-up thanks to the grammar school system. Hers is a story, too, about geography, for she was a proudly provincial woman. She was born in Nuneaton, Warwickshire, which isn't so very far from Oxford in miles, but is otherwise on a different planet. She spent much of her adult life as an art teacher in a school in Shropshire – deep, leafy England, far away from the metropolis. Her greatest enemies were the wealthy, powerful and entitled media grandees of central London.

But this is first, of course, a story about values. Whitehouse was always a Christian moralist. She was a keen member of the Student Christian Movement, before joining Moral Rearmament, the pre-war campaign for revived spiritual values founded by Frank Buchman and warmly supported by, among many hundreds of thousands of others, the novelist Daphne du Maurier. Like the Queen, she was outspoken about her Christian faith, writing in her autobiography: 'it is nearly 50 years since I asked God to take my life and use it . . . Nothing has altered the conviction that came to me all those years ago that God could and would work miracles in the big and little things in life if I lived in the expectation of them.' Finally, this is a story about the growth of sophisticated campaigning and media manipulation, because behind her famous butterfly-wing spectacles Whitehouse was a brilliantly deft persuader – indeed a campaigner of genius who created stunts, talked herself on to front pages and cleverly created a network of powerful supporters so that she became one of the most potent public figures of the 1960s – in her way, as much of a mid-century media star as were David Frost, Tony Benn or Joan Bakewell.

Most accounts of Mary Whitehouse's life agree that she began her crusade against moral decline after becoming alarmed at the attitudes of teenagers at her school when she was put in charge of their sex education in 1960. She believed that 'a tidal wave of permissiveness' originating in Sweden and Germany was harming British children, asking: 'how could "chastity" and "fidelity" possibly survive, even as words, in this maelstrom of atheist humanist clap-trap?' What lit the blue-rinsed touch paper, detonating the launch of a national organization, the National Viewers' and Listeners' Association, was an early example of liberalism on British telly. Whitehouse's most famous target was Johnny Speight's sitcom *Till Death Us Do Part*, shown on BBC1 from 1965 to 1975 and starring Warren Mitchell as Alf Garnett, the pugnaciously patriotic and racist patriarch of an East End working-class family.

Whitehouse loathed the programme for its bad language (merely 'bloodies' in the early days) and its mockery of religion. To the modern viewer, the show is still shocking because of Alf Garnett's hostility to black immigrants ('coons'), Jews and women. Speight had created Garnett as a backhanded portrait of his own London docker father, whose racism he abhorred, but he later had to accept that many viewers tuned in because they *agreed* with the Enoch Powell-supporting character and cheered on his every word. The show's producer, Dennis Main Wilson, said he feared (too late) that his big audience might have been laughing with Alf's prejudices rather than against them.

But Mary Whitehouse understood almost from the beginning that Alf Garnett was a satirical creation. She believed his character had been deliberately created to deride reasonable, mainstream political beliefs. Her National Viewers' and Listeners' Association briefing on the programme attacked the BBC's Director General, Sir Hugh Carleton Greene, for glorying in its assault on 'certain prejudices'. What might these be, she wondered? The *Radio Times* itself listed them – and they make interesting reading today:

> Alf Garnett. He is working class, skilled at his trade, three gener-ations behind the times and is well endowed with the most natural human failings . . . He is also a Tory and a monarchist but has

never forgiven Edward Heath for trying to get us into the Common Market. It need hardly be said, therefore, that Harold Wilson and the Labour Party are utterly wrong as far as he's concerned. The same goes for General de Gaulle, the Russians, the Chinese . . .

Whitehouse wrote to the BBC's new Chairman Sir Michael Swann in January 1974: 'Johnny Speight has made it perfectly clear, on a number of occasions, that the motivation of this series is political. He portrays Alf as he does in the hope that the public, in rejecting him, will reject also these things which he holds dear.' However, she went on, rather shrewdly, 'That it has not worked out that way is no fault of Mr Speight's.'

She never stopped campaigning against the programme, and Johnny Speight seems to have almost enjoyed tangling with her stream of protests. After she had successfully brought a libel action against him in 1967, he imported her into the show. In one episode Alf Garnett is found reading her latest book and defends her against his sniggering son-in-law: 'She's concerned for the bleedin' moral fibre of the nation!' That was certainly so. Nevertheless, this particular show ended with her book being ceremonially burned.

Many of Mary Whitehouse's targets look, from the vantage point of the twenty-first century, misplaced or merely ridiculous. She attacked the BBC *Panorama* programme for revisiting, in a documentary about the broadcaster Richard Dimbleby, the Belsen concentration camp whose liberation he had witnessed. Here, her ire was directed at showing dead bodies – hardly avoidable, given the subject. In 1977, she successfully launched a private prosecution for blasphemy against *Gay Times*, over a poem by James Kirkup in which a Roman legionary imagines having sex with Jesus. For much of the gay liberation movement this seemed outright homophobia and she was reviled for it. Her 1980 prosecution for obscenity of Howard Brenton's anti-colonial National Theatre play *Romans in*

Britain, which portrayed a scene of anal rape, felt to many in the theatre like an attack on free speech itself; Mrs Whitehouse had to admit that she had never seen the play herself.

Some of her other campaigns, however, look better and stronger with hindsight, not weaker. For instance, the late 1960s and 1970s saw, as part of sexual liberation, a determined campaign to legalize sex between adults and children. The central propagandist for this, working through parts of the gay liberation movement, was the Paedophile Information Exchange or PIE. At one point the paedophiles infiltrated, and had some influence in, the National Council for Civil Liberties. Mary Whitehouse campaigned ferociously against PIE, at one point in 1978 delivering to Downing Street a 1.5 million signature petition against child sexual abuse.

She brought in an American expert on paedophilia to try to persuade the then Labour government to change the law and outlaw child sexual images: finally achieving this through a private member's bill, after winning the backing of the new Leader of the Opposition, Margaret Thatcher. At one point, to explain her case in full to the head of the Catholic Church in Britain, Cardinal Hume, she was asked to send some of the relevant material to him. So, Mary Whitehouse ended up posting a catalogue advertising child pornography and 'boy magazines' to the eminent cleric. Her campaigning group ABUSE (Action to Ban Sexual Exploitation of Children) persuaded 1.6 million people to sign up.

In the middle of the campaign, Mary Whitehouse received death threats and promises to burn her house down. Trolls, it seems, existed long before social media. Today, after the Jimmy Savile scandal, and so many revelations of abuse in British boarding schools and religious institutions, plus increasing public anxiety about paedophile porn on the internet, Mary Whitehouse seems on this subject ahead of, not behind, her times. A broader point could be made about pornography generally, which moved from obscure and dingy bookshops in British back streets to become mainstream and ever more explicit during the Queen's reign. Mary Whitehouse campaigned against shopkeepers displaying magazines where children could see them; and against a deluge of pornographic films such as Linda Lovelace's *Deep Throat* of 1970. What would she have made of a world in which millions of children can view explicit pornography handily available on their electronic tablets and smartphones?

Again, at the time, Whitehouse was much mocked by expensive barristers and filmmakers. A soft-porn magazine was even named after her. Yet it should be recorded that Linda Lovelace herself – real name Linda Boreman – later told the horrific story of her exploitation in a memoir, *Ordeal,* in which she said of her male controller Chuck Traynor:

> My initiation into prostitution was a gang rape by five men, arranged by Mr. Traynor. It was the turning point in my life. He threatened to shoot me with [a] pistol if I didn't go through with it. I had never experienced anal sex before and it ripped me apart. They treated me like an inflatable plastic doll, picking me up and moving me here and there. They spread my legs this way and that, shoving their things at me and into me, they were playing musical chairs with parts of my body. I have never been so frightened and disgraced and humiliated in my life. I felt like garbage. I engaged in sex acts for pornography against my will to avoid being killed.

Unsurprisingly after that, Boreman became an anti-pornography campaigner. She would say later on that anyone who watched *Deep Throat* was watching her being raped. Again, from the perspective of twenty-first-century revelations about Harvey Weinstein, Kevin Spacey and other powerful men in the film world, can we say confidently that on this subject Mary Whitehouse was a reactionary figure? Interestingly, when she addressed student audiences in the 1980s, young feminists often applauded her.

A final and much more dubious issue is blasphemy. Attacking the *Gay News* poem, she launched a private prosecution for blasphemous libel, a law that was finally abolished in 2008. But again, in expressing outrage at public attacks on Christianity, she spoke for many more than herself. In 1970–1, along with missionaries, bishops, the Salvation Army, many Church groups and other public figures like the writer Malcolm Muggeridge and the pop star Cliff Richard, Mary Whitehouse was involved in an evangelical anti-sexploitation movement called the Festival of Light.

At giant rallies in Trafalgar Square and Hyde Park in London, 100,000 people heard speakers proclaim the importance of Christian values to heal a corrupt and drifting Britain. A message of support was read from Prince Charles. But this was far from a top-down movement: Frank Deeks, a trade union shop steward from Dagenham, spoke for many: 'We ordinary people have allowed, through apathy, our television sets to become sewers . . . Our churches (and may God forgive them) have often been compromising, hesitant and plain scared to give a lead.' The Festival of Light, partly because it drew together so many different religious groups and partly because its aims were too vague, never made much progress against heathen pop music and broadcast cynicism. But it, and Mary Whitehouse, were as much part of the story of the British in these decades as were the Rolling Stones.

Among the worried Christians was the Queen herself. We know this because in the mid-1970s Whitehouse launched a campaign to ban a Danish filmmaker, Jens Jørgen Thorsen, who intended to make a film about the sex life of Jesus Christ, from coming to Britain. Roy Jenkins point-blank refused to ban Thorsen. But the Churches were with Whitehouse – the then Archbishop of Canterbury Dr Donald Coggan said he would oppose the making of the film 'with every power in my being' and threatened to use blasphemy laws going back to the 1600s. At this point a young supporter of Mary Whitehouse's campaign, Michael Hastings, wrote to the Queen and, against all previous practice, she gave explicit permission for her reply to be published. In it she expressed hostility to such an 'obnoxious' film being made in Britain – a very rare example of her intervening in public controversy, which shows how strongly she must have felt.

Today, the settlement in towns and cities of millions of Muslim Britons has lent an entirely new edge to the blasphemy debate. Hindu protesters have also invoked blasphemy. Whatever side you are on in this, it is hard to deny that Mary Whitehouse was pointing an angry finger at the future, not simply crooking one towards the past.

Comedians and journalists would treat her as a figure of fun. As we shall see, she was the target of a dramatic protest by the Gay Liberation Front in 1971. In the heat of the culture war going on in Britain in the 1960s and 1970s, Whitehouse was also considered an extremely dangerous figure by parts of the establishment. For some eleven years, she was effectively banned from the BBC, and any mention of her name on air had to be referred up to senior managers. The only other person of whom this was true was Enoch Powell.

Hugh Carleton Greene, the brother of the novelist Graham Greene, who had been a journalist and propagandist during the war, and was Director General of the BBC throughout the 1960s, loathed her and refused to meet her. Indeed, he had a portrait painted by the Wigan artist Jim Isherwood, of Whitehouse nude, with five breasts, at which he would throw darts – behaviour which today would be regarded as sinister or sick rather than witty. Greene was a determined and uncompromising modernizer. He was right to see Whitehouse as his enemy; and she was right to see him as hers.

He spoke bluntly about wanting to clear out from the BBC:

> accumulated dust from what seemed to my journalistic, rather than philosophic, eyes to be, at the end of the 1950s, a rather stuffy institution, out of touch with the young and the rebellious, appealing to a rather narrow section of the public. To keep pace

with the values of a changing world you have in fact to keep a bit ahead and in the case of the BBC it meant trying to shift its position from being a recognised part of the establishment into a very different posture from which it could radically, and sometimes irreverently, question accepted establishment attitudes and beliefs.

Ever since then, successive directors general of the BBC have struggled to cope with the consequences of his change of direction.

Many of the most eminent people in television, in ITV as well as the BBC, believed that if she was listened to seriously Whitehouse would destroy the industry in Britain. And she wasn't always shrewd. Her inability to distinguish the merely smutty and suggestive – as in the lyrics to Beatles songs, for instance – from genuine moral corruption made it easy to mock her. From today's viewpoint, the biggest charge against her is that she was homophobic. She always denied this, describing cordial conversations with 'the Gays', and she seemed genuinely shaken in October 1977 when a young gay man during a debate at Birmingham University Students' Union told her in tears, 'I am a homosexual . . . I go in fear and trembling of my life because of you – I am anathema to you.'

Like many Christians, she distinguished between sexual practices and orientation – a distinction rejected by LGBT Britons then and now. She said, 'When I say what is true – that I'm not against homosexuals as people, but believe homosexual practices to be wrong, I'm very conscious of the inadequacy of what probably sounds a very negative declaration. Homosexuals have as much right to be fully understood, to be treated with compassion and love as the rest of us.' But, she went on, perhaps revealing more of the deeper feelings: 'The natural repugnance which most people feel when homosexuality and lesbianism is mentioned can result in a harshness of attitude and thinking which is, at least, unhelpful and certainly as unChristian as the perverse practices which are condemned.'

Part of the story of modern Britain has been restless liberalization and so, today, these views put her beyond the pale. But there is no doubt that Mary Whitehouse hit some real targets – violent and misogynistic pornography, paedophilia – and hit them hard. Nor can there be doubt that she was a pioneer campaigner, finding new ways to influence opinion which were then exploited by others. She was a quiet expert at manipulative stunts, such as the delivery of large petitions to Downing Street or Buckingham Palace. She would call up useful experts from abroad and cajole them into coming to Britain to make more news. Despite those early broadcast nerves, she soon became a pungent, often humorous and forceful speaker, happy to take on some of the best-known names in television in their own studios. She knew the power of bombardment, albeit with an old-fashioned typewriter and a GPO telephone rather than a Twitter feed. She was an expert organizer, able to muster millions of signatures on petitions and drum up large audiences, mainly of women, almost anywhere in Britain. She knew how to leak information, persuade editors to give her front-page stories and exploit legal loopholes to devastating effect. All of these techniques would be followed by many other organizations, pursuing many other interests. But their maestra was Mary Whitehouse.

How many Britons did she speak for? Since she pursued so many campaigns against so many targets, that is an impossible question to answer. No doubt some of the people who signed her petitions against BBC filth then went home and rather enjoyed the very programmes they pretended to be outraged by. But there was a considerable anti-liberal and traditionally religious part of the country, pushed to one side during the Swinging Sixties, but never pacified and never conquered. It was this quiet congregation of disregarded Elizabethans for whom she spoke.

15

GRAHAM, A VERY NAUGHTY BOY?

In 1971 Whitehouse came up against one of the most powerful weapons of social liberalism, humour. And this confrontation starts with a man who seemed, from the outside, the absolute embodiment of mid-twentieth-century British heterosexuality. Graham Chapman was addicted to tweed jackets, a briar pipe, rugby and pints at the bar with fellow sportsmen. He was at the centre of a dishevelled platoon of comedy writers and performers who by the late 1960s were making Britain laugh in a new way. Chapman himself was en route to becoming a fully qualified junior doctor at St Barts Hospital in London and was up for all the alcohol-fuelled boyish japes expected of medical students at the time. With fitting surrealism this future Python had been persuaded to turn away from medicine and towards comedy by the Queen Mother who, after a chance conversation, urged him to join a comedy tour of New Zealand.

At around the same time, Chapman realized that he was gay. His sexuality had not been clear to him, either as a Leicestershire schoolboy – he was the son of a police officer – or as a young student at Cambridge. But, on a writing holiday with John Cleese and others on Ibiza, which in 1966 was a permissive haven, Chapman met and fell in love with his long-time partner David Sherlock. It was the year before homosexuality was partially legalized in Britain. It was still the era of aggressive 'aversion therapy' for gay people. Making his sexuality public would have destroyed Chapman's nascent career as a doctor, and probably on television. Nevertheless, he courageously came out to friends, including his former girlfriend, and most of the future cast of *Monty Python's Flying Circus*. John Cleese believed he was still fundamentally angry about the issue:

> Graham, at that point, decided that everyone was gay; it was just a question of the extent to which they were gay. Gay until proven innocent. And I don't think he was very comfortable about this, because I think he needed to see that everyone else was gay. He didn't want to be gay on his own, and what was complicated about Graham is he thought of himself, or his image of himself, as very virile, which ties in with the rugby and the mountaineering and all that sort of stuff. And what he couldn't stand was 'camp gay', he hated the equating of gayness with being effeminate, and that made him very angry, and he didn't like gays who were effeminate.

Chapman threw himself into support for the new Gay Liberation Front, founded in Britain in 1970 at the London School of Economics by students who had been inspired by the new gay pride movement in New York. The GLF held its first protest marches the following year. One of its key targets was Mary Whitehouse and the Festival of Light. Graham Chapman was about to become one of the few well-known figures who had come out openly, using a live TV interview with George Melly, the jazz singer, himself bisexual, a surreal conversation in which Chapman is clearly drunk. He may have needed the drink: even in entertainment, very few other gay men were out.

To start with, he limited his practical support to attending weekly gay liberation meetings at All Saints Church in Notting Hill, where he munificently funded a tea urn to provide for the up to 400 people regularly turning up. There is something profoundly British-Elizabethan about a radical comedian who had been promoted by the Queen Mother deciding that what gay liberation most needed was a decent cup of tea. In November 1971, Chapman went further. Fans of *Monty Python* will be unsurprised to know that he provided nuns' habits for gay activists to disguise themselves when they entered a Festival of Light evangelical rally at Westminster Central Hall. Once inside, the 'nuns' released live mice, brandished bananas, clapped and cheered satirically and danced a conga.

All of this, however, was a mere flea-bite compared to the controversy that Graham Chapman, John Cleese and their colleagues would provoke at the end of the decade when they released the 1979 film *Life of Brian*, an assault on various idiocies, religious and political, seen through the story of a Christlike messiah called Brian Cohen. Although John Cleese applied to play the role of the Messiah, this went to Graham Chapman, who was then finally managing to confront his lifelong alcohol addiction. It gave him his most famous role by far, made him a hero to a generation of young people and brought him the further enmity of Mary Whitehouse and the Festival of Light.

Although they picketed the film and managed to persuade some British councils to refuse to allow it to be shown, this publicity helped the movie rather than the reverse. In New York, to the Pythons' delight, *Life of Brian* was picketed by real nuns, while in Sweden it was advertised as the film that was so funny it had been banned in Norway. There is no evidence whatever that this carefully written film, which nowhere refers to Christ, has done any damage to the reputation of Christianity. In fact, in a final pleasing rebuke to the blasphemy lobby, its best-remembered scene, the 'What have the Romans ever done for us?' argument between the People's Front of Judaea and the Judaean People's Front, is a take-down of the contemporary squabbling between far-left Trotskyist groups. The dangerous gay campaigner had ended up choosing to skewer Marxists not Methodists.

Chapman, who was a thoughtful social observer as well as a sharp comedian, argued that the great achievement of the Gay Liberation Front was to start to end the exclusion of lonely men and women across Britain:

> If it means that people are prepared to stand up and say 'I'm gay,' and someone hearing about it in, say, Oldham will be able to think, 'Thank God, I'm not so abnormal after all,' it gives a lot of comfort, and it means that the predominantly homosexual man or woman will be able to lead his or her own life instead of making a disastrous heterosexual marriage just in order to have children.

Chapman believed older gay people had been imprisoned in an exaggerated and effeminate world from which they now had to be freed, whether they wanted to be or not: 'The older homosexuals are afraid – they really do mince and talk in funny high voices and they are homosexual without admitting it and having to suffer the consequences. They think the GLF will ruin it for them. Any liberating force is important. But when the slaves were liberated in America, they didn't particularly like the idea . . .'

Apart from the highly questionable parallel, was this not uncharitable about all the gay lives limited before the age of liberation? Yes, the world in which words like pansy, nancy and fairy were openly bandied around, and 'queer-bashers' roamed the streets, was a world of fear, self-hatred and self-harm for uncomfortable numbers of gay men and women in Britain. Yet it is simply not true, and makes no human sense, to think that there was no kind of tolerable gay life in Britain before 1967.

16

OTHER HOMOSEXUALITIES

On the surface, few social attitudes have changed as much in Britain during the Queen's reign as that towards homosexuality. Traditional hostility to same-sex relationships goes back in Britain, as in other European countries, to the dawn of modern history. In England, the 1533 Buggery Act made such behaviour punishable by death, and throughout the first fifteen years of the modern Elizabethan period – until 1967 – homosexual behaviour between men was a crime, punishable by imprisonment. Today, by contrast, the United Kingdom is measured as having one of the highest degrees of liberty in the world for its LGBT people. In 2015, an international gay rights organization gave it the highest score in Europe, with 86 per cent progress towards 'respect of human rights and full equality' for LGBT people, and 92 per cent in Scotland alone.

Tales of the dark ages have become part of gay folklore. Stories of men entrapped by 'pretty police' in public toilets and having their lives publicly upended are legion. And during most of the twentieth century class was no protector of gay men, in particular. In 1931, Lord Beauchamp, a member of the Lygon family who owned the grand country estate of Madresfield (the original for

Marchmain, the splendid house in Evelyn Waugh's *Brideshead Revisited*) was accused of 'rampant buggery' by his politically hostile brother-in-law, the Duke of Westminster. It was true. Beauchamp had a weakness for footmen in particular. Westminster, Britain's wealthiest man, was livid that his divorces had excluded him from George V's court while Beauchamp seemed to be getting away with it. When he told the monarch about him, George V is alleged to have replied, 'My God. I thought that men like that shot themselves.'

A clique of Tory aristocrats arrived at Madresfield and confronted Beauchamp, giving him a choice of immediately leaving the country or being publicly shamed and ruined. He resigned most of his public offices and eventually left for the continent. Initially he planned to kill himself, as the King had kindly suggested, but was talked out of it by his children. His daughters, by the end of the Second World War, were living in comparative poverty. One had had so many love affairs it was delightfully said of her, 'My dear, that woman knew every ceiling in England.'

Beauchamp was the victim of a particularly poisonous family feud, of course: many gay men were able to carry on their lives without public disgrace, and the existence of gay clubs throughout the twentieth century gives the lie to the idea that all homosexuals found life impossible or intolerable. But by the early 1950s there was a renewed campaign against gay men, with the Metropolitan Police operating out of public toilets across the capital, both exploiting and choreographing a wave of media hysteria, about a supposed 'epidemic of sodomy' sweeping Britain. One of their most famous victims was the great actor John Gielgud, caught importuning an undercover policeman in a public toilet in 1953. Despite giving a false name in court, he was spotted by a journalist and became front-page news.

Gielgud was rehearsing a play with, among others, Dame Sybil Thorndike, who told him, 'Oh John, you have been a silly bugger!' The producer of the play, Binkie Beaumont, feared the public would stay away, but at his first appearance in Liverpool the extremely nervous actor found himself cheered to the rafters as he walked on to the stage. The spontaneous applause was repeated later in London. Yet there is no upbeat ending here: later in the run of the play, Gielgud found he was suffering from double vision, had a full nervous breakdown and was forced to quit acting in public for a while. It was often the psychological pressure on gay men in an essentially censorious public atmosphere that was the biggest danger.

All this said, some words of caution are appropriate. First, although the media and many politicians, as well as judges and senior police officers, were outspokenly hostile to homosexuality, there is much less convincing evidence that ordinary members of the public felt the same way. Second, the notion that we have left an age of darkness, in which most people loathed homosexuals and entered an age of brightly lit tolerance is not something many gay people today would agree with. Social change happens much more patchily and raggedly. Finally, whether we call it classic English hypocrisy, or admire the decorous discretion of another age, there is another side to this story. And it takes us to one of the greatest composers Britain has ever produced.

The reconsecration in May 1962 of the rebuilt Coventry Cathedral was a pivotal moment for post-war Britain. It was an assertion of the country's cultural rebirth after the war. The new building was yoked to the shell of the medieval St Michael's Cathedral, which had been destroyed by the Luftwaffe during the Coventry Blitz of November 1940. Its architect was Sir Basil Spence, one of the most influential modernist voices of the age. Its artwork included major pieces by the two most famous British artists of the period, a vast tapestry by Graham Sutherland, then seen as only a step behind Picasso, and a huge, incandescent window by John Piper.

The Queen's opening of the cathedral was intended as a bold statement of reconciliation in a Britain where German-hating was still something of a national pastime. In the immediate aftermath of the 1940 bombing, Coventry's senior priest Richard Howard had written the words 'Father, forgive' on chalk on the blackened back wall of the destroyed cathedral. He was much derided. A month later, Howard had told listeners to BBC radio that he was determined that after the war Britain must help 'to build a kinder, more Christ-child-like world'.

Because of the shattering effect of the siege of Stalingrad, Coventry was twinned, in a world first, with that Soviet city, and then in 1956 with Dresden, which had been fire-bombed by the RAF in what many believed had been a revenge attack for the eradication of medieval Coventry's city centre.

So this was a moment to ponder Britain's status as a peace-loving country, in relation not only to Germany but, at a very dangerous time in the Cold War, to the Soviet Union as well. What kind of musical statement was appropriate? Coventry Cathedral had made a choice which was both obvious and yet bold. They had commissioned – though they tried hard not to pay him – Britain's greatest living composer, Benjamin Britten, a man now firmly part of the cultural establishment, to write a war requiem Mass. What was bold about that? For one thing, Britten was a well-known and outspoken pacifist. And for another, he had been living openly as a gay man long before decriminalization.

Britten had contemplated writing a major requiem Mass twice before, once after the nuclear attack on Hiroshima, and then again after the death of that great hero of non-violent action, Mahatma Gandhi. This time, he dedicated the Mass to four friends who had died during or after the war, three of them gay, and one the object of an early passion of his. The text interleaves the Latin Mass for the dead with nine anti-war poems by Wilfred Owen, the popular (and gay) Great War poet. Britten told the Australian artist Sidney Nolan that he saw his *War Requiem* as an act of atonement or restitution: 'Really what the whole thing is, it's a kind of reparation.' To underline this, he planned the main solos to be sung by three artists from different warring countries – his own lover and partner Peter Pears, the German baritone Dietrich Fischer-Dieskau and the Russian soprano Galina Vishnevskaya.

Britten had heard Vishnevskaya sing when she came with her husband, the cellist Mstislav Rostropovich, to his own annual music festival at Aldeburgh on the Suffolk coast. Now, how much does this matter? How much have the high arts ever really affected the national mood? Classical music is much loved by a passionate minority; but can it be said that a composer such as Britten, unquestionably great, reaches out beyond a limited and specific natural audience? In his case the answer must be yes. First, in the late 1950s and early 1960s, classical music provided a rare bridge between the West and the Soviet world. Benjamin Britten was revered by Soviet musicians, who had invited him to Moscow. In turn, the great Russian composer Dmitri Shostakovich was invited to London and became a firm friend of Britten's.

In the end, despite all of this, the Soviet authorities refused to allow Galina Vishnevskaya to sing in Coventry. Britten said that the combination of a cathedral and the notion of reconciliation with West Germany had been too much for them; the Russian Minister of Culture, Ekaterina Furtseva, tartly asked the singer: 'How can you, a Soviet woman, stand next to a German and an Englishman and perform a political work?' Still, after the performance of the consecration, Vishnevskaya was allowed to take part in a recording, conducted by Britten, which sold 200,000 copies as a two-record set when it was released at the beginning of 1963. And the *War Requiem* has already enjoyed a considerable afterlife: it became a firm favourite of the anti-nuclear movement and the Sixties counterculture.

This was remarkable enough. But Benjamin Britten's bold ability to ignore official British hostility to homosexuality is even more striking. As a younger man, he had been part of the W. H. Auden and Christopher Isherwood gay, left-wing set, cutting his teeth as a composer on pioneering documentary films. When he left Britain in 1939, it was with Peter Pears, who had been a close musical collaborator: almost as soon as they got to the United States, where Auden and Isherwood were awaiting them, they became lovers and were close, lifelong partners thereafter. Despite the illegality of living as gay men in post-war Britain, they both registered as conscientious objectors, performing frequently together. As they became more and more famous, Pears and Britten made no attempt to hide their relationship, without going out of their way to advertise it either.

'Everybody knew' – including the Queen and Prince Philip, who in 1953 joined them at a private dinner party to listen to a run-through of the opera specially commissioned in the aftermath of the Coronation, *Gloriana*. Those at the dinner party thought the royal couple had thoroughly enjoyed themselves; afterwards, Prince Philip took the trouble to study the libretto closely, and shortly after its first performance Britten was made a Companion of Honour. By the time of the Coventry commission, he was celebrated as the composer of a string of much loved operas – *Billy Budd, Peter Grimes, Albert Herring, The Turn of the Screw, A Midsummer Night's Dream* – as well as piano and violin concertos, many song cycles and numerous other compositions. His sexuality, so far as the British establishment was concerned, seems to have been a matter of sublime indifference.

By the first performance of the *War Requiem*, having two openly gay men taking centre stage among the archbishops – eight of them, no less – seems to have provoked almost no comment. In 1967 the Queen and the Duke of Edinburgh came to open Britten and Pears's new concert hall in Snape. Pears was awarded a CBE in 1958 and eventually knighted. Britten joined the most exclusive royal honours circle in 1965, becoming a member of the Order of Merit. In that year, we should remember, less prominent gay men were still being arrested by the police and faced ruin, even prison.

One could argue that this was a classic case of English – and indeed monarchical – hypocrisy. As Britten was composing his vast musical blast against war, he had to close his ears, and shut windows, against the USAF bombers screaming overhead as they left their nearby base. The Queen, titular head of the British military, gave her blessing to what ought to have been seen as an act of profound dissent. As her police officers leaped out of booths in public urinals to collar frightened homosexuals, she and her husband listened to Pears singing accompanied on the piano by his partner and lover Britten.

To a modern eye the case is even odder than this. For Benjamin Britten had a very well-documented and also well-known fascination for teenage boys. After a passionate love affair with a strikingly good-looking adolescent German boy, which may well not have been consummated physically, he was forever adopting and making favourites of schoolboys, preferably around the age of thirteen. The writer John Bridcut, who knew Britten, gave a list of them in his book *Britten's Children*. And it's a long list. Some of them were recruited as singers in operettas and song cycles. Others were helped with their musical ambitions. Often, they were piled into his car for local trips, or he simply played with them in his garden.

By the twenty-first century, with its profound anxieties about paedophilia, this behaviour would simply not have been tolerated. And yet, as Bridcut makes very clear after extensive interviews, there is no evidence the composer interfered with the boys. Rather, he seems to have had a Peter Pan complex of his own, a desperation to return to schooldays which had been abruptly terminated so that he could attend music school in London. He adopted the childish patois of the English schoolboy, and threw himself into games of cricket, tennis and so forth as a way of escaping the pressures of his professional musical life.

Nothing about this is simple. Judging by letters and anecdotes, there was a half-hidden romanticism about his boy obsession, which flowed into his music. Boyish trebles became very important to

Britten's sound world, conveying innocence, purity – but occasionally seduction too. The composer Michael Berkeley, who was Britten's godson, said that the sound of boys' voices was 'The key to a door for him. It opened a door to his emotional landscape.' This emotional landscape did involve what looked to outsiders like love affairs – including, for instance, with David Hemmings, who later became one of the most famous of English actors. Britten then became entranced by the young son of one of his librettists, a boy called Roger Duncan. Bizarrely, he asked his father whether he would 'share' his son. Even more bizarrely, the father, Ronnie Duncan, agreed. Mentioning his daughter he explained: 'We've always got Briony.' Letters between the composer and the young boy are full of kisses and expressions of love.

Perhaps it is too easy to jump to conclusions. Perhaps this is one part of the atmosphere of the lost Elizabethan world we can't now recapture or understand. According to John Bridcut, Roger, having been teased by other boys at his school, Harrow, 'became embarrassed about it. He did not dilute the effusion in his letters, but "we talked about it and I told him that I wasn't homosexual, and he respected that. He used to kiss me, and that was about all."' In later life, Roger explained that Britten had been very proper, even straitlaced: their conversation on walks was mainly about why Stravinsky and Shostakovich were better than Schönberg: 'I think my father trusted Ben not to . . . seduce me, to be straightforward. And my mother likewise. I was a pretty precocious, articulate person, and if I'd had any concerns I would have told them, and I didn't.' This might be dismissed as one lucky escape – except for the fact that so many of the boys befriended by Britten looked back on him in later life with affection and delight rather than embarrassment or horror. Many of them went on to be successful musicians and even composers. To attract the composer's eye might have been a lucky thing rather than the reverse.

We are here deep in a thicket of confusion that divides the

Britain of the mid-twentieth century from today's attitudes. In the 1950s we were a country of single-sex boarding schools; of chapels and churches with unquestioned male priestly authority; of scoutmasters and cadet forces, and of family beds shared in crowded working-class households. Shame and privacy were stronger forces. This was a culture that barely mentioned predatory paedophilia. That it existed is borne out in personal anecdotes, including some the author has heard from prominent figures today, and in some fictional writing, for instance by Laurie Lee. To that extent, we can give a simple round of applause for the more frank (and frankly suspicious) atmosphere of the twenty-first century. Teacherly paedophiles and boy-molesting priests find life a lot harder now.

But Benjamin Britten, were he somehow able to join the conversation, might ask whether something has not also been lost – the very notion that it is possible for adults to have healthy, nourishing and relatively innocent friendships with children. For the culture of the mid-twentieth century was also one of personal restraint, which didn't see individual sexual fulfilment as one of the great goods of life, and in which self-repression could be seen as admirable rather than simply sad.

For if one major reason that Benjamin Britten 'got away with it' as an openly gay man in an era of rampant homophobia is that he was a genius, and genius has always played by its own rules, a second reason is that he wasn't *that* open. 'Everyone knew' – that's broadly true. When Britten was offered the job of Musical Director at Covent Garden in 1952, a powerful clique gathered against him. His rival composer William Walton remarked: 'There are enough buggers in the place already, it's time it was stopped.' Michael Tippett said that anti-Britten composers such as Constant Lambert, along with the poets Dylan Thomas and Louis MacNeice, 'had great chips on the shoulder and entertained absurd fantasies about a homosexual conspiracy in music, led by Britten and Pears . . .

[Walton] once let out a great cry, saying "Everyone is queer and I'm just normal, so my music will never succeed."'

Yet visitor after visitor to the Britten–Pears home in Aldeburgh noted that the two men kept separate bedrooms. They were private, fastidious and discreet men. Stephen Reiss, one of the managers of the Aldeburgh Festival, said he believed that Britten was highly sexed, like many creative people: 'But he was also, I think, highly controlled, and held himself in check, and didn't do it.' Straitlaced local housekeepers who came to work for them saw no sign of sexual activity.

All this allowed them to project a civilized mid-century equivalent of 'don't ask, don't tell' – a quiet determination to keep private lives private. It allowed for close relationships with the Queen and Prince Philip, including visits to them at Sandringham. Britten liked the Queen and confessed to being 'a bit of a snob'. More political and outspoken gay friends were irritated by his discretion and social climbing: this is probably what caused him to fall out with his old friend and collaborator W. H. Auden, for instance. A friend of Auden's said: 'It was what seemed Ben's lack of daring, his desire to be the Establishment, that irritated Wystan most; the playing it safe, settling for amiability as a guard against his queerity . . .' Maybe so: but this was one way of being gay in Britain in the middle of the twentieth century, and for some lucky men it worked exceptionally well. Others had a very different experience.

So far, we have discussed gay men. There was a powerful lesbian subculture too, particularly in London, though it has been less frequently and less vividly described. But, like the male gay culture, its watchword was discretion and behind closed doors it allowed a remarkable amount of social mixing, of a kind rare outside. Barbara Hosking, the disabled Cornish daughter of a shopkeeping family, would rise to become one of the most influential civil servants of her generation, working for, among others, Edward Heath, Harold Wilson – in Downing Street – and Tony Benn during his technological phase. She had started as a rising star in the Labour Party machine during the 1950s, and ended as one of the midwives of breakfast television in the 1980s. From an early age, she knew that she was attracted to women. When she first arrived in London and was looking for a room to rent she was, by happy chance, taken in by a lesbian couple who eventually introduced her to the Gateways club in Chelsea.

She takes up the subject in her autobiography. At the Gateways, Hosking:

> met an extraordinary range of women, from prostitutes to university lecturers. I danced with them all, memorably with Jeanette, a plumpish nineteen-year-old prostitute from Yorkshire with a beautiful smile, and as wholesome as freshly baked bread. She was an only child, and as I grew to know her she told me her story: of the father who had raped her from the age of twelve, and of the mother who found out when Jeanette was sixteen and threw her out of the house. She lived entirely outside the law. Everything was paid for in cash, and a friendly shopkeeper in the Edgware Road, who sold cigarettes and sweets, became her banker. She took him her earnings every day and he kept her money safe, giving her cash when she wanted it. Jeanette had two pieces of luck, I reflected: she was not run by some petty criminal pimp, and the shopkeeper was honest. One evening, she appeared with a black eye; on another with a cut lip. When I asked her what happened, she laughed it off and changed the subject.

Bit by bit, Barbara Hosking's colleagues came to intuit her sexuality, yet it was never referred to; and was certainly not something she was ever challenged about by work colleagues in Whitehall. What happened in the club stayed in the club. As she said of the Gateways, 'Many of the women at the club were careful to keep their private lives private and were reluctant to trust newcomers.'

So in some ways Hosking's experience is close to the contours of Benjamin Britten's – a quiet, parallel gay world which existed thanks to a public atmosphere, not of the aggressive homophobia of a few judges or politicians, but of a more widespread and civilized 'don't ask, don't tell' culture. But that is only one part of the story. There was a much rougher and more dangerous country, either forced upon homosexual people or occasionally deliberately chosen by them; and in that respect Jeanette, without her surname, is as good an example as any. Another, better-known and more celebrated case of walking on the wild side is the story of an argumentative artists' model and unlikely media star.

In most respects, Quentin Crisp's treatment of his sexuality was the negative, or opposite, of Britten's. He came from the same generation – Crisp was born in 1908, Britten in 1913. His background was, similarly, in the respectable middle classes. Crisp's father was a City solicitor, Britten's a Lowestoft dentist. Both men effectively left their families behind and were drawn into the bohemian and literary gay world of inter-war London. Crisp was born with the almost comically flat name of Denis Pratt, in suburban Surrey. He lacked something Benjamin Britten had, genius, but against that he had remarkable courage.

Far from trying to subdue or hide his identity Crisp painted his nails, dyed his hair red, or blue, and sashayed around London – including through the Blitz – with naked feet and floating clothes. He was regularly abused and beaten up by outraged Londoners – an easy target, the epitome of camp, the lord high exhibitionist of twentieth-century London, a relatively impoverished man who carried on as if he was a flamboyant Regency rake.

By the beginning of the Queen's reign, London had a well-developed gay underworld, consisting of tea shops and bars in Soho and Fitzrovia, where gay bachelors, rent boys and lesbians would gather and exchange news. The war had brought, along with a million American servicemen, most of them passing through

London, a supercharged street sexuality, which included a lot of furtive gay sex. Crisp had been one of those who took an American lover during the war. His favourite cafés included the Black Cat, the Low Dive, Tony's, the Scala and the Partisan, where outsiders of all kinds – homosexuals, thugs, deserters from the armed forces and young criminals – would mingle. With his long, painted nails, his extraordinary hair and thick make-up, he would hold court. As soon as he was out on the streets, he risked being attacked. Today, transvestite men, such as the comedian and Labour Party activist Eddie Izzard and the artist and documentary filmmaker Grayson Perry, still run the risk of being jeered at or shouted at. But when Crisp brought flamboyant cross-dressing to the streets of mid-twentieth-century London, he was doing something even braver.

Crisp kept body and soul together by working first as a commercial artist and then later as an artist's model, but his breakthrough into fame came in 1975 after his 1968 autobiography, *The Naked Civil Servant*, was made into a film starring John Hurt. More books, theatre performances and broadcast work followed before Crisp left London and moved to New York in the early 1980s. He always said he was not much interested in sex, describing it as 'the last refuge of the miserable'. For him, the essence of his sexual identity was the creation of the exotic image. According to his biographer Andrew Barrow, 'the dream was far more important than sex and sex became not only unnecessary but a contradiction. He wanted to be out of reach and would in future wear heavier and heavier make-up partly in order to be rejected, even to avoid being accosted.'

By one of those quirks of style history, Crisp then found that in the swinging London of the 1960s his hair dye, bare feet and flowing silk scarves were being adopted as a uniform by young people. It was, perhaps, inevitable that the gender-bending David Bowie would discuss making a musical based on Crisp's life. But just as he had been crazily stubborn on the streets of London as a younger man,

Crisp refused to allow himself to become a symbol of sexual liberation. As he grew older, he became more hostile to the growing gay
lib movement, causing outrage in Chicago by referring to AIDS as
a 'fad' and declaring in a later book: 'Passive sodomy is an addictive
habit that leads to the abandonment of all reason . . . No one who
practises this vice can count on living happily ever after, or even
long after.' He was hostile to the idea of gay marriage, attacked gay
people for being 'mad about their rights' and engaging in endless
marching and protesting and grumbling and said, 'Wild, pink horses
would not make me turn the adjective "gay" into a noun.'

Unsurprisingly, he was equally hostile to Princess Diana. Crisp
was one of those nettle-tongued individualists who was determined
to keep offending any fashionable target right to the end. But every
small boy who experiments with lipstick, or puts on his sister's shoes
to totter defiantly to the local shops, owes a tiny something to the
shape-changing chutzpah of Denis Pratt of Sutton.

17

HASHTAG METOO AND THE STORY OF TED

One day in 1990, a seventeen-year-old British actress, Kate Beckinsale, knocked on the door of an American film producer's room at the Savoy hotel in central London. The producer answered it wearing only a dressing gown. Later, he claimed that he simply could not remember whether or not he had sexually assaulted her. Beckinsale declined to work with Harvey Weinstein after the incident, provoking bullying and verbal abuse from him.

The encounter became one telling piece of evidence in a huge surge of allegations against Weinstein, accused of sexually bullying, harassing and raping young women, actors and models, who might depend upon him to further their careers. By October 2017, more than eighty women had come forward with accusations, including the British model Cara Delevingne and the actor Lysette Anthony, who said she had been raped by him after answering the door at her home. As women began naming men who had sexually harassed them in the film world, in theatre, in politics, in law, in the media and in the charity sector, a hashtag was born: MeToo. In February 2020, Weinstein was found guilty of two of the five felonies with which he had been charged, and was sentenced to twenty-three years in prison, initially in New York.

Some of the MeToo allegations were relatively trivial – a hand on a knee, a passing remark – while others involved groping, extreme violence and rape. Cabinet ministers, prominent charity workers and others were all named and shamed, losing their jobs and reputations. Not every allegation was about men behaving inappropriately with younger women – the actor Kevin Spacey, who was gay, was accused of harassing young men – but almost all involved the abuse of power, particularly at work. A new national conversation began about relationships, and what was acceptable or appropriate. Some men said they were being lied about and victimized themselves. French feminists argued that the entire movement had gone too far, because it risked outlawing flirting and romantic male behaviour. The #MeToo debate was clearly some kind of attitudinal turning point, but the issues it raised go back to heterosexual behaviour throughout the Queen's reign. Here too, as with gay experiences, a little history is a useful antidote to twenty-first-century self-absorption.

In the raw February of 1952, a tall, striking Cambridge undergraduate, already turning heads as he strode around in his dyed black clothes and long sweeping coat, wrote to his elder sister. Excitedly, he pointed out that the King's death meant that they were both now Elizabethans, the first people to be Elizabethans since the time of *Hamlet*. He hoped to be the poetic soul of a new English Renaissance. Shortly afterwards, another student had stopped him in the street, shaken his hand and stuttered, 'Ted, Ted. Thank you for saving England.'

The undergraduate had mistaken Ted Hughes for Ted Dexter, the cricketer, who had just made his Test debut. But as one of Hughes's biographers later put it, the spirit of the tale was true: 'saving England by re-embodying the heady spirit of Elizabethan poetry was indeed our Ted's mission'. Hughes would go on to become one of the most loved and also most lampooned of modern

British poets, a man with an authentic and unmistakable voice of his own, who became a personal friend of members of the royal family, above all of the Queen Mother. He would be made Poet Laureate, and would be installed alongside Britten as a member of the Order of Merit by the Queen, a personal fan of his poetry.

Yet across much of the world none of this is how he is now remembered. Four years after his exuberant boast about being an Elizabethan, at a party given to celebrate the publication of a new poetry magazine, Hughes approached a young American poet, over in Cambridge on a scholarship. She was called Sylvia Plath. Their first meeting, on 25 February 1956, has become a literary myth, with each of them contributing vigorously to it. They danced. She thought him a 'big, dark, hunky boy, the only one there huge enough for me', with a 'colossal' voice. They danced some more. And then, she told her diary,

> he kissed me bang smash on the mouth and ripped my hairband off, my lovely red hairband scarf which has weathered the sun and much love, and whose like I shall never find again, and my favourite silver earrings: hah! I shall keep, he barked. And when he kissed my neck I bit him long and hard on the cheek, and when we came out of the room, blood was running down his face . . . such violence, and I can see how women lie down for artists.

From his side, Ted Hughes wrote in a poem published much later in *Birthday Letters* that her eyes were a crush of diamonds, and 'You meant to knock me out / With your vivacity. I remember / Little from the rest of that evening / . . . And the swelling ring-moat of tooth-marks / That was to brand my face for the next month. / The me beneath it for good.' This was clearly unlikely to be an everyday romance.

Hughes and Plath were quickly married. To start with, she seemed the lesser poet. He was a rising star of literary Britain, a man admired by T. S. Eliot, a winner of prizes, whose early volumes were published simultaneously in Britain and America. He was hailed as an exhilarating force of nature, sweeping away the painstaking classicism and charming surrealist embroidery of previous English poets. Then, following a long visit to the United States, Sylvia Plath began to emerge at least as formidably, perhaps more so – often greeted as most important female English-language poet since Emily Dickinson.

To begin with, their marriage was intense and exclusive, generous on both sides, as they shared ideas and images. This reached the point where, according to Jonathan Bate, Hughes's biographer, 'they were becoming one soul . . . They did not plagiarise each other; they achieved synchronicity of vision through their shared imagination and observation, their conversation, their healthy competition, their daily and nightly bond of love and work.' Plath said she would not be writing as she was without his help: Hughes suggested that two people so sympathetic to each other, 'who are compatible in this sort of spiritual way, in fact make up one person'.

This blast of love and mutual support could not last for ever. Ted Hughes had a huge, almost insatiable sexual appetite. Sylvia Plath was a brilliant but clinically depressed woman, who had tried to kill herself at college, had undergone electroconvulsive therapy and was prone to outbreaks of violent temper. Later, in the eyes of the legions of their devoted admirers and haters, they became symbols of their respective nations: Hughes, the gruff, slightly brutal North Country Englishman, with his instinctive understanding of the natural world and its creatures – old-fashioned, unabashed about his animal needs, a caster of horoscopes and a self-described sadist, stomping through life – versus Plath, the very image of the new American woman, carving her unique path through what had been a self-congratulatory male world, the devoted mother of two young children even as she pursued her literary ambitions, glamorous and vulnerable both.

These are caricatures, not real people. In life Ted Hughes was a sensitive and devoted father, happy to wash up the dishes and generous about promoting the talent of his wife. Sylvia Plath was a tough and highly ambitious woman, not above trying to seduce other men. But the caricatures were strong enough, and Hughes's baroque love life was extensive enough, that when the marriage broke up because of his adultery, and Sylvia Plath gassed herself, he became the very model of the violent and predatory male.

His timing was bad. The first generation of the American feminist movement was finding its voice. Hughes's poetry brimmed with images of violence and appetite. To some women, he was almost irresistible. Erica Jong, author of *Fear of Flying*, remembered him as being 'fiercely sexy, with a vampirish, warlock appeal. He hulked. He was tall and his shoulders were broad. His hair fell against his broad forehead. He had a square jaw and an intense gaze and he reeked of virility. Moreover, he knew how irresistible he was in the Heathcliff fashion, and he did the wildman-from-the-moors thing on me full force when we met. He was a born seducer . . .' And, indeed, a serial one. Assia Wevill, a German Jewish refugee, whose affair with Ted Hughes contributed to the break-up of his marriage to Plath, also killed herself – and their child – by gassing in 1969, despairing at the poet's infidelity. So when radical feminism began to spread across campuses in the United States – Valerie Solanas's *SCUM (Society for Cutting Up Men) Manifesto* was first published in 1967, and Germaine Greer's *Female Eunuch* in 1970 – and with Sylvia Plath's story world-famous, Hughes was an obvious target.

Robin Morgan, a radical feminist, anti-war activist, editor and poet in the United States, lit the fuse. In 1972, she published a poem which, in its original version began: 'I accuse / Ted Hughes / of what the entire British and American / literary and critical establishment / has been at great lengths to deny / . . . the murder of Sylvia Plath.' She went on to accuse him of rape, unfaithfulness, brainwashing and plagiarism – and, for good measure, of murdering Assia as well. And Morgan finished by fantasizing about cutting off his penis, stuffing it into his mouth, sewing his lips around it and then shooting him through the head. She ended: 'Hughes, sue me.'

Hughes never did sue. But his life was never quiet again, either. At poetry readings and during foreign visits, he was pursued by demonstrations and heckled by women shouting 'murderer'. Sylvia Plath's gravestone, which carried her full married name of Plath Hughes, was repeatedly vandalized, with the 'Hughes' hacked off; and the English poet faced endless hostile articles and books. Plath herself was an unlikely feminist martyr, deeply though she resented household drudgery: she was fascinated by fashion, fine clothes, excellent food and flirtatious men. With sad inevitability, their children were caught up in the controversy. After Plath died – much later – their son also took his own life.

By the time Hughes himself died, in 1998, he was still a successful British establishment figure, accustomed each year to fishing in Scotland with the Queen Mother and deer-stalking with Prince Charles. Other poets regarded him as one of the great adornments of their craft. But the disaster of his marriage to Sylvia Plath remains, today, the thing he is most remembered for. As Britain again begins to debate the consequences of unrestrained male sexuality, the sad and salutary Tale of Ted deserves to be remembered alongside his own fables about Iron Men, Moon People and Mermaids.

He himself was long reluctant to write that story. His first response to Morgan's attack was to fall into a defiant, decades-long silence about his marriage. As he explained: 'I preferred it, on the whole, to allowing myself to be dragged out into the bullring and teased and pricked and goaded into vomiting up every detail of my life with Sylvia.' Eventually, in 1998, he published *Birthday Letters*, a genuinely sensational collection of confessional poems giving his side of the story. To his critics, he still seemed to be letting himself off the hook by presenting Plath's suicide as virtually preordained. But there was a final surprise in store.

He had written (but perhaps had not finished) a 'last letter' about the events around the time she died, in which he revealed that he was in bed with one of his current two lovers when she turned on the gas. Melvyn Bragg, a friend of the poet, published the poem in the *New Statesman* in 2010 and, again, Team Plath were outraged by Hughes's description of his two lovers. Plath's friend the writer Al Alvarez wrote brutally in the *Guardian* that Hughes was like a man pleading guilty in the dock:

> but the crimes he was pleading guilty to were treachery, double-dealing and shabby behaviour, and there was nothing noble or tragic about them. He had abandoned Sylvia and gone off with Assia Wevill; now he was betraying Assia for a fling with Susan Alliston. The poem implies it was not his fault: his 'numbed love life', he writes, was being fought over by two crazy tattooists, each trying to mark him as her own; what could he do? What indeed? In the end, making good poetry out of the mess he had created was beyond him. But what did that matter compared to the mess his behaviour had created for Sylvia?

This is a conundrum that perhaps cannot be resolved at the moment. On the one hand, there is the need to chase down and call out unacceptable male behaviour, as part of a radical rebalancing of relationships between the genders. Much more than a moment in history, modern feminism marks a pivot in relationships that will long outlast all Elizabethans. On the other hand, many of Ted Hughes's friends and fellow poets felt that he was having his own most intimate life and memories ripped open and disgorged into the public arena. To what extent do we own our own lives, our own memories? How much do we value privacy, the right of a fallible, guilty, self-reflective mind, to do its own business in its own way? This is becoming a dilemma played out almost daily on social media and affecting all parts of British society. But there is a case for saying that it began with a wild dance and a bitten cheek, one evening in Cambridge in 1956.

18

THE BRITISH JOURNALIST

So far, in this first part of the book, we have described some of the big social issues during the reign of Queen Elizabeth II – class, race, education, sexuality, relations between the sexes and moral disagreements. Almost every one of these stories was also a media story, influenced by broadcasting or newspaper treatment of it. The media is always changing, and always matters. At the beginning of the reign, Britain was criss-crossed by big-selling, heavily staffed and influential local newspapers, as well as by national papers based in London, Manchester, Glasgow and Edinburgh. Much of that romantic, inky world has now vanished, replaced by Instagram influencers and Facebook advertising algorithms.

What hasn't changed is that the media remains controversial, a target of conspiracy theorists. The number of people who believe that Britain would be a dramatically different country if only it wasn't for the BBC, or for overseas tycoons, or for the malign effect of modern social media, is astonishing. It surprises, or ought to, because it gives so little agency to everyone else.

The overall story of the British Elizabethan media is the erosion of hierarchy, driven by technological change. At the beginning of the Queen's reign, the BBC had a broadcasting monopoly. It was an establishment organization, prim and notoriously deferential to politicians, albeit with some louche fringes in its radio schedules. The then Director General, Sir Ian Jacob, was a retired lieutenant general, who had been secretary to Churchill's war cabinet. It was a closed, imperturbable, self-confident and didactic world. Competition came only after the Television Act of 1954. But it has never ceased to destroy and rebuild creatively ever since.

On the first night of commercial television, 22 September 1955, the BBC ruthlessly killed off Grace Archer, matriarch of the Archers radio clan, in a house fire, to try to discourage Londoners from turning to Associated-Rediffusion. The commercial imperative was seen by BBC mandarins as disgraceful, even corrupting. But the new company, partly owned by Associated Newspapers, was hardly a threat to the establishment: its General Manager, a retired naval captain called Thomas Brownrigg, wanted commercial television to be as near as possible to the BBC, except with some adverts. The legislation had already ensured that British television programmes, unlike American ones, would not be sponsored.

Yet this was an important moment in British cultural history. From then on, broadcast competition became driven by popular demand rather than by what the establishment thought people should watch. The BBC took note and followed the commercial companies. It changed as well. Game shows became popular, as did increasingly cheeky comedy – including the kind that so outraged Mary Whitehouse. There was less of the cut-glass Joyce Grenfell and more written by working-class writers such as Speight.

Radio's trajectory was a little different. Here the BBC had been changed by the war. The wartime popularity of Forces' Broadcasting, with more music and jokes, had already spawned the Light Programme, alongside the Home Service (today's Radio Four). The success of wartime broadcasting to occupied countries meanwhile hatched a permanent BBC Overseas Service. In radio the BBC faced no serious domestic competition, although from the 1930s onwards

Radio Luxembourg had broadcast in English to the UK. For people interested in the new popular music, there was American Forces Broadcasting – the signal was better the nearer you lived to one of the military bases. But overall this was a tightly controlled environment.

That changed with the arrival of pirate radio stations in the 1960s. They originated with the simple realization that any station moored in international waters was beyond the control of British parliamentary regulation. Radio Caroline, set up by the Irish entrepreneur Ronan O'Rahilly in 1964, began broadcasting from a former Danish cargo ship named *Caroline Kennedy*. It was swiftly followed by Radio London, created by a Texan, Don Pierson, who wanted to replicate the diversity of services he could hear at home, and which broadcast from a converted former US wartime minesweeper, the *Mi Amigo*, moored three miles off Frinton-on-Sea, Essex. These introduced disc jockeys, better music and informal chat.

Immediately, they sounded more like ordinary Britain and they introduced a stream of young broadcasters who would become nationally famous (often on the BBC) such as Tony Blackburn, Kenny Everett and John Peel. In 1967 the British state, in the form of Harold Wilson's Labour government, passed a new law outlawing the pirate stations offshore, which duly irritated younger voters. But the arrival of relatively cheap and transportable transmitters by the late 1970s and early 1980s produced a surge of onshore 'pirate' stations and a lengthy game of cat and mouse with the British state. The mice won: by 1989, there were said to be more than 600 pirate stations operating across Britain.

Accepting that the world had changed, Edward Heath's government legislated for legal and commercial radio in 1972. The following year, LBC in London became the first legal commercial challenger to the BBC, followed by Capital Radio, also in London, then Radio Clyde in Glasgow, BRMB in Birmingham and Radio Piccadilly in Manchester. Today, almost every part of the UK has its own commercial radio station. Since then, digital radio and internet-based radio have expanded choice even further, so that innumerable music and talk choices are available throughout the UK. It is one of the BBC's unsung modern successes that its main radio stations continue to hold their own: competition should rarely be resisted in general, and never in the media.

In television, similarly, the old, slowly dividing British landscape – BBC, then ITV, then BBC2, then Channel 4 and so on – has been blown away by the arrival of fast domestic broadband, bringing the big American companies such as Amazon and Netflix with streamed movies and their 'box set' system of expensively made, expertly written and highly addictive dramas. As with so much else in the modern world, from defence to food standards, the traditional status quo has been upended by the spread of what is technologically possible.

In broadcasting, this presents Britain with formidable challenges. Does a divided and modestly scaled (in world terms) television drama industry have the money and the raw talent to compete not just with America but with the scores of well-made continental and other television imports? The answer, longer term, is no. So the second question is, does that matter? This is harder, because the values, structures and instincts of so much imported television are very similar to the television that might be made here. Yet the Americans, and the French and the Scandinavians, see Britain very differently from the way Britons do.

Since so many younger viewers now virtually ignore traditional broadcasting in favour of the easier and more predictable attractions of imported products, this cannot help but mean that the next generation of Britons will be, imaginatively, 'less British'. In terms of national identity, this technological drenching, which comes alongside the more subtle influence of programmers working for Facebook, Twitter, Instagram and other social media sites, may be more important than – say – leaving the EU.

At any rate, the overall picture is clear: a crumbling of traditional authority, driven by technology and competition, and the greater financial heft of overseas competitors. There are parallels in the newspaper world. Early in the Queen's reign, the British newspaper scene was dominated by the great names of pre-war British journalism. Lord Beaverbrook, as stentoriously pro-Empire and anti-Common Market as ever, still presided over his chained crusader at the *Daily Express*. The Manhattan-born English milord John Jacob Astor still had control of *The Times*. The second Viscount Rothermere, son of the brilliant, mercurial, pro-Nazi and putative King of Hungary, Harold Harmsworth, who had co-founded the *Daily Mail*, was running it rather successfully.

Another Harmsworth family member, Cecil King, was in charge of Britain's most popular newspaper, the *Daily Mirror*, with its brilliant editor Hugh Cudlipp providing the style and the stunts. And Viscount Camrose, of the Welsh Berry family, was still, if rather doddery, at the helm of the *Daily Telegraph*. Most of these men had been firm supporters and friends of Winston Churchill. Observing them from a safe distance, a little loftily, was the *Manchester Guardian*, about to change its name and relocate to London (1959). It was still very clearly under the posthumous influence of its great editor C. P. Scott ('Comment is free, but facts are sacred') and was owned by a trust, then chaired by his son. Finally, Odhams Press published the Labour-supporting *Daily Herald*, still popular among older male readers but clearly in decline.

The British press was, in short, a comfortable, familiar but not applecart-overturning medium, through which the vast majority of British people still got their news, and which helped them shape their arguments. None of it was republican. All of it was in different ways patriotic. *The Times* and (to a slightly lesser extent) the *Telegraph* spoke to and for the Conservative political elite. They were regarded as impeccably accurate and neutral in the news coverage. The *Daily Mail* and *Daily Express* were angrier and more suspicious: they spoke to and for the tax-harried middle classes, who had often enjoyed the Empire and were most nostalgic for the more powerful Britain of the pre-war years.

The *Guardian* represented an internationalist, liberal-minded middle class that was becoming more important, and Labour had the *Herald* to cling on to in good times and in bad. There was something for almost everyone – Marxists had their sober *Daily Worker.* These papers were, by modern standards, long-winded and serious; even the Sunday *News of the World* would carry complex diplomatic stories on its front page. Decency was tightly enforced by editors across the political spectrum. In that more papers supported the Tory cause than the Labour one, it was an unfair system. (And the once mighty Liberal England was barely repre-sented at all.) Yet the press reflected, and almost universally accepted, a parliamentary division of spoils in which the parties were rivals, never enemies. In terms of gender, sexuality and what we would call today identity politics, it was all highly conventional.

This began to change on 16 September 1964, when a young Australian from a modest newspaper dynasty, Rupert Murdoch, acquired the *Sun*. It had been created as a rather dull broadsheet by the then owners of the failing *Daily Herald*. Working with a chippy, hungry and risk-taking northern editor, Larry Lamb, Murdoch turned it into a tabloid newspaper and aimed it directly against the *Daily Mirror*, whose sales had topped 5 million, a record, but which they felt was becoming self-satisfied, stodgy and over-staffed.

The myth is that Murdoch's *Sun* was from the beginning a 'Tory rag' designed to corrupt the working classes. In fact, its first edition included an interview with then Prime Minister Harold Wilson; Larry Lamb was a Labour supporter; and the paper proclaimed itself as being more of the left than the right. Much more important was its impact as a cultural force – the obsession with sex, gambling, television celebrities and sport at the expense of politics; the breaking of taboos such as the use of topless models and extracts from sexually explicit books; and the provocative, aggressive, punch-you-on-the-nose style of headlines.

In a sense, Murdoch and Lamb just took another part of the common national conversation and put it into print. If, in the saloon bar, they were talking *Daily Mirror*, arguing about the new Education Act and what was going on with the rebellion in Kenya, as well as who was going to win the Grand National, then perhaps in the snug bar they were talking about who was shagging whom and having a very rude laugh at the expense of that pompous git on the telly. In other words they were talking *Sun*. Another way you could put the change is to say that Murdoch was simply copying directly from Harmsworth in his glory days when he created the *Daily Mail*. Harmsworth made clear that he had a horror of licking the boots of politicians and told one of his reporters: 'The three things which are always news are money things, sex things and health things.'

But the impact of the Murdoch *Sun* on the top-down British newspaper system was even greater than the impact of Harmsworth's *Daily Mail* had been at the beginning of the century. As its figures rose, and those of the *Daily Mirror* began to plummet, the other papers rushed to mimic aspects of the Murdoch style. Any last vestiges of deference in the British media began to be torn away. The so-called mid-market papers, the *Express* and the *Mail*, learned a lot too. Traditional, drily factual political coverage began to fall out of fashion. Even *The Times* eventually ditched its parliamentary coverage page, finally going tabloid in 2003–4. Rupert Murdoch's politics were driven by his business needs: hostility to European regulation, and the vice-like, infuriating grip of the print trade unions, drove him further and further to the right and he became a prime – if not the prime – supporter of Margaret Thatcher.

Under a new editor, Kelvin MacKenzie, and under pressure from another downmarket competitor, the *Star*, owned by the *Express*, the *Sun* became ever more outrageous, smearing Labour politicians and trade union leaders, jingoistically jeering during the Falklands conflict and making up stories, including about gay celebrities such as the singer Elton John. Fake news long preceded the internet. Its most raucous headlines, such as the air-punch of 'Gotcha!' when the Argentine battleship *General Belgrano* was sunk (323 sailors, some of them young sea cadets, died) or 'Freddie Starr ate my hamster' (he didn't), may have made much of Britain laugh or cheer, but they undoubtedly coarsened the atmosphere. Meanwhile, following the principle of staying close to real power, and because of his contempt for the Tory Prime Minister John Major, Murdoch smoothly switched his support from the Tories to Tony Blair's New Labour.

Time brings in its whirligig of revenges. Journalists will do almost anything for a story, and British journalists in particular have long been notorious for bending and twisting the facts to forge a good headline. But it was the discovery that it was possible, even relatively easy, to 'hack' into a generation of mobile phones and listen to messages which had been left on voicemail that gave Parliament its opportunity for revenge against an increasingly contemptuous newspaper culture.

In the early 2000s, it became clear that journalists working for Murdoch's *News of the World* had been listening to private messages on the phones of politicians and celebrities, and some members of the royal family. By 2011 it also became clear that the phone of a schoolgirl who had been murdered, Millie Dowler, had been eavesdropped on. The same had happened to the phones of dead British soldiers, and of the victims of terrorist attacks. A huge public row ended only after the *News of the World* had been closed entirely after 168 years of publication, and key Murdoch lieutenants had resigned – though some were reinstated later. Murdoch's News Corporation cancelled its proposed takeover of the satellite broadcaster BSkyB.

Further attempts, on the back of all of this, to introduce a new system of state regulation of the British press have – at the time of writing – failed. It cannot be said that increased competition in the British press has changed very much in the country. It is always too tempting and too easy to assume that if only newspapers had taken a slightly different stance Labour would have won a particular election, or the miners would have won their strike, or the pro-EU side would have won the Brexit referendum. The ownership, structure and political bias of the mainstream media certainly matter; but in a market system almost all of these organizations have to respond to the public mood, as much as making it. And in the event the real challenge for newspapers and broadcasters alike came not from legislation or new regulation, but from the competition of the so-called social media.

This has allowed a new generation of Britons to communicate directly with one another, generally avoiding the mediation of any editorial or professional organization at all. The biggest advantage has been speed. Nobody now needs to wait for a news bulletin or the publication of newspapers to find out what is happening in the world. But the biggest disadvantage has been that, because users of Facebook or Twitter choose whom to follow, they can become unwittingly entombed in a small echo chamber of their own prejudices, no longer open to challenge or surprise. The self-righteous anger of many who turn on their television sets and find they are confronted by people who (pass the smelling salts) have a different view shows that we are pulling back into smaller and smaller tribal groups.

19

BAD BEHAVIOUR: REAL WOMEN BREAK THROUGH

The history of art and social history are very different. But sometimes they go together; and art provides a useful sidelight on the changing influence of professional women during the Elizabethan age. Someone growing up with an interest in painting in the 1950s would have found that almost all the big figures being discussed were men – either the European greats, like Picasso, Matisse and Braque, or the famous British painters, from arch-reactionaries like Sir Alfred Munnings to modernists such as Walter Sickert, Graham Sutherland, Henry Moore and Stanley Spencer.

It's not that there weren't good female British painters and sculptors. The Bloomsbury group was led artistically by Vanessa Bell, who was a more distinguished painter than any of the men in it – though she was rivalled by Dora Carrington. Winifred Nicholson was as interesting and unexpected as her husband, the abstract pioneer Ben Nicholson. These days, by common consent, Gwen John is regarded as a far better painter than her flamboyant brother, Augustus; and many would deem Barbara Hepworth as formidable a sculptor as Henry Moore. Laura Knight's paintings of gypsies, war workers and circus performers were sensationally popular up to and beyond the Second World War.

But overall the visual arts were still a male preserve, in which bearded libertines wearing excessive headgear swaggered and shouted at one another as they downed bubbling pints of dirty brown ale, sniffed each other's testosterone and fought about Picasso. The great teachers, Henry Tonks before the Second World War, and William Coldstream and David Bomberg after it, attracted schools of eager young men, who learned by copying, and by drawing undraped female nudes.

This had a wider impact. The male gaze in art produced a public accustomed to seeing women portrayed in a particular way – naked, passive, supplicant and demure. British artists, learning from greater figures abroad, took dancers or prostitutes as their subject, or, alternatively, put-upon, defeated-looking domestic women. Whether it was Moore deconstructing and drilling holes through his nudes or Stanley Spencer producing shockingly anatomical depictions of his wife Patricia Preece, the second sex was to be stared at, or – literally – looked down on, not to make the pictures themselves. In gallery after gallery, the male was voyeur-creator. Art, as much as association football or trad jazz, was a boys' club.

By the beginning of the Queen's reign, this was starting to change. Up and down Britain, art schools were expanding very rapidly. This was partly because so many demobilized servicemen were keen to enrol but it gave opportunities for women students as well. Both Prunella Clough, who studied with Henry Moore before the war, and the great abstract pioneer Gillian Ayres found teaching jobs to supplement their painting. Bridget Riley studied at Goldsmiths and the Royal College of Art. All three were driven and self-confident women, happy to use their elbows to advance in a male world – Roger Hilton, a prominent abstract painter, told Gillian Ayres once that she couldn't be a painter because she didn't have a penis.

In photographs from the time, she is seen in pubs and around dinner tables with a slightly quizzical expression and a half-pint of beer. But Ayres had a boldness – a streak of wildness even – which her male counterparts largely lacked. In the spring of 1957 she was introduced to a young architect called Michael Greenwood, who was redecorating South Hampstead High School for Girls and asked her to do a mural for the dining room. In the spirit of Jackson Pollock, unknown in Britain in those days, Ayres decided to put her boards on the floor and throw the paint on them:

> I covered the whole lot in an hour, to start with. It was the end of term in July and the windows were open. It was in the school room. I just threw all the paint and turps over the panels, and the workmen rushed out. Then the architect came in. He shut the door, and said, 'They've all gathered out there. They think you're a madwoman.' We just laughed.

None of these female painters, to use a later expression, produced obviously 'gendered' art. Clough's muscular industrial scenes, Riley's op-art paintings and later abstract works of colour, which followed the pointillist artist Seurat, and Ayres's exhilarating yet controlled explosions of pigment, becoming thicker over time, were not works which the viewer would have identified as being by a female artist. But all these women were more dedicated, bolder and simply worked harder than most of their male rivals. Decade by decade, as more and more female artists have come first to rival the male art scene in Britain and now to surpass it, the subject of art has begun to change, in ways which will ripple out far beyond schools and galleries, sometimes unexpectedly.

In 1998, one young artist's life was running out of control. She later explained: 'I was then at a point in my life when I was pretty low. I hadn't got out of bed for four days and I hadn't eaten, properly, for a few weeks, I was drinking like an absolute fish. I went out and got paralytically drunk and came home and didn't get out of bed for four days . . .' She woke up one morning so dehydrated that she feared she was going to die, crawled to her kitchen for a drink of water and crawled back again. At this point, Tracey Emin looked afresh at her bedroom and saw it plain. 'It was disgusting, absolutely ugly.' But she realized that it was, possibly, also her deathbed and that, surrounded by used Kleenex, tampons, bottles of water, cigarettes and a certain amount of unsightly detritus, it might show a strange beauty. Carefully reassembled, it became Emin's signature artwork, shortlisted for that year's Turner Prize at the Tate Britain Gallery, and a sure-fire, ready-made, handcrafted British public scandal. The bed, which has since been sold on by art collectors for many millions of pounds, became a symbol of all that had gone wrong in the British art world – an obsession with celebrity, youth, sex and shock-value at the expense of talent, craft and hard work.

If that was the top and the bottom of the story, it would be a pretty dull one. Tracey Emin was a member of the so-called Young British Artists or YBAs, most of whom had graduated from Goldsmiths art college in London in the late 1980s. They included Damien Hirst of pickled-shark fame, Emin's friend and collaborator Sarah Lucas, Gary Hume, Gillian Wearing, Matt Collishaw and Fiona Rae. Some of them – Fiona Rae in particular – were mainstream painters, but what united them was a sense that art could be made out of anything, and a voracious appetite for publicity. It would be ridiculous to say they were untalented or anything other than very sharp, but what made Tracey Emin different was her clear-sighted and contemporary sense of a subject: 'I realized that I was much better than anything I had made . . . I was my work. I was the essence of my work.'

And by making herself her own subject, Emin introduced an entirely new theme into the British art world. She came from the down-at-heel seaside town of Margate, the child of unmarried parents – her Turkish Cypriot father had twenty-three children he acknowledged. Margate in the 1970s was a place of fairgrounds, discos, cheap pubs and a great deal of underage sex. As a thirteen-year-old, Tracey Emin had sex with numerous older men. She would criticize partners who had exploited her, using her loneliness and emotional openness for their own erotic purposes. Her memoir describes anal rapes, the jeering abuse she suffered and her love for her family. In it she exposed herself shockingly:

Have you ever longed for someone so much, so deeply that you thought you would die? That your heart would just stop beating? I am longing now, but for whom I don't know. My whole body craves to be held. I am desperate to love and be loved . . . I want to be physically a part of someone. I want to be joined.

She was joined. She was joined, via her art, to strangers all over Elizabethan Britain. Emin had found a new subject, beyond the range of any male artist. She displayed a directness, a frankness about female experience – the pain and hope of a young woman on the margins, fighting for recognition in London, a woman who was unapologetic and blatant about sex and frank about her drinking – which connected to many British women and girls who were otherwise alienated from the art world completely. But contemplating her drawings of herself masturbating, and her photographs of herself naked in the bath, the grander parts of the art world were – satisfactorily, from her point of view – alienated.

Emin was easy for a newspaper reader to get wrong – although, interestingly, tabloid newspapers, fully immersed in gleeful self-revelation and unshockable personal stories, were kinder to her than the broadsheet press. For instance, a later famous work, *Everyone I Have Ever Slept With 1963–1995*, made in the latter year, which was a cheap, disposable tent decorated with appliquéd names, was widely seen as a crude boast about how many sexual partners she had had. In fact, the tent included the names of her twin brother,

her mother and her grandmother and was just as much about the intimacy of sleep as anything else. She is easily misunderstood, though rarely by her target audience. As she told Melvyn Bragg in a *South Bank Show* television interview, she was much disliked by middle-minded Middle England, but 'I have got lots of kids on the street going, "You're cool."'

Her story is a contemporary echo of the spirit of Diana Dors, further down the coast at Folkestone. It is also a final example of how the art world both leads and mimics wider social change. Tracey Emin was lucky to coincide with the later 1980s and early 1990s, which were good times for wily cultural entrepreneurs. A strange curdling of Thatcherite individualism and the unchained media of the Blair era, from the wildness of the *Sun* to the icon-breaking transgressiveness of Channel 4, gave new opportunities to smart kids on the make. Art was an obvious example. But it wasn't the most powerful one.

20

OUT OF CONTROL: NEW WAYS OF MISBEHAVING

Neither Alan McGee nor Chris Donald were predictable Thatcher-era business successes. Born a few months apart – McGee in East Kilbride, south of Glasgow, and Donald in Newcastle – both were conspicuous failures at school. McGee left his school, aged sixteen, with just one exam pass at GCSE level. Donald failed his A-levels and started work as a clerical officer in a local social security office. Both boys were natural rebels. McGee co-founded a punk band, the Drains, while Donald scribbled down spectacularly rude parodies of D. C. Thomson children's comics in his bedroom. But both were given a crucial leg-up by Margaret Thatcher.

Viz was launched by Donald, his brother and a friend in November 1979. To start with, they sold about 150 copies of the comic, which had been produced as a photocopy in their local Prontaprint store. A decade later, it was selling more than a million copies five times a year and was the target of major takeover bids by established publishers. A sense of the *Viz* style, heavily based on the *Beano* and *Dandy*, can be gleaned from some of the titles of its most popular strips – Buster Gonad, Cockney Wanker, The Fat Slags, Millie Tant and Sid the Sexist. In its brutal Anglo-Saxon verbiage, it's as unexportably British as brown sauce or Boris Johnson, and its preferred subjects for mockery include piles, bottoms generally, fat people and snooty intellectuals.

Existing in a fictional quasi-1950s Britain, childish, outrageous and profoundly politically incorrect, *Viz* has absolutely nothing to recommend it – except that to millions of bored and anti-authority British people it happens to be very funny indeed. But when Margaret Thatcher launched schemes in the early 1980s to encourage people to move from unemployment benefit to start their own companies, Sid the Sexist was probably not exactly what she had in mind.

These were the bleakest years for British post-war unemployment, as the squeeze of monetarist economics throttled inefficient companies across the country. In January 1982, total unemployment rose above 3 million for the first time and Thatcher, along with her Chancellor Geoffrey Howe, was under ferocious internal attack by Tory critics such as Michael Heseltine. She had no intention of reneging on her economics, but she was looking for ways of softening its impact on the jobless figures. Among the initiatives that came at the time were the Business Expansion Scheme which offered tax relief of up to £40,000 to individuals investing in non-public UK companies, and the Enterprise Allowance Scheme. This gave £40 a week for up to a year to unemployed people who wanted to start their own businesses.

It was a classic expression of Thatcherite moral economics: the best replacement for outdated businesses was the creation of new ones, by enterprising risk-takers, prepared to stand on their own two feet and try something new – anything to get off the humiliation of the dole. Although many of the early EAS start-ups failed, and it never had a huge effect on British unemployment figures, because most of the new companies employed only their founder, overall the EAS helped 325,000 people to become self-employed. But the trouble with entrepreneurs is that, almost by definition, you don't know what they're going to do next.

Not if they're Chris Donald. Not if they're Alan McGee, either. The 1980s were a good decade for British music, as rock began to morph not only into punk but into psychedelia, and dance clubs popularized a new generation of drugs, demanding a new music to dance to. House music had spread to Britain from Chicago by the early 1980s. By the middle of the decade, the dance scene in Manchester (or 'Madchester') was being transformed by the availability of MDMA or ecstasy, and within a few years British youth culture was going through its liveliest times since the 1960s. McGee became the manager of one of the key independent bands of the early 1980s, the Jesus and Mary Chain, from East Kilbride, and also signed the Glasgow band Primal Scream, led by his schoolfriend Bobby Gillespie, part of the acid house scene.

As in the 1960s, drugs, hedonism and fresh music went together, and soon people were talking of a second 'summer of love'. With MDMA, new pop-up clubs and acid raves, British youth found a loved-up, glowing, psychedelic refuge from the bitter politics of the miners' strike, privatizations and anti-nuclear protest. The new drugs were never as safe as their promoters claimed; an Essex eighteen-year-old, Leah Betts, became the face of anti-drugs concern when she died after taking ecstasy in 1995. The ravers and the new bands insisted that MDMA was, nevertheless, a lot less dangerous than heavy drinking. Despite Roy Jenkins, not even the newly formed SDP was quite as much fun as leaping around for hours to Primal Scream. Young entrepreneurs using new-fangled mobile phones created instant mass parties, sold tickets, and made serious money. If it wasn't for the fact that the drugs put them well beyond the pale for the Conservative hierarchy, they would have been ideal Thatcherite role models. But if you are determined to free the people, you can never be absolutely sure just what you are freeing them for.

At the other end of the scale from proto-Tory entrepreneurs working out of London, dishevelled young anarchists and travellers created their own outdoor festivals, either in fields or in industrial buildings easily accessed from major motorways. On one famous occasion, a giant rave took place on the spring bank holiday in 1992 at Castlemorton Common in the Malvern Hills.

Many thousands of people, alerted by telephone messages, descended on a stretch of farmland and partied all night, causing local outrage and pompous questions in Parliament. Carl Hendrickse, whose band Back to the Planet played there, later told the BBC that outdoor raves were happening because people were not given the right to gather: 'There were no facilities for people to come and dance, gather with like-minded people, and that is why they started happening illegally, because there were no proper facilities for people to have these kind of events.' In its plaintive tone, it's very 1968.

Meanwhile something slightly different was happening with Alan McGee. After receiving help from Margaret Thatcher's enterprise allowance, his label Creation Records had signed a stream of inno-vative new bands, while McGee immersed himself in the acid and rave world. Perhaps too deeply: on the edge of bankruptcy, he sold half his company to Sony Records in 1992, the year of the Castlemorton rave. But now McGee found that one recent signing was becoming a sensation, an aural goldmine. The Manchester bad-boy brothers Noel and Liam Gallagher were becoming the biggest-selling band of the decade with their Beatles-influenced *(What's the Story) Morning Glory?*

Self-marketing has always been a British enthusiasm, and now came the so-called Britpop years, with Oasis and Blur pumping up their boxing-ring rivalry, sardonically observed by the coolest of the new bands, Pulp. Watching all of them, with the unblinking atten-tiveness of a leopard observing gambolling impala, was the New Labour leader Tony Blair. 'Cool Britannia', the punning slogan first used in the 1960s by the Bonzo Dog Doo-Dah Band, and later appropriated to sell a popular brand of ice cream, was about to be reborn.

The new Queen's coronation…
But behind the pageantry, another
country was already taking shape.

Nepali-Indian Tenzing Norgay and New Zealander Edmund Hillary. A great 'British' triumph on Everest.

Jan Morris, the Welsh trans writer who accompanied the expedition and broke the story of their success.

Shirley Williams (left),
American-influenced radical.

Helen John (above), hugely
influential anti-war campaigner,
paid a high family price.

U and Non-U sent
half of Britain mad.

Diana Dors, the original 'It Girl', was the toughest of tough cookies.

Dors's much weaker co-actor, Ruth Ellis.

Quentin Crisp: snobbish, vain and extraordinarily brave.

Notting Hill's original black rights activists, with genial anti-drugs
restaurateur Frank Critchlow on the right.

Dan Dare, an alternative vision of a
great British future.

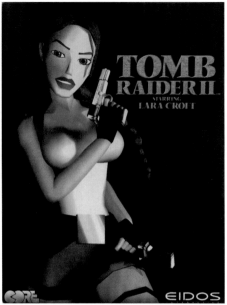

Lara Croft, pumped up for the
American market.

Enoch Powell (left) and
Tony Benn (below),
Washington-sceptic
radical allies against a
Greater Europe.

(Monty) Pythins pose,
but tortured stories lay
behind the grimaces.

Tony Crosland (left) and
Roy Jenkins (right), two
of the most culturally
influential politicians of the
post-war period.

The formidable decency
campaigner Mary Whitehouse.

Sylvia Plath and Ted Hughes: 'Me Too' before the hashtag.

Glorious Dusty Springfield, there before the Beatles.

Tracy Emin and her bed – making the artist establishment think again.

New Labour was at its zenith – just before it was actually elected – when Tony Blair was invited as the guest of honour to the February 1996 Brit Awards. Blair, thanks to his aspirational working-class father, had been sent to the posh Edinburgh private school, Fettes College. The Labour Party was now in the hands of a public-school-educated barrister (which, because it had done so little to democratize the British education system, was really its own fault). Blair was sensitive to the criticism that he didn't come over well enough to working-class voters, particularly young voters.

In short, like so many public-school-educated boys in modern Britain, he badly needed to acquire some cool. So, as he arrived at the awards, smartly dressed, he seemed just a little nervous. The Gallaghers, after all, were notorious. He need not have worried. They were off their heads. Heavily influenced by large amounts of ecstasy, when Noel Gallagher received the award, standing alongside McGee and others, he announced to the world that there were just seven people in the room 'who have given a little bit of hope to young people in this country'. They included himself, his brother Liam, Alan McGee – and Tony Blair. The room erupted. McGee later reflected that it was a stupid thing to say but was just the kind of thing that happens when you are off your face.

He too was using a very large amount of Class A drugs at the time and angrily berating politicians for what he saw as their gross hypocrisy on the subject. But this didn't stop him, soon afterwards, from presenting Blair with a gold disc at a Labour youth conference. There the Labour leader promptly seized on Creation Records as an example – not of Margaret Thatcher's employment policies but of his own vaulting ambition: 'It's a great company. We should be really proud of it. Alan has just been telling me he started twelve years ago with a thousand-quid bank loan . . . and now it's got a £34 million turnover. Now, *that's* New Labour!' A little later still, after he'd been elected Prime Minister, to ram the message home, Blair invited McGee and Gallagher to a glitzy, much photographed party in Number 10, where the rock star ambled around and made awkward conversation with Blair's children.

On TV news broadcasts and newspaper front pages, it did make Blair look cool. Later, McGee said that 'We got conned but, you know, what can you do? I mean: me . . . and the rest of the country.' It was, at the time, a quite brilliant piece of PR. But no PR lasts for ever. McGee would later accuse Blair of being a control freak out of George Orwell's *1984* and, in due course, speak of his admiration for a new Tory leader, David Cameron. Curses! By 1999, McGee was suffering burnout, caused in part by his drugs intake and disillusion with the music business, and Creation Records closed.

In so many ways, this story demonstrates not how much has changed during the Queen's reign, but how little. Angry, talented and sometimes dangerous working-class people, elbowing and arguing their way up, have always attracted upper- and middle-class politicians keen to buy a little street credibility. It's part of the strange foxtrot of showbiz democracy. Back in the early 1960s, the louche arty crowd hanging around with the Kray twins fascinated the Tory peer Lord Boothby; and Harold Wilson wasn't thinking entirely of their musical importance when he persuaded the Queen to give the Beatles MBEs. The British bands of the Blair era were as authentically working class as those of the 1960s. And the atmosphere of acid parties in the 1980s and 1990s seems to have been similar to the original summer of love, even if the drugs had moved on a little.

The real difference is the impact mass deindustrialization has had on popular culture. Music and media stars in the 1960s were living in a small bubble of working-class hedonism, admired from afar by the millions who remained grumpily but safely disciplined by work, unions and Churches. After the collapse of so much of Britain's manufacturing during the 1980s, the customers for MDMA, raves and exciting new music were less tethered. From Newcastle to East

Kilbride, they wanted more of the fun for themselves. They weren't looking on at a few lucky ones. They were climbing the fences. Margaret Thatcher may have expected that her drive to create more entrepreneurs would eventually turn out dark-suited conformists and modestly sized engineering companies. But the market was now for dark, anarchic humour and getting off your head. These were wild times.

21

LARA CROFT AND HER BOYS

We have looked at new cultural attitudes in the media, in art and in music. But the biggest technological change in the later part of this second Elizabethan period, the microprocessing and internet revolution, also produced new cultural industries. In content, they tended to emphasize violence and adventure over reflection or analysis; fantasy worlds over history; and male perspectives over female ones. Britain had some big successes in computer gaming. These too involved awkward questions about female identity in a new age which prides itself on equality.

In 1994, as Alan McGee and Oasis were romping ahead, the Japanese company Sony were about to launch their new computer games console, the PlayStation. Its 3D graphics, detailed and richly coloured, would allow a much more immersive and gripping experience, although of course this would only 'grip' anybody if the game and its story were good enough.

One man who got an early glimpse of the new console was Jeremy Heath-Smith, the founder of a small gaming company, Core Design, in Derby. He drew his team together and asked them to come up with stories. One very young designer, Toby Gard, from Chelmsford in Essex, who had joined the company when he was sixteen, responded with an idea for a treasure-hunting adventure set among the Egyptian pyramids. This, he argued, would be new and original because its hero would always be seen on screen, both part of the embedded story and directly connected to the game-player.

By 1995, as Gard began to develop the game he was now calling *Tomb Raider*, his boss became increasingly worried. Heath-Smith realized that their hero archaeologist was too close to a certain popular film franchise: 'When Toby first showed it to me, it was a male character . . . He did look like Indiana Jones, and I said, "You must be insane, we'll get sued from here to kingdom come!"' Gard was already interested in the possibility of making the main character female, partly because he had been told that this broke every rule in the book laid down by American marketing men. He was also determined that she should be British. To start with he called her Laura Cruz. Her character seems to have come from a mélange of sources, from Gard's sister to the character Tank Girl from the increasingly fashionable Japanese manga comics.

He imagined her as feisty, belligerent and cool, a classic strong woman for the new times. American clients didn't like the name – too Hispanic, probably – and so he changed it to Lara Croft. An actress with a fairly cut-glass accent, Shelley Blond, was hired to be her voice. So far, so 1990s. But the needs of boys in what was still an overwhelmingly male market could not be gainsaid and inch by inch, bust to legs, Lara Croft mutated into a martial-arts sex symbol, the Page 3 girl Toby Gard has always recoiled from. For this and other reasons, he quit the company just as the game was about to take off. It can't have been an easy thing for a young man to do. Heath-Smith told him: 'This game is going to be huge. You're on a commission for this, you're on a bonus scheme. You're going to make a fortune, don't leave. Just sit here for the next two years. Don't do anything – you'll make more money than you've ever seen in your life.'

But Toby went one way and Lara went another. He went on to a very good career in gaming design. She chose world domination. The games (for the first was followed by many more) became number-one bestsellers in Asia and America, were credited with the huge success of the Sony PlayStation and earned massive amounts for the London company, Eidos, which eventually acquired her after a series of complex takeovers. Along with the Spice Girls at about the same time, of whom more later, Lara Croft was a great British export and did much to promote the idea of strong female heroines or – in the phrase of the time – *girl power*. A series of blockbuster Hollywood films followed.

Yet alongside that, while advertising almost everything you can imagine, Lara Croft was also a profoundly old-fashioned, outdated sex symbol, marketed for her pert bosoms and lean bottom as much as for her skill in fighting wild animals and looting ancient artefacts. Lara Phwoar. No decade is just itself: in the middle of the 1990s, the spirit of the 1970s doggedly refused to die. You can't imagine her earlier in the reign of the Queen – too in-your-face, too violent – but she wasn't modern Elizabethan either.

For it's hard to overstate the speed and drama of changes in our attitudes to class, gender, sexuality and religion during the reign of Queen Elizabeth II. It's easy to spot how our physical appearance has altered. A thinner, whiter, more drably dressed, behatted nation has become multicoloured, fatter and sloppier. We are all familiar with the speed of technological shifts between 1952 and the present day – new ways of transport and entertainment, invasive gadgets and algorithms which observe and plot our daily lives. But more fundamental than any of this is how quickly we have changed inside our heads as we think about identity, class, gender – in essence, *how* we think about *who* we are. This kind of change is harder to capture but it matters more.

Part Two

———◆———

ELIZABETHANS
IN THE WORLD

22

DOES BRITAIN HAVE FRIENDS?

We turn to Britain's place in the world, and our attitude to the way the wider world has arrived and changed our lives at home. For us, this is a time of pivotal change. In or out of the EU, we no longer bestride the world. If nothing else, the coronavirus crisis of 2020 showed how interconnected, in humour, science and attitudes to government the contemporary world still is. Throughout the Elizabethan period Britain enthusiastically imported ideas and culture. We have imported many people, our new fellow citizens too.

As a result, we are not, physically or imaginatively, quite the people we were. Do you feel alarmed about this? Or do you feel cheered by it? Britain faces big choices now, about whether we lean more towards America, and American culture, or towards Asia, or whether we try to reconnect to our damaged European identity. But, just as much as with new attitudes to gender, culture or class, being reminded about some of the lesser-known parts of our recent history is a useful aid to thinking ahead.

In the small hours of 8 October 2019, Arron Banks apologized. Sometimes, it is the small things which speak eloquently about where a country is going. Banks, co-founder of the Leave.EU campaign which helped win the 2016 referendum for Brexit, and a record-breaking donor to anti-Brussels campaigning, was not one of life's natural apologizers. A pugnacious, unstoppable provocateur, he had attacked journalists investigating his financial background in insurance and South African diamond mines; a wide range of British politicians; and even the anti-climate-change activist Greta Thunberg. His general approach when rebuked was to say that he'd been joking, and that the accuser was some version of a pathetic, whingeing, limp-wristed snowflake. His many followers on the libertarian right of politics adored his unapologetic and cheerful aggression.

But this time a tweet from Leave.EU, which followed a difficult conversation between Boris Johnson and the German Chancellor Angela Merkel, had made even Arron Banks think twice. It showed Merkel, her right arm held aloft as if in a salute, and carried the words 'We didn't win two World Wars to be pushed around by a Kraut.' Andy Wigmore, the other founder of Leave.EU, deleted the tweet and announced, 'We're sorry.' Banks himself said that the message had 'gone too far . . . on reflection the point could have been made better'.

Fractious, seemingly endless and bitterly divisive, the arguments about how and whether Britain could leave the European Union had thrown up old questions about our identity. Millions of people who had never shown much interest in the arcane and often faceless power system of Brussels discovered that they were, after all, emotionally European. Here is an irony: Europeanism became, thanks to the referendum vote and for the first time, an authentic and popular part of British identity. But at the same time millions of other British people – the majority, on the day – were rediscovering a national patriotism rooted in suspicion of the European continent, and the experience, still in living memory, of the Second World War.

The first group, waving blue and gold EU flags, regarded the second group, waving Union Jacks, as pathetically nostalgic, outdated xenophobes – old people endlessly dribbling on about the Spitfire, ignorantly sneering at the French and the Germans, unable to cope with the big changes in world status since 1945. That Leave. EU tweet seemed to confirm the caricature. It was too crude, too embarrassing, too unfunny. Even after a few weeks of spittle-flecked infighting, when pro-EU Remainers had been seen as surrender-loving traitors, liberal pessimists and not true British patriots, this mockery of the 'Krauts' had gone just a yard too far. It was polit-ically self-defeating. There were some lines not to be crossed after all.

By this point in the extraordinary political autumn of 2019, the possibility of Britain leaving the EU without a deal seemed very high. The Prime Minister Boris Johnson had given wrong advice to the Queen about proroguing Parliament and had lost compre-hensively at the Supreme Court. There was a real sense that the British political system was coming apart at the seams. Economists, officials and business people were warning that leaving without a deal would be extremely damaging to British prosperity, security and power. But committed Leavers, fed up to the back teeth with the endless delays and complexities, did not believe the warnings. They were responding in the spirit of the famous David Low cartoon, first published by the London *Evening Standard* in June 1940, at the low point of the war, which showed a British infantryman standing against a stormy sea and waving one fist defiantly in the air, with the simple caption 'Very well, alone'.

The twenty-first-century truth was that Britain, like any other medium-sized economy in a closely connected world, was not alone and could not afford to be alone. We were no longer a country which could afford to insult foreigners, or offer 'take it or leave it' deals to our nearest competitors. If we were not haggling with Brussels, then we would be haggling with Washington, or Beijing. Just a few months later coronavirus dramatically anaesthetized the angry political divisions of the previous winter, at least temporarily. But coping with the pandemic brought a great deal of haggling, and sideways-gazing at different strategies and scientific advice across Europe and around the world.

One of the oldest questions of the Queen's reign kept coming back: where did we want to stand in the world and, just as important, with whom? Coronavirus brought a great deal of mistrust of China. Had its communist government been properly frank about the origins of the epidemic? But it also raised questions about our historic closeness to the United States, as an angry President Trump closed borders and withdrew funding from the World Health Organization. France, with her centralized political system, and Germany, which had invested more in her health system, offered interesting parallels for Brexit Britain. There were, for conservatives as much as for social democrats, questions about our core values, and our natural friendships.

Throughout the reign, British governments had struggled to replace the Empire lost before the Queen's reign with some kind of 'Greater Britain'. The smoothest and most obvious alternative was the British Commonwealth, later rebranded the Commonwealth of Nations, which sought a close, friendly and trading alliance without the clanking, flag-and-garrison imperialist military machine of Empire. This low-fat vegetarian replacement for the original bloodier project caught the imagination of the young Princess Elizabeth, and stayed with her throughout her life. At first sight, it seemed an entirely benign, sunlit lounge among the furniture of the post-war world. But it was never so simple. First, there was the so-called Old Commonwealth of white former British subjects in Canada, Australia and New Zealand. Did they wholeheartedly embrace the black and Asian citizens of newly independent countries in other parts of the world? Was the Commonwealth under the Crown really all in this together?

This was not just a question about religion or skin colour, but about global politics. No longer subject to British power, Commonwealth nations were seeking their own interests and their own, separate destiny. For many, that meant looking for alliances which brought their governments more immediate material help, including armaments and strategic support, such as Soviet assistance during the Cold War. For others, it meant concentrating on their own part of the world, even at the expense of old British ties. Following the Second World War, and Britain's military humiliation in Singapore, Australia increasingly recalibrated herself as an Asian power. In a cascade of changes when he took power as leader of the Labor Party in 1972, the Australian Prime Minister Gough Whitlam summoned home Australian troops from Vietnam, established relations with China, voted in favour of sanctions on apartheid South Africa and Rhodesia, and loosened links with the Crown. It was a dramatic and controversial assertion of Australianness, which raised obvious questions about the real value of the Commonwealth.

So, for different reasons in different parts of the world, the Commonwealth of Nations was tugged by centrifugal forces, too strong to be calmed down by royal speeches or pained admonishment from Whitehall. Independent African countries became Marxist people's republics. Canadians and citizens of Caribbean nations looked increasingly to the US, the global giant on their doorstep, rather than to far-off London. Any global system that does not reflect the underlying realities of power will decay. And throughout the Queen's reign, Britain was not economically and militarily powerful enough to hold together her global network.

Important symbolic failures in the late 1960s and 1970s underlined this truth. After the devaluation of sterling in November 1967, and then in June 1972, with the imposition of exchange controls to prevent a haemorrhage on the foreign exchange markets, the once mighty sterling area, which at its peak had brought British financial influence across seventy-four other nations, territories and dependencies, began to collapse entirely. It is painful to say it, but the death of the pound as an international currency was one of the most important markers of the journey of the Elizabethans in the wider world.

It was far from being the only problem the Commonwealth faced. Even as other ex-Empire countries observed British decline and sought their own destinies, so too the British were obliged to confront a powerful magnetic pull nearer to home. This was hardly a new force. Throughout her history Britain had been plunged arm-deep in European politics, long before the world wars. For at least 400 years, her overwhelming strategic aim had been to prevent the emergence on the continent of Europe of any single dominant power, whether it be Habsburg Catholicism, Bourbon France, Napoleonic Empire or a reunited Germany. So it was inevitable that as soon as French, German and other continental political leaders began discussing the creation of a single European market and alliance in the late 1940s, Britain would face the dilemma that has dominated her politics in recent decades: should we be part of this new continental system, or should we stand aside, Ourselves Alone?

This is about identity as much as it is about democracy. Were the British islander-Europeans essentially similar to the Danes or the Dutch, or were they deep-blue-sea internationalists, even if without the global naval power they once enjoyed? Continental merchants or saltwater traders? For sceptics about Brussels, that became a more difficult either/or choice, as the EU's rules tightened. Eventually it became a dilemma that tormented modern Elizabethan Britain. If we chose Europeanism, the Commonwealth trading system had to be discarded. If we clung to the Commonwealth, and fostered post-imperial global links, we could not be normal Europeans. For nearly forty years Britain fudged this, until by the twenty-first century a hefty chunk of political Britain decided it could no longer stomach the taste of fudge.

That is a metaphor which might suggest a somewhat abstract

problem, something to be mumbled about and chewed over in London's civil service clubs, parliamentary committee rooms and foreign policy think tanks. And there was indeed much mumbling and much chewing. But for millions of Britons the choice was more pungent and immediate. It was about the people living next door, or down the road in the housing estate. The Empire had never been something most British people encountered directly. A steady stream of soldiers and administrators had been packed off to the colonies. Scottish tobacco and opium traders had brought back fortunes. Early twentieth-century branding on beers, biscuits, cigarettes and shops reflected the Empire. But *actual* Nigerians, Indian Hindus, black Caribbeans or Asian Muslims, never mind Romanians and Bulgarians, had rarely been encountered by the British themselves.

Now, in the new Queen's reign, with cheaper shipping and mass air travel arriving, this was no longer true. Imperial or European? The choice would affect exactly who was living and welcome on British streets, the smell of restaurant food, the people appearing on British television screens. If Britain was to be an enthusiastic member of a new Commonwealth of peoples, then she could hardly reject fellow members of that Commonwealth when they wanted to come and live in the 'home country'. In this spirit, immigrants from the Caribbean, the Indian subcontinent and Africa had a message for chilly white natives: 'We are only over here', they would say, 'because you were over there.'

A parallel question was raised by British membership of the European Union. If – *if* – we were now truly Europeans, then what could be the objection when, as many of us migrated to Spain and France, Poles, Lithuanians and Hungarians chose to come and live among us? The British, if not exactly lazy, seemed no longer prepared to do a range of jobs, from working in care homes to driving mini-cabs, which poorer migrants would undertake. During the coronavirus crisis of 2020, the reliance of the British NHS, and the country's system of residential care homes, on foreign-born workers was glaringly obvious. But beyond that, as fruit and vegetables rotted in the fields, it seemed that even at a time of high and rising unemployment, British people were not prepared to do agricultural labour. The UK might be out of the EU, and airlines might have shut down most flights, but after pleading from farmers, Romanian farmworkers were being hurriedly brought back into the country once more.

The politics of this is not simple. It would be naive to assume that every migrant group linked arms in solidarity with every other: during the 2016 referendum, British Pakistanis and British Chinese had been encouraged to vote to leave the EU on the grounds that more of their relatives would then be able to come here, once Christian East Europeans were no longer able to. As with the history of modern New York, each group of immigrants tends to look at the next one arriving with some suspicion.

So choices about where Britain stood in the world were also choices about who was living next door to you, what food was available in the corner supermarket and whose children yours would make friends with in the playground. Because of that, decisions made in Whitehall changed the tone and tenor of everyday life. In a globalized and much more quickly connected world, 'foreign policy' and neighbourhood consequences became the same thing. Although Britain has always been marked by immigration, the scale of late twentieth-century population movements was unprecedented.

Meanwhile, Britain's engagement in modern Europe had a personal, visceral impact in both directions – on all those people who came to live here, but also on all those who moved to the continent. The British learned to eat differently, to speak differently and even, up to a point, to dress differently as a result of their European immersion. Better-off, older Britons retired to southern Spain or bought sprawling vacant farmhouses in rural France. Some of them actually learned Spanish and French. Their children emerged from holidays with Portuguese, Polish or Greek girlfriends and boyfriends on their arms.

For British policymakers, meanwhile, the great dilemma was how best to project power. Their luxuriantly bearded, frock-coated predecessors had expected to make a big noise around the globe – to be deferred to, listened to and, whenever necessary, to be at least a little feared. They assumed this status while by and large keeping foreigners out of Britain itself and not paying them that much heed. This was possible only because Britain was one of the prime industrial and military powers of that age. But was it possible for the British in the reign of Queen Elizabeth II to remain both truly powerful in the old way and properly independent? The answer being no, which way should we look? And in all of this, how loyal a supporter should we be of our half-sister superpower, the United States?

These were issues that the Queen's prime ministers, from Churchill at the beginning of the reign to his biographer Boris Johnson towards its close, could never ignore. But Europe-or-America? was also a dilemma experienced all around Britain by the Queen's subjects. If US filmmakers rewrote our Second World War history or the story of the British royal family in ways we didn't like, did we shrug and reflect that in the end after all they were 'sort of' on our side? If a struggling business eventually collapsed under the weight of regulations imposed not by British politicians but by Brussels, did we accept that as a price worth paying to be 'Europeans'? From sport to food, commerce to culture, the big choices about where we find our new place and allies in the world defined much of what it was to be British in the second Elizabethan reign.

23

MOUNTBATTEN AND THE NAVY

One of the biggest changes in our national life is the decline of the British military. In saying 'decline', I cast no aspersions on the courage or intelligence of today's serving personnel. I mean the falling away in numbers, relative punching-power and budgets that have been the fate of the British Army, Royal Navy and RAF since the 1950s. But I mean something more profound too. Because of National Service and the fresh memory of the war, the military retained a central position in the British imagination until the 1960s. Schools had cadet forces. From haircuts to shoes, the influence of the Army was physically present on millions of British male civilians. Military tattoos, bands and parades were immensely popular. Fondly or bitterly, men talked in local servicemen's clubs about their days in the Army. London projected herself to the rest of the UK through grand national and royal ceremonial occasions, with military parades almost always part of that.

Some of this remains true today but the military atmosphere in British life has been pushed to one side, as it were, around the corner. This is despite the growth of fervour in response to Remembrance Days in the century after the First World War. We still have recruiting adverts, TV programmes about military life and royal birthday parades. However, sometimes it seems almost as if the military have become a kind of old-fashioned, respected but slightly odd cult. Politicians don't talk about this, but they know it. Military budgets have been cut, and cut again, with little voter reaction. Britain's Army, Navy and Air Force are currently the smallest they have ever been in modern times. Senior staff officers worry that they don't have the manpower and weaponry any longer to project major-power force. Just as, bit by bit, we became a secular country, so, without any great national discussion, we also became a fundamentally less warlike one.

This might seem a strange judgement. After all, throughout the Cold War, Britain maintained nuclear submarines and bomber forces which could devastate much of the planet, as well as a major mechanized army (albeit more visible in West Germany than on home turf); moreover we fought a series of vicious post-colonial wars against guerrilla armies. Indeed, from Malaya, Cyprus and Suez through to Afghanistan and Iraq, Britain was at war far more often than she was at peace. But this is part of the explanation for today's pacific turn in the national character. The Cold War, with its threat of mutually assured annihilation, created an undercurrent of hostility not just to nuclear weapons but to the whole military enterprise. The anti-insurgency wars were never very popular at home. And finally, when the Cold War threat ended, so too did that sense of imminent and real danger.

The historian Helen Parr reflected on the changes happening during the 1980s:

> The armed services came to be regarded much more as another professional occupation. Many more officers had a university education and married women who wanted to maintain their own careers. Over time, the army was forced to adjust . . . perhaps in the future if historians look back on the 1970s and early 1980s, this period would appear to be the end of the era defined by

total war. The ways in which manhood was linked to the responsibility of military service – the final trial of the stiff upper lip
– will seem dated, perhaps even absurd.

The popularity of military-mocking television shows such as
Blackadder and the shrinking of English poetry in schools to anti-war
poets from 1914–18 are small but quietly elegant examples of this.

In a book reflecting on the history of the Parachute Regiment,
to which she had had a family connection, and the Falklands War,
Parr continued: 'The connections between national character,
manhood and society were already beginning to be transformed
soon after 1982, more intently so after the end of the Cold War
in 1991. Armed service is now regarded less as a burden of masculine duty to be accepted without complaint, and more a set of
special skills that can be taught to all people, not just to men.'

By contrast, 1950s Britain was suffused with the brisk ethos of
military masculinity, not just in boys' comics and popular novels,
but on the screen as well. And it was the Navy that was the 'Senior
Service', with a special call on British hearts. The culmination of a
series of hugely popular black-and-white war films came in 1960
with *Sink the Bismarck*, starring the ubiquitous Kenneth More. The
gala opening in Leicester Square in February that year was a kind
of naval reunion, as the Duke of Edinburgh, who had served in
the Mediterranean and Pacific fleets during the Second World War,
shook the hand of the actor – who was himself the son of a Royal
Naval pilot, and a wartime veteran of the cruiser HMS *Aurora* and
the aircraft carrier HMS *Victorious*. Observing them was Lord
Mountbatten of Burma, Prince Philip's uncle, who had just stood
down as First Sea Lord.

Sink the Bismarck was praised for its realism both in Britain,
where it was the highest-grossing film of the year, and in America.
It gave birth to a popular song. But the film's story is a poignant
one, featuring the destruction not only of the German battleship,

but of Britain's HMS *Hood*, which had been blown to pieces during the pursuit. The most realistic scenes had been created thanks to Lord Mountbatten. He had been approached by the film's producer, who happened to be his son-in-law John Knatchbull, Lord Brabourne. Mountbatten told the Navy to do all they could to help. They certainly came up trumps: the ship that stood in for both the *Hood* and the *Bismarck* was nothing less than Britain's last battleship, and indeed the last battleship to be launched anywhere, HMS *Vanguard*.

The Navy had been cut to pieces since the end of the Second World War, a giant selling-off and scuttling of giant ships such as it had never experienced. The 1953 Queen's Coronation Fleet Review is still an extraordinary spectacle to watch on archive news film – vast numbers of formidable warships lined up off Spithead, letting off thunderous cannonades. In 1945 the Royal Navy had ended the war with the largest fleet it had ever possessed, and indeed the second biggest in the world after the United States. It boasted nearly 9,000 vessels and a personnel strength not far short of a million. Dramatic post-war cuts had to be made to get highly qualified RN personnel back into the civilian economy and to save money.

For a while, in the late 1940s and early 1950s, the Navy was partially protected because it was thought necessary to protect the Empire and then the Commonwealth. But the shrinking of Britain's worldwide role, and the arrival of nuclear weapons, initially to be carried by RAF bombers, meant that yet more big cuts were needed. The naval historians Duncan Redford and Philip Grove argue that Britain 'was not just the keeper of a huge and global naval instrument – it was also effectively bankrupt . . . Having been the defender of the nation for centuries and the steadfast protector of its empire, the Royal Navy now found itself in turbulent and mystifying times.' In essence, what this meant was that its role shrank from global capability – even the wartime Pacific Fleet had been vast – to defending the North Atlantic and North Sea as part of an essentially

European anti-Soviet force. So the story of this Elizabethan Royal Navy is inextricably tangled up with that of Britain's reduced place in the world.

The figure at its heart was Lord Mountbatten, hirer-out of HMS *Vanguard*. He was First Sea Lord from 1955 to 1959, and then Chief of the Defence Staff until 1965. He was also one of the most glamorous and best-connected figures in the post-war British establishment. He was born Prince Louis Battenberg to German parents, part of Queen Victoria's extended family, who visited Tsar Nicholas II of Russia and his family before the revolution. Mountbatten was a close personal friend of Edward VIII, served in the Royal Navy in both wars, became the last Viceroy and Governor General of India and in due course Prince Charles's 'honorary grandfather'. Long after his death, released FBI files anonymously described him as a 'homosexual with a perversion for young boys'.

Whether the FBI was fair or not, in terms of his politics Mountbatten was regarded by senior Tories as a dangerous radical. He was a leading opponent of Sir Anthony Eden's 1956 plot to seize the Suez Canal from Egypt – and had to be ordered not to resign in protest as First Sea Lord. His greatest success in saving the Navy from deep cuts came after a long battle with the then Minister of Defence Duncan Sandys. The latter was a pro-European Tory with a proud wartime record of his own but was nicknamed in Whitehall 'the mincing machine', for his ruthless focus on numbers as against tradition.

But Mountbatten won him round by using tradition ruthlessly against him. He hosted a dinner for Sandys in the historic and poignant surroundings of Horatio Nelson's cabin aboard HMS *Victory*, and followed up with a long weekend at the grand Mountbatten family mansion, Broadlands. Both admonitory and sinuously flattering towards the minister, and deploying every ounce of his famous charm, he freed the Royal Navy from the deepest proposed cuts and even won a vague promise for more aircraft carriers to project British power in the nuclear age. In every conversation the setting matters, and a handsome royal who wears a uniform well can still be a deadly weapon.

Mountbatten turned heads. In the mid-1960s, right-wingers and rebellious military officers who plotted a coup against Harold Wilson's Labour government sounded him out as a potential dictatorial figurehead. He, however, dismissed the idea as treason. At the time, Mountbatten was again a crucial figure in trying to defend the Royal Navy, working on the inside, against Labour cuts. Whatever can be said about the rest of his reputation, he proved a wily and successful politician. The Navy was now being pitted against the RAF in vicious internal battles about how Britain's nuclear bombs would be delivered. Eventually the Navy and its submarine fleet proved victorious. But such political battles didn't win Mountbatten many friends. Sir Gerald Templer, the splenetic Chief of the Imperial General Staff, is said to have told him: 'Dickie, you're so bloody crooked that if you swallowed a nail, you'd shit a corkscrew.'

Denis Healey, who as Wilson's Defence Secretary had to push through cuts, was a cold-eyed judge of the man, complaining of Mountbatten's 'monarchical characteristics', including the need for a personal court:

He was immensely proud of his royal birth. When he was standing in line with Edna and me at a reception for a thousand attachés and their wives in the Banqueting House, Edna turned to him after shaking several hundred hands and said that her wrist was feeling sore. Dickie looked down at her and pronounced: 'My great aunt – the Empress of Russia – used to have a blister on the back of her hand – as big as an egg – at Easter – where the peasants had kissed it. She never wore gloves.' There was no answer to that.

Healey, however, spotted that this foreign-born royal, who had never been welcomed by the British aristocracy, was anti-establishment: 'It is said that he answered the door at his country seat, Broadlands, to a Tory canvasser during the 1945 general election. "I don't have a vote because I'm a peer," he told her. "If I did, I'd vote Labour. But I think my butler's a Conservative."'

Notwithstanding his private amusement and enjoyment of Mountbatten, Healey as Secretary of State for Defence sacked him and then proceeded radically to reduce the surface fleet in order to maintain Britain's nuclear submarine deterrent force. Eventually the battle was lost for a new aircraft-carrier-building programme and then, ship by ship, the big ones went. It was a failure the Royal Navy never forgot. In the twenty-first century, it would finally get back two aircraft carriers, at a cost of more than £6 billion – HMS *Queen Elizabeth* (named after the first Queen Elizabeth), and then HMS *Prince of Wales*. They are a robust modern assertion of British nautical pride. How useful they will be remains to be seen.

Meanwhile, back in the 1960s, the Admiralty itself disappeared. With its origins going back to Tudor England, and the proud possessor of Britain's first purpose-built office building – a U-shaped, elegant structure put up in 1726 in Whitehall – the Admiralty had directed naval operations against Napoleon, Hitler and all around the British Empire. Healey, with a strongly developed sense of history, was well aware of this, even as he prepared his bureaucratic wrecking-ball: 'The Royal Navy was proud of a history which went back to the Armada. Living as I did in Admiralty House, surrounded by paintings of Captain Cook's expeditions to the South Seas, eating under the marble eyes of Nelson and the great admirals of the eighteenth century, I was not likely to forget it.'

Yet he had to reduce defence spending from over 7 per cent of the nation's output to 5 per cent and was proud of the fact that 'When I left office, for the first time in its history, the state was spending more on education than on defence.' So much for the

Admiralty. Since it had brought together senior admirals and politicians, its elegant rooms had hosted debates between great commanders such as Lord Hood (after whom the doomed Second World War battleship had been named), Anson, Howe and Sir George Cockburn, who had burned Washington in 1814. Politicians who had served there before Healey included Winston Churchill, Pitt the Elder and Arthur Balfour.

The Admiralty had had its periods in the doldrums. It had been touched by scandal. It had wallowed in inefficiency. But for centuries it had been absolutely at the heart of how Britain saw her place in the world. And then, in 1964, it was killed off and its corpse walled into the bleak anonymity of the Ministry of Defence. Lord Jellicoe, son of the British commander at Jutland in 1916, was the last professional Lord High Admiral. The ancient title was then taken by the Queen herself, who held it for forty-seven years before passing it to her husband the Duke of Edinburgh, who had given up a promising naval career to marry her, as a ninetieth-birthday present in 2011.

Lord Mountbatten would have liked that. But as the Admiralty went, so did much of the Navy for which he had fought so hard. It was taken apart in a series of new defence reviews under both Tory and Labour governments. Denis Healey's review of 1965 during Wilson's first government was one of the most devastating, but it was followed by another bleakly savage cutback under Sir John Nott, Margaret Thatcher's Defence Secretary, in 1981. By then, despite the promises made to Mountbatten, the Navy had just one aircraft carrier in service at any one time, no bigger ships at all, and was losing its destroyers and frigates. In 1981, shortly before the Argentine invasion of the Falkland Islands in April 1982, Nott had been arguing that surface ships were no longer necessary to the Navy at all. Among his cuts was the ice patrol ship HMS *Endurance*, the only Royal Navy vessel regularly in the South Atlantic.

This seemed to give the green light to the Argentine dictatorship to invade the islands they called the Malvinas; and British history was changed. Although many, including the US administration, regarded the project of recapturing the islands as militarily impossible, the diminished Royal Navy was able, just, to assemble a task force of forty-three vessels, plus another eighty-four auxiliaries and requisitioned vessels. Power could still be projected across the Atlantic. More than 900 British and Argentine people were killed, but the islands were retaken and, enjoying a wave of patriotic enthusiasm, Margaret Thatcher's Conservatives were triumphantly re-elected the following year.

Never has a botched defence review produced such an unwonted political bonus. Sadly, Lord Mountbatten's thoughts on all of that will never be known: he had been murdered by the IRA in a bomb hidden on his pleasure boat off Northern Ireland in the summer of 1979.

24

NEW-FANGLED WARS, OLD-FASHIONED HEROES

The dirty war in Northern Ireland, which involved so many murders and so much brutality, undermined the reputation of British soldiers for many watching at home. The lowest moment for the Army's reputation came on 30 January 1972 when the 1st Battalion, the Parachute Regiment, fired at protesters during a demonstration in the Bogside area of (London)Derry, killing twenty-eight unarmed civilians, at least some of whom were running away at the time.

After the involvement of senior military figures in shadowy plots against Harold Wilson and growing public hostility to some of the anti-insurgency, post-imperial actions abroad, there was already a widespread belief on the left that the Army was no longer neutral, but had become the politically loaded weapon of a Conservative British state and so could not be trusted by progressives. The London-Irish singer Declan Patrick McManus, who performed as Elvis Costello, captured this anti-Army mood in his 1978 song 'Oliver's Army'. Influenced by seeing the British armed forces in Northern Ireland, Costello sings of mercenaries and imperial armies around the world, with working-class boys 'from the Mersey and the Thames and the Tyne' being the ones expected to do the killing and with 'one itchy trigger' creating 'one more widow, one less white nigger'.

There was always profound support for the military in other parts of British society; after the IRA bombings in Birmingham, London and Warrington, many saw the Army in Northern Ireland as the good guys protecting them against terrorism. Perhaps some of the cultural divisions that would become apparent in the 2016 referendum on British membership of the EU were already present, or began, with a deeply divided view of the British Army and therefore of British history too. The romantic appeal of Britain's military history did not vanish quickly. We know this because of the popularity of a sequence of modern British soldiers – old-fashioned heroes fighting by and large new-fangled wars.

The first was Lieutenant Colonel Colin Mitchell, an Argyll and Sutherland Highlander. A young wartime soldier who had stayed on in the forces, Mitchell had seen action against the Jewish guer-rillas in Palestine, including the arrest of a future prime minister of Israel, and witnessed the bombing of the King David Hotel. The friends he made at the time among both Arabs and Jews included the great Israeli general and politician Moshe Dayan. Mitchell later fought in the Korean War, and then in a series of smaller post-imperial fights, in East Africa, Cyprus and Borneo. But he will be remembered in history for his leadership during the Aden insurgency of 1967.

Aden, a small port city on the southern tip of Somalia, overlooking the Arabian Sea, had been a strategically important British posses-sion since the early days of Queen Victoria's reign, and a key port and coaling station for the Royal Navy throughout the age of imperialism. By 1963, under the influence of growing Arab nation-alism, there was a low-key guerrilla uprising against British rule, particularly in the mountainous hinterland to the north.

By the summer of 1967, this had spread to the city of Aden itself. There was special trouble inside the small, cramped suburb of 'Crater', so named because it had been built inside the crater of an extinct volcano. Soon after the Argyll and Sutherland Highlanders arrived, they suffered a lethal ambush there, with eight troopers killed. British soldiers withdrew to the perimeter of the area, while politicians and generals back in London agonized about what to do. Eventually, running out of patience, Mitchell ordered the Argylls to retake Crater, which they did with swaggering success, bagpipes playing. This gung-ho attitude in 'the last battle of the British Empire' delighted much of the British press, who christened the no-nonsense, clipped, self-certain young Lieutenant Colonel 'Mad Mitch', as if he was a figure from a boys' comic.

However, as his troops took control of Crater, Mitchell's techniques seemed to some observers excessively brutal, even barbarous. He bluntly told the television cameras that his policy was to be 'extremely firm and extremely mean'. If 'some chap' came at British troops with a grenade or pistol, 'we will kill them, quite rightly'. For Mitchell, any criticism of what became known as Argyll law was 'poppycock and wet tripe'. But this assumption of British rights over bolshie 'wogs' was already, in 1967, out of date. In November of that year, despite the old-fashioned bravery of the Argyll and Sutherland Highlanders going into a warren of streets almost made for ambush, their political masters had had enough and the British abruptly quit another tiny speck of Empire.

Mitchell's story, however, remains relevant today. He might have lost the argument with his military superiors, but he was entirely modern in the ruthless sophistication of his public relations. He had personally summoned journalists alongside him when he marched into Crater. He made absolutely sure the cameras were on hand to record his statements. He delivered stories to the patriotic press in Britain so carefully crafted that they hardly had to be edited. In short, he gave a large section of British public opinion exactly what it wanted – an us-and-them, highly coloured, gung-ho adventure from the glory days of Empire. Mitchell realized that in the new world, if Britain was going to fight wars abroad, she had to have public opinion roaring approval of her heroes. This was a view which previous British warriors had shared – think, for instance, of Horatio Nelson and how he encouraged his personal cult. And later in the twentieth century other fighters would remember 'Mad Mitch' with special interest.

Fifteen years younger than Colin Mitchell, Herbert (or, as he always preferred, 'H') Jones had missed most of the end-of-Empire actions, although he had served in the Devon and Dorset Regiment at the tail end of the Cyprus emergency, and in British Guiana before independence there. The child of a wealthy, slightly raffish Anglo-American family, he had been educated at Eton and Sandhurst. After he was killed charging a machine-gun post in the Falklands and had been awarded the Victoria Cross, an Etonian contemporary wrote of Jones:

> He loved military books in general and tales of heroism in particular; he was a romantic who even then could be seen measuring himself against Beau Geste . . . He was to an alarming degree resistant in any boyhood trial in the endurance of pain. Above all he had a highly developed sense of honour; if he somehow formed a conclusion that he ought to act in a certain way nothing, but nothing, would deflect him.

Jones, who had not been an outstanding schoolchild or young officer, nonetheless rose quickly as a soldier, training as a paratrooper, before returning to his regiment at the beginning of the Northern Ireland troubles in 1970. During his training as a staff officer, a colleague described Jones in a way that uncannily reflects the Eton judgement: 'His moral courage was as great as his physical courage, if not greater. He had all the qualities of a G. A. Henty hero, a Bulldog Drummond or a Richard Hannay. Without a doubt, he would have distinguished himself equally well at Waterloo, Omdurman or Rorke's Drift.' He sounds almost like Mitchell reborn. This was the man, unconventional in his origins in the British Army, who was steadily promoted through the junior officer ranks until, by the time of the 1982 Falklands War, he commanded as a lieutenant colonel the 2nd Battalion of the Parachute Regiment.

The Falklands dispute was nothing if not old-fashioned. The islands off the coast of Argentina had been taken by the French Empire and then by the Spanish, who bought them in 1776. Britain and Spain nearly came to war over them in the eighteenth century, and when, in 1820, Argentina became independent of Spain she inherited the Spanish claim to the islands. In 1833 a British ship landed on East Falkland after the Argentine settlement had been destroyed by an American bombardment. British sovereignty was claimed, although Argentina never accepted it. This was therefore a long-standing but obscure dispute and, for most British people, a frankly confusing one. By the 1980s there were only 1,763 English-speaking people living on the Falklands. As we have seen, naval cuts by London suggested that the United Kingdom was no longer terribly interested in the remote archipelago.

Towards the end of 1981, Argentina's somewhat desperate dictator President Galtieri was looking for a popular cause, as his country was demoralized, politically riven and weakened by inflation. There is, of course, nothing like a war to cheer people up. Galtieri directed Argentina's armed forces to retake the islands and this was done, relatively efficiently, in April 1982. Margaret Thatcher felt she had no choice in how to respond. She immediately declared that Britain would take the islands back, and commissioned a task force including twenty warships, and 15,000 men to sail to the South Atlantic. This was the largest mobilization of British forces since the 1950s. Colonel 'H' Jones, gripped by the unexpected drama, was determined that his parachute battalion would not miss the action. Nor did they.

What followed for the British paratroopers were battles that felt more like First World War skirmishes than late twentieth-century fighting. After a successful landing Jones ordered a full-scale assault on Argentine trenches at Goose Green, on a key isthmus. The plan was announced ahead of time by the BBC, to Colonel Jones's fury. But he possessed old-fashioned British military confidence. He told his troops that 'All previous evidence suggests that if the enemy is hit hard, he will crumble.' The result was a charge uphill on rough ground, with bayonets fixed, against dug-in machine guns. Many British soldiers died. They did, however, capture the trenches, which might have been inspired by Colonel Jones's own exceptional courage: he charged one of the trenches himself and was killed by covering Argentine fire.

Although some military historians and commentators argue that his actions were reckless and ultimately unnecessary, this was soldiering heroism of the kind generations of British boys had been brought up to admire. The citation for Jones's Victoria Cross read, in part:

> It was clear to him that desperate measures were needed in order to overcome the enemy position and rekindle the attack, and that unless these measures were taken promptly the Battalion would sustain increasing casualties and the attack perhaps even fail. It was time for personal leadership and action. Colonel Jones immediately seized a sub-machine gun, and, calling on those around him and with total disregard for his own safety, charged the nearest enemy position. This action exposed him to fire from a number of trenches. As he charged up a short slope at the enemy position he was seen to fall and roll backward downhill. He immediately picked himself up, and again charged the enemy trench, firing his sub-machine gun and seemingly oblivious to the intense fire directed at him . . .

The war, fought in freezing and muddy conditions by soldiers who, despite air cover and bombardments from modern warships, conducted themselves very much in the same way as wartime British Tommies, was a modern British victory which had spectacular political repercussions. It helped destroy General Galtieri's dictatorship. In Britain, it may have saved Margaret Thatcher, who was at a low point, threatened by the fast-rising new centre party, the SDP. Having taken the decision to go to war herself, and dominating the Commons during it, suffering private grief at British losses, she then milked the victory, making it personal to her. Britain agreed. In June 1983, on the back of the Falklands War, she gained a massive second general election victory, winning 397 seats in the Commons, against 209 for Labour and just 23 for the SDP.

So it is not hyperbole to say that the big changes in British society during the 1980s – the curbing of trade unions, the privatizations, the unleashing of the City – came about in part because of what Colonel Herbert Jones and his soldiers did on the wet, tussocky and dangerous territory of Atlantic sheep farms. Yet, in the story of Britain's military culture, this seemed more like the end of something – an unusual, old-fashioned war, fought in the old-fashioned way by old-fashioned heroes – rather than any prefiguring of the coming new warfare of drones, cyber-attacks and super-fast missiles.

A more modern, and considerably more brutal, war later produced an alternative military character for the British to admire, one whose fame tells us about how the country has changed. Colonel Tim Collins, Belfast-born, commanded the 1st Battalion of the Royal Irish Regiment as it prepared to help invade Iraq at the beginning of the 2003 war. He was a thoroughly professional and formidably well-educated modern soldier.

The invasion of Iraq to oust the dictator Saddam Hussein was a great modern disaster. A fast and almost one-sided military victory over Saddam's over-hyped forces eventually resulted in the deaths of hundreds of thousands of Iraqi civilians. Iraq became a haven for the most fanatical and deadly Islamist terror group of all, Al Qaeda, and Shia Iran rose to become a major regional influence. In Britain, the war had been unpopular from early on. Many believed that because of the lack of clear UN approval it was effectively illegal. It split Tony Blair's Labour Party, and he never recovered his reputation. It created the 'Stop the War' coalition, and one of the biggest demonstrations the streets of London have ever seen.

In the end, much of the criticism was about the purpose of war in the modern world and how it could be conducted. And this is where Colonel Collins and his famous speech come in. The speech cannot be claimed to have changed much. Although it is said to have been framed and hung in the White House, little of its profound message was properly heard by the US-dominated invasion coalition forces.

What was that message? Over to Colonel Collins:

We go to liberate, not to conquer. We will not fly our flags in their country. We are entering Iraq to free a people and the only flag which will be flown in that ancient land is their own. Show respect for them. There are some who are alive at this moment who will not be alive shortly. Those who do not wish to go on that journey, we will not send. As for the others, I expect you to rock their world. Wipe them out if that is what they choose. But if you are ferocious in battle remember to be magnanimous in victory. Iraq is steeped in history. It is the site of the Garden of Eden, of the Great Flood and the birthplace of Abraham. Tread lightly there. You will see things that no man could pay to see – and you will have to go a long way to find a more decent, generous and upright people than the Iraqis. You will be embarrassed by their hospitality even though they have nothing. Don't treat them as refugees for they are in their own country.

Their children will be poor, in years to come they will know that the light of liberation in their lives was brought by you . . .

This is such an interesting speech to be made by a British soldier because, although it touches old traditions of military thinking, in its noble humility it seemed to offer an alternative and better way forward for Britain to conduct herself across the world. Both 'Mad Mitch' and 'H' Jones were brave, charismatic, rebellious and complicated military heroes: but it was Colonel Collins, rather than they, who spoke more clearly for contemporary Britain.

25

BOB THE GOOD

By the 1980s, television had become a prime driver of public attitudes to foreign affairs. Britain's readiness to engage in wars abroad was heavily affected by the work of star correspondents such as Kate Adie of the BBC, whose reports on the break-up of former Yugoslavia, Rwanda and Sierra Leone had a big impact, not least on the government of Tony Blair. But television could be used to reshape public opinion for other causes than military intervention; and in the spirit of the Collins speech the Britain of the late twentieth century was beginning to realize that global influence can come in many varieties.

On 23 October 1984, another of the BBC's most experienced overseas correspondents brought the world a first-hand account of a famine from a refugee camp in the small community of Korem in Ethiopia, where the rains had failed. Michael Buerk, working with a Kenyan cameraman called Mohammed Amin, kept his voice dry and (almost) unemotional. Buerk was the epitome of reporterly restraint, so admired by Corporation executives. But the words he chose, as much as the pictures he broadcast, would change, at least for a time, the modern world.

His report began:

Dawn. As the sun breaks through the piercing chill of night on the plain outside Korem, it lights up a biblical famine – now in the twentieth century. This place, say workers here, is the closest thing to hell on earth . . . Thousands of wasted people are coming here for help. Many find only death. They flood in every day from villages hundreds of miles away, dulled by hunger, driven beyond the point of desperation. Fifteen thousand children here now – suffering, confused, lost. Death is all around. A child or an adult dies every twenty minutes. Korem, an insignificant town, has become a place of grief.

The relief agencies do what they can. Save the Children Fund are caring for more than 7,000 babies. Every day they weigh them on a sling then compare their weight with their height. By this rule of thumb one in three is severely malnourished, starved to the point of death. This morning another 114 babies have arrived. The choice of who can be helped and who can't among the constant stream of newcomers is heartbreaking. There's not enough food for half these people. Rumours of a shipment can set off panic. As on most days the rumours were false. For many here there will be no food again today . . .

Images of children no bigger than kittens, and of men and women with emaciated legs running desperately on the mere rumour of food arriving, combined with Michael Buerk's mingling of almost religious language and harsh statistics, had an immediate effect on public opinion. Long before the internet could be relied upon to spread images, the BBC report was picked up and broadcast around the world by no fewer than 425 television stations.

Perhaps it would have remained just another horrifying missive on evening-news programmes – more bad news just around supper time – had it not also been watched, in their Chelsea house, by an Irish rock musician whose career was on the slide and by his young television-presenter partner, Paula Yates. At the end of the report, she ran upstairs, crying, to check on their new baby: he felt a mixture of anger, disgust and shame.

Bob Geldof wrote later that:

> From the first two seconds, it was clear that this was a horror on a monumental scale. The pictures were of people who were so shrunken by starvation that they looked like beings from another planet. Their arms and legs were thin as sticks, their bodies spindly. Swollen veins and huge, blankly staring eyes protruded from their shrivelled heads. The camera wandered amidst them like a mesmerised observer, occasionally dwelling on one person, so that he looked at me, sitting in my comfortable living room surrounded by the fripperies of modern living which we were pleased to regard as necessities.

Known in the music world for his intemperate and often foul-mouthed diatribe directed at rival rock bands, Geldof had been brought up a rebellious Catholic in Dublin. Perhaps Michael Buerk's religious imagery struck a particular chord. Bob Geldof reflected: 'Buerk had used the word "biblical". A famine of biblical proportions. There was something terrible about the idea that, 2,000 years after Christ, in a world of modern technology something like this could be allowed to happen as if the ability of mankind to influence and control the environment had not altered one jot.'

After a bad night's sleep, Geldof woke to find that Paula Yates had already left for work, heading to Newcastle to record the TV programme *The Tube*. But she had left a handwritten note stuck to the fridge door. It read, 'Ethiopia. Everyone who visits this house from today onwards will be asked to give £5 until we have raised £200 for famine relief.'

Geldof felt the same way. He would send some money. But then he thought that this would not be enough. To allow the famine to continue would be tantamount to murder. He, however, was only a pop singer and by now not a very successful one: 'I could not help the tottering man to carry his burden. All I could do was make records that no one bought.' Instead, that very day, he suggested making a record to raise money for the Ethiopians. He phoned Paula Yates and she liked the idea too. Christmas was not so far away – perhaps, if enough people were touched, a Christmas record might raise serious amounts of funding. But Geldof, nothing if not self-critical, feared that if his own band, the Boomtown Rats, made the record it wouldn't sell very well.

He would have to bring others in. He began by ringing Midge Ure of Ultravox, an old friend, and then telephoned the Geordie rock star Gordon Sumner, better known as Sting, of the Police. Passing an antiques shop on the King's Road, he noticed Gary Kemp of the band Spandau Ballet inside, and popped in to persuade him. Bit by bit, call by call, Geldof persuaded, wheedled and cajoled an impressive number of the pop stars of the mid-1980s to join him in singing the song he composed with Midge Ure, 'Do They Know It's Christmas?' It duly stormed into the charts at number one.

Rock and pop music is as competitive as any other part of business life. Now, however, old rivals and enemies made peace, at least for a while, and performed together under the collective name Band Aid. For a famously combative man this was quite an achievement. But Geldof also had a shrewd and underused business brain. Despite the wild image, he had positioned the Boomtown Rats as the new-wave band whose material was nevertheless safe for the BBC. He was always frank about his desire to make money.

Now this Dublin boy, who had been scarred by a chaotic upbringing, turned his hard-edged, impatient negotiating skills to persuading chain stores and trade unions to give up their cuts on the song. It was an extraordinary moment. That Christmas, street singers could be heard around Britain singing what had become, in effect, a new carol. By early in the new year, Band Aid had more than £5 million in its bank account. Geldof went out to Ethiopia to see for himself what was happening.

During the first months of the following year, 1985, Geldof monitored how the money was being spent and, as he was touring with his band around the world, reflected on what should happen next. A man who always thought big, he devised the idea of a globally broadcast concert of rock music, beamed simultaneously from the United States and Britain, woven together by satellite and transmitted across the globe. With manic energy he now persuaded most of the biggest names in rock at the time, from David Bowie and Mick Jagger to Bob Dylan and Paul McCartney, to take part in this 'global jukebox'. Although a few rock stars refused to commit themselves (including Bruce Springsteen and Michael Jackson), some iconic but splintered bands, including the Who and Status Quo, re-formed for the event. Queen, of whom more later, would eventually steal the show. Much of the commercial underpinning, from stadium rentals and air flights to design and advertising slots forgone, was given free after yet more Geldof confrontations.

Live Aid – the name was thought up by Geldof – was finally broadcast on 13 July 1985 to an audience of 1.9 billion people in 150 countries, or 40 per cent of the world's then total population. At one point during the live broadcast Geldof responded to a presenter reading out an address for money by saying 'Fuck the address, let's get the [phone] numbers.' People responded in huge quantities. It became almost a frenzy of donation, by far the biggest event of its kind ever. It is now thought that around £150 million was raised directly from the concert.

Live Aid provoked perhaps inevitable controversies. Had Geldof signed enough black singers and bands? (No, but it wasn't for lack of trying.) Were all the band sets of a high quality? (Umm, no.) And most important: did all the money raised go to the right people? (Probably not all of it: there were criticisms about the involvement of the Ethiopian leader Mengistu Haile Mariam, accused of siphoning off some of the funds to buy Soviet weaponry. Geldof responded that he would do a deal with the devil in order to get money to the famine victims.)

That moment in the summer of 1985 did not mark a step change in Western attitudes to aid. More famines, disasters caused by war, tsunamis and earthquakes followed, and stretched the willingness of affluent Westerners to hand over money. It was, no doubt, a self-important and preening meeting of Western pop and Western technology, in which the competitive self-interest of rich musicians played a part. But here's what matters: without Bob Geldof's manic determination, many people who are alive today would have died.

In later life, Geldof would face much personal misery. Paula Yates, the young presenter who stuck that note on the fridge door, later divorced him and died of a heroin overdose in 2000. Their second daughter, Peaches Geldof, a columnist and model, was found dead, also by heroin, at the age of twenty-five. But the Irish rebel, later knighted by the Queen, did more to help his fellow men and women than any other Elizabethan. Dishevelled, foul-mouthed, prone to bragging and not one of the *very* greatest musicians of the age, he deserves to be remembered as Bob the Good. Some have satirically mocked him as 'St Bob'. But he was a kind of saint; and where in the historical record does it say that saints are generally easy or happy people?

26

WOMEN AND WAR

In the run-up to Easter 1983, Margaret Thatcher's Press Secretary Bernard (later Sir Bernard) Ingham, a jowly, red-faced former Labour supporter from Yorkshire, had a wizard wheeze. The government was worried about a blizzard of dangerous negative publicity over its latest defence planning. But this 'will secure less airtime and have less impact if something more newsworthy in television terms occurs . . . What would take the trick would be press and television pictures for release on the evening of Good Friday and/or Saturday newspapers of Prince William in Australia.' Long before Tony Blair's government got into trouble for trying to 'bury bad news', their Conservative rivals had been up to just the same thing. The Thatcher government was discussing the use of what was, in British popular media terms, the ultimate nuclear weapon: cute pictures of a toddler prince. But what was the dangerous blast of hostile publicity requiring such a heavy-duty response?

The person perhaps most responsible for Bernard Ingham's anxiety was a quietly spoken nurse and midwife from Wales, who had five children and a calm determination to do her bit to prevent nuclear war. There had been growing publicity in Wales at the time about the possibility of nuclear materials being stored there, but there was a much bigger global context, too.

Since the mid-1970s, the Soviet Union had been deploying hundreds of what the Russians called RDS-10 Pioneer missiles, but which were known in the West as SS-20s. These lumbered around the countryside on mobile transporters and could be launched almost instantly, with a range of more than 3,000 miles. The Soviet Union and its allies had a big advantage over NATO in conventional weapons – tanks, artillery and troops. Soviet commanders feared, therefore, that if they attacked Western Europe, NATO would quickly respond with nuclear weapons. To prevent that, or get their retaliation in first, Warsaw Pact generals intended to use these new intermediate-range, mobile missiles. Following the game of nuclear tit for tat, NATO decided to respond with its own new generation of intermediate- and short-range nuclear missiles to be deployed across Europe, including in Britain. The previous Labour government, under Jim Callaghan, had agreed to this deployment in 1979.

What many European politicians particularly feared was that the United States now intended to fight a nuclear war in Europe alone, keeping the American homeland out of it. This profound suspicion of American intentions would spread the anti-nuclear message more widely among voters than ever before. So the Welsh midwife, whose name was Helen John, was walking into the most sensitive of political issues when she got together with a smallholder called Ann Pettitt in early 1981 to found a new organization, Women for Life on Earth.

A few months later, in late August 1981, a total of thirty-six women, four men and some children began a ten-day, 120-mile march to the Greenham Common airbase in Berkshire. There, the Tory Defence Secretary Francis Pym had said in July 1980, the first of the new American Tomahawk cruise missiles were due. Greenham Common had a long American history. Ever since 1942 it had hosted US fighter squadrons, flying Mustangs and Thunderbolts over Nazi-occupied Europe. Later, as the Cold War became hot in Korea, and during the Berlin airlift, American bomber squadrons had been welcomed back to the RAF base, where they had remained until 1964.

The people of nearby Newbury had just become used to the tranquillity of not having the US Strategic Air Command as their neighbours – until this latest episode in missile competition got going again in the 1980s. Now, Helen John and her comrades were determined to send the Americans home once again.

The trouble was, that original march was paltry in terms of numbers. The media was distinctly unimpressed. So, to try to grab headlines, some of the marchers chained themselves to the gates of the base, and this worked. Good pictures; headlines followed. To start with, none of the protesters had intended to stay long at Greenham Common. But now some dug in.

As the autumn of 1981 wore on, a cold, muddy, open-air protest, huddled around an open fire on top of a concrete base, gradually became bigger and better organized. Water came from a standpipe. Tents and sleeping bags were donated. Numbers grew. By February 1982 a key decision was made: this would be a women-only protest. Male protesters, thought to be more confrontational, were now excluded, hurt and offended though they might be. Throughout the rest of the year, the women made many attempts to blockade the base. These were followed by complex legal battles and evictions, and scores of arrests. But the protest kept growing.

For Helen John, as for many other women, it would mark a personal crisis in her life. She and husband divorced and from then on she saw little of her five children. In this, which she deeply regretted, she was not unusual. For many of the protesters the camp was about even more than cruise missiles. It was a protest against an entire male-dominated way of thinking and acting, the 'patriarchy'. Eventually, the Greenham Common protest camp would become the single biggest all-female protest in modern history, copied around the Western world – though not, of course, in Soviet Russia.

This was still, just, a world before the internet. In December 1982, the old-fashioned technology of a chain-letter passed by pillar box around the UK resulted in 30,000 women arriving at the camp to 'embrace the base' by linking arms – producing striking aerial photographs and garnering massive TV coverage. On New Year's Eve, forty-four women used ladders to clamber over the barbed wire and got into the base, where they eventually climbed on to the missile silos and danced. Thirty-six of them were arrested and sent to prison. The following April, 200 women protested by staging an enormous teddy bears' picnic, and there was another human chain, this time involving 70,000 people.

Such was the rolling wave of anarchic, comic, colourful publicity and protest that had so worried Margaret Thatcher's press secretary. The newly appointed Defence Secretary, Michael Heseltine, also had a flair for publicity. He visited Greenham Common where (just because it was raining, he said) he accepted the offer of a combat jacket to put over his suit. He also appeared to suggest that women who got into the base in future might be shot. But not even 'Tarzan' in a 'flak jacket' complaining about 'one-sided disarmament' could undermine what Helen John had started.

In the end, it wasn't the protesters but their other great opponent, President Ronald Reagan (against whom they had launched a court case in New York), who got the Tomahawk cruise missiles out of Britain. When he met the new leader of the Soviet Union, Mikhail Gorbachev, at their famous summit in Reykjavik in October 1986, the two men caused widespread amazement by agreeing that all intermediate nuclear weapons would be removed from the European theatre. Gorbachev was already worried that the nuclear arms race was causing such economic devastation to the USSR that the entire system might collapse – as indeed it soon did. In 1987 the two sides signed a treaty to get rid of the weaponry. Russian observers were then ushered through the same gates that the protesters had attempted to storm so often. The last missiles were taken away from Greenham Common in 1991.

Greenham Common protesters were widely derided by the conservative press as dirty, family-deserting extreme feminists. The columnist Nigel Dempster, writing in the *Daily Mail* in January 1983, was typical: 'Tinkerbell is alive and well . . . really believing that if we all wish hard enough, nuclear bombs will just go away, and everyone can live happily ever after.' But the protests were so big that they dug deep into the self-image of the British left, in ways which reverberated for decades afterwards. To have been one of the Greenham Common 'Wimmin' soon became a badge of considerable pride.

Helen John herself became a full-time and lifelong anti-war and anti-nuclear protester. From 2001 to 2004 she was a vice chair of the Campaign for Nuclear Disarmament and was prominent in protests against the use of military drones, the proposed 'star wars' space defence system and British military engagement in Afghanistan and Iraq. In 2001 she was one of the key people who created the Stop the War Coalition, formed to protest against Western fighting in Muslim countries deemed responsible for the 9/11 Twin Towers attacks in New York. The coalition brought together traditional anti-war politicians such as Jeremy Corbyn and Tony Benn and left-wing intellectuals such as Harold Pinter and Tariq Ali, plus a mélange of Trotskyist, communist, Muslim and other groups. In February 2003, its mass protest march in London against the invasion of Iraq produced crowds of between 750,000 and 2 million and is seen still as the largest single such demonstration in British history.

Since that war went ahead anyway; and since the Tomahawk cruise missiles were removed from Britain because of an agreement between two presidents, can we say that 'anti-war' protesting has achieved anything real at all? In conventional political terms, as soon as Jeremy Corbyn was elected as the leader of the Labour Party it could certainly be said that the worldview of the protesters had captured one of Britain's biggest political parties. More generally, the underlying atmosphere of the country, as it continues to change, has become more feminized and has therefore eased further away from the essentially male, military nation of the beginning of the Queen's reign. Put it another way: which has been the more influential figure for contemporary Britain; Helen John or Colonel 'H' Jones? VC or not, I would suggest that the answer is obvious.

27

GETTING OUT

The speck of the British Empire that in the 1950s had a special place in the affections of patriotic Britons was surely Malta. These three small Mediterranean islands between Sicily and North Africa had been part of the Empire since they were taken from Napoleonic France by Nelson. They became pivotal during the Second World War. From Malta, the RAF and Royal Navy were able to disrupt convoys supporting Rommel's Afrika Korps, and to mount raids themselves. Because Malta was crucial to the fight for North Africa, from 1940 it became itself a major target for German and Italian attacks. The siege of Malta, from 1940 to 1942, when half-starving and ill-supplied islanders held out against ferocious air attacks, was remembered in Britain later with almost the same intensity of emotion as the Battle of Britain itself. The story of the three Gloster Gladiator biplanes – not, in fact, named Faith, Hope and Charity – defending the island was known to all British schoolboys. In April 1942 King George VI awarded Malta the George Cross, which can still be seen on its red and white flag.

By the early 1950s, the cost and pain of decolonization were becoming all too clear. The self-congratulatory story that Britain, unlike France and other colonial countries, had managed to get rid of her Empire peacefully was still widely believed, although it could not be taken seriously by anybody with a passing knowledge of the Indian subcontinent or Africa. Under Mountbatten the partition of British India between largely Hindu India and Muslim Pakistan inspired an orgy of intercommunal violence. Some 10–12 million people were displaced and became refugees, and up to 2 million people died, though the true figure will never be known.

The historian Piers Brendon records as much as we need to remember about the reality of what happened:

> Muslims and Hindus also perpetrated every outrage summed up in that grotesque modern euphemism 'ethnic cleansing'. They roasted babies on spits, impaled infants on lances, boiled children in cauldrons of oil. They raped, mutilated, abducted and killed women, sometimes hacking off the penises of their dead husbands and stuffing them in their mouths. They subjected men to frenzied cruelties, burning them alive in their houses, stabbing them in the streets, butchering them in hospitals, strangling them in refugee camps, torturing and forcibly converting them in desecrating temples, mosques and gurdwaras . . .

Scenes of almost equal cruelty, though involving fewer people, took place from 1952 to 1960 in Kenya, during the Mau Mau uprising against British rule. This was essentially a struggle over the limited amount of good farming land, with the white farmers and their African allies pitted against the majority Kikuyu people, led by Jomo Kenyatta and his Kenyan African Union (KAU). The arrest of the KAU leaders by the Governor Sir Evelyn Baring and the declaration of a state of emergency in October 1952 began a cycle of horrific violence. Mau Mau insurgents swore bloodthirsty oaths which intimidated the Europeans, committed murders and subjected pro-British Africans to terrible collective punishments.

The British responded with racist demonization – Oliver Lyttelton, the Colonial Secretary, compared Kenyatta to 'the horned shadow of the devil himself'. British troops responded by massacring Kikuyu rebels and inflicting a wide range of sadistic tortures in prison camps, which led to them being compared to the Waffen SS. Indeed, one of those who did the comparing was the Attorney General of the British administration there, who wrote to Baring that the mistreatment of detainees was 'distressingly reminiscent of conditions in Nazi Germany or Communist Russia' and urging him to go more softly. 'If we are going to sin,' he said, 'we must sin quietly.'

In January 1959, in one of the British camps, at Hola, the Commandant demanded that the detainees undertake physical work. When they refused, eleven were beaten to death by the guards while another seventy-seven received serious permanent injuries. This finally caused a huge political row in Britain. During an impassioned Commons debate, the Tory MP Enoch Powell pointed out that what had happened was a stain on British values:

> We cannot say, 'We will have African standards in Africa, Asian standards in Asia and perhaps British standards here at home.' We have not that choice to make. We must be consistent with ourselves everywhere. All Government, all influence of man upon man, rests upon opinion. What we can do in Africa, where we still govern and where we no longer govern, depends upon the opinion which is entertained of the way in which this country acts and the way in which Englishmen act.

Trying to disengage from an empire which held, by force, so many different people from around the world was very difficult to do while maintaining basic standards of decency. Race was still an important idea to many British people. There were, even now, 'lesser breeds' and 'African' or 'Asian' standards. This racism had the usual consequences. According to the Kenyan Human Rights Commission, some 90,000 Kenyans were killed, tortured or maimed during the

British crackdown, while 160,000 were kept prisoner in terrible conditions. What was becoming clear, from Malaya to Africa, Cyprus to Palestine, was that a Britain which had been bled to exhaustion by world war was neither financially strong enough nor militarily effective enough to repel the demands for independence from well-armed and persistent locals. Yet in many parts of the world there was still great goodwill for the British and a reluctance to cut all ties immediately. Which leads to the great question: was there an alternative? Was there another way the British could have dealt with at least some of the vast, now-being-dismantled Empire, beyond the choice of either brief, embarrassing repression or simply scuttling?

This takes us back to the brave and impoverished islands of Malta. Here were a people who, having seen off Saracen and Ottoman invasion attempts and lived much of their modern history under the rule of Crusader Knights of St John, were undeniably European, Christian and now pro-British. The Empire and its economy went together. Malta's capital, Valletta, had been the headquarters of the British Mediterranean Fleet for more than a century, and the Fleet provided much of the work there.

Dom Mintoff's upbringing in the years after the First World War was, therefore, in many ways classically Maltese. His father was often away working offshore as a Royal Navy cook. His mother was a Catholic matriarch, watching over her brood of six boys and three girls. Mintoff was a young, bright rebel who escaped from his upbringing. As a left-wing student he won a Rhodes Scholarship in 1939 to Hertford College, Oxford, training as a civil engineer during the war. Working in Cheltenham, Mintoff married his landlady's daughter, the aristocratic Moyra de Vere Bentinck, who was related to both the dukes of Portland and the dukes of St Albans.

These are grand connections: the eighth Duke of Portland, who served in Malta himself, is a third cousin of the Queen. Once Princess Elizabeth had married Prince Philip, it was almost inevitable that they too would end up in Malta, where he had served as first lieutenant on HMS *Chequers* before getting his own command. In the early 1950s, as the Queen was enjoying the nearest she ever got to a quiet private life, and going dancing at the newly opened Hotel Phoenicia, Dom Mintoff, by now an architect, was rising up the ranks of the Maltese Labour Party. Their paths would cross again: the Queen was also Queen of Malta from 1964 to 1974, while Mintoff was Malta's dominant political personality; but it was he who terminated that arrangement, taking the island to republic status as he became increasingly anti-British.

The intriguing thing about this story is that, unlike almost anywhere else in the British Empire, Malta came quite close to actually becoming part of Britain. From 1955 until 1958 there was a serious project, backed by Mintoff and other Maltese politicians, and by a wide range of Tory, Labour and Liberal MPs at Westminster, for Malta to 'integrate' with the UK, sending three MPs to Westminster and enjoying a similar status to Northern Ireland. It would have been a little bit of 'real Britain' in the warm waters of the southern Mediterranean.

This is not so outlandish an idea. After the war, the French Republic treated some of her overseas colonial possessions in the same way, making them full French departments, with representation in Paris. Today, there are twenty-one senators from 'overseas France', including the Caribbean islands of Guadeloupe and Martinique, French Guiana and a string of Pacific islands. Being fully French has brought them financial benefits that former British colonies have never enjoyed; could the British have done the same?

The idea was first floated by Mabel Strickland, daughter of a former Maltese Prime Minister, Sir Gerald Strickland, and editor herself of the *Times of Malta*. In that newspaper she wrote in April 1946, with the glow of wartime heroism still bright and hot, 'The war has shown that Malta is as much a part of Britain as Portsmouth or Croydon. The one practical solution to Malta's constitutional and economic post-war problems would then be for political unity with Britain . . . Let Malta be a county of England, as an integral part of the United Kingdom represented in Parliament at Westminster.'

Mintoff, though no great fan of Mabel Strickland, picked up the idea. It appeared in his Labour election manifesto of 1950 and when he became Malta's Prime Minister in 1955 'Integration or self-determination' was his slogan. He proposed three Maltese MPs at Westminster, but always wanted the British to pay a substantial price. 'Equivalence' was the word he used for Maltese workers getting the same rates as British workers, and the same level of Social Security, while paying the same rates of tax.

To start with, this was greeted with enthusiasm at Westminster. A grand cross-party round-table conference on the subject in September 1955, which included the former Prime Minister Clement Attlee and the Liberal leader Clement Davies, concluded that sending Maltese MPs to Westminster was 'practical and reasonable'. Most of the relevant ministers in Anthony Eden's Tory government agreed. On that basis, a Maltese–British merger was put to the people of Malta in February 1956.

The idea was opposed by the Maltese Catholic Church, whose leader Archbishop Michael Gonzi regarded the flamboyant, cigar-chewing Mintoff as a dangerous atheist, and probably a communist. If Mintoff, who was no keener on the Archbishop than the Archbishop was on him, had hoped that merger with a Protestant nation would clip the wings of the immensely powerful local clergy, then Gonzi feared exactly the same thing. Nevertheless, the vote for a merger was won by 76 per cent. The turnout, however, was only 59 per cent, meaning that fewer than half of all eligible adults had actually voted to become British.

If this suggested a slight waning of enthusiasm in the Mediterranean, it turned out there were bigger problems emerging in London. The most fundamental was that some Tory MPs and senior officials didn't regard the Maltese, however loyal and brave, as truly British

– and hated the idea of former colonial subjects exercising any power in the House of Commons. Sir Norman Brook, the Cabinet Secretary, suggested that 'We should then be headed towards a Parliamentary assembly representing, not the United Kingdom, but "the United Kingdom and Colonies".'

In a Commons debate in March 1956, the Tory MP for Brighton Pavilion, Sir William Teeling (an early enthusiast for a Channel Tunnel), put it even more bluntly: 'If we go on indefinitely in this way we shall reach a stage where a number of representatives from the colonies might make a serious difference to this country at a general election.' Perish the thought! Harold Macmillan, then the Chancellor, who would become the great advocate for rapid decolonization, put the matter even more bluntly: 'The trouble is that, I suppose, it will mean three Labour seats.'

A second substantial problem concerned economics. Britain was close to being bankrupt at the time. The 1957 defence review had emphasized the importance of the British nuclear deterrent far above conventional weaponry. In that situation, how much did Britain really want to pay to maintain a traditional Royal Naval base in the middle of the Mediterranean? It was a genuinely difficult question. Dom Mintoff's insistence on equivalence meant that he would be getting a considerable British subsidy for Malta, in return for an absolute long-term guarantee that the islands would remain British and loyal.

After the loss of the huge, sprawling base at Suez in 1954, and with a terrorist campaign ravaging Cyprus, Britain was now fast losing ground in the Mediterranean. The Chiefs of Staff would have liked to keep Malta for the Navy; and at a time when other colonies were keen to break away Maltese Britophilia felt like rare good news. Macmillan told Churchill: 'at this moment in our history the voluntary and patriotic desire of Malta to join us is something we ought not to repel. Centrifugal forces are very strong at the moment . . .'

But Anthony Eden, Foreign Secretary and soon to succeed Churchill as Prime Minister, was well aware that simply taxing the Maltese at the same rate as the British would not be a good financial deal. Maltese families (Dom Mintoff's included) tended to be large, and even in the dockyard Maltese incomes were relatively low. The Governor of Malta at the time, Sir Robert Laycock, told the British government, therefore, that 'the proposal for the introduction of British social services into Malta, with the single *quid pro quo* of the United Kingdom taking Maltese direct taxation, is simply a means of securing a large and continuous flow of United Kingdom funds into Malta.'

Invited to pay to bind Malta into Britain, the Tory government of the mid-1950s was not inclined to do so, and the bold plan for integration began to unwind rapidly. By 1958, the mood at Westminster had soured and Mintoff was leading violent protests on the islands, with strikes, marches and boycotts of British produce. His original slogan had always been two sided – 'Integration or self-determination'.

Now Malta went for the latter, achieving independence from Britain in 1964. After the Queen of Malta had been deposed in 1974, notwithstanding the lovely time she had had there twenty years earlier, Mintoff's Republican Malta pursued socialist policies. The special power of the Church was broken, adultery decriminalized and laws brought in for secular marriage, equal pay for women, maternity pay, children's allowances and widespread nationalization. Later, Mintoff became something of a political thug, bullying opponents and cosying up to Marxist dictators – including North Korea's Kim Il-Sung, China's Mao, who funded a dock extension at Valletta, and Marshal Tito of Yugoslavia. After various leaseback arrangements, the British military base closed in March 1979, with HMS *London* sailing out of the port where in August 1942 the survivors of the famous 'convoy of Santa Maria' to relieve the island had been welcomed with delirious joy.

Could things have gone differently? Undoubtedly. For more than a year, the argument was balanced very finely at Westminster, though for how long the Maltese and British would have willingly shared common citizenship under the Queen is unknowable. A modestly sized but exuberant Maltese community emerged in East London around the Docklands. If the British had been willing to share sovereignty with anybody at any time, it would surely have been with the Maltese in the aftermath of the island heroics of the war. But the idea of the British integrating constitutionally (rather than by immigration) with former colonies now died.

Harold Wilson, Labour Prime Minister from 1964, received integration proposals for some of the smaller Caribbean islands in 1965 and then, two years later, from the Chief Minister of Fiji in the Pacific. He rejected them, more or less out of hand. By that stage, skin colour or 'race' was becoming a major issue in British politics.

28

THE EMPIRE LOYALIST

At the beginning of the Queen's reign, there had been few black people living in Britain. The most famous moment in the British immigration story remains the arrival of a former Nazi passenger ship, renamed the *Empire Windrush*, which steamed into Tilbury from Jamaica in summer 1948, carrying 493 West Indians looking for work, many of them ex-RAF. But this was the very beginning of the story, not its climax.

The economic background to migration at the beginning of the reign was a severe shortage of skilled labour. When the war was over there was a lot of rebuilding to be done. Eastern European refugees whose countries had been overrun by the Soviet Union – Poles, Latvians, Lithuanians and Czechs – had been actively encouraged to stay in Britain to work.

They were just one segment of the 12 million displaced people in Europe at the war's end, and from London to Lancashire modestly sized European immigrant communities now sprang up. But, given the scale of the demand, the numbers of available workers weren't enough. Refugee camps were closing as the International Refugee Organization was wound up at the beginning of 1952. 'Border-crossers' from the other side of the Iron Curtain continued to arrive, but of these the British were highly suspicious. As *The Times* reported, they 'have had to be scrutinised very closely ever since half of those arriving in a single month were found to be communist agents'.

So more migrants were needed. To begin with, it wasn't obvious that they would mainly come from the Caribbean. The author David Olusoga estimates that in 1948 there were probably fewer than 20,000 black people in Britain. Between then and 1952, there was a modest trickle of West Indians arriving, lured by the severe British labour shortages, which were advertised in Caribbean newspapers. British Rail, London Transport and British hoteliers were all particularly eager recruiters. Then nature, and the Americans, intervened. A terrible 1951 hurricane, which hammered Jamaica, was followed by severe new US restrictions on immigration. Together, these increased the flow to the UK. In 1953, the number of Caribbean workers arriving in Britain reached 3,000, and then 10,000 the following year. By the mid-1950s, around 45,000 West Indians were arriving for work each year.

They were entering Britain profoundly confused and divided about issues of race and belonging. On the one hand, with the old Empire tottering as the full cost of the war became apparent, there was an optimistic drive for a new, multiracial Commonwealth of Nations, formally announced at the London Conference of 1949. The British Nationality Act of the previous summer had given all Commonwealth citizens the right to enter Britain – a liberal measure which was supposed to reflect the reality of this new, open global network. From 1949, migrants such as those coming down the gangplank at Tilbury had an absolute right to come and settle in the UK. For many white British people, their first experience of black skins had been the arrival of more than 100,000 black GIs during the war. As we have seen, despite occasional attempts to whip up racial panic over mixed marriages, they were generally made welcome; and there was quite a lot of self-congratulation that the British were not as prejudiced as the 'color bar' white Americans were.

There seems to be some truth in the self-congratulation. David Olusoga tracked down a 1959 social science study on British attitudes towards coloured immigration. Of those sampled, 76 per cent agreed that 'coloured people are just as good as us when they have the same training and opportunities'. Some 68 per cent agreed that a lot of 'coloured people here are very clever' and almost the same percentage thought that 'if we all behaved in a more Christian way there would not be any colour problem'.

Yet many British people were still profoundly racist and their political leaders were deeply uneasy about the idea of non-white people settling here in any numbers. The assumption had been that Australians, Canadians and New Zealanders might well choose to move home but that Africans and others were much less likely to. Churchill's government worked hard to see whether there was any way of keeping West Indians out. Churchill told the Governor of Jamaica in 1952 the alternative was that 'we would have a magpie society: that would never do'. It was even reported that Churchill contemplated as an election slogan 'Keep Britain White', though his colleagues swiftly dissuaded him.

The Notting Hill and Nottingham riots of 1958, when gangs of white youths attacked black homes and passers-by, helped change the public mood or at least spook politicians. The early 1960s were marked by new laws to tighten black immigration. They were tentative, and not nearly enough for Enoch Powell, who made his hysterical 'rivers of blood' speech in Birmingham in 1968, warning of the impact on the racial composition of the country of black people who had already been born here.

Immigration, however, continued. Taking a wider historical sweep, it is perhaps odd that there was not more unease and protest: the British of the 1950s had been brought up to believe that their Empire was a great force for good in the world, but also that race mattered. Churchill himself spoke ceaselessly of 'the British race'. Britons were brought up with the word 'Imperial' as a common prefix. Yet at just the same time as Britain was frantically divesting herself of colonies and dominions around the world, the composition of the 'mother country' was now also changing. Harold Macmillan, whose 1960 'winds of change' speech in South Africa acknowledged the growth of national consciousness, had himself abolished Empire Day two years previously.

At other times and in other places this might have produced an almost revolutionary backlash – think of the trauma of France and her defeat in Algeria. In Britain, most people seem to have absorbed coming down in the world quite philosophically. Most, but not all. There were Elizabethans who wanted absolutely no truck with any new world order or imperial surrender, still less an entanglement with Europe. During the 1950s and early 1960s, Tory leaders were pursued and heckled, and found themselves the objects of numerous stunts.

The League of Empire Loyalists was small in number but determined and creative when it came to grabbing publicity. Its members would hide under Conservative Party platforms and leap out to yell abuse at the likes of Anthony Eden and Harold Macmillan. They dressed up in military and ecclesiastical garb to gain entrance to public meetings, which they then heckled. They hauled down and stamped on the United Nations flag. They pursued Russian leaders during visits to Britain with megaphones and cries of 'murderers'. They harassed and ridiculed the left-wing Movement for Colonial Freedom.

The League of Empire Loyalists' most famous and bloody confrontation came in October 1958 at the Tory Party's Blackpool conference. The party was expecting trouble and had brought in Special Branch officers from London, but the conference had already been thoroughly infiltrated. Bugles were used to sound the 'retreat' from Empire, and one after another hecklers took on the Prime Minister, Macmillan. The response was brutal. Labour MPs present as observers said it was the worst violence they had ever seen at a public gathering and there were cries of 'Kill her, kill her' from Tory delegates when one female LEL member interrupted Macmillan. According to an account by the *News Chronicle*, one of the protesters had his arms held fast to his side by a steward while another gripped his nose, 'a third covered his mouth and a fourth lunged at what could be seen of the rest of his face, while an outraged Tory matron assisted by twisting his testicles. He was then carried, kicking and struggling, to an office near one of the Winter Gardens entrances. Holidaymakers in the foyer heard his cries for police help . . .'

Officially launched at the Caxton Hall in Westminster on 13 April 1954, the LEL had attracted military types, former colonial civil servants and some formidable female campaigners, including the novelist Graham Greene's cousin, Margaret or 'Leslie' Greene. Adept at manoeuvring its way on to newspaper front pages and into editorials with its stunts, its later targets included the anti-bomb campaigners, CND. It is now remembered as little more than a ripple on the calm surface of the Tory years. But this is not quite right. It was also a progenitor of the more formidable and violent right-wing movement of the 1970s, the National Front. It didn't change the course of British history, but it certainly soured the mood. And to understand why, we need to understand the man who created it.

He was Arthur Kenneth Chesterton. 'A.K.' was a cousin of the famous Catholic writer G. K. Chesterton. Born near Johannesburg in South Africa in 1899, he went to school at Berkhamsted with Graham Greene and fought well in the First World War, winning the Military Cross. Then, between the wars, Chesterton made his way as a hack writer and journalist, producing at least one play, before joining Oswald Mosley's British Union of Fascists, where he rose to become its director of propaganda. For that he had a real gift, and it was now that his fanatic streak became apparent. His wife, a Fabian socialist and pacifist, thought of him as a kind of rebel angel: 'In a strong, rugged, cadaverous way, he is handsome.

There's something at the same time noble and rebellious about him, like Satan in *Paradise Lost*. A light seems to be smouldering in his eyes as if he were aware of a great mission to perform . . .'

But the light was an evil one and the mission exceedingly dangerous; for 'A.K.' was a dedicated and vicious anti-Semite. In 1937, for instance, as the Blackshirts were marching to Trafalgar Square they faced counter-demonstrations by Jewish and working-class Londoners, whom Chesterton described in the most extreme terms. These enemies of the fascists were the 'wildest and most obscene animals in creation . . . Packed into the street and bidden to roar, and howl, and rave . . . These apelike creatures literally danced along the road – a dance of sheer hysterical rage . . . This public hostility of London's hideous underworld of Jewish and synthetic Jewish morons . . .'

Arthur Chesterton, whom even Britain's would-be fascist leader Sir Oswald Mosley found too anti-Semitic, is the connecting link between the fascists of the 1930s and the neo-Nazis of more modern times. Behind the schoolboy stunts and under the conspiracy-laden prose of his regular journal *Candour* was a worldview that rejected the entire direction of modern British history. 'A.K.' was against not simply the communists and immigration, but the EEC, NATO and other multinational organizations such as the General Agreement on Tariffs and Trade (GATT). In effect, he wanted to abolish the modern world. For a dozen years the LEL was funded by a million-aire Englishman exiled in Chile. When that money ran out, it folded; and in 1967 Chesterton co-founded the National Front. The League of Empire Loyalist pranks, which so irritated mainstream politicians and delighted newspaper editors, were an early signal that fascism and racial politics had not after all gone away for ever.

It would be wrong to see the League as just a bunch of batty outsiders. The LEL said rudely and raucously in public what many more mainstream figures thought in private – the military leaders horrified by the decline in the Army and Navy, politicians aghast at the winding up of the Empire, eminent believers in the purity of the British race and anti-Semitic writers at the heart of the London establishment. A good example of the kind of person Chesterton could attract in the 1950s was Edmund Ironside, the first Baron Ironside, who had been Chief of the Imperial General Staff at the beginning of the Second World War. A huge man nicknamed 'Tiny' in the Army, he had fought in the Boer War and ended the First World War as the youngest major general in the British Army. He was fluent in around a dozen languages and was said to be the original for John Buchan's hero Richard Hannay.

His entry in the *Dictionary of National Biography* is so irresistibly vivid it demands to be quoted at some length. Ironside, reports the *DNB*,

> was warm, sensitive, impetuous, mercurial and blunt. He had virtually no appreciation of music or poetry, little of theatre, none of dance . . . No stranger to the vulgar racial, cultural and gender prejudices of his class, nation and time, he made harsh judgements even of friends and often shattering criticism of others – especially air marshals, timeserving soldiers, politicians, pacifist university dons, diplomats, shipboard companions, nearly all women in what he considered the male domain, and most foreigners. Certain of British superiority, he professed special dislike of the Irish, Jews, Latins and 'lesser races' – that is, most of mankind.

He sounds very like Uncle Matthew in Nancy Mitford's satirical novels.

Some of Ironside's motivation, as it was of Chesterton's, was an agonized nostalgia for a sunlit Empire in which the white man was boss. The pain of the loss of Empire spread throughout the United Kingdom, among families who had been brought up in Kenya or Bengal, Egypt or South Africa, and who felt adrift and dispossessed in rain-streaked bungalows in Edinburgh or Cheshire. The vivid, confident and brightly coloured world of their childhood had suddenly vanished and their belief in the greatness of the British race, despite the recent victory over Nazi Germany, was everywhere rejected and mocked. The vast majority of people who felt this way did nothing much about it – shrugged, kept on keeping on and learned to absorb change. Many would become assertive campaigners against British integration in Europe, quietly chuckle at Alf Garnett and applaud Lord Beaverbrook's *Daily Express*. But there was an angry minority who loathed the arrival of black and Asian people in Britain and deeply resented the decline in British status.

Many of them would be gathered into the unlovely ranks of the National Front, who brought back to the streets of 1970s Britain something of the tone of the Blackshirts in the 1930s. The writer David Olusoga, quoted a few pages earlier, remembers growing up on a council estate in the North-east of England where he felt profoundly unwelcome:

> Despite our mother's careful protection, the tenor of our times seeped through the concrete walls into our home and into my mind and my siblings'. Secretly I harboured fears that as part of the group identified by chanting neo-Nazis, hostile neighbours and even television comedians as 'them' we might be sent 'back'. This, in our case, presumably meant 'back' to Nigeria, a country of which I had only distant memories, and the land upon which my youngest siblings had never set foot.
>
> At the zenith of its swaggering confidence, the National Front – the NF – made enough noise and sparked enough debate within Britain to make the idea of sending 'them' 'back' seem vaguely plausible . . . the political aether had been polluted by the politics of hate.

This was in part the achievement of the Military Cross-wearing journalist and playwright A. K. Chesterton – the man who had marched with Mosley against the Jews, and who lived to chair the organization now marching against the blacks. But there were equally committed people on the other side, and changes in race relations would come from unexpected places.

29

FARROKH BOMI BULSARA

Immigration from the former British Empire touched almost every aspect of British life, including what we hummed. The story of a gawky, toothy Zoroastrian whose Indian parents fled a nationalist revolution in Zanzibar for unglamorous Feltham, West London, makes the point. As a teenager at a traditional British-curriculum boarding school in a North Indian hill town, Farrokh was remembered as polite, enthusiastic, a keen cricketer with a flair for art. His father, a minor British government official, had had to save hard to send his son across the Indian Ocean and pay the school fees. So far, this was a classic late-imperial family story of graft, 'fitting in' and modest aspiration.

Farrokh's story could have fitted into a book about the Elizabethans under many different headings. It could have been partly about how Britain learned to export 'soft' or cultural wealth – a tale to sit alongside those of Dusty Springfield and the Beatles. It could have been part of the stories of gay lives. Farrokh Bulsara renamed himself Freddie Mercury, after the messenger of the gods, and became, with his band Queen, the most successful rock performer in the world; a famous participant in the 1970s London and New York gay scene, he would die of AIDS, aged forty-five, in 1991.

And it could have been a story of hard graft and professionalism – because, behind the big hair, outrageous costumes and high jinks, Queen practised more intensively and took bigger commercial risks than almost any other band.

Almost nobody would consider Freddie Mercury's story to be one about race or immigration. But that's the point. Today, to be 'mixed race' or of 'mixed heritage' is an almost unqualified bonus in the worlds of music, fashion, theatre or television. It offers enough of the exotic and interesting to flavour bland old British whiteness. If you came from Hounslow today, and you wanted to make it, telling people you came from Zanzibar, as a devotee of an ancient Persian religion Zoroastrianism, is just the kind of thing you might invent. Yet Freddie never discussed it, almost as if he was ashamed. He wasn't ashamed of his parents; nor were they of him.

It is more that, at that time, being British was more glamorous. His biographer Lesley-Ann Jones, who knew him, points out that back in the 1970s rock stars were supposed to be white American, black American or to come from either Liverpool or London. Having traditionalist parents who had been born in Gujarat, of an Iranian exiled family who followed a conservative religion which abhorred homosexuality, was definitely not cool.

After Freddie's parents had fled African-majority hostility in Zanzibar (part of today's Tanzania) and arrived at Heathrow with little more than a couple of suitcases, like many other recent immigrant refugee families they found they had to accept a bump down in status – no mansion or servants here. His father found a job as a cashier for a catering company and his mother worked a till at Marks & Spencer, while Freddie went to art college, in Ealing. This, as we shall see later, was an almost compulsory rite of passage for young men reinventing themselves in the 1960s. Sleeping on friends' floors, sketching and learning to dress fashionably, Mercury became obsessed by the great guitar showman Jimi Hendrix, criss-crossing the country to see him. Through a network of similarly music-fascinated friends, he met Brian May, an Imperial College student studying physics and astronomy. The essence of Queen had come together (Mercury chose the name not as a tribute to Her Majesty but as a wry wink at gay culture). May and the drummer Roger Taylor had a band called Smile. Freddie eventually persuaded them to take him on as frontman. The usual story of missed opportunities, brief alliances with other musicians, early failures and breakthrough gigs followed.

By now Mercury was at least two different people. On stage, he was, as it were, perfectly mercurial – flamboyant, restless, strutting, outrageous. He had an extraordinary vocal range which opera singers would notice and envy and the ability to hold high tenor notes for an astonishingly long time. Offstage, he was quiet, polite and ravaged by insecurities. He both hated and was proud of his unusual teeth. He probably had four extra teeth, an hereditary condition, which made him look buck-toothed, something he was extremely sensitive about. But he also believed that his teeth were somehow connected to his singing ability and resisted suggestions that he should get them 'fixed'.

He was also complex in his sexuality, something he strongly disliked talking about, at least to journalists. He had many gay lovers and a later, almost marital long-term gay partnership; and he was a fixture at the iconic London gay club Heaven, which opened just south of Trafalgar Square in 1979. Among his friends were some of the best-known gay people in Britain, such as the radio DJ Kenny Everett. He was the first really well-known rock star to die of AIDS. However, alongside all of that, his closest emotional and sexual relationship was with a glamorous and loving woman, Mary Austin; and all his life he particularly enjoyed the company of women. Precise sexual taxonomy has become a contemporary British obsession, but often these things are too personal, too psychologically complex to be clear to anybody else. Or, for that matter, very interesting.

Great performers often depend, anyway, upon an element of mystery. Queen's hits, from the gargantuan 'Bohemian Rhapsody' to air-punch anthems such as 'We Will Rock You' and 'Hammer to Fall', are part of the mental furniture of millions of Elizabethans – and indeed of middle-aged people all around the world. Queen were the stand-out, triumphant success at Live Aid discussed earlier. Freddie Mercury has been taken to the hearts of millions – an instantly recognizable entertainer of whom we are proud. He would have liked that. He wanted to change his new country, but by loosening it up, cheering it up, and no more than that. He would not have wanted to be thought other than British. Mercury looked exotic but for him Britain had been a land of opportunity. The lands of his origins, homophobic, angry and socially conservative, were best forgotten. He spoke of his Indian-African heritage almost dismissively as 'something inbred', which allowed him to walk around like a 'Persian popinjay'. Other migrants, at around the same time, took a very different view.

30

JAYABEN DESAI

One of the most persistent and headline-grabbing aspects of public life in Britain from the 1960s until the 1980s was the confrontation between organized labour, represented by the trade unions, and capital, represented by private companies and the state. We had railway strikes and council strikes and strikes in the car industry. We had the titanic confrontations in the coalfields and strikes in the dockyards (of which more later). We had the most political strikes between newspaper proprietors, such as Rupert Murdoch and Eddie Shah, and printers and journalists. School students went on strike and university students went on strike. Eventually even gravediggers went on strike. For a while, if you weren't on strike, you can't have been paying attention. But before Margaret Thatcher launched her legislative and physical campaign against the national enthusiasm for striking, we had Grunwick. And this is a story about race as much as about industrial relations.

From the summer of 1976 until the spring of 1978, a battle in a North London suburb over the right of workers in a photographic processing plant to have union recognition defined and explained much of what would follow. At Grunwick, the mutual misunderstandings, and the raw struggle for power, which had affected British working life for decades were played out like morality theatre. At Grunwick, each side saw themselves as the David against an opposing Goliath. But this time, on the one side were an Asian boss called George Ward and his British managers; and on the other, women from India, Pakistan and Africa. It was an intimate battle, about respect, in the new Britain. Female Asian workers, obliged to ask permission to go to the toilet and to accept mandatory overtime and long hours, saw their young white male managers as alien, tinpot tyrants. They had no intention of knowing their place.

Jayaben Desai, the tiny Asian woman who became a symbol of the strike, told her contemptuous manager Malcolm Alden: 'What you are running here is not a factory, it is zoo. But in a zoo there are many types of animals. Some are monkeys who dance on your fingertips, others are lions who can bite your head off. We are those lions, Mr Manager.' Week in, week out, in her sari and overcoat, Desai led other Asian women on a picket line where they were jeered at and abused by furious managers. She was a hard woman to shake, however. When she felt the trade union movement was letting her down, she promptly went on hunger strike outside the TUC headquarters. To many on the left in Britain, she remains one of the great unsung heroes of the Queen's reign.

Born in Gujarat, not far from where Freddie Mercury's family had started, Desai married a factory manager and settled in East Africa. She arrived in Britain in 1969, one victim of the wave of expulsions of Asians from Tanzania, Kenya and Uganda in the 1960s by African nationalist leaders. Better off than many Africans, and keeping themselves to themselves, Asians had been regarded with deep suspicion by the newly independent nations. Asian businesses were taken over; prominent Indians were harassed; and under Uganda's Idi Amin they were abruptly ordered to leave. Ted Heath agreed that Britain should take tens of thousands of these refugees of Empire. Many would end up in Brent, North London. One sociological study suggested that these new Britons were both abnormally well qualified and abnormally badly paid.

Desai fitted that mould. She was tough, eloquent and unusually political – as a young girl, she had been an avid admirer of Nehru and Gandhi. Her core motivation was not more money but respect from her white managers. Although Grunwick's owner George Ward defended his company as a progressive and humane environment, for many of his women workers it was stifling in every sense. They had virtually no autonomy about when they worked. Short loo breaks had to be begged for. Holidays and time off were regularly refused. Again and again, they complained that they were being treated like animals. 'A person like me, I am never afraid of anybody,' Desai warned the managers.

Migrants from Africa and the Indian subcontinent were much less likely to join trade unions and were ready to work harder in worse conditions for less money – which is why, it was alleged, the Grunwick photographic business, facing ferocious competition from larger multinationals, was employing so many of them. So when Devshi Bhudia, Chandrakant Patel, Bharat Patel and Suresh Ruparelia left their jobs in the mail-order office after a row over overtime working, they didn't know what a trade union was. Nor did Jayaben Desai. She and they would rely on the Citizens' Advice Bureau and a local telephone directory to finally make contact with APEX, the union who embraced, recruited and backed them.

George Ward, himself an Anglo-Indian who had experienced racial discrimination as a young man, saw the world very differently. More than anything else, Asian migrants would be business creators and entrepreneurs in contemporary Britain. Ward had built up his small photographic enterprise from scratch. Most of its profits came from developing and printing holiday snaps. Using an early mail-order system, he was managing to undercut large multinational rivals.

But profit margins were tight and Ward needed his workers to back him all the way, working ferociously long hours. He believed the strikers were supported for cynical political reasons by communists. Britain, he wrote, was engaged in an ideological struggle between two fundamentally different forms of society: 'one is the Big Brother society, whether state and the union bosses control everything, and people are not free to choose their own lives. I cannot understand how anyone could wish to live in this kind of society, but I suppose that there is such a thing as the fear of freedom.' In his view, he was the underdog, standing up to corporatism.

It is not going too far to suggest that the struggle between Desai and Ward changed British politics. It became a cause célèbre which energized and put steel into the political free-market right. George Ward attracted the support of the National Association for Freedom (NAFF), an anti-trade-union and free-market pressure group whose founder Ross McWhirter had been shot dead by the IRA. Margaret Thatcher was an early and avid follower of the Grunwick dispute, praising Ward as a champion of freedom. Sir Keith Joseph, her John the Baptist, said in a speech at Doncaster racecourse in 1977 that the dispute represented 'a make-or-break point for British democracy, the freedoms of ordinary British men and women . . . the Grunwick siege shows how far self-styled democratic socialists and self-styled union moderates have allowed themselves to be hijacked by the men of violence and coercion.'

So when Thatcher and Joseph came into power in 1979, they would follow many of the demands made by Ward, including repealing the closed-shop legislation, extending democracy inside unions and limiting picketing. The famous Thatcher trade union legislation changes might have happened anyway, without this dispute, but they were certainly given focus and urgency by it.

On the left its influence was even greater. For most trade unionists involved, this was their first experience of almost militarized policing tactics by the state. Strikers and their shocked union

organizers reported incidents of brutality, intimidation and harassment. In their account of the dispute from the strikers' point of
view, Jack Dromey and Graham Taylor say: 'the police seemed to
be at the beck and call of management. The police did nothing
against the dangerous driving of company vans and cars, even when
pickets were knocked down. Managers would even threaten pickets
with their fists in front of police and nothing would be done. By
Christmas 1976 not one striker retained his or her original respect
for the British police.' Certainly, the London Metropolitan Police
Special Patrol Group (SPG), which became known for their use of
sledgehammers, baseball bats and other unorthodox weapons, took
a prominent role against the Grunwick strikers. They would later
become notorious during the miners' strike and Anti-Nazi League
demonstrations.

The managers saw the violence very differently. As more and
more trade union members arrived to back the strikers, they believed
the intimidation of workers who wanted to carry on working was
becoming intolerable. The most militant parts of the trade union
movement came to London to support the Grunwick strikers –
Arthur Scargill led Yorkshire miners there, for instance, claiming,
'We will bring down thousands of miners from the whole of the
membership of our union. We will not allow the trade union
movement to be defeated.'

In his account, entitled *Fort Grunwick*, George Ward described
standing inside his factory looking down at scenes of disorder:

> Every time one of our employees got near the gates, moving
> through the gap in the picket lines that the police were struggling
> to keep open, toughs would surge forward in an attempt to get
> to him; there would be three or four more arrests required in
> order to get a single worker through to the plant. That mob in
> the street was not trying to coax our workforce: it was throwing
> insults and threats at them.

The day when the pickets were led by Scargill 'was a day of savage violence. It was the day when PC Trevor Wilson had his head cut open by a milk bottle, while left-wing pickets howled, "Kill the bastar'."'

As the strike dragged on, it became an epic battle in Parliament, in the courts, through the arbitration system, and on the streets. The company devised increasingly ingenious ways to obtain the raw materials and deal with suppliers; the strikers kept going for far, far longer than anyone expected though they regarded the final settlement, influenced by an increasingly nervous and unpopular Labour government and the Trades Union Congress, as a sell-out. Grunwick deeply entrenched attitudes on both sides. It was the curtain raiser for the epic industrial fights of the Thatcher years.

In the wider sweep of history, however, it also marked a turning point in attitudes to race by many working-class British socialists. Since the beginning of time, the British trade union movement had been fundamentally conservative on race issues – or indeed openly racist. In 1968, East London dockers and porters from the Smithfield meat market marched in support of Enoch Powell's anti-immigration 'rivers of blood' speech. Recently declassified MI5 papers suggest that both marches were led by right-wingers – Harry Perman, a supporter of Moral Rearmament, and a fascist, Dennis Harmston. But they may not have had to work very hard. In the last age of heavy industry, the bulk of the unions had overwhelmingly white – and mostly male – members. Coal miners, shipyard workers and railwaymen were easy to persuade when told coloured immigrants were coming to undercut their wages.

But Desai toured union conferences and meetings, relentlessly making the case that her struggle was also that of white workers, and that she needed and deserved their financial and physical support. When the Grunwick strikers needed the backing of local postal workers (who were, in turn, threatened with the sack), their leader drily explained to his men, 'You don't say "no" to Mrs Desai.'

A vivid, charismatic, colourful figure on the picket lines, standing up to policemen several feet taller than she was; giving punchy television interviews and above all addressing meetings of other unions, Jayaben Desai showed that recent immigrants could be as uncompromising trade unionists as any white worker; and by doing all that, she won hundreds of thousands of them to her cause.

In the end, like Arthur Scargill later, she lost her strike. Characteristically, she did so only after a three-day open-air hunger strike in freezing conditions against her own temporizing union on the steps of Congress House. But her real achievement was to have changed the landscape of the union movement and left-wing attitudes to migrant workers. Thanks to her, white trade union bosses made speeches in favour of the Grunwick Asian workers at their national conferences. Thanks to her, tens of thousands of white British workers gave up their weekends to come down to London and march in support of Asian women. After the strike was over she reflected, 'We have shown that workers like us, new to these shores, will never accept being treated without dignity or respect.' And, she added, 'We have shown that white workers will support us.'

31

THE IDEA OF A NATION

In very different ways, all these stories centre around the idea of nation – what 'Britain' means today. At a time when American culture is so intense and invasive, how much Britishness do we want on our pages, in our theatres and on our screens? How much British humour, how much British taste and sound? These cultural, even philosophical, investigations of national identity touch parts of all our lives; but they become active when they are shaped by political imagination. Patriotism is an emotion we feel fluttering inside us. Nationalism, a political idea, is something else. It happens outside, on the streets.

Both Enoch Powell and Tony Benn were romantic men with a passionate, throbbing sense of British history. Both believed, almost above all other things, in parliamentary democracy and the potency of the House of Commons. Neither liked the idea of the European Community, though for very different reasons; and they were both deeply sceptical about modern American power, again for almost opposite reasons. Understand Enoch Powell and Tony Benn, and you will understand quite a lot about the dilemmas of British nationhood during the reign of the Queen.

As a boy, Enoch Powell, born in Birmingham to a Welsh family, was both absurdly, almost offensively clever and hilariously ambitious. His parents came from determined, self-improving working-class families. His father, the son and grandson of scrap-metal dealers, had become a primary school headmaster. His mother was the very bright daughter of a policeman. Powell himself was reading fluently by three, and while still at school fell heavily under the heady, dangerous influence of the German philosopher Friedrich Nietzsche.

Even as a young man he had an intimidating face – lean, glaring; as a schoolboy he was known as 'Scowelly Powelly'. As a scholarship student at Cambridge he effortlessly immersed himself in classical Greek and Latin, winning prize after prize and then one of the top degrees of his year. He studied in London to learn Urdu, since he had quietly decided to become Viceroy of India. He seemed to learn foreign languages as easily as other people read newspaper articles. By the age of twenty-five he was a full professor of classics in Sydney, Australia, and a formidable, much admired poet who had learned part of his craft from A. E. Housman, of *A Shropshire Lad* fame.

He was a convinced imperialist. During the late 1930s, however, Powell was obsessed by the coming threat of war, by the cowardice of the British government in response to that threat and by the horrors of a country he intellectually admired, Germany. He developed something close to a genuine death-wish, talking again and again about his thirst to kill and to be killed. When the war started, he left Australia and enlisted as a private in the Royal Warwickshires, briskly working his way up to become an intelligence officer. As such, he helped plan the British victory over Rommel at El Alamein.

In Egypt, he came across his first Americans. It was loathing at first sight. He regarded the US desire for total victory over Nazi Germany as barbaric and inhumane, and individual Americans he met as gauche and amateurish. In a letter home in 1943 he suggested that, after beating Germany and Japan, 'if the present hostilities do not actually merge into a war with our terrible enemy, America, it will remain for those of us who have the necessary knowledge and insight to do what we can where we can to help Britain be victorious again in her next crisis'.

Even as a relatively young man, Enoch Powell was extremist by instinct. Much later in his life, asked how he would like to be remembered, he brutally replied: 'I should like to have been killed in the war.' For him, anti-Americanism was a basic given. One might have guessed that he would therefore continue a staunch supporter of the Empire and then of its successor, the Commonwealth.

And indeed, after leaving Egypt, he went to India, where he rose to be the youngest brigadier in the Army. India, where Powell again drenched himself in its languages and culture, intensified a profound, romantic love of Empire history. But, as that Empire collapsed, Powell responded almost as a spurned lover. If the mighty project was no longer mighty, then let it go, say goodbye and don't be sentimental. He saw the Commonwealth as a rather pathetic and demeaning mimicry of the genuine Empire and never had much time for it.

Romantic, pessimistic and yet with a streak of almost coarse realism, Powell developed his notion of the British state during the 1950s and early 1960s. We have spoken of the Navy. Powell rammed home to audiences in speeches that the glory of the Empire had vanished 'as surely . . . as the Imperial fleet from the waters of Spithead'. But as he rubbed noses in the reality of British decline, he found his true inspiration not in the political project of modern Britain, still less in the United Kingdom, but in Englishness. Despite his Welsh surname, England was what mattered for Powell.

Sounding more like the poet-novelist Thomas Hardy than a modern politician he spoke about the timeless continuity of the English, going back through the centuries to medieval villages and churches, from where the essential native people still looked on, like ghosts, at modern times:

What would they say? They would speak to us in our own English tongue, the tongue made for telling truth in, tuned already to songs that haunt the hearer like the sadness of spring. They would tell us of that marvellous land, so sweetly mixed of opposites in climate that all the seasons of the year appear there in their greatest perfection; over the fields amid which they built their halls, their cottages, their churches, and where the same black-thorn showered its petals upon them, as upon us . . .

Above all, the old English would remind their modern successors of the central importance of democracy, or, in Powell's inflamed words, 'a palace with many chambers and one lofty hall, with angel faces carved on the hammer beams, to which men resorted out of all England to speak on behalf of their fellows, a thing called "Parliament", and from that hall went out men . . . to judge the same judgements, and dispense the same justice, to all the people of England.'

Where did it lead, this institutional romanticism, this view of the nation which would have been comfortably familiar to Victorian historians, albeit now shorn of their Empire? First, Powell's anti-Americanism did not drive him towards Europe. As a scholar, he sympathized with much in the cultures of Germany, Italy and Greece, but he always regarded the European political project as a profound and direct threat to British parliamentary sovereignty and, therefore, to the highest expression of English continuity he could think of. This would be war to the knife. In the Commons, Powell would hack away at British involvement in the European Community for year after year. He himself was no caricature Little Englander. Multilingual, a lover of India and Australia, and later a Unionist MP in Northern Ireland, his central mission was nevertheless to defend 'the unbroken life of the English nation over a thousand years and more' by maintaining parliamentary supremacy.

On this, his influence would become enormous, perhaps decisive.

It took time. For long periods, he was hugely unpopular, including during the mid-1970s, when Britain voted overwhelmingly to stay inside the Common Market. But Enoch Powell's unyielding hostility to Brussels would influence successive generations of Tory politicians, including Margaret Thatcher and the anti-Maastricht campaigners during the 1990s, and then the creators of the UK Independence Party, and many of those such as Nigel Farage who led the successful campaign for Britain to leave the EU in 2016. He was also, separately, a high priest of anti-big-government and free-market thinking and would, in these crucial areas, be a key influence on the Thatcher revolution.

If this were all – and it's a lot – then Powell would deserve to be remembered as one of the most influential Elizabethans of his age. But of course it isn't all. Immigration was beginning to become a political issue in the West Midlands by the early 1960s. Powell was a Wolverhampton MP. On his doorstep, Indian and West Indian immigrants doing tough jobs in heavy industry were beginning to take up large amounts of the worst housing that had been used by poor white families.

To start with, Powell wrote in his local papers about the importance of better integration of different communities and promised to serve immigrant constituents just as well as any others: 'I will always set my face like flint against making any difference between one citizen and another on grounds of his origin.' As a health minister, Powell himself had encouraged West Indians to come to Britain to work in the NHS.

But by 1968 he felt the issue could no longer be ignored. He was politically frustrated and casting around for a cause. With the Tories now in opposition, he was being sidelined by Edward Heath in the shadow cabinet. So Powell devised a speech on immigration which he promised a friend would go up 'fizz' like a rocket. He delivered it in the upstairs room of the Midland Hotel in Birmingham which had, no doubt, heard many political speeches before. What made this one different was the mixture of intellectual, classical references with the coarsest and the most provocative language that had been heard on matters of race from any leading British politician in the post-war period. He quoted a white constituent who, Powell said, had told him that he wanted to emigrate because 'In this country in 15 or 20 years' time the black man will have the whip hand over the white man.'

Acknowledging that this was a horrible thing to say, Powell then insisted that this was what hundreds of thousands of British people were thinking: 'Those whom the gods wish to destroy, they first make mad. We must be mad, literally mad, as a nation to be permitting the annual inflow of some 50,000 dependants, who are for the most part the material of the future growth of the immigrant descended population. It is like watching a nation busily engaged in heaping up its own funeral pyre.'

Then he read out what he said was part of a letter from an elderly woman living in Wolverhampton who was afraid to go out: 'Windows are broken. She finds excreta pushed through her letterbox. When she goes to the shops, she is followed by children, charming, wide-grinning piccaninnies. They cannot speak English, but one word that they know. "Racialist" they chant . . .' And Powell ended his speech, probably the most notorious modern British political oration, by alluding to Virgil's *Aeneid*: 'I see wars, horrible wars, and the Tiber foaming with much blood.'

Fellow Tory shadow cabinet ministers were disgusted and made it clear to Edward Heath that unless he sacked Powell they would resign. To Powell's great surprise, Heath did sack him. Powell insisted to his dying day that he was not racist, but merely conveying the deep fears of his constituents. If his motives included personal advancement, the speech was a disaster. For Heath, and most of the Tory establishment, it had inflamed and deliberately damaged race relations, making the problem worse, not better: and that was certainly how it was received by many West Indians and other immigrants.

But it was, initially, a *popular* speech. We should never forget that. Within a few days, Enoch Powell had received 20,000 letters of support. As we saw in the Grunwick story, East London dockers and other workers had marched in their thousands, telling Parliament 'We want Enoch.' Now admittedly marches and letters are hardly a scientific assessment of real public opinion. But by the end of the month the polling company Gallup found that 74 per cent of those they asked agreed with Enoch Powell and only 15 per cent disagreed.

These are huge numbers and give the lie to the far too easy modern assumption that Enoch Powell was out of touch with twentieth-century Britain. He was in touch with the majority view. The more interesting question is why he wasn't successful. His popular support was enormous. Tory Party conferences were almost hijacked by his backers; docks and factories went on strike in support; he got enormous media coverage. Privately, senior Labour figures such as Dick Crossman acknowledged that Powell spoke for many working-class Labour voters. During the late 1960s and early 1970s, Powell extended his campaign, covering almost the entire economic agenda, foreign affairs and the right to free speech. Facing student demonstrations and bans in universities, he was embroiled in exactly the kind of 'no platform' controversies that became common in the Britain of the twenty-first century.

It's possible to imagine an alternative history in which Powell swept Heath from power as Tory leader (many people at the time thought he would), and then went on to impose the kind of radical changes Britain would not experience until Margaret Thatcher's government in the early 1980s. He could have been the leader of a popular upset as dramatic as the 2016 European vote.

But it never happened. Far from making him a potent political tribune, as he had expected, his aggressive stance on race and immigration pushed him away from the centre of national life. By the time of the 1975 European referendum campaign, when he was fired up and full of energy, his support for the 'no' side was actually damaging. Seven years after the 'rivers of blood' speech, serious-minded people didn't want to be seen on the same side as Powell. So again, why? What went wrong?

One answer is that, with the memories of the Second World War still fresh and the cinema newsreels of Dachau and Auschwitz having provided a new definition of political hell, for a large number of moderate, mainstream conservative Britons the possibility of racism becoming respectable was horrifying. Whatever people felt late at night in the privacy of their homes, for anyone who considered themselves respectable public expressions of racism were becoming a red line.

Challenged repeatedly on whether he was racist, Powell gave two kinds of answers. First, he would say that if racism meant that he believed one racial or ethnic group was superior to another then he emphatically wasn't. But, second, he would then go on to discuss the numbers of immigrants, as in a *Daily Mail* interview he gave in 1968: 'We are all racialists. Do I object to one coloured person in this country? No. To 100? No. To 1,000? No. To a million? A query. To 5 million? Definitely.' By moving beyond this to advocating voluntary repatriation – his critics insisted that, if his numbers were right it would soon have to be compulsory repatriation – Powell crossed that line.

It wasn't just angry students campaigning against him. Quintin Hogg, a prominent Tory of the period, sharply reminded him in public of the Greek saying against extremism – moderation in all things. Much more aggressively, Tony Benn, once almost a friend of Enoch Powell's, warned a meeting in London against 'filthy obscene racialist propaganda' and said that 'the flag hoisted at Wolverhampton is beginning to look like the one that fluttered over Dachau and Belsen'.

Such warnings seem to have struck home. Despite his popular support, Powell was disinvited by universities and even, to his fury, by the commanding officer of the British Army of the Rhine. There was just something about him – his staring eyes, his hypnotic West Midlands voice, his brimming self-belief – that made middle Britain shudder. White voters were concerned about the scale of black immigration. But they didn't want to be part of a nation that was rounding up fellow citizens and sending them 'home'.

There is one final explanation for his failure which is dull but important. During the critical period when he was at his most popular and dangerous as an insurgent, Powell stuck by the rules and codes of the Conservative Party. He disliked Edward Heath. He teased him. He criticized him. But he accepted that Heath was the party's elected leader and never mounted a direct challenge. So he didn't have the mechanism for a popular revolt. Had, somehow, Enoch Powell been allowed access to an earlier referendum on immigration, then our history might have been very different indeed. (Against that, as a stickler for parliamentary democracy, he would probably have rejected the idea of a plebiscite, even one in his favour.)

While Enoch Powell was serving the British Army in Egypt, the young Anthony Wedgwood Benn was serving in the Royal Air Force further south in Rhodesia – which later became Zimbabwe – and in South Africa. On opposite sides in politics, the two men shared many similarities. They both came, to start with, from intensely high-minded and hard-working families.

Benn's was by far the more political. His great-grandfather had been heavily involved in the politics of London's East End. His grandfather and his father were both progressive MPs. With his other grandfather on his mother's side a radical Scottish MP, this was a family saturated in the politics of the non-Marxist left. Benn's own father, William Wedgwood Benn, began as a Liberal, then joined Labour in the late 1920s, being appointed Secretary of State for India, a job in which he jousted with Winston Churchill. A pilot in the First World War, he rejoined the RAF in his sixties and was much decorated. William Benn ran a house that was austere, disciplined and much concerned with principle. His mother was a feminist Christian, with a nonconformist suspicion of hierarchies. Unlike Powell's, this was a privileged household: politicians of the eminence of Lloyd George visited it. The hugely successful actress Margaret Rutherford was a cousin.

The young Tony Benn was strongly religious, and all his life believed that the teachings of Jesus Christ, if not his divinity, were of fundamental importance. But it was an idiosyncratic religion: 'I came to believe that Marx was the last of the Old Testament prophets, a wise old Jew sitting in the British Museum describing capitalism with clinical skill, but adding a moral dimension . . . Marx added a passion for justice that gave his work such unique political and moral power.' Benn's privilege and idealism meant that he would be mocked mercilessly throughout his life by the mainstream British press; but, with his family deeply involved in helping Jewish refugees, and his horror at the behaviour of the British in Africa, he was tapping into a deep vein in the British imagination which is perhaps under-remembered today – nonconformist, internationalist and idealistic.

Benn's commitment to English tradition was, in its way, just as romantic as Powell's, but derived from an almost opposite edition of history. In Tony Benn's book, the key period was the revolutionary uprising against the reign of Charles I and his doctrine of Divine Right. As he later explained in a speech commemorating the Levellers, they had believed in the sovereignty of the people:

> Their message was spelled out very clearly in 'An Agreement of the Free People of England' which outlined a new and democratic constitution for Britain. It was published on 1 May 1649 while the leaders of the Levellers were imprisoned in the Tower of London, and the key words are these: 'We, the free people of England, agree to ascertain our government, to abolish all arbitrary

power and to set bounds and limits both to our supreme and all subordinate authority and remove all known grievances.'

Christian proto-socialists had argued for state schools and hospitals, anticipating the welfare state by 300 years. Tony Benn, quoting a writer of the times, saw them as being grounded in Christ:

> The relation of master and servant has no ground in the New Testament; in Christ there is neither bond nor free . . . There is no ground in nature or scripture why one man should have £1,000 per annum, another not a pound. The common people have been kept under blindness and ignorance and have remained servants and slaves to the nobility and gentry. But God hath now opened their eyes and discovered unto them their Christian liberty.

Just as Enoch Powell believed that the British, after the loss of the Empire, had to fall back on their ancient institutions – Parliament above all – so Tony Benn thought that the radical, progressive tradition initiated in Britain in the seventeenth century could only be protected by parliamentary democracy.

Two journeys emerged at the same place. Benn's vision of Britain also depended, albeit for different reasons, on the supremacy of the House of Commons. Writing as early as 1948, in words that eerily foreshadow Powell's thinking, Benn defended British democracy against communism: 'We in the English-speaking world have created a wonderful machinery for peaceful change in parliamentary democracy. It has taken 1,000 years, and we should not and cannot expect it to grow in Russia, Eastern Europe or primitive countries which have not our history of peace, plenty and stability. But we must treasure it ourselves and use it to achieve our own ends.'

Like his older colleague Michael Foot, Benn's deep belief in parliamentary democracy provoked a rising fear that it was threatened by the prospect of European union. For him, the emphasis on a 'single market' was less to do with peace on the continent than with security for the capitalist system. The Common Market was, to use an old socialist phrase he liked, a 'bankers' ramp'. For Tony Benn and his many followers on the left (including Jeremy Corbyn), 'Europe' was an anti-democratic capitalist plot.

One of Benn's most complete explanations of his hostility to the European project came in a speech in March 1972, when he warned the Commons:

> If the British people are herded into a federation against their will, the whole fabric of our society will be threatened. First, we shall find ourselves governed by laws we did not make and cannot change. Second, we shall find ourselves taxed by people we did not elect and cannot remove.
>
> Third, we shall find ourselves locked in to economic policies that may harm us and cannot be altered because they were devised to meet the needs of others. Fourth, we shall be governed by European bureaucrats elected by no one for whom Ministers are only needed as a rubber stamp. Fifth, we may find ourselves sucked into a European military machine with its own nuclear weapons shared by France, Britain and possibly Germany, over whose use the British people will have no control at all. When the British people wake up to realise what is happening, there will be a veritable explosion of rage.

Tony Benn was by no means the only, or even the most prominent, Labour anti-Common Market politician. Michael Foot, Peter Shore, Hugh Gaitskell, Barbara Castle and many others shared his suspicions of Brussels. But because Benn went on to foment and lead a major left-wing rebellion inside the Labour Party during the 1970s and early 1980s, when he became the standard bearer of the so-called hard left, his influence was particularly important. For a generation, he was the anti-Tony Blair, the leader of the peace movement, the man who rejected the pro-market manoeuvres of New Labour. By the time of his death in March 2014, the one-time iconoclast 'Wedgie' and hate figure of Conservative newspapers had been transformed into a safe, almost cuddly and reassuring national treasure – the pipe-smoking grandad whose diaries told his own extraordinary story.

Under Tony Blair, Labour had become almost fanatically pro-EU, even to the extent of wanting, for a time, to ditch sterling for the euro. Benn, it seemed, was no longer relevant. But this was – it almost immediately turned out – absolute nonsense. Just over a year after Benn died, one of his most devoted followers, Jeremy Corbyn, was overwhelmingly elected leader of the Labour Party. This was, among other things, a posthumous triumph for Benn's brand of socialist parliamentarianism. Part of that brand was scepticism about the European Union; and in the 2016 referendum Labour's enthusiasm for staying in was, to put it politely, pretty muted.

Tony Benn and Enoch Powell were two of the most divisive, loved and loathed politicians of the Queen's reign. Neither achieved conventional political success. But Powell's influence on the Tory right, and Benn's on the Labour left, climaxed in the 2016 referendum. Together, their ideas overwhelmed the establishment, pro-European consensus of the time.

32

THE LEAPING SALMOND

The British establishment was nearly overwhelmed from another direction. On 18 September 2014, more than 1.6 million Scots voted to leave the United Kingdom and form an independent country. This would have ended a union formed a little more than 300 years earlier and it had been, in the words of the Duke of Wellington, a damned close-run thing. Opinion polling just before the ballot itself had suggested a win for the pro-Scottish Nationalist 'yes' side. Cautiously but clearly, the Queen had warned against jumping into the unknown. And on the day a shade over 2 million Scots stuck with the Union. This was a personal achievement for Alistair Darling, the former New Labour Chancellor who had led the 'no' side. He suffered ferocious personal condemnation for doing so.

The referendum campaign had been dominated by issues such as the ability of an independent Scotland to survive economically; what currency it would use; how easily, if at all, it would be able to remain inside the EU; and the future of the British military, including its nuclear bases, as well as the monarchy, in an independent Scotland. All these were argued about, at a high level, in major speeches and interviews. Throughout the campaign there were marches and demonstrations but not a hint of violence.

There was, however, vituperation – a lot of it. In what turned out to be a trailer for some of the nastier aspects of the Brexit referendum two years later, passionate and sometimes extreme nationalists exchanged deeply offensive, menacing and repeated threats with equally outraged unionists. People who had lived in Scotland for most of their lives but were opposed to the SNP were told to 'go home' and warned they would not be welcome in an independent Scotland. For some, flying the Union Jack was an act of rash provocation.

What this showed was at one level humdrum and banal: that riled people will say things anonymously online they would not contemplate saying face to face. More important, it showed just how passionate and visceral feelings of national belonging still were. If part of the motivation for leaving the EU had been the subdued, sneered-at pain of 1945 British 'Spitfire' patriots, and a certain amount of English nationalism, then two years earlier came a crest in the wave of profoundly felt Scottish national feeling, harking back to the glory of 1314 and the rhetoric of the Declaration of Arbroath.

It should have been no surprise. The SNP had been on the rise for years, despite an attempt by Labour to head off nationalism by refounding the Scottish Parliament in 1999. Its success was heavily down to the charisma, pugnacity and energy of one politician in particular. The man who formed the SNP's first Edinburgh minority administration in 2007, and became Scotland's First Minister, had been pushing relentlessly for the referendum ever since. Alexander Elliot Anderson Salmond, or 'Wee Eck' to his enemies, was Scotland's Elizabethan change-maker.

The coronavirus crisis made everything in wider politics uncertain. Before the virus arrived in Britain the Scottish leader to whom Salmond handed power after losing the referendum, Nicola Sturgeon, had been promising a further independence referendum in 2020 or possibly soon thereafter. There was at that point a narrow majority in the polls for independence. Four years earlier Scotland had voted heavily to stay inside the EU and the prospect of the United Kingdom breaking up as a result was real. However, the Scottish government's approach to handling the virus was not very different to that of London and a common threat had produced a vague 'we're all in it together' mood in the spring of 2020.

Among those watching and waiting from his Aberdeenshire home was Alex Salmond. He was recuperating from being cleared in one of the most sensational trials Scottish politics has ever witnessed. In August 2018 he had left the SNP after allegations of sexual misconduct during his time as First Minister had been made against him. He believed the Scottish government, now run by his old protégée Nicola Sturgeon, had handled the allegations improperly. In the summer of 2018, he launched a judicial review and was awarded a remarkable, punitive £500,000 towards his costs. Just sixteen days after this triumph, in January 2019, he was arrested and charged with fourteen offences against women – two attempted rapes, nine charges of sexual assault, two of indecent assault and one of breach of the peace.

The SNP is, for most of the time, a quiet, tidy, discreet organization. Its dirty washing is dealt with in a well-guarded scullery. The sex allegations blew this apart. Some MPs at Westminster and Holyrood broke ranks to defend the man who for them was simply 'Mr Scotland'. Others tried to form a shield wall around their heroine, Nicola Sturgeon. It was widely believed that the trial must destroy one of the rival river-fish. Salmond's defence team had used a warrant to obtain material which they believed showed that the actions of Sturgeon's government had been unlawful, even prompted by malice.

All of political Scotland was agog when the trial began in November 2019, with Salmond pleading not guilty to all charges. But the private material on the government was not allowed to be heard in public by the court; and when Salmond was cleared of all charges in March 2020, just as the viral threat was at its height, it remained under wraps. This is not the end of the story. The Scottish Parliament is pursuing its own inquiry and will be able to obtain the messages gathered by Mr Salmond's team. Only then might the damage to the SNP high command become clear. Alex Salmond himself may yet return to politics and the party he led for so long. If so, it would be only the latest twist in a career that has been utterly remarkable – perhaps matched in modern British history only by that of the leader of the Irish nationalists more than a century earlier, Charles Stewart Parnell.

Salmond had not come from a nationalist family. When he was born in Linlithgow in 1954 there were not, frankly, many of those. His parents were civil servants and his mother, according to Salmond, was a 'Winston Churchill Conservative'. Linlithgow is the kind of historic town which can provoke an interest in history; it is home to one of the great palaces of the old royal families of Scotland. At university in St Andrews in the 1970s, Salmond studied economics and medieval history and became gripped by the history of Scotland. He was a left-winger in politics, but London Labour had already seemed grey and lustreless and, provoked by an English girlfriend, Salmond turned to the Scottish National Party.

The SNP dates its origins to the 1930s, when its founder parties had drawn support from both right and left – from grandees such as the Duke of Montrose to communist poets such as Hugh MacDiarmid. It had never quite settled on the left–right spectrum. Salmond, as one of the founders of the left-wing 79 Group, helped push it leftwards, as it began to emerge as an alternative to the Labour Party, which had tended to regard Scotland as its natural territory. It was a long slog. In his first general election as SNP leader in 1992, the party failed to win any new seats. The 1997 election, the New Labour landslide for Tony Blair, saw them increase, but only from four seats to six. Nevertheless, in the Blair years Salmond became one of the most recognizable and provocative MPs of the time, opposing foreign wars and trying to have the Prime Minister impeached after the invasion of Iraq. No one thought he would ever return to Scotland.

A passionately enthusiastic follower of horse racing, and now a television presence, he was no longer the lean left-winger of yore and began to attract business support. Both Donald Trump and Rupert Murdoch admired him at times. In both cases, the admiration cooled. In Trump's, the falling-out was spectacular. Salmond resigned as SNP leader in 2000, only to return again, winning three-quarters of the votes, in 2004. In Scotland one of his most notable achievements was persistently and determinedly winning the backing of working-class Catholics. At earlier periods in SNP history, it had been seen as effectively a Protestant party. By changing that, and by championing left-wing causes such as opposition to the Iraq War, Salmond positioned the nationalists to take advantage of the collapse of Labour in Scotland, a party that had become weary and complacent.

Eventually, after 2014, Nicola Sturgeon, with a strikingly different style and greater caution, inherited the leadership of the SNP. But it is hard to imagine the breakthrough of the SNP in recent times without the fire and gumption of the pugnacious, charismatic and deeply flawed Salmond. Time and time again, he has been written off – finished, beaten, sunk. Time and time again he has resurfaced, like a rotund tartan life jacket in a storm. He has weathered political and personal scandals, objections to his friends and his business connections, and straightforward electoral defeats. But he reminds us that there is more than one idea of the nation in the UK today, and that while he lives above ground the Scottish question won't go quiet. Under Queen Elizabeth II, the United Kingdom held together – but only just.

33

THE REV. DAN DARE

Children's comics were one of the less political arenas in which the fight for British values and identity never ceased. During the 1950s and 1960s, usually as ballast in the holds of ships, large numbers of American Marvel Comics were being imported. Superhero characters now well known from the screen – Spiderman, Batman, Captain America – first made their way on yellowing, garishly coloured pages into British playgrounds and the grubby fingers of Scottish, Welsh, Irish and English children.

Not everybody was happy about this. American popular culture, allegedly more 'trashy' and 'violent' than British, was criticized by broadcasters, publishers and churchmen. The war had increased the flow of American publications, but debate about the influence of comics was nothing new. As early as 1940, George Orwell published an influential essay, 'Boys' Weeklies', in which he argued that not enough attention was paid to the cheap over-the-counter comics sold in British corner shops. These were, he argued, 'the best available indication of what the mass of the English people really feels and thinks.'

Concentrating on boys' comics, Orwell listed ten popular, locally written titles, produced by Amalgamated Press, or by D. C. Thomson of Dundee: 'They are on sale in every town in England, and nearly every boy who reads at all goes through a phase of reading one or more of them.' Most of Orwell's essay was a spirited attack on the more old-fashioned weeklies left over from the Edwardian era, the *Gem* and the *Magnet*, with their schoolboy stories of Billy Bunter at Greyfriars, which he found hideously snobbish, racist and badly written.

But when Orwell turned to the more modern papers, featuring tough and aggressive heroes, he included a telling sideswipe at the contemporary American magazines. It is worth quoting:

> There is a great difference in tone between even the most blood-thirsty English paper and the threepenny Yank Mags, *Fight Stories*, *Action Stories*, etc. (not strictly boys' papers, but largely read by boys). In the Yank Mags you get real blood-lust, really gory descriptions of the all-in, jump-on-his-testicles style of fighting, written in a jargon that has been perfected by people who brood endlessly on violence. A paper like *Fight Stories*, for instance, would have very little appeal except to sadists and masochists.

By the 1950s, D. C. Thomson, then a sectarian company which declined to employ Roman Catholics, had gone some distance to answer Orwell's lament about the lack of authentic working-class figures. In the *Victor*, Alf Tupper was a working-class welder and champion sprinter with a heart of gold, constantly foiling the dastardly plots of jealous 'posh boys' from the universities. In the *Rover*, Matt Braddock was an ace bomber pilot, whose father had been a boilermaker and who had worked as a steeplejack before the war, attending elementary schools across the North and Midlands of England.

Then, in the hugely popular *Dandy* and *Beano*, which were jointly selling more than 2 million copies a week in the 1950s, there was a cheerfully anarchic range of still-famous working-class characters

– Dennis the Menace, Minnie the Minx, the Bash Street Kids, Roger the Dodger and Billy Whizz. These were heroes and anti-heroes aimed at the working classes. But the Yank Mags continued to pour in, and so the fear of crude American values polluting British children remained a lively issue.

The Rev. John Marcus Harston Morris was one of the concerned. And Morris was a considerable moral warrior. Born in Preston, Lancashire, the son of a canon of Liverpool Cathedral, he had gone to Oxford on a scholarship, transferred to the austere Wycliffe theological college and was ordained in 1939. Serving during the war as an RAF chaplain, he then returned to Lancashire as Vicar of St James's, Birkdale, Southport.

There Morris showed startling signs of publishing ambition, relaunching his humble parish magazine as the *Anvil* and persuading luminaries such as the famous broadcaster C. E. M. Joad, the rising Conservative politician Harold Macmillan and the 'Narnia' novelist C. S. Lewis to write for him. Like George Orwell, although in his case from a Christian perspective, Morris was particularly worried about American influence on the young.

He represents a popular undercurrent of hostility to the US which must be placed against the elite intermingling of the American and British political classes, through scholarships and lecture tours, described at the beginning of this book. According to an *Observer* interview with him in March 1954, Morris felt there was a sadistic influence coming into the country. He didn't like comics which emphasized the 'tit-for-tat revenge motive' and, after writing a newspaper article protesting against 'comics that bring horror into the nursery' he determined that British children should be offered something more wholesome.

Morris clearly wasn't your average provincial vicar. According to a newspaper profile at the time he was a 'slight sandy-haired man . . . nervously quick in his movements. He dresses gaily, goes in for light suits, bright ties . . . and is often taken for an actor.' The author of his entry in the *Dictionary of National Biography* said that later in life he was tall, striking and chain-smoking, 'like a sardonic Leslie Howard'. Morris now roped in a talented Southport graphic artist called Frank Hampson. His first idea, perhaps just a little optimistic, was to attract the young reader with the adventures of an inner-city pastor called Lex Christian.

Pastor Lex failed to excite the children of Britain and in 1950, now heavily in debt, Morris ordered dummies of a new comic, featuring a large-jawed superhero space pilot, wearing an RAF-style uniform, called Dan Dare. He showed the proofs to the magazine publishing house of Hulton Press in London, who loved them. The *Eagle* – the very name was based on the oaken eagle forming his church lectern – took flight. So, too, would sister publications aimed at girls and younger readers – *Robin*, *Swift* and *Girl*.

Dan Dare, whose adventures were imagined happening in the 1990s, had a great influence on generations of British schoolboys, the current writer included. Dare implied that the future could be British as much as American, and that old-fashioned values of fair play and decency would prevail, even in space and even against foes as hideous as Vora, 'the bestial overlord of Saturn'. When Dan formed alliances, they were with horse-riding Russian and Indian allies. His was a (cautiously) multiracial as well as intergalactic world.

Dare blasted off weekly from 1950 until 1967, making less regular fly-pasts in the 1970s and 1980s. To oversee the *Eagle*, Morris moved to London, becoming a successful magazine executive. He ended up as General Manager of the National Magazine Company – a subsidiary, ironically enough, of the Hearst Corporation of America. Among the publications he launched in later life was *Cosmopolitan*, though it was markedly different from the *Cosmo* of today. But he always remained the Rev. Marcus Morris, becoming the assistant priest at St Bride's Church in central London, where he preached almost every week. According to the *Observer* in 1954,

'Morris . . . bases his editorial policy on a favourite quotation from Chesterton in praise of honest blood-and-thunder literature, "as simple as the thunder of heaven and the blood of man".' There were virtually no sexual references of any kind in his magazines, and compared to US comics the violence was 'mild and wholesome, even naive'.

In terms of Elizabethans who had a real impact on their fellow subjects, the sandy-haired, slightly flashy Reverend of Southport deserves to be well remembered. But he also reminds us that the change-makers were not all politicians or campaigners or soldiers. Our changes in attitude come as much from our tastes and habits as from our ideas; from our fingers and guts as well as from our minds. What has been the great appeal of Europeanism, for instance? Don't study the speeches, just close your eyes and sniff . . .

34

ELIZABETH DAVID, GOOD EATING AND EUROPE

British attitudes to continental Europe have always been affected by class. For hundreds of thousands of working-class British males, Europe was, above all, the place where they had fought. The continent was a territory of recent danger; and in the immediate aftermath of war it was an unappealing sprawl of shattered cities, impoverished people and incomprehensible politics. In the early 1950s, demobilized officers and their families might well agree: for those with itchy feet there were friendlier, warmer, post-imperial destinations to choose from – Australia, Kenya, South Africa.

And yet for wealthier, more cultured Britons, the European continent remained exciting and enticing, a place of better food, the very latest in art and design, philosophy and music. Copenhagen boasted modernistic, cool furniture and kitchenware that couldn't be found in London. Rome was already a mecca for film lovers, with Visconti, Rossellini and Fellini all hard at work, and Sophia Loren and Gina Lollobrigida on their way to becoming household names.

But it was France that had the biggest magnetic pull, rather as English travellers had immediately flocked there in 1802, when the

Peace of Amiens brought a short break in the Revolutionary and Napoleonic Wars. Painters, philosophers, designers and photographers, again feeling cut off from Paris, rushed back there in 1945–6. In her autobiography the designer Mary Quant explains its allure:

> London was dead. Paris was different. In Paris, the food was better: life was better. In every bar and restaurant, the French thumped their elbows, raised their fists and raged, arguing politics long into the night. Politics was fun. French film stars tended to be Communist millionaires and Maquis heroes, making long, angry films. Every Frenchman had a Gitane stuck to his lip, lived on hard-boiled eggs and drank black coffee in dark green cups with gold rims. All French men were intellectuals. They danced differently, spinning you round until you got vertigo . . . I found it impossible not to fall in love with the city . . .

London, by contrast, was a city waiting for the modern world with patient despair:

> The grown-ups had won a war and lost an empire without realising. They returned to their gardens and allotments and waited while everything calmed down, hoping that life would revert to how it was before the war. For ten years, rationing not only went on but became worse. No butter, no eggs, no meat, no sweets, no transport – yet there was still a prevailing attitude of 'don't rock the boat'. Government control had become a habit. London was a bombsite and the only thing that thrived was the buddleia. Burnt-out basements became jazz clubs or children's secret smoking dens . . .

Before cheap air travel, journeying to the continent was expensive, slow and difficult. The British faced severe restrictions on the amount of foreign currency they could buy and carry out of the country

– passports had to be filled in and stamped to show this. For those intrigued by European lifestyles and cultures, it was more a case of bringing them home to Britain than journeying forth to wallow in them overseas. And in this transaction nothing mattered more than food.

For some time, the modern Elizabethans did not eat well. It was an historic problem. The world's first industrial economy had long relied on imported, tinned and processed foods. The connection between soil, countryside and the table had been broken. The working classes' diet was stodgy and so lacking in nutrition that Second World War rationing visibly improved the health of millions of children and adults. What wealthier people saw as privation, the poorer found a treat. But even the middle and upper classes tended to eat a limited range of roast and broiled meats, overcooked vegetables and bland, soggy puddings. Of course, there were many exceptions – fine restaurants, good local kitchens. But the British were notorious across Europe – and among Americans who had lived here during the war – for terrible cooking; and with good reason.

By 1952 the range of available food was beginning to change, though not fast. Some of the most popular new products were American imports. The Brooklyn-born taxidermist Clarence Birdseye had developed his fast-freezing techniques for fish in America and Canada in the 1920s. His Birds Eye company was importing food into Britain before the war and in 1955 launched its famous fish fingers, giving the current writer (and millions of others) a sizzling, lightly crisped childhood memory. Proust had his madeleines; we, fish fingers. The mighty Heinz Corporation had made its first inroads in the previous century, with its bottled sauces and boldly marked tins piled high at Fortnum & Mason's, no less, from 1886. In 1910, its cream of tomato soup arrived in Britain, while Heinz salad cream was a staple of British restaurants and homes throughout the war and beyond. Heinz tomato ketchup had vanished from Britain in 1939 but returned triumphantly in 1948.

None of this made, however, for real eating as the French, Italians, Greeks or Spanish would have understood it. This was hardly the fault of the early British Elizabethans. Outside the natural cold-store that was winter in Britain, refrigeration was still uncommon: as late as 1960, only about a fifth of British households had fridges. Canned food, including a lot of canned beef from Argentina, was plentiful. But the supply chains which today provide exotic fruit and vegetables out of season simply did not exist. The yam, the avocado and the mango were merely unlikely rumours.

What the early Elizabethans did have, though, was a powerful appetite for better food. We were a salivating people. Immigrant Chinese from the Hong Kong New Territories had begun to spread Chinese restaurants across Britain during the 1950s. Bangladeshi sailors had begun to take over empty fish and chip shops and corner stores to sell basic curried food, though the big expansion of Indian restaurants was yet to come. Britain's first Wimpy Bar opened in 1954, offering burgers and hot dogs, and was an immediate success. Gaggia coffee machines were bringing good coffee for the first time to milk bars up and down the country. Small numbers of Italian grocers were spotted in Soho and Scotland.

Overall, however, the most notable thing was how profoundly the British were cut off from gastronomic cultures across the Channel. After the war, the British didn't know about Europe, and Europe didn't know about Britain. During the troubled and ominous 1930s only the richest and most inquisitive had travelled much to the continent. Now, after the war, with much of Europe wrecked and hungry, few people bothered.

Among those who did was a strikingly beautiful aristocratic woman who was spotted charging up and down Italy, taking busy notes as she gobbled and nibbled away through the cuisines of Venice, Tuscany and Rome, testing risottos and pastas, pizzas, olive oils and good local cheeses. Just as much as the Rev. Marcus Morris, Jayaben Desai or Tony Benn, she would be a genuine Elizabethan change-maker.

Elizabeth David had been variously a debutante, painter, actress and fashion assistant. She had been partly educated in Paris and later eloped with an older married man on a boat journey through the canals of France and across the Mediterranean to Italy and Greece. She had narrowly avoiding being imprisoned as a spy at the beginning of the Second World War. She ditched that man but was encouraged to write by the novelist Norman Douglas. She learned to cook in Greece and then in Egypt. After further adventures, including marrying a British officer and going with him for a spell to India, David returned to post-war Britain. Flush with her experiences of real food under a sparkling Mediterranean sun, she was horrified to discover what her huddled, rain-soaked countryfolk were eating: 'There was flour and water soup seasoned solely with pepper; bread and gristle rissoles; dehydrated onions and carrots; corned beef toad in the hole. I need not go on.'

She need not – though we can, for she was not exaggerating. In the 1950s, reputedly, olive oil was sold by chemists and used to clean out earwax. This was the era of those suspicious rissoles, of claggy macaroni puddings, of bleak plates of clammy cold meat and damp salad, of spam fritters leaking more oil than a burst pipeline. On an exceptionally good day, you might come across a moistly inviting semicircle of creamed swede. Real Italian food and real French food were virtually unknown. Lyons Corner Houses (a feature of urban Britain from 1909 until the mid-1970s) offered homely restaurant meals with French names. Under the names could be found doggedly British 'translations' – fried gammon, mayonnaise-coated salads, treacle puddings and uncompromising, rubbery custards.

In a tribute for the *Observer* newspaper, written after Elizabeth David had died, the food writer Simon Hopkinson recalled trying to imagine what she was up against, by going through cookery books for British housewives written at the beginning of the Queen's reign: 'Before me', he recalled, were the least appealing recipes ever written: mock marzipan cobbled from haricot beans and almond essence; 'eggs' that were tinned apricots fried in bacon fat. I opened one book and realised with a horrible gulp that I was looking at advice for cooking crow. 'Boil it up with suet,' said the writer, 'to keep the meat as white as possible.' There was a recipe for sparrow pie too – though the Ministry of Food did not 'encourage' the eating of these tiny birds.

Into this plated horror strode David, who now discovered that her real talent was not in fact for eating, or adventuring, or love affairs. She could cook, yes, but she was above all things an extraordinarily vivid writer. Now she began one of the most effective propaganda campaigns in modern British history. First in magazine articles and then in a sequence of famous and influential books, she dedicated herself to explaining to the British just what good eating could be like – to rubbing their noses, as it were, in the suet-cooked crow. *A Book of Mediterranean Food* was published in 1950 and *French Country Cooking* a year later. Her frantic note-taking in northern Italy and Sardinia appeared as *Italian Food* in 1954.

A passage from her French book gives a sense of the gastronomic pornography with which she assaulted her British middle-class readers. She told them to go and search out a better world, crammed with:

> the cheeses and creams, the fruits preserved in potent local liqueurs, the fresh garden vegetables, pulled up before they are faded and grown old, and served shining with farmhouse butter, the 'gallettes' . . . The mushrooms gathered in the forest, the mountain hares, pigeons, partridges and roebuck . . . The fried trout straight from the river, the sustaining vegetable soups enriched with wine, garlic, bacon and sausages, the thousand and one shellfish soups and stews, the *fritures de golfe* . . . of France's lovely prodigal coast . . .

This was writing as potent as anything in the best British novels of the time; and it pointed to a Europeanism far more effective than accounts of the creation of a European Iron and Steel Community, intended (as *The Times* put it bluntly on 9 January 1952) 'as the first genuine segment of a supra-national European Union'. During the Elizabethan reign, whatever they felt about the growing power of Brussels, the British middle classes would become steadily more entranced by, and entangled with, continental lifestyles. This was a natural human solidarity of the nostrils, the tongues, the fingertips and the browned skin, not of political structures, votes or regulations.

Cultural Europeanism would take many forms, from the popularity of *Asterix* and *Babar* books in British classrooms to the slow realization that cycling was something that could be done without a coat, muffler and pannier, and even for long distances at speed. But Elizabeth David should be remembered as one of the genuinely influential figures of the period. Her pleasure gospel spread through kitchens and restaurants across Britain, and is still followed attentively in creased, olive-oil-stained volumes on pine tables in every part of Brexit Britain. The *Observer* concluded that she had led this country 'from the greyness of austerity to an exotic world of fresh herbs and garlic'. And so, thank God, she did. But alongside the aromas, Europe always came with inescapable political choices. And during the reign of Queen Elizabeth II, they have caused us more heartache and division than almost anything else.

35

EUROPA, AND BRITISH EUROPEANS

Almost all the modern Elizabethans whose stories are told here are contemporary flesh-and-blood people, who either spent their lives in modern Britain or came and settled here during the Queen's reign. But there is one obvious seductive exception, a princess from long ago, from the coast of what is now Lebanon or Syria, who has haunted and disrupted the modern British story from 1952 to the present day. She is, of course, Europa, abducted by Zeus, who had disguised himself as a beautiful white bull and persuaded the Phoenician girl to jump on his back so that he could swim away with her to Crete.

This early and disgraceful episode of people-trafficking has been part of European storytelling from the start. Europa became, from ancient Greek times, a symbol of the European people and European culture. Today Europa is a name used for everything from one of the moons of Jupiter to a new urban development in Paris, an early (1928) European currency, an orchestra and the building inhabited by the European Council in Brussels, as well as an EU website and a European rocket. Does that also mean, therefore, that Europa belongs to the British people, and that she is part of British culture?

Well, that is the question. We have met two of the most politically influential anti-European Union figures in British culture. It is time now to turn to the other side of the story, a passionate enthusiasm for the European dream, which included leading politicians but also, more important than them, millions of ordinary British families. They had fallen under the spell of Elizabeth David. They had gathered at espresso bars and learned to drink Italian coffee. With a certain amount of spluttering and coughing, they had smoked French tobacco. And now they wanted part of all of that – the sunlight, the olive groves as well as the olive oil, the long evenings with singing crickets.

But before the English middle classes had recolonized Gascony and bought their way across the Côte d'Azur, the less well-heeled of Britain had led the way to the beaches of Mediterranean Spain – even today the single most popular destination for British tourists.

The first recorded British intervention in the area was led by a portly, red-faced admiral, Sir George Rooke, who spent almost all his life fighting the French and his gout. The gout defeated him entirely, the French only periodically. In the early 1700s, during the War of the Spanish Succession, Rooke, commanding British and Dutch vessels, more or less ruined the small town of Torremolinos. His countrymen would complete the job during the twentieth century in what had become a quiet village. Torremolinos by the late 1950s was attracting international stars searching for good seafood and quiet beaches. Frank Sinatra and Grace Kelly were early visitors. Artists were sketching under its pines. In a similar spirit, Ted Hughes and Sylvia Plath had visited Benidorm, further up the coast, for their honeymoon.

One man who passed through Torremolinos on a motoring holiday in 1948 when it was 'a sleepy fishing village' was a slightly chubby, bespectacled young Briton of Russian origin called Vladimir Raitz. Nobody, not even Elizabeth David, would be more influential in the real British–continental post-war story than he. But Raitz started his revolution not in Spain but in the French-owned island of Corsica.

A year after he had driven through Torremolinos in 1949 Raitz, a twenty-seven-year-old working for the news agency Reuters, had been invited to a camp at Calvi in Corsica. A Russian colleague had asked him to join the annual gathering of an émigré Russian water-polo club, the White Bears. Raitz was greeted by his friend Baron Nicholas Steinheil, the son of a landowner from the Caucasus; and one of the original water-polo players, Dimitri Filipoff, whose family had been famous bakers in Tsarist Russia. They were gathered under the fourteenth-century citadel of Calvi. It is genuinely difficult to imagine a less likely beginning for the British post-war mass-tourism boom.

The club was housed in surplus US Army tents left over from the war. There was a cheap bar. Sanitary arrangements included making creative use of the local vegetation. But Raitz, fresh from a forty-eight-hour marathon journey by railway and boat, was entranced:

> Everyone seemed to have a wonderful, carefree holiday. The beautiful Calvi beach of fine sand was almost deserted, although it was the August holiday season, and the Mediterranean was clear and unpolluted. A short distance away, there was magnificent rock swimming to be had; and snorkels and underwater spearguns were just making their appearance in France. At night, there was a club bar and dance floor, all the opportunity of visiting 'downtown' Calvi. Here you had the choice of two bars . . .

Raitz and the Russian Baron, seeing that there was an American wartime runway nearby, built in 1943 for the invasion of southern France, had the idea of chartering planes to bring sun-starved Britons to Corsica for all-inclusive holidays. Realizing this was a big idea,

Raitz went on to Majorca to see whether that too would be a potential holiday destination. Back in London, he threw in his job and used an inheritance of £3,000 from his grandmother to set up a company he called Horizon Holidays.

A long and complex struggle with the British authorities followed before he could get permission to fly holidaymakers south. The aircraft were available – old wartime Dakotas – but this was still the Britain of stifling bureaucracy, where the state carrier British European Airways enjoyed something close to a monopoly. Eventually, after opening his first office in Fleet Street, next to the famous Cheshire Cheese pub, Vladimir persuaded civil servants at the Ministry of Civil Aviation that he could operate his flights, although only for students and teachers. Raitz obediently advertised these new holidays in publications such as *The Teacher's World* and *The Nursing Mirror*.

This being post-war rationed Britain, food was an important part of the offer. Holidaymakers, recalled Raitz, 'would sleep under canvas, enjoy delicious meat-filled meals and as much local wine as they could put away; and we would have return flights to Corsica for the all-inclusive charge of £32 and 10 shillings'. Bookings and requests for more information poured in, and the first Horizon Holidays-chartered Dakota took off from Gatwick Airport, still a modest strip, in May 1950.

The next decade would see a dramatic expansion of holiday flights, changing the way Britons understood the world around them. The figures are remarkable. In 1950, around 2 million British people travelled abroad every year, often by ship and train; by the end of the millennium the figure was nearer 30 million. Nothing on that scale had ever happened to the British before, and it's worth asking what was so different about the first decade of the Queen's reign.

First, and very basically, most British workers now had paid holidays. In the mid-1930s, only about 3 million people had this right, but legislation in 1938 gave all industrial workers, roughly

11 million people, one week's paid annual leave. The outbreak of war meant that this new right had barely been exploited by the early 1940s. And by then the economic crisis produced new problems. Clement Attlee's government banned foreign holidays to countries outside the sterling area until 1948, while business travellers going abroad were limited to £8 spending money a day. That same year Britain's best-known travel company, Thomas Cook, which collapsed in 2019, was nationalized.

But as soon as the restrictions began to be lifted, would-be travel companies had one huge advantage: vast numbers of cheap aircraft, left over from wartime manufacturing, plus surplus airfields almost everywhere. Most important, there was a simple yearning to get away from the austerity and greyness of post-war Britain. It was a pent-up ambition which took time to fulfil. In 1952, two years after Vladimir Raitz's first holiday aircraft had taken off, a newspaper survey showed that only half of British people took any kind of holiday at all. Of those who did, a grand total of 3 per cent went abroad.

Yet a year later, in the year of the Queen's Coronation, rival companies to Horizon, such as Universal Sky Tours, were already opening for business. The government raised the adult limit for carrying money out of the country to £40 and even stuffy old carriers such as BEA began to get in on the act. It was all still pretty basic. As late as 1961, Heathrow Airport's international travellers were being accommodated in ex-RAF huts. But over Mediterranean islands, and increasingly over the long Mediterranean coast of Spain, the sun seemed inclined to keep rising, and drinks remained cheap, and there was plenty of roast meat to eat; and the tourism boom began. In 1957, as a marketing gimmick, BEA renamed 120 miles of the south-east Spanish coast near Valencia the 'Costa Blanca'.

The fascist dictator Franco was still in control of Spain, and his ministers realized that mass tourism was a potentially important source of foreign currency. The fishing village of Benidorm, like

Torremolinos, would be transformed. In 1958, the Queen opened Heathrow as London's new international airport. Vladimir Raitz was by now operating holidays in Corsica, Sardinia and France and on most of the Spanish coast. Again, it wasn't tourism as we know it today. One of the odder features of the first great expansion were the rules restricting prices and profits for the tour operators. Individual booking was frowned upon. To get around the rules, closed groups were formed purely to book planes and fly south – bird fanciers from West Hartlepool or the Society for Wine Appreciation in the Home Counties.

It wasn't just the British, obviously. Germans, recovering from the disaster of the war, also found Franco's Spain a welcoming place for sun and relaxation. The French began to move out of France. Benidorm became the place in the world with the most high-rise buildings per head – proportionately more, for instance, than New York. How much did this really change the way the British thought about 'overseas'? Famously, the Spanish coast established, alongside the gimcrack hotels, a large number of British fish and chip shops, English and Irish bars, and newsagents selling British popular newspapers. It was possible to sit and broil on the beach, reading your favourite columnist from back home, and down a few pints of reliable Watney's Red Barrel, before going to fight with that nice family from Bremen about which sun lounger to occupy for the afternoon. But although the caricature has an element of truth – familiar food and drink made 'abroad' less intimidating for conservative-minded working-class travellers – it's only part of the truth.

For a start, there were many, many different kinds of holiday. Raitz's Horizon Holidays also carried Catholic pilgrims to Lourdes in France; rival companies specialized in bringing large numbers of British tourists to visit castles in Spain or famous Italian hill towns; or in introducing younger Britons to the Greek islands, and even parts of Europe beyond the Iron Curtain, such as Bulgaria. Millions of people travelled for the first time in the 1950s and 1960s to the Mediterranean. Not all of them were uninterested in local culture, languages and people. Some eventually bought homes of their own. Some learned French or Spanish; some made French or Spanish friends. Eventually their children would take part in exchange holidays with foreign penfriends. Many returned to the industrial cities and towns of Britain with a more adventurous attitude to food, which would in turn encourage the development of Italian and French restaurants in Britain.

Whatever their politicians felt about parliamentary sovereignty and the deep history of the English people, the British themselves were slowly becoming Europeans, at least for a few weeks of the year. In various ways, the Kremlin has sought to alter the course of modern British history, but perhaps it was the White Russians of the Corsican water-polo school, not the red Russians of Moscow, who had the greater impact. This is now an important part of Elizabethan history. But was that continental turn inevitable? After all, there was an alternative variety of sunlit, outdoors, good-food culture on offer from English-speaking people further around the globe.

36

THE BRITISH CALIFORNIA

Britain was not always a magnet for migrants wanting to start afresh. During the first part of the Queen's reign, more people were trying to get out of Britain to start new lives than were trying to get in. The most popular destination was Britain's California, the sunlit open spaces of coastal Australia. Academic surveys about why so many people left suggest a wide range of reasons, but in answers to questionnaires the dreariness of post-war Britain, with its shapeless utility clothing, its rationing and its shortage of decent housing after the Blitz feature heavily. So does the climate.

Between the end of the war and the 1970s more than a million British people emigrated to Australia. They did not simply want a warmer and more spacious life, but were also attracted by Australia's apparently more open, democratic culture. As with Americans heading west earlier in the century, they saw Australia as a place of opportunity and hope where hard work would bring big material rewards, without the settled elites and snobbishness of the old country.

Australia, in turn, wanted British immigrants for basic reasons. The Second World War had brought Japan close to invading this relatively empty and undefended continent, while the Royal Navy was tied up for much of the war defending the Atlantic convoy routes, supplying Russia and supporting the Eighth Army in the Mediterranean. The fall of Singapore and some stunning Japanese naval victories underlined just how vulnerable Australia was. An air raid on Darwin in February 1942, killing around 240 people, as well as surface and submarine attacks, did nothing to calm fears. Proudly pro-British governments in Canberra, a city then only thirty years old, found themselves relying almost entirely on American help. This was not how things were supposed to be.

Between the wars, a British Empire self-sufficiency scheme had attempted to tie British and Australian destinies together. Both Whitehall and Canberra would subsidize selected immigration. From the early 1920s until 1933 more than 200,000 British people were paid to go out and work, mainly in agriculture. The 'Big Brother Movement' began in 1928, long before George Orwell's novel *1984* gave the phrase a sinister undertone. It imported British youths to work in farms on the Australian outback.

After 1945, when the Australian assisted-passage scheme was launched (New Zealand followed two years later), there was an openly racial purpose to the policy, to combat the prospect of more Asian immigrants. In 1938 the Archbishop of Perth had welcomed the arrival of young Britons by warning Australians: 'If we do not supply from our own stock, we are leaving ourselves all the more exposed to the menace of the teeming millions of our neighbouring Asiatic races.'

In 1945 a newspaper editorial welcoming more Catholics from Britain thumped the same drum: 'At best, the war with Japan is postponed. Asia presses from the north and the most effective ramp that we can raise is a human one.' The Labor government's slogan was 'Populate or perish'. Prime Minister Ben Chifley set a target of 70,000 immigrants every year and his Immigration Minister Arthur Calwell made it clear that these migrants had to be mainly white British: 'for every foreign migrant there will be ten people from the

United Kingdom'. In fact, the Australian scheme never managed to achieve anything like this proportion, and it was later extended to other white Europeans – Germans, Greeks, Dutch and Italians.

For British and Irish emigrants, the assisted-passage scheme meant that the governments ensured they were charged only £10 a ticket for every adult. Younger children went free and older ones got £5 tickets. Since the real cost of a ticket was about £120, this was a massively attractive subsidy, bringing the cost of crossing the globe well within the pockets of almost every potential British emigrant. Former troopships and dilapidated cruise liners were pressed into service. Between 1945 and 1982, of the 1.6 million British people who settled in Australia, 1.18 million had been assisted – the so-called 'Ten Pound Poms'.

The scheme made it much likelier that Britons who had had enough of their lives at home would choose faraway Australia. As the historians of this phenomenon have put it, the scheme 'gave Australia a competitive edge over the other destinations . . . Without the £10 scheme Australia would have struggled to compete with Canada – which was much closer to home – or indeed with the "New Towns" that were being built around the edges of British metropolitan centres and which also offered a better life for workers and their families.'

To whip up enthusiasm there was a massive publicity campaign, featuring billboards and posters of the bright new future awaiting emigrants; publicity films for cinemas; sponsored newspaper features, and special newsletters. In Australia, the British were told, the standard of living was higher, more people had motor cars (rationing meant they were still hard to obtain in Britain) and, along with sun and surf, it provided excellent schools and a familiar, British way of life. No mention was made of aboriginal Australians or land rights. One Australian journalist working in London in the early 1950s believed that the publicity caught the imagination of Britain because it 'added up to two things – sun and meat'.

Not all the British emigrants found the life they were looking for. Homesickness, being confined to special camps before jobs and houses could be found and the pain of torn-apart families meant that hundreds of thousands came back to the UK. Those who then remembered the British climate and returned to Australia were known as 'boomerang Poms'. But the majority settled and contributed to the long boom in Australia's post-war economy, even as the country changed its policies and brought in more and more European and Mediterranean migrants to reinforce its non-Asian atmosphere. Modern Australia is a genuinely multicultural nation, with large numbers of Japanese, Chinese and other Asian migrants, and this is a period in its history most Australians would prefer to forget.

None of it was necessarily a good deal for Britain: the United Kingdom lost many of the most ambitious, talented and hard-working people from its workforce just when they were needed for the huge task of post-war reconstruction. Though there is no such thing as a typical 'Ten Pound Pom', a large proportion were from the skilled working class and lower-middle class – people with marketable trades and business experience which could be easily translated to Australia.

That left obvious gaps at home. Partly, these would be filled by equally driven refugees from Eastern Europe, fleeing the Soviet empire. But the numbers were too small, and this explains, in turn, British openness to immigration from the Caribbean by the mid-1950s. Ironically, that too encouraged some to leave for Australia. A Londoner, Connie Ward, told researchers that 'That was one reason I was glad to leave England, because whenever you went on a plane, a train, you were the only white person. It used to aggravate me . . .'

So why did British governments collaborate with Australian governments to encourage one of the largest voluntary migrations of modern times? The short answer is that, for Whitehall, nostalgia for the Empire and enthusiasm for the 'White Commonwealth' of Australia, New Zealand and Canada had enormous resonance. If Britain was going to remain a major world player, her white dominions needed to stay strong and stay British: and if that, in turn, meant an infusion of British blood, then so be it. Thus a big and under-discussed social experiment took place; and it wasn't just about numbers.

The people who left changed both Britain and Australia by doing so. The Gibb family of Manchester, for instance, emigrated to Queensland where the boys formed a band and became the Bee Gees. On the other side, John Lennon's raffish father Alf came quite close to emigrating with his young son to New Zealand. Had he done so, of course, Britain would never have had the Beatles. Australian prime ministers were also part of the great emigration – Tony Abbott's family emigrated from London, and Julia Gillard's from Barry, South Wales. These are only a few of the most famous names, and behind that story there is a much darker one.

Some great change-makers stumble upon their cause almost by accident. Margaret Humphreys was a social worker in Nottingham, who had lost both her parents at a young age. Her father had died of cancer when she was twelve, and her mother followed a few years later. Perhaps because of this she had developed a strong sensitivity to the needs of orphaned and adopted children. In 1984, following a change in the law nine years earlier which made it easier for adopted adults to get access to their birth certificates and therefore to track their birth parents, Humphreys set up small local meetings to work with adopted people.

Out of the blue, she got a letter from Australia from a woman who said she had been sent there aged four and knew nothing of her family origins except that she had probably come from Nottingham. Not long after, by pure coincidence, Humphreys came across a local woman whose brother had also been sent to Australia as a child. She began to investigate.

What she discovered was one of the major scandals of the post-war Commonwealth. Up to 150,000 children had been deported from Britain to distant parts of the Empire – Canada and Zimbabwe, which was then Rhodesia, as well as Australia and New Zealand. They had been taken from private children's homes, from orphanages run by organizations such as the Catholic Christian Brothers and Barnardo's, and from local authority care.

Some were genuinely orphans, but many had been placed in care by single mothers or impoverished families unable to cope with them. Often without their families being told, they were embarked on ships and sent to start a new life. Records about them were hidden or destroyed. Far from being fostered with sympathetic, caring overseas families, many ended up in brutal institutions. The worst abuse appears to have happened in Australia, which became the favoured destination after 1945. It happened at Bindoon Boys' Town, run by the Christian Brothers in Western Australia; and at Fairbridge Farm School in New South Wales. Boys and girls were sexually abused, savagely beaten and ritually humiliated. But for many of them the worst thing of all was that they were without any information about their original families. They were children without mothers and fathers.

Margaret Humphreys, depending on private donations, set up the Child Migrants Trust and dedicated much of the rest of her life to trying to discover the origins of these forcibly emigrated children – and, where the parents were still alive, reuniting families. She faced a wall of obstruction from the Churches, the British government and many of the charities involved.

Digging into dark secrets some people thought best left untouched, she was also subject to angry personal abuse and even death threats, particularly in Perth, Western Australia. By the end of 1992 the Child Migrants Trust had received more than 20,000 individual enquiries. A documentary film and then, in the same year a TV drama about English children wrenched from their families and sent to Australia, *The Leaving of Liverpool*, at last made these cases a cause célèbre.

Things should never have gone that far. As early as July 1948 the Child Welfare Department in Western Australia investigated the conditions under which the British children were being kept. Their report on Castledare Junior Orphanage, for instance, reported that boys as young as three were being kept on urine-saturated mattresses and under 'miserably thin' blankets which were 'totally inadequate both in quantity and quality to provide necessary warmth for children of tender years . . . subject to the chilled conditions of winter . . . Practically all pyjamas seen under the children's pillows were grubby and dirty, damp with urine.'

The abuse went much wider than cold, wet bedding. A British parliamentary report in 1998 described it as widespread, systematic and exceptionally depraved. In 2017 around 2,000 former child migrants were still alive. One of them was David Hill, who migrated to Australia with his elder brother and twin brother, leaving Tilbury Docks in April 1959 aboard the SS *Strathaird*. Because his mother, who later emigrated to Australia herself and was reunited with the boys, believed it would be good for them, they were sent to Fairbridge Farm. Hill, who later ran the Australian Broadcasting Corporation, estimates that around 60 per cent of the children sent to learn farming and household skills on such schemes were sexually abused. Britain's California had bright, white beaches – and dark cold shadows.

37

CHURCHILL, EUROPEAN DREAMER

The European dream had entranced British politicians ever since the Second World War ended. There was nobody who had the deep, steeped British romanticism of Winston Churchill himself. And yet it was Churchill, still recovering from the shock of losing office in 1945, who made the great clarion call for European unity, at a speech at Zurich University in September 1946. Surrounded by the pomp, ceremony and comparative wealth of the neutral Swiss, Churchill extolled Europe as 'the home of all the great parent races of the western world . . . It is the fountain of Christian faith and ethics . . .'

Yet, he reminded his audience of aged academics and young students, because of German militarism Europe was shattered: 'Over a wide area a vast, quivering mass of tormented, hungry, careworn and bewildered human beings gape at the ruins of their cities and homes, and scan the dark horizons for the approach of some new peril, tyranny or terror. Among the victors, there is a babble of jarring voices; among the vanquished, the sullen silence of despair.'

Alluding to the danger of Stalin's red armies to the east – Churchill had already shocked the world and offended even some Tories with his 'Iron Curtain' speech in Missouri – he then warned Europeans that tyranny could yet return. But there was a remedy for all of this. If it was adopted it could miraculously transform everything and make all Europe free and happy: 'It is to recreate the European family, or as much of it as we can, and provide it with the structure under which it can dwell in peace, in safety and in freedom. We must build a United States of Europe.'

Churchill's Zurich speech is little remembered in Britain and often misunderstood. Could this most patriotic of parliamentarians really have suggested a United States of Europe? Surely he meant something else? But this was no passing fancy, rhetorical fantasy or loose language. Churchill meant what he said and repeated the argument frequently over the next few years. During the war, he had made the case in private, hoping for the creation of a Council of Europe as a first measure.

His vast admiration for the United States of America meant that the 'USE' echo was a deliberate one, and in a broadcast of March 1943 he directly addressed the idea of European integration. It was his hope, he told his listeners, 'that we shall achieve the largest common measure of the integrated life of Europe that is possible without destroying the individual characteristics and traditions of its many ancient and historic races'. The historian Felix Klos, who has made a close study of Churchill's views on European integration, points out that 'Churchill did not say that his earliest hope was to see an integrated Europe without destroying the *sovereignty* of its many ancient nation states. That would have been a contradiction in terms . . . he implicitly embraced the partial abrogation of national sovereignty as the primary prerequisite for unification.'

So, did Churchill ever envisage Britain giving up some sovereignty to achieve European integration? He certainly believed that sovereignty would have to be surrendered for the union to work. In a parliamentary debate in 1950 on the European Iron and Steel Community, the forerunner of European federalism being forged by France, Germany and other original member states, Churchill told MPs: 'National sovereignty is not inviolable . . . It may be resolutely diminished for the sake of all the men in all the lands finding their way home together.' But Britain? Britain with a shared language and history, looking across the Atlantic at the United States? Britain, victor in the Second World War? Britain, still with her residual Empire? *Britain?*

To start with, Churchill dodged that one. By the time he returned to power in 1951, he made no attempt to unpick the Labour policy of shunning the Iron and Steel Community. (In one of the most famous scenes in the story of British involvement in European integration, Herbert Morrison, Attlee's Deputy Prime Minister, had told officials when they cornered him in a restaurant with a French ultimatum, 'It's no good. We can't do it. The Durham miners would never wear it.') At the time Churchill, too, disapproved. In office he was distracted by the need for an anti-nuclear-war summit between Washington, London and Moscow and discouraged by the lack of enthusiasm for European integration shown by the old Commonwealth countries. He was also very old.

So no, in the end, Churchill was not pushing for Britain to become a founder member of the European Community. He did envisage some kind of special relationship, or extraordinary deal, between Britain and her European neighbours – not so very far from what some British politicians were trying to achieve in the post-Brexit negotiations of 2016–20. Yet the original ardour and idealism of the Zurich speech shouldn't be forgotten or diminished. Churchill saw the need for European integration and his lesson was remembered by many in the Tory Party, and it explains part of its determination under different leaders – Macmillan, Heath, Thatcher, Major – to keep Britain 'at the heart of Europe'.

Since the 2016 referendum on British membership of the EU, and the clear vote to leave it, things seem very different. This story goes far deeper than ordinary politics. It is about who we are. It's about how we think of other European peoples who look like us, whose cities and cultures much resemble ours, and who have been used – as we are – to moving across old borders as if they don't exist. The allure of Europe also provides a philosophical challenge to British democracy. Our most potent national myth is that we have been powerful and successful not because we are cleverer, braver or more hard-working – definitely not the latter – but because we have been living under a rather brilliant political system based on parliamentary sovereignty.

This has allowed us to correct our big mistakes and, after a few years of frustration, get rid of our most incompetent commanders. But a democracy depends on the idea of there being one people, who can debate with one another in one language, who understand and recognize leaders and ideas, and who agree together that when one side loses, it accepts defeat. It demands, in other words, an integrated political community, bound emotionally together.

Can such a community successfully sprawl across many different languages and ancient nation states? In our case, could the British come to regard Guy Verhofstadt or Beppe Grillo as 'our' politicians, in the same breath as Rishi Sunak or Keir Starmer? If the answer is no then there must, logically, be a limit on the amount of political integration the British could accept without losing their old system of parliamentary sovereignty. Yet the lure of Europe has been so strong – peace, after so many wars; the easier exchange of food and cars; near-at-hand, delicious and sun-kissed holidays – that for a long time, almost lazily, staying 'in' seemed more enticing than confronting the political conundrum.

During the first really critical period of British relations with the organization then known familiarly as the Common Market, Europa's suitors and enemies were mostly military men, marked by the Second World War. Edward Heath was the Tory Prime Minister who devoted his life to getting Britain into the Community. He had been doubly successful, first in signing the crucial Treaty of

Accession in 1972, and second in helping lead the winning side in a referendum to confirm British membership in 1975 – by which time he had lost power to Labour's Harold Wilson.

A proud, lonely, brilliant man whose reputation was later smeared by lurid, completely unproven, sexual allegations, Heath was one of the genuine representative political stars of mid-twentieth-century Britain. A believer in the European dream, he was firmly supported by politicians across the political spectrum, perhaps most notably by Roy Jenkins. So far, we have seen him only through the eyes of his enemy Enoch Powell. It is now time to look at him directly.

Perhaps it is glib to define politicians by reference to their formative years. Everybody can change their mind later. But the core political instincts of Heath do seem to have been shaped early, and then stayed constant. While he was still a student at Oxford, he travelled to Nazi Germany. He went to see one of the Nuremberg rallies and was invited to a cocktail party where he met key Nazi leaders including Heinrich Himmler, architect of the Holocaust, Hermann Göring and Reich propagandist Joseph Goebbels.

Heath's revulsion was further hardened by a visit to Spain, at a time when Nazi and Spanish fascist forces were throttling the last redoubts of the Republic. Among the people he met there was his later trade union opponent Jack Jones, fighting with the British Battalion of the International Brigades. Heath himself went on to fight in the Second World War in the Royal Artillery, taking part in the Normandy landings and seeing at first hand the devastation caused by war to northern Germany. Other people, having had Heath's experiences, might have returned home simply loathing the Germans, but he drew the opposite conclusion and became a lifelong believer in the idea that only European political unity could save the continent from another catastrophic conflict.

Heath was elected as an MP in 1950, and his very first speech in the House of Commons was a plea for Britain to join the plan to bring together the iron and steel industries – the same one the

Durham miners were allegedly so much against. A young modern-izer, he rose quickly through the parliamentary party, becoming Harold Macmillan's Chief Whip. One of his most difficult tasks then was to calm down Tory imperialists, irate after the Suez fiasco, as the party struggled with the Malta episode, described already, and the return of Archbishop Makarios to Cyprus. This made him enemies on the Tory right.

As deputy to Alec Douglas-Home, then Foreign Secretary in the House of Lords, Heath led Britain's first attempts to join the European Common Market. This would have been virtually impos-sible had it not been for the veteran French leader General de Gaulle. He was worried that the European project was veering towards federalism, and rather hoped the British would arrive and help stop that kind of nonsense. But in the early 1960s it proved impossible for the British to join anyway. This was, inevitably, both about food and about Britain's place in the world.

The French were shaping the new Common Agricultural Policy, which would shovel money into the pockets of French farmers; Britain, on the other hand, still very Commonwealth-focused, wanted guarantees to protect New Zealand and Australian farmers. To complicate things further, Britain had in 1960 formed a rival group to the Common Market, EFTA, and was still obliged to fight the interests of Norway, Switzerland, Iceland and its other fellow members.

Heath's negotiations to get in, very much like Theresa May's negotiations more than half a century later to get out, became horribly bogged down in the detail, earning Heath the mocking *Private Eye* nickname of 'Grocer'. As his biographer Philip Ziegler explains, once it became clear that every commodity 'from butter, through bananas, to kangaroo meat was to be the subject of lengthy bargaining, it became obvious that the negotiations would be protracted, tedious and faintly absurd . . . The noble concept which Heath cherished was almost lost in a welter of trivial haggling.'

This is not a small point. Throughout Britain's relations with the EU, its core mechanism, a legal machine to bind countries together politically by yoking together their trade and industrial arrangements, meant that political idealism kept toppling over into a bog of arguments about widgets, turnips and the self-interest of lobby groups.

But, as Powell had noticed, 'the noble concept' was always about political identity. Edward Heath knew it from the start, writing later that 'the myth has become fashionable – that we were concerned only with economic affairs . . . Nothing could be further from the truth. The main purpose of the negotiations was political.' Anti-Brussels critics in the Conservative Party would call Heath a traitor for trying to hide the effect on British sovereignty of European membership; and it was a charge widely repeated when the UK Independence Party was formed. This was Britain's version of the 'stab in the back' explanation for a great national mistake.

It was never quite true. Heath did say what he was up to and did acknowledge early on that it would have an effect on British sovereignty. But he also understood the incendiary effect of this on right-wingers in his own party. Ziegler gives a balanced judgement: Heath 'did not seek actively to mislead the British public about his expectations, but he did not feel it necessary or desirable to spell out the full implications of British membership in any detail'.

Heath's great virtue as a political leader was his stubborn refusal to surrender on what he saw as the biggest issues. He was like a great, grumpy First World War tank, slowly lumbering down into shell-holes and up over tangled barbed-wire fortifications yet never deviating from his objective. When, in January 1963, General de Gaulle gave his devastating 'non' to British membership – as a French nationalist, he eventually decided that Britain was too close to the United States – Heath was personally devastated. One journalist found him 'frozen into profound depression; his cheeks grey, his eyes glazed with fatigue'. But he refused to give in, telling British, French and German reporters that Britain was not going to turn its back: it was 'part of Europe by geography, history, culture, tradition and civilization'.

He soldiered on. In 1970–1, as Prime Minister, having already ditched the old British currency of pounds, shillings and pence, he finally got his way and negotiated British membership of the Common Market. 'Grocer' was always a rotten nickname for him. An awkward, brusque and intensely proud man, Edward Heath was driven by a horror of war and those early memories of having seen Nazi evil up close and personal. He was quietly determined that Britain's place was in Europe. Compared to Powell's romantic and emotional view of the nation, Heath's approach might have seemed that of a brutally pragmatic modernizer. But he was as driven by idealism as his enemies, something that was still true of the rival tribes during the battles over Europe in the twenty-first century.

After the 1975 referendum, one of the politicians on the losing side, Neil Kinnock, told a meeting of journalists that 'Only an idiot would ignore or resent a majority like this . . . We're in for ever.' It took more than four decades, but another referendum would prove Kinnock wrong. And if we ask why the British people changed their minds so dramatically, or rather, who influenced them most, then the answer has to be none of the men so far brought into Europa's story, but a woman. The obvious woman. Margaret Thatcher. Although she had been dead for three years before that referendum campaign, and outside active politics for much longer than that, it was Thatcher's instincts – about money, democracy, immigration and the liberal elites – which carried the day. She was hugely influenced by Enoch Powell, but it was through her, and under her, that his ideas were transmitted.

She had begun as a fairly conventional supporter of Britain's membership of the European Community. This was partly loyalty to Heath, her boss. But in the early years of British membership,

Lord Mountbatten: the man who saved the Navy, and the flashiest new Elizabethan of them all.

A. K. Chesterton, fascist, empire loyalist and hugely influential racist.

The Aden Emergency, an anti-Imperial uprising that discomfited Whitehall.

The geeks will inherit the Earth: Clive Sinclair and his game-changing ZX Spectrum computer.

The Comet, an Elizabethan dream that fell to Earth.

Some Elizabethans were genuinely
world changing in their attitude
to man and other animals.
Gerald Durrell (top) and David
Attenborough (right) were quiet
revolutionaries. So was the
remarkable Anita Roddick (bottom).

John Lennon, Paul McCartney and Yoko Ono. Racism played its part in how many Beatles fans reacted to John's new love.

Foul-mouthed and properly moral – Bob Geldof at Live Aid.

A small woman with a
big vision: Jayaben Desai
at the Grunwick protests.

She reminded a hungry country that Europe was about much more than voting and bureaucrats: the great Elizabeth David.

David Lammy, Tottenham MP, remembers his friend the artist and Grenfell Tower victim Khadija Saye. Her photography was featured in the 'Breath is Invisible' public art project.

Bringing back the engineering spirit: Sir James Dyson.

From the marshes of Iraq, Queen of the Curves Zaha Hadid.

Director Ridley Scott on the set of *Alien* in 1979.

All of us together: Patrick Hutchinson carries a protester to safety during a Black Lives Matter confrontation.

Clapping for Carers.

Captain – now Sir – Tom, who aimed to raise £1,000 for the NHS but by the morning of his 100th birthday had surpassed £30 million.

she was in favour for the same reasons so many Conservatives gave. It was the era of the Cold War and Soviet Russia was a genuine threat: European democracy seemed a useful defensive barrier to communism. Second, with the Labour left rampant, the pro-market orthodoxies of continental countries seemed a way of limiting and constricting domestic socialist dreams. Third, British membership exposed British industry to the more dynamic and better-managed competition of continental companies: it was hoped that British managers and workers would be forced to take heed, becoming as productive as their rivals in Bavaria, northern Italy and the Netherlands. To mainstream Tories, Europe was the sensible choice.

So, in June 1975, Margaret Thatcher had herself knitted a hideous woolly jumper, with all the flags of the European nations displayed across her chest; and she called on the housewives of Britain to vote for Europe because 'In the Common Market we can be sure of having something in the larder.' In office during the 1980s, she changed her mind fundamentally. Her biographer Charles Moore has argued persuasively that she was never a really enthusiastic pro-European. Her shift of direction is however very important in the story of Elizabethan Britain. By becoming an ever more outspoken and articulate opponent of European Union, Mrs Thatcher led a vast swathe of the British press (the *Sun*, the *Daily Mail*, the *Express*) away from their earlier Tory Europeanism; and she gave her party as her legacy a guerrilla army of utterly committed, entirely relentless, anti-Brussels campaigners who would make the life of her successor John Major almost intolerable and would end up by taking over the party itself.

Without the inspiration of Margaret Thatcher's anti-integrationist beliefs, it seems most unlikely that this would have happened. Many of those credited, or blamed, for the vote to leave the EU in 2016, from Michael Gove and Boris Johnson inside the Conservative Party to Nigel Farage and Arron Banks outside it, had hailed her as their heroine, and self-consciously derived their hostility to Brussels from her. This is no small matter. How and why she shifted so dramatically is among the most important issues for anyone studying the Thatcher years.

The answer comes in three parts: it was about money; it was about culture; and it was about personalities.

Margaret Thatcher always took a profound economistic view of politics. Balancing the books was crucial. Waste was despicable. Soon after she had won her first landslide election victory, in November 1979, she found herself at a summit in Dublin with her fellow European leaders. On the other side of the table was the President of the Commission, her one-time ally in that referendum four years earlier, Roy Jenkins. This was the period of the most radical Thatcher budgets – taxes cut, public spending slashed back. Cash was very tight. She told one of her private secretaries before the summit: 'I get more and more disillusioned with the EEC. We are going to have a real fight over the budget and by one means or another we have to get our way. We need the money.'

The fight that followed at Dublin was remembered by nobody with much fondness. Jenkins recalled other Europeans describing Thatcher's lengthy and repetitive four-hour tirade, in which she kept insisting 'I want my money back' as the behaviour of a true grocer's daughter. The German Chancellor Helmut Schmidt pretended to fall asleep. The French President, Valéry Giscard d'Estaing, allegedly took refuge in a newspaper. Thatcher's case was strong. Although by head one of the poorer countries in Europe at the time, Britain was paying out contributions to Brussels second only to those of Germany. The British were being penalized for two virtuous things. British trade with the rest of the world was higher than that of most of the EC countries. And British agriculture was much more efficient and modern than the continent's, particularly that of France, whose farmers were given massive subsidies.

After another exceedingly difficult confrontation at the summit

in Strasbourg, when Mrs Thatcher kept arguing late into the afternoon, as the other leaders were desperate to get away for a grand
dinner and some good wine, she finally began to shift the debate
and started the process of getting 'my money back'. But a deep-
rooted suspicion took hold, which never left her, that behind the
grand rhetoric of European peace and reconciliation Brussels was a
giant subsidy machine designed to make life easy for those who
had first designed it. Arguments over money, however, are the very
stuff of politics, and generally get sorted out in the end.

Just as important was the culture clash between British politics,
the Westminster style, and the way power was handled in Brussels.
British politics, in the 1970s and just as much today, is adversarial,
aggressive, vivid and noisy. To be a Commons leader you have to
be fast with the put-down, have a brutal and unfair sense of humour
and drive arguments towards caricatured extremes before they are
resolved by vote. It is still a raucous political culture which would
be recognized by eighteenth-century political ranters. Benn, Powell
and Thatcher herself partly achieved their own positions by giving
no quarter in the bearpit of the House of Commons. Further, British
prime ministers are able to dominate their cabinets, should they
choose to do so, in a way that has no continental parallel. The
satirical 1980s television show *Spitting Image* famously showed the
Thatcher cabinet sitting round the table, she having ordered a steak.
'What about the vegetables?' asks the waitress. 'Oh, they will have
the same as me,' snaps Thatcher, glaring at the men around her.

The Brussels style could hardly have been more different. In the
interests of being 'good Europeans', the leaders gathered at EC
summits are supposed to defer to the agenda of the unelected
Commission officials, and to put the interests of their own elector-
ates second to the higher and nobler cause of European unity. Where
there are national differences, these should be deprecated and
smoothed away rather than tussled and argued over. Decision-
making is interminably slow, cautious and consensual. In a relatively

new organization composed of so many different countries, speaking so many different languages, this was to an extent inevitable. But it drove Margaret Thatcher mad with frustration and irritation.

Finally, and connected to this, there were serious clashes of personality. Thatcher never liked Giscard d'Estaing. Her first French President was a very grand centrist – descended not just from King Louis XV but also from Charlemagne – who had been born in Germany during the French occupation of the Rhineland. He had a languidly aristocratic demeanour and took the pomp of the French presidency extremely seriously, upsetting Margaret Thatcher, for instance, by requiring that he be served first at dinner. 'He is very *noble*,' she said drily afterwards, not meaning it as a compliment. She got on slightly better with his successor, the Socialist President François Mitterrand, who at least flirted with her, famously describing her as having 'the mouth of Marilyn Monroe and the eyes of Caligula'.

But she absolutely couldn't stand Schmidt's successor, the German Chancellor Helmut Kohl. She never understood his passionate concerns for German unity and European Union, born out of his wartime experiences. Fat, provincial and speaking only German, Kohl and his love of a pig-based diet horrified her. He, accused of falling asleep during meetings, had no time for her ferocious work ethic. Once, when she was on holiday near Salzburg in Austria, she found herself bored and suggested an impromptu policy discussion with Kohl, who was nearby, also on holiday. He told her that he was too busy: shortly afterwards, walking crossly in the street, she came across him sitting outside a tea house, eating a huge cream cake. 'My God! That man is so German!' she would say.

At one level, these things are trivial, mere political gossip, and yet when individual leaders don't get on on a personal basis, much else can unravel. As time went on, Margaret Thatcher became increasingly suspicious of the entire European project. Finally, in September 1988, she travelled to Bruges in Belgium to deliver a speech which would ricochet and resonate down the years in British politics. The beautiful medieval Flemish town had been carefully chosen – as Margaret Thatcher pointed out, the first book ever printed in English by William Caxton had been produced there; and Chaucer had been a frequent visitor. After insisting that Britain was a fully European country, which wanted to co-operate with her neighbours, Thatcher launched an unbridled attack on the central project of the EU, as it took on many of the characteristics of a state – flag, anthem, currency and the rest of it. She told modern Europe that:

> To try to suppress nationhood and concentrate power at the centre of a European conglomerate would be highly damaging and would jeopardise the objectives we seek to achieve.

Europe will be stronger precisely because it has France as France, Spain as Spain, Britain as Britain, each with its own customs, traditions and identity. It would be folly to try to fit them into some sort of identikit European personality . . . working more closely together does not require power to be centralised in Brussels or decisions to be taken by an appointed bureaucracy.

It was ironic, she said, that:

> just when those countries such as the Soviet Union, which have tried to run everything from the centre, are learning that success depends on dispersing power and decisions away from the centre, there are some in the Community who seem to want to move in the opposite direction. We have not successfully rolled back the frontiers of the state in Britain, only to see them re-imposed at a European level with a European super-state exercising a new dominance from Brussels.

This speech is worth remembering because it set in motion one of the most successful insurgent campaigns in modern British politics.

The anti-integrationist Bruges Group was formed the following February as a home for Tories hostile to Brussels and its project. As Margaret Thatcher's successor John Major struggled with the competing demands of deeper European integration and more profound scepticism about the project in his own party, Brugesites challenged and tried to frustrate him at every turn. After he had lost power, and the Brussels-enthusiastic Tony Blair became Prime Minister, Thatcherites continued to fight against the European dream.

In 1993, they founded the UK Independence Party. The following year, the financier Sir James Goldsmith founded the Referendum Party to campaign for a plebiscite on Britain's EU membership. More significantly than either of these, however, the number of anti-EU Tories grew and grew, to the point where, having been a small minority of 'swivel-eyed' obsessives, they were able to challenge David Cameron's leadership and persuade him to commit himself to what became the 2016 referendum. On the surface of British politics, and in the boardrooms of the British companies, it was unthinkable that the UK would not continue to be a member of the European Union, but in towns and villages all over the country, something entirely different was stirring. Europa was no longer wanted. And Margaret Thatcher was the Elizabethan most responsible for that.

38

THE ROAD TO BREXIT

Those roots of British Euroscepticism would break surface and rise as new growths during the 1990s and the first decades of the new century. The consequences of Margaret Thatcher dogged Major from 1990 onwards. He knew he was taking over a party with two mutually hostile traditions. On the one hand were those who believed that Britain could no longer wield great influence by herself but could not fail as part of Europe. As Major himself summed up their views: 'Narrow-minded nationalism should be cast aside; the Conservative Party was the party of Europe and should remain so.' On the other hand were those who argued that Britain had always been a proud, self-governing nation with a strong Parliament. 'Our history in the twentieth century', Major wrote, 'had been the polar opposite of our European neighbours: we had not been invaded, did not practise consensus politics, we traded around the world. We should not yield any more power from the British Parliament: it was not in our national self-interest to do so.'

What made John Major's task even harder was that on the continent there was a fresh drive for deeper integration. Under Jacques Delors, the European Commission was determined, at last, to lay deep foundations for a superstate, based on common social rules, a single currency, the euro and a common defence system. This came to a head in the Dutch border town of Maastricht in December 1991 when Britain seemed suddenly isolated. The timing, so close to the end of the Parliament, could not have been worse for the British Prime Minister.

At the time, the direction of European policy was a pathological source of division within the Conservative Party. 'The wounds from Margaret Thatcher's departure were still fresh, and showed little signs of healing,' Major wrote. Against the odds, working through the night and in a quiet triumph for British diplomatic persistence, he won opt-outs from the most objectionable parts of the new plan. He was briefly applauded as a hero by his MPs. Then the Thatcherite and Powellite anti-Brussels campaigners got to work to undermine him, fomenting endless Commons rebellions and rumours of plots to unseat him. In doing so they greatly eased the way for that most enthusiastic pro-European Tony Blair to succeed him in 1997.

Rebels as various as Richard Shepherd, the fastidious and independent-minded constitutionalist; John Biffen, a Powellite, and one of the most liked MPs in the House of Commons; the abrasive and outspoken Teresa Gorman; and Nick Budgen, who had inherited Enoch Powell's seat, essentially took the same view of British nationhood as Powell himself. Allied with others who were profoundly upset by Mrs Thatcher's departure, they were now determined to win over the Tory Party. It happened away from the cameras, by and large, in passionate conversations in Conservative associations all around the country. Powell might have been disgraced by the accusation of racism after his 'rivers of blood' speech, but his views on the nation had always been popular inside the Tory Party.

Although John Major was an opponent of Powell's speech, he was well aware that many in his local party in South London had liked it a lot. Now all over the country those local Tories, who regarded Margaret Thatcher as the greatest leader the party had had since 'Winston', began to mobilize. Discreet pressure was put on uncommitted MPs. Anti-Brussels candidates began to find it easier to be selected. Far away from Westminster, a quiet national rebellion was bubbling. William Hague was the first post-Thatcher Tory leader to embrace it. By the time David Cameron became leader in 2005, it was too late to put the fires out. He eventually conceded the idea of a national referendum on British membership of the EU after more than 100 Tory MPs had written to Downing Street, threatening to unseat him if he refused. Without Enoch Powell, without Margaret Thatcher, there might have been no such demand in the party and therefore, no Brexit referendum. Sometimes the biggest political achievements are posthumous.

39

BREXIT WARRIORS

There are many problems with referendums. They tend to be binary, but few serious problems are binary. The questions that fit neatly on a ballot paper tend to be too simple for the answers that, in the modern world, most questions require. This was even the case with such a simple-seeming question as whether or not Scotland should be an independent country. Did 'independent' mean independent of the European Union? What currency would this self-governing country require? Would an independent Scotland have a full and policed border with England?

As we now know, in the internet age referendums can also be manipulated by outsiders with deep pockets. Their appeal seems limited until one considers the one, very considerable advantage referendums have over ordinary parliamentary political contests. They summon outsiders. For a short time, the traditional political class loses its monopoly.

During Britain's 2016 EU referendum, there were many players who came from outside ordinary politics – business people, PR gurus, Arron Banks and Tony Blair's former communications chief, and author, Alastair Campbell. But there were two who stood out, and became etched in the public imagination, both of them attracting admiration and loathing from different quarters.

One was an investment manager and marketer. Gina Miller was widely described in the press as the most hated woman in Britain and faced multiple death and rape threats. She beat the government twice in the Supreme Court. Her first victory came in September 2017 when the court ruled that MPs should have a say over triggering Article 50 of the Treaty on European Union, which took Britain out. Her second came two years later when it ruled that Boris Johnson's decision to prorogue Parliament was unlawful. Both defeats changed the political weather and made life much harder for Leave politicians.

On the other side of both arguments was a Kentish cricket fanatic and former metals trader, seen by liberal Britain as the most dangerous populist in the country – Nigel Farage. Together their stories tell us a lot about the Britain which became embroiled in Brexit towards the end of the Queen's reign.

In their autobiographies, Miller and Farage are equally conventional in taking for granted that their early lives had a huge impact on what happened later. During Gina Miller's girlhood (she was born in 1965, in what was then, just, still British Guiana, now Guyana), children were more likely to experience old-fashioned British values in the former colonies than they were in the United Kingdom itself. Miller was the daughter of an impeccably dressed, charismatic Guyanese lawyer and a tough mother who had had to grow up fast, helping run a business after her own father was murdered. She was the disciplinarian in the family and dealt with her daughter's misbehaviour with a cane. Before being sent to a boarding school in England, Gina was taught in a traditional way: 'back in Guyana, I'd attended a very strict convent and was taught English with a precision that came from terrifying nuns. We had to learn pages of proverbs and compete in spelling bees.' At home, her formidably moral father regaled her with stories from court, after she had completed her chores: 'All of this meant that, from an early age, I was raised with a very strong notion of worth and value. My father instilled me with core values of equality, justice and fair play.'

After having to cope with the inevitable bullies at school and some bad relationships, Miller gave birth to and brought up a mentally handicapped daughter. Her inner toughness showed through repeatedly. After the breakdown of her second marriage, during which her husband had beaten her, she and her daughter struggled to live a normal life.

> It's a fault of mine that I can be very proud. I was too ashamed to ask other people for help. I tried to rent a flat for the two of us, but every time the estate agent wanted my permanent address, my bank account details, where I last lived. I didn't have anything because I had no paperwork. I had no documents. We stayed the odd night in a bed and breakfast. When I ran out of physical cash Lucy-Ann and I slept in the car, with all our possessions stuffed into a couple of bags in the boot. More than once, we slept in a multi-storey car park.

This was the 'entitled', smug and elitist woman later demonized by Brexiteers.

Trained in law, Miller spent much of her career in marketing before devoting herself, with her third husband, to campaigning against the misselling of financial products. In the City her victims called her 'the Black Widow Spider'. Among her earlier experiences, which she discussed during the MeToo era, were numerous acts of sexual harassment, including a rape during her student years. She was also frequently on the receiving end of racist taunts. We could say, in other words, that Miller's experiences were, sadly, not unusual for a black professional woman finding her own way in the Britain of the late twentieth century. Her brief autobiography brims, however, with self-certainty, assertions of the importance of standing up for oneself and an utter conviction in her own rightness.

On the surface, you could hardly find a more different story than that of her deadly foe Nigel Farage, the leader of the UK Independence Party through the Brexit storm. Exuding all the chirpy, cheerful certainties of a golf club saloon bar in the Home Counties, Farage is seen by his political enemies as a closet racist or at the very least an old-fashioned xenophobe. Like Gina Miller, however, he idolized his father, an alcoholic who dried himself out and rebuilt his career in the City, was strongly marked by early and traumatic family experiences, in particular his parents' divorce, and – like Miller – remembers blissful times rambling in the countryside away from all authority, though in his case it was rural Kent rather than steamy Guyana. He too got a lot of early rote-learning and, like Miller, was convinced early on of his own rightness. In his own words: 'I must have been a cocky little sod, sorely in need of challenging . . .'

After attending the elite Dulwich College in South London, where he misbehaved frequently, was always argumentative and fell under the spell of radical Tories including Enoch Powell and Keith Joseph, Farage became a metals trader in the City. As a white, upper-middle-class man he did not, of course, face either the unwanted sexual attention or the casual racism that Gina Miller faced, but Farage's earlier life wasn't without its complications. He was very nearly killed after stepping out, drunk, in front of a Volkswagen, and an aggressive testicular cancer convinced him that he was likely to die.

The parallels between Nigel Farage and Gina Miller may seem trivial. What they show is that two individuals who chose to take prominent and controversial roles on opposite sides of the most bitter political argument in modern British history had been toughened by early experiences, and were disciplined, strong minded, argumentative. More important, I would argue, is that they both harked back to a world of clearer and better rules.

Gina Miller's father introduced her early on to notions of fairness and equity, while her experience of racism and sexual harassment made her particularly alert to any illiberal shifts in the political weather. Nigel Farage grew up as a schoolboy in the political chaos of the 1970s. From an early stage, he had enjoyed attacking conventional wisdom, at that period dominated by the left – John Lennon's hugely popular song 'Imagine' with its dreamy peace-and-love message was a plinky-plonk sermon the teenage Farage particularly loathed. He was marinated in the male, golf- and cricket-fixated rules-are-there-to-be-broken atmosphere of the City during the wildest 'Big Bang' years. Although he joined the Tory Party, he found it a tedious organization and was never – like Gina Miller – a natural party-political loyalist.

And, in the strangest of strange turns, neither of them seems to have been, at first, terribly interested in the European Union. Gina Miller discusses EU issues only in passing in her autobiography: she is much more concerned with traditional British values, historical heroes such as the suffragettes and the British Victorian philanthropists, and with the absolute importance of standing up for yourself. She is critical of the political class. Sometimes, reading both their accounts of themselves, it can be hard to be sure which devoted enemy is which. Who is this? 'I'm never short of an opinion or six, so I said some typically politically incorrect things about how certain women held out as heroines of diversity are more like men in skirts . . .' No, not Nigel but Gina. And who is this? 'I think it's more useful to be independent because I don't have to pledge my allegiance to anyone. I don't have to join any club. I don't have to toe the party line. I'm free to speak where others fear to.' Again, Miller, not Farage. And which of them, explaining why they voted Green in the 1989 European elections, said: 'I am a green at heart. I firmly believe that we should all cultivate our own gardens and that the greatest danger comes from those so alienated as to be bent on saving the entire planet according to one philosophical or political prescription'? That's not Miller but muesli-munching Farage.

Farage has devoted his entire political career to getting Britain out of the EU, but judging by his writing his real concerns seem to be nearer to home. He shows a strong enthusiasm for the traditional British constitution, laws made under the Queen, imperial measurements and a belief in the importance of variety and distinction, of small platoons, not large regiments. As he puts it: 'The individual and his or her own community are best able to react appropriately to their own circumstances in accordance with their needs, priorities and conventions.' Without being needlessly provocative, it may be worth pointing out that Gina Miller doesn't seem a million miles away from this either.

When she took the UK government to court in the Article 50 battle, she insisted that her real concern was nothing to do, really, with the European Union: 'My point was that the rule of law had to be properly observed. Parliament is sovereign. You could not have a government rolling back our constitution and behaving in an authoritarian manner . . . Leaving the EU without a parliamentary vote would have been profoundly unconstitutional. In truth, I was seeking to defend our democratic process . . .'

So here we have two people who both believe that they are defending traditional British values, both passionate, tenacious and self-righteous, and both natural outsiders from the party-political system; and who end up on completely different sides in the biggest political choice modern Britain has had to make. Why? The more one reflects on Gina Miller's autobiography, the more clearly one sees a figure moulded by immigrant and female experiences during the Thatcher period, and the years afterwards. She was brought up, as were so many immigrants, on a rose-tinted and romantic notion of Britain, a country 'of fair play, tolerance, justice, civility and the rule of law'. Just as much as anyone in UKIP, she was brought up to be passionately Anglophile. Her mother collected royal-themed

Wedgwood china and the family listened to the BBC World Service every evening: 'My siblings and I grew up thinking Britain was the highest pinnacle of all that was best in the world. It stood for everything to which we most aspired. At school, I learned about Queen Victoria, Dickens and Shakespeare. I was taught to speak English with perfect grammar by British nuns: no "couldn't" or "wouldn't", it was always "could not" or "would not".'

But Gina Miller's adult life has been one long and distressing overturning of these illusions. She arrived in a sloppy-tongued country which sneered at her as an immigrant, in which she was constantly told that she wasn't up to this or that. From boarding school through university to City boardrooms, she felt disrespected. Far from being the world capital of morality and courtesy, she found Britain a place of slovenly professors and lazy, corrupt professionals, none of them living up to her immaculately turned-out and high-minded father.

She argues that societies can best be judged by what they teach their children: 'And what is it we are teaching our children? What are the lessons they are seeing in politics, media and in public debates? We are teaching them it's okay to lie, to cheat, to be irresponsible, to be misogynistic, to watch porn, to make up anything as you go along, to treat other people with disrespect, to be discriminatory.' Some of this, at least, she blames on the new technology of smartphones and endless internet browsing. Her campaign against the government's handling of Brexit was as much a demand for old ways of doing things, made by a cultural conservative, as it was a cry of rage about the rise in anti-immigrant and racist opinion which she blamed on the referendum campaign.

Nigel Farage is blamed by many people on her side of the argument for much of that. A wide range of opinion was angered by an anti-EU poster he unveiled during the referendum campaign, showing a curving queue of migrants coming towards the camera, a photograph originally taken in Slovenia, with the headline

'Breaking Point'. It was reported to the police as an act of racism. Against that, in the world of modern politics, when so much is recorded, and with such a garrulous, unstoppable speaker, it is noteworthy that no explicitly racist comments or speeches by Farage have ever emerged. So would it be fairer to say that, although once married to a German wife, a Frankfurt government bond broker called Kirsten Mehr, Farage is just an old-fashioned xenophobe?

No, he insists: he loves exploring the people and churches of the continent of Europe, and had Asian and Afro-Caribbean friends at school. No doubt he did. And yet, in 2013, a letter was published from a former Dulwich College teacher to its then head teacher in 1981, following the Brixton riots, arguing that the young Farage should not be made a prefect because of his 'publicly professed racist and fascist views'. She said also that he had once marched through a Sussex village singing Hitler Youth songs – a charge he later rejected as 'utterly untrue'.

Lacking documentary evidence and however hard we scrub, it is difficult to make a window into anyone's soul. But after years of reading his speeches and other writings, and listening to Nigel Farage both on the record and talking privately around television studios, it seems to me that he is driven mainly by a loathing of homogenization and bureaucracy. He seems motivated more by a dislike of the political class (influenced, perhaps, by his repeated failures to join their ranks at Westminster) and by a self-perception as the perennial upstart, telling truth to a bewildered establishment, than by an urgent dislike of brown or black or Polish fellow citizens. This writer has, for instance, also interviewed the leader of the French far right, Marine Le Pen: she is a much angrier and darker individual. Nigel Farage's greatest limitation is perhaps a radical lack of curiosity about or empathy for the experiences of so many black and Asian British people. Along with that goes a far too easy and self-congratulatory contempt for 'politically correct' feminists and others. In short, the impermeable and flushed self-confidence of the nineteenth hole or the dining room at Lord's cricket ground seems to be at the origin of this populist rebel.

As younger Britons, particularly university-educated ones living in the great cities, have become progressively more liberal, more ethnically mixed and more at home in a globalized shopping culture, so another Britain, throwing abuse and empty beer cans at the 'elites', has felt shunned, cut out and disorientated. At earlier periods in our history, the country was held together, even across warring classes, by a common patriotic pride in Britain's role in the world. Because of our confusions over Europe, our ambiguous feelings about our own imperial history and our lack of economic and military heft, we haven't been able to enjoy that unifying sensation of late. There remain genuinely excluded groups, noticed by the rest of the country only when there is some disaster to push them on to the front pages, such as, to use a phrase popularized during the coronavirus crisis – 'key workers'. But how can people be both key and marginal?

40

FROM BURNING TOWER TO HOSTILE ENVIRONMENT

The so-called Windrush scandal broke in 2018. Large numbers of Commonwealth citizens, mostly from the Caribbean, who had come to Britain entirely legally and worked all their lives here, paying taxes, suddenly found themselves accused of being illegal immigrants and facing deportation. It originated in a Conservative panic about sharply rising immigration numbers and the political threat from the UK Independence Party – the same threat that later led to the 'Breaking Point' posters.

The 2014 Immigration Act required that landlords rent only to those with a legal right to live in the UK. It attempted to block so-called health tourism, foreigners visiting to seek free care on the NHS. As with housing, the burden would now be on individuals to show documents justifying their right to be here. Nurses and doctors, along with the owners of flats, would be legally obliged to ask for, and check, documentation. That was not all. As the then Home Secretary, Theresa May, told the Commons in October 2013 when announcing the measure:

The Bill will also introduce new rules to crack down on illegal migrants accessing banking products and services in the UK . . . Having tackled the ability of illegal migrants to work, access health care, rent property and open bank accounts, I also want to ensure that illegal migrants are denied driving licences. The Bill will give legislative force to the current administrative practice, but the measures go further, giving us the power to revoke licences. We will do everything we can to make it harder for illegal migrants to establish a settled life in the UK when they have no right to be here.

The background to creating this 'hostile environment' was surging support for UKIP, which won twenty-four seats and more than 4 million votes in the May 2014 European parliamentary elections. Elections of MEPs to the EU Parliament were not normally considered either exciting or important, but this earthquake in Middle England shook David Cameron's Conservative Party to its core. The 2014 vote had been heavily influenced by hardening attitudes to immigration. The latest of the regular NatCen Social Research British Social Attitudes surveys found that nearly a quarter thought the main reason immigrants came to Britain was to claim benefits. It was a change in the weather. There was also a big fall in those who believed *legal* immigrants who were not British citizens should have equal legal rights. Nearly three-quarters of those surveyed said it was important to have been born in Britain to be considered British.

This growing hostility to immigration hadn't come out of the blue. The year 2013 had seen the highest number of migrants coming to Britain, well over 200,000. And from 2009 until 2013 the average number of people being granted British citizenship each year was 195,800. This wasn't primarily an EU issue: China, India, the United States and Australia were all among the most popular countries of origin. But the fact that free movement of peoples inside the EU meant that the British government was unable to control migration from other European countries made it politically toxic.

There was a second, mostly subterranean connection. Residual racial hostility to black Britons, and growing hostility to radical Islam, fuelled by a series of terror attacks in London, Manchester and elsewhere, turned many British people against all immigration. White British people voting against the EU because they didn't like the scale of social and cultural change that Caribbean and Asian immigration had brought to Britain, were joined by black British voters who were being promised – to put it brutally – that leaving the EU would result in fewer poor white Europeans turning up.

The inability of the British government to limit immigration while inside the EU, and profound scepticism about the ability of the Home Office to manage Britain's borders generally, were behind Theresa May's aggressive new law. The idea, which had originated inside the Home Office as early as 2009, was to make life so difficult for illegal immigrants that they would decide to go home and, in the official phrase, 'self-deport'. All of this was done frankly, and openly, and with the support of all but a few MPs (one of them being the future Labour leader Jeremy Corbyn). Mrs May herself explained: 'The aim is to create, here in Britain, a really hostile environment for illegal immigrants.' This would protect the Tories from insurrectionist challenges.

Advertising vans were sent around London boroughs bearing the rubric 'In the UK illegally?' and the instruction 'Go home – or face arrest'. As the debates around the 2014 Act make clear, these measures, meant to mess up the lives of illegal immigrants, were dressed up in the language of technical improvements to 'chaotic' previous regimes. The Home Office had not proved a particularly adept organization. Since Britain had no form of national identity cards, it was difficult to count and track individuals. But in 2018, by which time she was Prime Minister after the fall of David Cameron, Theresa May's chickens came home, very loudly, to roost.

On 14 June 2017, a hideous fire shocked the nation and made many people think again about disparities in wealth, and about how decently many British people of colour were being housed. Grenfell Tower, in a poor area of Kensington and Chelsea, one of Britain's richest boroughs, suddenly erupted in a blaze which appeared to be spread by its outer cladding. It killed seventy-two people, with a further seventy-four being hospitalized. The survivors, their friends and supporters blamed the council for the poor quality of the building work, and the Conservative government for years of cuts which had left so many people vulnerable.

Although this wasn't fundamentally a story about race, in Britain membership of an ethnic minority and poverty very often go together. At Grenfell, many of those who died were Muslim, or black, or refugees. Theresa May went to listen to the Grenfell families, which took some courage. She was shouted at, expressed deep sorrow and heard them out. The anger was not surprising. Grenfell was a man-made disaster caused by years of cheeseparing savings in government expenditure, incoherent housing policy and lack of interest in the black and Muslim people who find themselves at the bottom of the economic pile.

The 'Windrush generation' is a vague phrase. It doesn't refer specifically to those Caribbean immigrants who arrived on the ship of that name in June 1948, but applies more generally to Commonwealth immigrants who came to the UK during the 1950s and indeed right up to 1973, when restrictive laws effectively ended Commonwealth immigration, except for some family members and holders of work permits. Nearly half a century later, Mrs May's government told people who had arrived before 1973 that they had to prove their right to be in Britain, and simultaneously targeted the children of the first immigrants.

At a time when much government bureaucracy was being outsourced to private companies, people who had thought themselves entirely British began to receive letters from a company called Capita telling them that they had no right to be in the UK. According to a study by Oxford University, some 57,000 people were affected by the change of policy, of whom 15,000 were originally from Jamaica, 13,000 from India and some 29,000 from Pakistan and Africa. Amber Rudd, Mrs May's successor as Home Secretary, was forced to resign after it emerged that there had been a hidden Home Office target system for deportations, despite what she had told MPs. Later, she was exonerated: she had been misled by her own officials.

This was not, however, fundamentally a story about rules and records, though physical landing cards, essential for people to prove their arrival, had been destroyed by officials. It was the intentional exclusionary policy of an incompetent state machine whose political masters were panicking about opinion polls. It produced a flood of sad, sometimes heartbreaking, human stories. As people were reclassified as illegal immigrants, thanks to the hostile environment policy described above, their lives quickly became almost intolerable. Elderly people, who had worked hard in this country all of their lives, were thrown out of their accommodation, lost their jobs, lost their rights to benefit and found themselves sleeping on sofas in relatives' houses, or with friends, or even living on the street.

The Labour MP for Tottenham, David Lammy, spoke of breaking down in tears after constituency surgeries where he met people who had been driven, remarkably quickly, into a shadowy underground life. Many were deeply depressed, and some were suicidal. From the other side of the political spectrum, the newly appointed Home Secretary Sajid Javid, whose parents came to Britain from Pakistan in the 1960s, announced that he was horrified by what had happened: 'It could have been me, my mum or my dad.' An investigation he ordered suggested that sixty-three members of the Windrush generation might have been wrongly and indeed perhaps illegally deported before a halt was called. It is all too easy, however, to discuss policy failures in abstract terms and fail to focus on the individual tragedies they produce.

41

KHADIJA SAYE

As these debates about race and immigration boiled over, at least one young British woman was having the time of her life. In 2017, aged only twenty-four, Khadija Saye, the daughter of two Gambian migrants to Britain, had made it as a global artist. She had been chosen for the new Diaspora Pavilion at the prestigious Venice Biennale, the festival where artists from around the world, championed by their home countries, are paraded in front of international gallerists and buyers. In a crumbling, grand old Venetian palazzo wedged between two small canals Saye's mysterious, smoky photographic portraits on tin, interrogating issues of identity and origin, had delighted critics and were selling well. 'At last I can say it. I'm an artist,' she would repeat, grinning broadly.

In so many ways, Khadija Saye was a living symbol of what was going right with immigration in Britain in the new century. She had been a flamboyant child, growing up in West London's Ladbroke Grove, and had been educated at a Roman Catholic girls' school before winning a prestigious scholarship to the private boarding school Rugby when she was fourteen. She found Rugby a culture shock, standing outside the 'you can do anything you want' assumptions of the more entitled pupils. But this modest example of social engineering worked well for Khadija. She had always loved photography and with the help of supportive teachers she went on to take a degree at the University for the Creative Arts in Farnham.

Successful artists need great skill and determination but, perhaps even more than that, they need a subject – something that drives them forward, and interests others. Khadija Saye had a subject. She was a young African woman in mostly white West London. Because her father was Muslim and her mother Christian, she attended both mosque and church, so she found herself at a crossroads of faith and culture. She became fascinated by her Gambian origins, and started to create self-portraits in which she posed herself in different costumes and holding an array of intriguing objects. The Venice exhibition of her 2017 photos was entitled *Dwellings: in this space we breathe* and was genuinely moving and eerie. Saye's pictures combined the archaic look of explorers' and anthropologists' photographs from the nineteenth century with the sensibility of twentieth-century surrealism, the world of Dalí and Man Ray.

This hybrid way of looking won over viewers. Horizons began to open for her. Saye's mentor was the British portrait artist Nicola Green who had painted, among others, the Pope and Barack Obama and was a personal friend of the supermodel Elle Macpherson. (Art collides worlds: Green was also married to David Lammy.) At her Venice show, Khalida was sharing exhibition space with really big, established artists such as the Nigerian-British Yinka Shonibare, who made dazzling sculptures using African textile designs and whose replica of Nelson's ship in a bottle had recently set sail from one of the plinths in Trafalgar Square. If there was anywhere where the bright, intriguing contradictions and celebrations of modern British multiculturalism could be displayed, here it was. Khalida was greatly looking forward to taking her mother, Mary Mendy, to see the Venice show. The two women lived together. Where? High up on the twentieth floor of a popular housing block overlooking the Westway road as it snakes into central London. It was called Grenfell Tower.

Then came 14 June 2017. Among those who died so horribly were the promising artist and her mother. The Grenfell disaster was not 'caused by racism', as was made clear by the official report, finally published on the day before Britain had been due to leave the European Union, 31 October 2019. It was a complicated story of financial cuts, short cuts by contractors and poor management. But because of the identity of so many of those who died, it can never be entirely disconnected from the wider story of race in Britain in the twenty-first century – the prosperity, political power and security of poorer new Britons.

During the 2012 London Olympics celebrations, Britain had presented herself to the rest of the world as a happily, warmly and securely multiracial and multicultural society – and had patted herself on the back for it with noisy self-congratulation. Six years on, Britain seemed a very different country. Was the change in any way connected to leaving the EU? The United Nations appeared to think so. In May 2018 its special rapporteur on racism, a Zambian-born Californian law professor, E. Tendayi Achiume, said she thought the environment before, during and after the 2016 referendum:

> has made racial and ethnic minorities more vulnerable to racial discrimination and intolerance . . . Many with whom I consulted highlighted the growth in volume and acceptability of xenophobic discourses on migration, and on foreign nationals including refugees in social and print media . . . The harsh reality is race, ethnicity, religion, gender, disability status and related categories all continue to determine the life chances and wellbeing of people in Britain in ways that are unacceptable and, in many cases, unlawful.

This verdict outraged many. Was this simply one multinational organization supporting another? Commentators and politicians pointed out that the professor had spent only eleven days here. But it was embarrassing. The judgement came at a time of alarm about the treatment of EU nationals here and when young black children were suffering from an epidemic of knife crime.

It was followed by a very different multicultural moment, the wedding of Prince Harry to Meghan Markle, a divorced, mixed-race American television actress. The ceremony was optimistically said to demonstrate the new, genuinely inclusive Britain of the twenty-first century. In the jewelled late-medieval casket of the chapel at Windsor Castle, a British gospel choir belted out an American pop song. Bishop Michael Curry, the African-American presiding head of the American Episcopal Church, gave a thrilling sermon, quoting Martin Luther King on the power of love and telling the new couple to follow the message of American slaves: 'They sang a spiritual, even in the midst of their captivity. It's one that says "There is a balm in Gilead . . ." – a healing balm, something that can make things right. "There is a balm in Gilead to make the wounded whole, there is a balm in Gilead to heal the sin-sick soul."' After this address, which left the Queen and the Duke of Edinburgh looking quizzical at best, a young black British cellist serenaded the mixed crowd in St George's Chapel.

If this seemed a new dawn in British race relations it was a false one. Harry and Meghan tangled with the famously prickly and intrusive British media, did not enjoy the grind of royal duties and effectively removed themselves from the royal family, decamping to start a new life with their child in Canada, then in California.

Far away from them, at around the same time, another black British campaigner discovered for himself just how conflicted parts of Britain still were about race. Trevor Phillips, the youngest of ten children born to parents from British Guiana, in North London in 1950, rose through the National Union of Students and a television career to become one of the best-known voices of the British left. As Chairman of the Equality and Human Rights Commission, he became increasingly worried about multiculturalism as a philosophy, creating divisions between communities rather than a single, equal national community. This, and his robust defence of free speech against charges of Islamophobia, put Phillips on a collision course with parts of the British left. Following their defeat in the 2019 general election, Labour leftists tried to throw one of Britain's best-known activists for equal rights out of their party.

So which is the real Britain of the twenty-first century? The country in which black and Asian citizens survive in shoddy housing and risk death in consequence, and where others live in fear of deportation, despite years of hard work and paying tax? Or the country of the Windsor Castle wedding? To answer 'both' would be meaninglessly glib. The truth is that, towards the end of the Queen's reign, the nature of the attitude of the majority to non-white British communities was still being vigorously fought over.

We just don't know what kind of country we are, in that respect. The liberal optimism of the Blair years, during which the essence of Britishness came close to being boiled down to a bland assertion of 'tolerance' (always far too easy) no longer feels right. But this just brings us back to business-as-usual during the Elizabethan years. From the League of Empire Loyalists to Rock Against Racism, questions of race and belonging have never been finally decided. If there is a genuinely tolerant and successful multiracial Britain some-where in the future, the journey towards it is a long and twisting one, with many blind corners.

During Britain's negotiations to leave the European Union some people seemed to give up on their country. They decided that the Brexit vote revealed Britain to be fundamentally xenophobic, mean-minded and arrogantly deluded about her own past. But a country doesn't change so quickly. Political events, whether the rise of New Labour or the Brexit vote, are more like searchlights playing across the scumbled surface of a gouged and craggy landscape. At each pass some facets of Britishness are highlighted and exaggerated in the passing gleam. Then the light bounces in from a different direction and everything seems completely different.

The truth is that demography and immigration are altering us for ever. Big, unstoppable world forces, including our own imperial history, are making Britain a much more ethnically mingled country. That will continue, more or less despite the EU. In general, younger Britons, many of them in relationships with people from other cultures, are more relaxed about this change. Many older people, hugging the warm memories of youth, often find such changes threatening. And the years pass and the balance shifts. Whether you choose to accentuate the relatively welcoming atmosphere of multicultural Britain, or whether you highlight a panicky anger about immigration, you are describing exactly the same country – one which has altered its make-up at an unprecedented speed and, so far, without serious violence. And if we are to have a tolerable future, we now have no alternative but to learn to live as brothers and sisters with people of other faiths and distant origins.

Part Three

—◆—

ELIZABETHANS AT WORK

42

DIDN'T WE DO WELL?

W hy couldn't we have the lavishly funded welfare state and NHS, and really well-built, safe, comfortable council housing, that political leaders dreamed of in 1945? Was it really down to incompetent planners or bureaucratic wreckers? Why, as the old Empire declined, couldn't we be a powerful, major force in the world, a counterweight to the United States and to Russia, with an awe-inspiring military presence and a big, influence-buying system of trade and aid to project our power? Was that because of random political mistakes, from Suez to Iraq? Was it because Whitehall was crippled by a mixture of colonial guilt and political correctness? Or perhaps because we no longer wanted to be a big force in the world, and were happier looking after ourselves?

In each case, the answer is no. It was about money. We were unable, during the reign of Queen Elizabeth II, to have the country people dreamed of in 1952 because we were never rich enough. We had ingenuity and creativity. We had brilliant scientists and engineers. We had cultural titans and fast-thinking entrepreneurs. We won many Nobel prizes. The British invented jet engines, hovercraft, much of the technology behind the computer age and novel, potentially world-changing materials and vaccines. During the Queen's reign, British creativity included musical innovation, from Benjamin Britten to the Beatles; globally famous artists from Henry Moore to David Hockney; new forms of finance and banking; and two discoverers of DNA, Francis Crick and Rosalind Franklin. Brilliant examples of British industrial design ranged from Robin Day's polypropylene chair and the Alec Issigonis Mini to Mary Quant's mini-skirt, Concorde under Sir James Hamilton, the Harrier Jump Jet and the Dyson family of cleaners and dryers.

Yet, despite all this, British industry was unable to make and sell enough products that were reliable enough, at the right price, to buy the British people the power and the domestic affluence they believed they deserved. If you want a single explanation for why New Jerusalem was never fully built and Greater Britain never reached its hands around the world then, reader, this is it.

Let us not overdo the self-flagellation. At the time of writing, Britain is the sixth largest economy in the world and her per capita GDP (perhaps the most useful of these kind of statistics) has the British about level-pegging with the French and not very far behind Germany. After coronavirus, we are all going down together, but Britain does not seem a peculiarly incompetent outlier. For all the dire warnings about the consequences of leaving the EU – those remain to be proven or disproven – the British financial sector remains one of the world's key hubs and, thanks to a weaker pound, in the immediate aftermath of the referendum, British manufacturing exports grew faster than for many years.

'Declinism' is an unseemly relish for believing that your country has been entirely taken over by the dogs. But it's all about perspective. When the Queen came to her throne, the British felt themselves a dominant global power, blessed by history and with a glittering, gold-plated future ahead. Being a little bit behind the Germans by the twenty-first century would then have seemed humiliating. Yet much of what has happened is merely the process of aligning unrealistic dreams with unremarkable realities.

What are we comparing? British productivity growth in the Victorian period was remarkable, but only because the Industrial Revolution and the tariff walls around the Empire had given the British a unique and one-off historical advantage. It was an unrepeatable special offer. Today, productivity remains a problem, yet the biggest gap in the world is not between Britain and her rivals, but between the advanced industrial nations of the West and the hungry rising powers of Asia. And since productivity is now so much about technological upgrading, in the age of robotics and automation many of the old truths about productivity growth can be upended in the blink of an eye.

All of that said, there is almost nobody who looks at the performance of the British economy from the 1950s until today who would not agree that the story has been disappointing. As the naturally bearish Chancellor of the Exchequer in Theresa May's government, Philip Hammond, put it: 'The productivity gap is well known, but shocking nonetheless. It takes a German worker four days to produce what we make in five, which means, in turn, that too many British workers work longer hours for lower pay than their counterparts.' This is almost exactly what overseas commentators were saying about Britain in the mid-1970s, except that then the gap between British workers and German, or American, or Japanese was even greater.

The reasons for it have been debated for years but certainly include weak industrial financing arrangements, low investment by both the private and the public sectors and poor labour relations. In the final part of this history, I want to focus on how we have (and haven't) 'earned our bread', but also to move beyond the familiar territory of metal-bashing exporters and wildcat strikes to look at British creativity and influence in some less expected areas.

For there is no going back – not to a world of massive factories employing thousands of well-drilled people, nor to a Britain which had such a technological lead over the rest of the world that it could dominate countries around the globe which were lagging in science and technology. That's all over. By moving away from it, we also change the way we live at home. Along with heavy industrial Britain, and military Britain, we have lost a largely masculine public climate, with its own disciplines, rituals and culture. In its place, we have seen a growth of casual gig-economy work, of call centres and retail parks often staffed by recent immigrants, though now we can see that version of Britain, in turn, being pushed aside by automation.

The more we stick to old ways of thinking about work and economics, the easier it is to become thoroughly depressed. But flowers and bushes have been blooming on the wastelands. A surge of small businesses, gaining ground in niche markets; a growth of cultural exports; the continued success of services; all these things, outside the clichéd representation of work as a mass, routinized activity imposed by capital on under-educated workers, are changing the shape of modern Britain. And that means that our influence is changing shape too. If a country, for instance, has a significant impact on global attitudes to wildlife or pollution or reshapes a part of youth culture (think of K-pop or Bollywood), then that may matter just as much as the power of its military or its voting in international bodies.

43

'HOUSES AND MEAT AND NOT BEING SCUPPERED'

So let's return, one final time, to Britain at the beginning of the reign. Riffle through *The Times* newspaper and it quickly becomes clear that in 1952 the British were quite close to bankruptcy. On 8 January, the paper warned its readers of plunging gold and dollar reserves across the sterling area, and predicted 'total disaster' after the worst crisis the pound had faced since the war. As things stood, 'it would be about nine months at this rate before the reserves were exhausted to their last bar of gold . . . The price of bread would be settled not in Whitehall but in New York, Paris and Zürich.' (Telling, isn't it, that the price of bread was thought to be properly set in Whitehall at all?) *The Times* then casually disposed of its own readers as if pampered children: the British 'persuade themselves that in the end something – whether American aid, another devaluation, credits from Europe or elsewhere, or a sale of foreign investments – will turn up to stave off the evil day. They are deceiving themselves.'

Winston Churchill's Tories had beaten off Clement Attlee's Labour Party the year before, in the general election of 1951, but had inherited an economic crisis triggered by the huge cost of rearmament for Korea – the first major shooting war with the communist world. Britain was spending on guns, not butter (which was still in short supply). Churchill made R. A. Butler, his Education Minister during the Second World War, the new Chancellor. But in classic Churchillian language, he had warned Butler to go easy on the working classes: 'In this crisis of our island life, when the cottage homes could so easily be engulfed in penury and want, we must not allow class or party feeling to be needlessly inflamed.' Churchill had summed up his government's overall policy in refreshingly direct terms as 'houses and meat and not being scuppered'.

But not being scuppered was difficult. Rearmament for Korea, and the huge building programme to replace all those homes destroyed by the Luftwaffe, was barely affordable. Britain was already importing too much. This was a hungry country and Britain was not exporting enough to pay the cost of food, industrial machinery and wartime loans. What could be done?

Butler met the head of the civil service, Edward Bridges, and his private secretary William Armstrong. They ate a dispiriting lunch in the grandly gloomy setting of the Athenaeum Club. 'Their story was of blood draining from the system,' Butler said in his memoirs, 'and a collapse greater than had been foretold in 1931. I returned home in sombre anticipation of what was to be dished up to me . . .' Like the editors of *The Times*, Britain's senior civil servants and leading politicians thought that the evil day could not be staved off for very much longer.

If Butler's lunch had been grim, what he was then obliged to dish up to the country was even less attractive. His budget would attempt to deal with the trade imbalance by slashing imports and forcing the country to export more. Today it's almost incredible to imagine a government ordering British companies only to sell a certain amount of their products to British people, but that is exactly what Butler did. By the end of January, just before the death of King George VI, *The Times* was reporting that 'home deliveries' of foods, clothing, furniture, motorcycles, toys, carpets, washing machines, television sets, bicycles, lorries and cars were all to be cut by a sixth; and that the travel allowance – the amount of money British people were allowed to carry abroad on holiday or business – was to be cut to £25.

Even Churchill found Butler's determination to export more, and to import less, admirable in theory but very hard in practice. He complained bitterly to his Chancellor that his old friend the statesman Édouard Daladier feared losing his seat in the French Parliament because of Butler's 'brutal' ban on the importation to Britain of glacé cherries.

Yet in the end the hysterical Cassandras were wrong, and this tough medicine began to turn Britain's weak economy around. Britain in 1952 was, after all, still a world workshop. The pages of *The Times* are also full of proud announcements of new engineering successes, from Britain's first twin-engine helicopter, the Bristol 173, making its maiden flight at Filton, to new airliners and the first all-British gas-turbine locomotive, being built by Metropolitan-Vickers of Trafford Park, Manchester. There are adverts for fine-looking cars made in Britain – Lanchesters, the Humber Super Snipe, the Wolsley 4/50, Rolls-Royces and Daimlers. It might be difficult for the British actually to get their hands on these sleek beasts, but they were still being designed, and being built, in Britain.

Even more striking is how much military hardware was also home-made. The RAF were getting their first ever jet bombers, Canberras, built by A. V. Roe, Handley Page, Short Brothers and English Electric – all home companies. Another, Hawker Siddeley, was delivering its stubby new jet fighter, which was beating world speed records. Churchill had great hopes of exporting the new model of the wartime Centurion tank, and indeed 800 of the lumbering monsters were bought by the United States – and then passed on to help rearm Denmark. In technological terms, the new Elizabethan age began with throaty, oily bass roar.

And the sound carried beyond aircraft and cars. Those industrial giants the General Electric Company (GEC) and Imperial Chemical Industries (ICI) were developing new drugs and fabrics in the English Midlands. Although competition from European yards and from Japan was just visible, a smudge of smoke on a distant horizon, the shipyards of the Clyde and the Tyne were welding and hammering out great merchant vessels. The skies above London, Glasgow, Belfast, Cardiff and the great industrial cities of the English North and Midlands were still thick with coalsmoke and the scent of oil, while the streets resounded with the muffled clank of machinery, albeit much of it of Victorian vintage.

Overall, at the start of the Queen's reign, manufacturing still accounted for a third of everything that Britain produced. (It's around 12 per cent today.) Despite the Luftwaffe, in 1952 Britain turned out a quarter of all the world's manufacturing exports. (It's around 2 per cent today.) Around four in ten of all British workers were employed in manufacturing.

Of course, we should not make a fetish of manufacturing. People can earn their bread in many different ways, and more enjoyable ways, in the modern world. But manufacturing had shaped the look, sound, smell and social structure of the country for more than a century. The world of factory work disciplined generations of British men, toiling on hot and dangerous production lines under the watchful eyes of their managers and shop stewards. If we were a more sinewy, disciplined people in the 1950s, this is partly why.

44

CATHODE TUBES AND ISOTOPES: NEW WAYS OF MAKING

B ut, despite the smokestack industries, we should not make the mistake of thinking that Britain in the 1950s was one sprawling industrial museum. Freddie Williams and Tom Kilburn were respectively Lancashire and Yorkshire grammar school boys whose mathematical brilliance had allowed them to play a major role in the development of radar during the Second World War. By the time of the death of King George VI, they had developed one of the world's first commercial computers at Manchester University, the Ferranti Mark 1, as well as an early method of storing memory using a cathode tube.

They were a relatively quiet, conventional pair, which may have cost them the level of posthumous fame enjoyed by, for instance, the tragic codebreaker Alan Turing, whose top-secret Bletchley Park Colossus machine had been destroyed on the orders of Whitehall as soon as the war was won. Williams and Kilburn preferred to stay close to home in Manchester. Kilburn holidayed in Blackpool and always returned for the first Manchester United game of the season. But their achievement was immense. For a while they put Manchester at the global forefront of the mysterious new world of computing. It is true that, at about the same time, the much larger IBM team in the United States were producing their first mainframe computers, but it wasn't clear who would win. Upgraded versions of the Ferranti sold in their scores during the 1950s. By 1962 the British company's Atlas computer was said to be the world's most powerful.

A similar go-ahead story could be told about the early nuclear industry. Calder Hall was the world's first commercial nuclear power station, supplying energy to the National Grid. It was opened by the Queen in August 1956. Constructed at the small Cumberland village of Sellafield, where during the war a high-explosive factory had been sited, it had been built by 5,000 workers employed by British engineering companies and construction firms such as Babcock and Wilcox and Taylor Woodrow – and it depended upon another British company, Parsons, for its turbines. Right across Britain, there was vast optimism about the coming 'new atomic age'.

Calder Hall, using magnesium alloy fuel containers, known as a Magnox power station, was supposed to produce electricity so cheap nobody would need meters – electricity for British households would become, to all intents and purposes, free. In fact, Calder Hall supplied relatively puny amounts of power to the grid and its true purpose was to support Britain's atomic warfare programme. But at the time it seemed another example of British imagination and technical skill. The much larger nuclear programmes of the Soviet Union and the United States had failed to produce any domestic electricity.

The Queen herself was cautious. As so often, she looked for a moral, telling the assembled dignitaries:

This new power, which has proved itself to be such a terrifying weapon of destruction, is harnessed for the first time for the common good of our community. A grave responsibility is placed upon all of us to see that man adds as much to his stature by the application of this new power as he has by its discovery. Future generations will judge us, above all else, by the way in which we use these limitless opportunities.

In all her long reign, the Queen has never spoken more wisely. What she could not know is that a mere fourteen months after she had made her cautious and cautionary speech, on 10 October 1957, Britain suffered her worst nuclear accident ever, just across the River Calder, at the Windscale nuclear piles. Windscale had been developed because immediately after the war the US government had passed the McMahon Act forbidding the sharing of nuclear secrets with any other countries, including Britain (which had provided many of the scientists used in the Manhattan Project). So during the early 1950s, with both Labour and Tory leaders determined to stay in the nuclear race, Windscale, which had been an old munitions plant, was used to produce Britain's first home-made hydrogen bombs.

The British had been greatly helped by information provided by Klaus Fuchs, the German theoretical scientist who had fled as a refugee to Britain in 1933. Later, he became the most effective Russian spy to infiltrate the nuclear programme at Los Alamos. But he also provided essential data to Britain. In 1957, the team of scientists at Windscale was under enormous pressure from the Prime Minister Harold Macmillan to produce plutonium for Britain's new bombs. In October, after a misguided attempt to speed up the process, a fire erupted in one of the nuclear piles. After a last-ditch attempt to use ordinary hoses to douse the nuclear inferno, Britain narrowly escaped an explosion on the scale of the Soviet disaster at Chernobyl. Nevertheless, a huge cloud of smoke containing radioactive isotopes floated gently across south-east England, before crossing the Channel and reaching Germany and Norway.

At the time, the British government launched a highly effective cover-up, claiming that the 'smoke' was harmless and had anyway blown in the other direction, safely out to sea. The radioactivity fell silently in streets, schools and factories across most of England. Many years later, it turned out that the radioactive cloud also contained polonium-210, the same extremely radioactive ingredient later used to kill the Russian Alexander Litvinenko, when his tea was spiked with it in a London hotel in 2006. The use of polonium-210 to kickstart the chain reactions for British bombs was a state secret at the time.

By the 1980s, the National Radiological Protection Board, which had previously estimated the death toll from the undetected nuclear cloud at around thirteen people, upped its assessment to a few dozen extra deaths at most. However, according to a statistician and anti-nuclear activist, John Urquhart, who discovered the release, because of the high radiological risks of polonium the cloud was dangerous enough to have killed around a thousand people across Britain. The writer on nuclear history Fred Pearce quoted Macmillan's grandson, Lord Stockton, who said his grandfather 'covered it up, plain and simple'. Pearce went on: 'the Atomic Energy Authority supported the cover-up on the grounds that, as its minutes explained, to tell the truth about the fire would "shake public confidence" and "provide ammunition for those who had doubts about the development and future of nuclear power"'. Which, on the basis of her speech a year earlier at Calder Hall, perhaps included the Queen.

45

CRASH! SIR GEOFFREY DE HAVILLAND

A further example of excessive British industrial optimism in the early 1950s comes from another 'first' – the world's first passenger jet airliner, the de Havilland Comet, which took to the air in 1949 and was built at Hatfield in Hertfordshire. At the time, all passenger aircraft were propeller driven. They were slow, noisy and uncomfortable. The assumption in the huge US aircraft industry was that jet engines gave too little thrust for the amount of fuel they needed for long journeys to be practicable. De Havilland got around the problem by making their new jets fly much higher, at around 40,000 feet, than their turboprop rivals. Higher flight meant thinner air, which meant greater efficiency.

The Comet, with its turbojet engines embedded in swept-back wings, looked unlike anything else then flying. It could carry people much more quickly to Africa, Asia and Australia – and later across the Atlantic too. When it arrived, it seemed to give Britain a sudden and dramatic advantage over the previously dominant American aero industry which had emerged from the Second World War. The Comet was a one-off design-engineering feat, essentially an entirely new aircraft, and it seemed a perfect example of British engineering genius.

The Comet had been the passion project of one of the most remarkable engineers of Edwardian and early twentieth-century Britain – Sir Geoffrey de Havilland. A vicar's son from Buckinghamshire, he was a pioneer in the Edwardian car industry before moving to aircraft, building his first flying machine in 1909. He designed more aircraft, and sold them to the Royal Flying Corps during the First World War, when he served as a pilot after teaching himself how to fly one of his own designs. During the 1920s and 1930s, he built up his own company and continued to produce new planes. He believed that Britain could have had jet fighters for the Second World War, although during that conflict de Havilland did provide the RAF with one of its most successful ever fighter-bombers, the Mosquito.

De Havilland carried on flying into his seventies, and indeed his company just missed getting its jet fighter, the Vampire, into wartime service. Meanwhile, Sir Geoffrey sat on the key committee tasked with deciding what kind of airliners Britain and her Empire might need when the conflict was over. Against a lot of official opposition, he fought for a jet airliner – the Comet. He used his privileged position to badger insistently, but in deepest official secrecy, for a radical new direction in British aeronautics; and it would be his plane, with his engines, that would make the breakthrough. Sir Geoffrey was intensely proud of it.

The Comet was highly advanced, its fuselage made from new alloys. Flying so high, the planes had to be pressurized, which meant more stress. With four engines, it was much quieter and smoother than previous long-distance air travel had been; and using large square windows and relatively few seats, it felt spacious, even luxurious, inside. On 30 June 1953, Sir Geoffrey hosted the Queen, Princess Margaret and the Queen Mother on the Comet's inaugural flight. There was huge optimism, and later the same year the British Overseas Aircraft Corporation (BOAC) was flying eight Comets a week from London to South Africa, Tokyo, Singapore and South

America. In its first year, the plane carried 30,000 passengers. Orders for Comets arrived from France, Japan, Air India and the United States.

Tragically, the plane was too experimental. There was a series of crashes on takeoff, and then two Comets broke up in mid-flight and were completely destroyed. Metal fatigue caused by pressurization and the long flights, it seemed, had opened up cracks around those attractive square windows. The planes simply blew apart. It is often argued that it was the squareness of the windows that caused the problem, but this is not so: the problem was more to do with the system of riveting, which put excessive stress on the edges of the windows.

As the writer Nicholas Comfort has pointed out, the aircraft, although sleek and modern looking, had been built in a very old-fashioned way: 'Like the excellent aircraft that had won the war in the air, the Comet and other post-war British planes were designed by engineers with slide rules working in imperial measure . . . Engineers noted that no two of the airframes had exactly the same dimensions.'

The story of the Comet would go on for a long time. Eventually new and safer versions were sold, but they had limited commercial success. The early crashes and the Comet's withdrawal from service gave American aircraft producers Boeing and Douglas exactly the time they needed to produce rival airliners, the 707 and the D8. By the time the final, strengthened version of the Comet, Comet 4, was commercially available the American jets were bigger and could travel further.

Comets continued to carry passengers until the beginning of the 1980s, but sold relatively puny numbers compared to the output of the big American companies. Eventually the Comet evolved into the naval spy plane, the Nimrod, which continued in RAF service until 2011. To a large extent, the Comet's failure was a consequence of being first into a ruthlessly competitive market. There were too many innovations that had to be made all at the same time. De Havilland engineers claimed that Boeing and Douglas admitted in private that they had learned from the Comet's mistakes and that, had it never been built, they would have made the same errors themselves. But the de Havilland story also showed the limits of relatively small, traditionally organized companies in the post-war world. Handmade is good, if expensive, for suits, but less so for big engineering projects.

Making do and winging it were no longer enough. British governments would try to force more efficiency by encouraging the merger of the country's remaining aircraft manufacturers, but rationalization too often meant turf wars and feuds – while the Americans, with a much bigger home market and increasingly aggressive attitude to selling into what had been British markets, began a remorseless advance.

46

THE ROBOT WE NEVER USED

Alongside these industrial challenges, Britain was attempting to stay a key player in the world economy. National prestige meant keeping the pound as a big international currency and the sterling area comprised all those countries either pegged to the pound or actually using the pound. These included the usual Commonwealth allies – Canada, New Zealand, Australia – and the African colonies. But other sterling area members were widely scattered – India, Pakistan, Kuwait, Bahrain, Iceland, Ireland, Jordan and the United Arab Emirates were all part of the system.

That seems impressive. But any country trying to maintain a global currency on the back of an increasingly weak industrial base hasn't got room for manoeuvre. It needs to keep its home economy modern and competitive. Weaker economies need floating currencies to balance them. For Britain in the 1950s, the apparently impregnable bastion of the sterling area was becoming a problem. Churchill's government investigated a secret and radical idea – floating sterling in world markets and allowing the convertibility of some sterling holdings to the dollar. In effect – jump out of the old cosy system and use a lower-valued currency to compete.

This might have given exporters the boost they needed. But the scheme, codenamed Robot, was scuppered by the Foreign Office, worried about its effect on Britain's global status. The value of a crisp paper pound, now with the new Queen's head on it, was as much part of Britain's world ranking as the size of her Navy – even if a high pound was making British goods too expensive abroad and quietly throttling investment at home. Most ministers, as one of them mordantly noted to Butler, 'preferred a genteel bankruptcy'.

Nor was there any appetite to shake up the industrial landscape in other ways. The wartime coalition had brought Churchill and leading Labour and trade union figures closely together. Despite public denunciations of one another, and the bitter blow to Churchill inflicted by the general election result of 1945, the Tory Prime Minister had absolutely no appetite for confrontation with his old socialist friends. Butler, the one-time appeaser of Nazism, even complained of his leader that, because of memories of the general strike of 1926, he 'was determined to pursue a policy of industrial appeasement'. Strong words, but prescient ones.

In the chill winter of 1953, Britain was on the verge of a major strike in the railway industry. The nation held its breath. Who would blink first? Butler got a call from Churchill telling him that he and Sir Walter Monckton, the Minister of Labour, had spoken to the union leaders privately and 'settled the rail strike in the early hours of this morning'. On whose terms? Butler asked. 'On theirs, old cock. We did not think it necessary to keep you up.'

In essence, long before the huge industrial confrontations of the 1970s, the political and managerial classes had lost confidence in their authority. They no longer really knew how to deal with an assertive working class, who had done so much to help win the war for everyone. But to see what this really meant in practice, we have to look at the failure of what was once another great British firm.

47

BERNARD AND NORAH: LET'S HAVE SOME FUN

Birmingham Small Arms had been a go-ahead company with a record of innovation. Started in the city in the 1860s by fourteen gunsmiths who wanted to mechanize armaments manufacturing on the American model, BSA realized that machine tools for revolvers and rifles could be adapted for the new craze, the bicycle. Then came the next obvious leap forward. In the years before the First World War, it was selling out its new range of motorcycles. Then, from guns to bicycles, to motorbikes, to cars. In 1910 BSA's new board member Dudley Docker, a go-ahead star of railway takeovers, engineered a merger with Britain's then-biggest car manufacturer, Daimler.

Between the wars BSA motorbikes, Daimler cars, then Lanchesters were all big sellers. During the Second World War, BSA made motorcycles for the British Army, and returned to its gun-making roots. It manufactured tens of thousands of .303 Browning machine guns – the weapons which, placed in Spitfires and Hawker Hurricanes, won the Battle of Britain. Daimler also made armoured cars and scout cars – one of which was seized and used by the German field marshal Erwin Rommel to escape after the battle of El Alamein. So BSA emerged from the war as a glamorous industrial titan. In the early years of the Queen's reign it was the largest motorcycle manufacturer in the world.

Dudley Docker died in 1944 and was succeeded as Managing Director of BSA by his only son Bernard, who also became Chairman of Daimler. Bernard Docker had the stolid, moon-faced demeanour of a caricature industrialist out of central casting. But he was a ferociously hard worker, and a major player in British business – a director of the Midland Bank, Anglo-Argentine Tramways and the travel agents Thomas Cook, alongside his day jobs with BSA and Daimler.

And this time central casting had got the wrong man. For Bernard was nothing if not fun-loving; and he got most of his fun with a Birmingham dance hostess, Norah Turner. Before the war, Norah had been a friend of the rich and titled, including the Duke of Marlborough. By the time she married Dudley Docker in 1949 she had already been married to an eminent wine and spirits businessman, Clement Callingham, and the salt magnate and Chairman of Fortnum & Mason, Sir William Collins, both of whom had died, not of high spirits. Dudley was her third millionaire hubby.

Throughout the early 1950s Sir Dudley – as he now was – and Lady Docker – as she now was – became celebrities. Norah Docker was famous for her flamboyant, outspoken and provocative style. She was the daughter of an upwardly mobile, free-spending Birmingham woman who had run pubs and hotels; and a father who had tried to pay the bills and ended up killing himself. Although Norah presented herself as just a chirpy, fun-loving girl, born above a butcher's shop and with the common touch, in truth she seems to have been a nasty piece of work. Dancing for a living and flinging herself at millionaires, she was highly manipulative and entitled; her greatest talents were spending money and causing rows.

Bernard, her doting third husband, commissioned a series of specially built Daimlers for her – cars such as the 1951 gold Daimler, trimmed with real gold and 7,000 small gold stars; the 1953 Silver Flash, whose accessories included scarlet fitted luggage made from crocodile skin; and the 1955 Golden Zebra, which, with gold replacing normal chrome, sported an ivory dashboard and upholstery covered with zebra skin. When she was asked about that, Lady Docker drily explained: 'Zebra, because mink is too hot to sit on.'

The Dockers always maintained that their cars were a form of advertising for Daimler. It's true that these remarkably flash cars were much discussed in the press, though they were far too expensive for ordinary customers. But advertising and promotion, it is fair to say, were not Bernard's main motivation. What he had realized was that, by putting his wife on the board, he could charge as business expenses her vastly extravagant lifestyle. This was just about defensible in good times and if done moderately. But moderate was not a word Lady Docker had ever come across.

Always quick with a salty, quotable comment, she became a favourite subject of the British popular press in its post-war heyday. They loved the wildly extravagant parties at Claridge's, where film stars and politicians mingled, and her descents on West End stores to gather minks, sables and diamonds, and other flights of fancy, as she made play with her humble origins. They enjoyed her rubbing shoulders with royalty while insisting she preferred bangers and mash to oysters and champagne. During a grey period in British history Norah brought primary colour.

In 1954 she was invited to visit a coal mine near Leeds, posing for the press and distributing booze. As a way of returning hospitality, she then invited forty-five miners, and the television cameras, on to Bernard Docker's huge, famous and opulent steam yacht, the *Shemara*. There she regaled them with champagne, cigars, lobsters and a vast spread of other foods – as well as the hornpipe, danced by herself. Smiling broadly in a yachting cap, Sir Bernard was filmed looking on indulgently, as he mostly was.

But the Dockers were setting themselves up for a fall. Sir Bernard was spending too much time having fun and not nearly enough on the company, which at one point had the potential to be the British rival to continental industrial combines such as Krupp and Thyssen. In 1952, the couple were banned from the Monte Carlo Casino after Lady Docker hit one of the waiters, telling the *Daily Mail* unrepentantly afterwards: 'It is quite true that I socked one of the little men at the Casino. I socked him good and hard, too.'

In 1956, she responded to the twilight of the age of austerity by turning up at the Paris motor show in a £5,000 mink and gold outfit, which she tried to claim as business expenses. And in April 1958, at the christening of Prince Albert of Monaco, Lady Docker tore up a floral flag of the Principality after a row with Prince Rainier and was promptly banned not only from Monaco but (because of an international deal with the French government covering criminal activities) from the whole of the French Riviera. She came back in livid, volcanic form and gave extraordinary press interviews about what she really thought of that royal family.

The British press, as is its habit, suddenly turned on her and her husband. What had been high jinks was now shameful vulgarity. What was once admirable plain speaking was now inexcusable rudeness. Norah suffered two huge thefts of her jewellery and didn't find much public sympathy. By then the shareholders of BSA had already had enough. At a tumultuous meeting in London on a rain-soaked spring day in 1956, Sir Bernard had been sacked as Chairman for his extravagant expenses claims. The Dockers, who had become household names across Britain, eventually retired, grumpily, as tax exiles on Jersey, which Lady Docker found exceedingly dull. Sir Bernard sold off his substantial shareholdings.

And what of BSA? What of the golden goose? In simple terms, it failed and was broken up – or cooked. Daimler, despite all the selfless work to publicize its cars undertaken by Lady Docker, was sold to Jaguar in 1960. Lanchesters had already disappeared. The once mighty bicycle division went to Raleigh, in 1957, shortly after Sir Bernard's departure. But the most damaging part of the story was the precipitous collapse of the motorcycle business.

BSAs and Triumphs had been world beaters, including in the United States. They were big, powerful, heavy machines, which had exploited the new popularity of Speedway motorbiking. But although by the 1950s smaller, much cheaper motor scooters from Italy, the Vespa and the Lambretta, were growing in popularity in Britain, the real threat was from further afield. Japanese-made bikes by Honda and Suzuki did not rely on a boot and a kick to get them started, but on a modern key. One twist, and you were off. These bikes were cheaper, less prone to breaking down and soon just as powerful. A final blow was that the US government changed the rules to favour gearshift and brake pedals as designed by the Japanese, not by the British.

Nicholas Comfort gives a fair and measured assessment of where it all left BSA in the context of British post-war industry generally:

> decades of underinvestment and mismanagement were coming home to roost. The industry was still dominated by craft-based production methods, with inflated workforces and the unions resisting new techniques that might have slimmed them. BSA – at its peak the largest motorcycle producer in the world – bucked the trend by installing a semi-automated assembly line . . . Sadly the workers did not adapt, the new models produced did not perform and the company's problems intensified.

Much of that sad story happened on Sir Bernard's watch. He had begun his post-war business career as a focused, admired and gutsy captain of enterprise. But the lure of a lavish life in the media bubble, choreographed by his wife, meant that he came to prefer the helm of his luxury yacht to the helm of his company. Too much fun, not enough work. He wasn't quite the first and he certainly wasn't the last. If the story of the Dockers was symbolic of British manufacturing in the first part of the Queen's reign, then this would be a dreary book indeed. Luckily, there were other change-makers with better lessons for us today.

48

TO POTTER IS TO FLY

British history and literature are crammed with a certain kind of rebellious son. He is the sensitive, daydreaming boy who reacts against a tyrannical but businesslike father. He is the boy who runs away from the family business to paint watercolours, compose poems or write music. Christopher Cockerell was a boy who rebelled in the opposite direction.

His father, Sir Sydney Carlyle Cockerell, was a great Edwardian aesthete, who made the Fitzwilliam Museum in Cambridge the wonderful collection it is. He adored the arts. He wrote to, and received letters back from, Leo Tolstoy. He numbered Ruskin and William Morris among his friends. Among those he welcomed into his home when Christopher was young were George Bernard Shaw, Rupert Brooke, Siegfried Sassoon and Joseph Conrad. But Christopher wasn't much interested in any of that. He liked electronics and building things – to his father's disgust and amazement. He built from scratch a steam engine to power his mother's sewing machine and equipped his school (where he knew the poet W. H. Auden and the later spy Donald Maclean) with a home-made and complete electronic wireless system.

Then, once he'd properly escaped from the cloying atmosphere of all that drippy art and pansy literature, Cockerell became a sensational engineer. Working for Marconi, he was responsible for the first ever BBC outside-broadcast vehicle and for the shortwave television aerials for Alexandra Palace. By the late 1930s, he had moved into research and development for Marconi. During the war his inventions included new radio communications, navigation and homing devices for Bomber Command; new beacons and receivers to allow Fleet Air Arm pilots to get back safely to their ships; and a new way to allow the RAF to identify German radar bases on the northern French coast before D-Day. Like Frank Whittle with the jet engine, Barnes Wallis and his 'bouncing bomb' and indeed Alan Turing at Bletchley Park, young Christopher Cockerell was a jolly useful chap.

But by the beginning of the new reign Cockerell was up to something very different and more than a little strange. Trying to maximize downward force, he had fixed a small industrial fan over a Lyons Coffee tin, with a smaller Kit-e-Kat tin inside it. He had used his wife's inheritance to found a new company, Ripplecraft Ltd, to build motorboats around the Norfolk and Suffolk Broads. But he wanted them to go very quickly, so had become fascinated by the problem of water drag. If it was to be a really quick boat, it would have to go just above the water, rather than cutting through it.

In what was almost a caricature of the lone inventor pottering determinedly away in his shed, Cockerell developed prototypes using balsa wood and the skills of a local boatbuilder. By 1955, with his fan and metal tins, screws and metal-cutting machines, he had invented the hovercraft – his name for what his patent patiently explained was 'neither an aeroplane, nor a boat, nor a wheeled vehicle'.

Today, hovercrafts are used around the world. They have been deployed for rescue and commercial purposes from Finland to Japan. The American military used them in Vietnam and again, with great success, in the first Gulf War. The Chinese Army use hovercraft.

So do the Norwegians, the Saudi Arabians and the Finns. The Russian Army, having developed a very large range of different hovercraft, is currently building a new generation of armed, troop-carrying hovercraft. These machines, remember, were invented in Britain and developed on the Isle of Wight.

And yet how many hovercraft used around the world today were built in Britain and exported? A few: the British hovercraft dream is not quite dead. Griffon Hoverwork in Southampton manufactured the two rather magnificent, brightly painted craft that still take passengers from Southsea on the Hampshire coast to Ryde on the Isle of Wight in just a few exhilarating minutes – currently the world's only commercial hovercraft route. Other British makers produce a few craft . . . but this is a tiny industry here compared with the dreams people had for it in the 1950s and 1960s.

Why such a commercial failure? Cockerell himself answered the question with a single word – bureaucracy. First, at a time of heavy government intervention in the economy, civil servants were slow to fund and slow to approve. A reluctant Admiralty had eventually encouraged the Ministry of Supply to put the prototype hovercraft on to its 'secret list' of nationally sensitive designs. In 1957–8 Saunders-Roe of the Isle of Wight, whose main business was seaplanes, developed a manned model. On 11 June 1959, the world's very first working manned hovercraft, SRN1, emerged from the huge hangar and was launched on to the Solent, looking for all the world like an offcut for a lost episode of *Thunderbirds*. Aided by the addition of the now famous rubber 'skirts' to increase power and thrust, SRN1 crossed the Channel on 25 July 1959. So far, so go-ahead. A new age was dawning in travel.

But when licences were issued to build hovercraft commercially, ministers insisted that the four winning British companies must be forcibly merged, at a stroke killing competition. They then also helpfully issued licences to foreign manufacturers such as Bell in the US and Mitsui and Mitsubishi in Japan – though a Russian application was rejected. Cockerell was furious. He thought this would hobble the development of a new industry at home while handing overseas rivals an early bonus.

He resigned and was given just eight days to clear off. Not everybody in the establishment was unimpressed by him. The Duke of Edinburgh, mustard-keen for innovation across the British economy, championed the invention, visiting the factory at East Cowes. Having persuaded its commander to give him a shot at the wheel, the Duke piloted SRN1 too fast across bumpy waves and managed to dent it.

Cockerell tried frantically hard to interest the British military, to no avail. As he later explained, 'The Navy said it was a plane not a boat; the Air Force said it was a boat not a plane; and the army was "plain not interested".' That wasn't the end of the hovercraft story in Britain, however. Cockerell created a new company to operate large passenger and car ferries, based on the later SRN4 model, across the Solent and the Channel. For a generation, British holidaymakers and business people travelled between England and France by hovercraft, until faster passenger ferries and then the Channel Tunnel hammered the economics of these huge craft. The Ministry of Defence finally became properly interested as well, when it became clear that hovercraft could destroy mines at sea without being damaged themselves – only for the programme to fall foul of defence cuts in the 1980s.

Sir Christopher Cockerell, as he became, went on to work on post-fossil-fuel energy and to campaign about the lack of decent technical education in schools. He thought every British school should insist on a curriculum which included science and engineering for all, and that universities should tilt towards hard-edged subjects and away from the long tradition of arts and humanities first. As he later complained, 'Unlike the Greek ideal of the whole man, we are a split society, nearly all of us being only half educated either on the one side or the other.'

This was not only a gentle riposte to his famous and anti-science father but was more or less exactly what was known as the 'two cultures' debate. Compared to France or Germany, or indeed the US, Britain had far more people at the top of the tree educated in Greek, literature or history rather than in engineering or the sciences. There was a strong anti-craft snobbery in the country, which goes right back to the failure of that original 1945 reform programme to do much about Britain's class system.

49

HOW OTHERS SAW US

By the mid-1970s, two decades into the Queen's reign, it seemed to many that Britain was finished as a serious economic centre, and that snobbery, in part directed against oily-fingered engineers, was part of the reason. A witty, biting American documentary of 1976 portrayed Britain as a country divided between an effete, idle and rather dim entitled upper class, who spent their time quaffing champagne at the Henley Regatta and wearing silly hats, and a truculent, idle industrial working class, expecting above-inflation wage rises as of right, and resistant to industrial modernization as they called for social revolution. It wasn't quite a binary picture; there was a harried, overtaxed middle class, watching their pensions vanish as inflation romped ahead.

Many Britons, announced the American commentary, were now thinking of leaving their tired, divided country and starting new lives somewhere else. Desolate factory scenes and images of elderly workers still attending to machinery from the first Industrial Revolution – steam-driven engines, cobwebbed looms – added to the impression of irreversible decline.

The US commentator explained that it was partly the fault of socialist governments who had persuaded the British to rely on a highly bureaucratic and incompetent state, and partly the fault of British capitalists who had refused to invest in their own country and instead sought their dividends in other parts of the world. The film was, to put it frankly, anti-British propaganda, which made droll use of music and shots of various classes of Britons caught fast asleep at the seaside. But if it is interesting as a hostile review of Britain in the mid-1970s (two stars) it also told an uncomfortable amount of truth.

Industrial decline would have enormous social consequences, not all of them bad. The identity politics of the twenty-first century, in which gender, sexuality, race all seem to matter more than class or traditional politics, had been pushed forward by the vanishing of the hierarchical workplaces and trade unions. To look back at footage of big union conferences from the 1970s is to glimpse a world as lost for ever as Victorian London or the monasteries of the Middle Ages. You see hundreds of calm white-shirted men (if there are any women present, they seem to be merely taking notes, and it's hard to spot any black faces at all) raising their hands in drilled unanimity to vote, after an impassioned speech calling for the overthrow of capitalism.

These are the same men who would walk out without a second thought if their shop stewards demanded it, and who kept a close eye on youths starting work. This was a period of victory for working-class people over their one-time social superiors: trade union leaders from the poorest backgrounds, with strong Midlands, Scouse or Geordie accents, wielded more power than managers in handmade suits. A combination of union power and galloping inflation meant that the real disposable income of men on factory lines, or in unionized offices, was growing, while that of the old middle-class professionals – accountants, teachers, solicitors and doctors – was falling.

In film, television and music, the sounds of provincial Britain began to elbow aside the cut-glass voices. The growth of working-class drama on television – these were the glory years of *Coronation*

Street, set in 'Weatherfield' or Salford, and *Crossroads*, set in a motel outside Birmingham – and the swaggering self-confidence of the second generation of rock music bands reflected what was beginning to feel like a gradual social revolution. Perhaps the most obvious example is a 1972 song by the Strawbs, a folk-rock band from Strawberry Hill, North London, which became a kind of anthem for the age. 'Part of the Union' began with the declaration, 'Now I'm a union man,' and goes on to say that the union man's company 'stinks' and that he instead pledges allegiance to the union and to bringing about the fall of the factories.

Some thought that this was a satirical attack on militant unionism, though the Strawbs denied it. At any rate, its chorus – 'you don't get me I'm part of the union' – was sung on picket lines and at union conferences for decades to come. There were many who symbolized this defiant, even reckless spirit, from Arthur Scargill of the miners and Vic Feather, the Yorkshire shop-worker who led the TUC against Heath, to Derek Robinson or 'Red Robbo' at British Leyland. But nobody, not even the young Scargill, had the provocative glamour of a young Scottish communist from the Clyde.

50

SUCCESS AND FAILURE ON THE RIVER CLYDE

At Clydebank, between the centre of Glasgow and the open sea, there stands a single, enormous crane. It is called Titan, and it was erected in 1905. Below Titan, in the days when it was surrounded by many other cranes, some of the greatest ships ever built in Britain slowly took shape. Their vast, sharp structures overshadowed the sandstone terraced streets all around as they were raised up by armies of riveters, welders and engineers. Atlantic liners, with beautiful lines, from the *Lusitania* to the *Queen Mary* and both *Queen Elizabeth*s; some of the greatest fighting ships of the twentieth century, including the gigantic HMS *Hood*, blown up by the *Bismarck*, and a vast array of lesser warships, cargo ships, tankers and cruise ships all emerged below Titan's armpit.

This part of the River Clyde was chosen as a great shipbuilding centre, because there is a smaller river, the Cart, on the opposite bank: the ships launched by John Brown Shipbuilding were so large that they couldn't fit into the Clyde and had to be launched in a complicated three-point turn. Tens of thousands of people who had paid to stand on nearby farmland to watch these launches were often drenched by the wave of river water, as the latest ship began her maiden voyage.

These were heroic industrial times, when shipbuilding was central to Scotland's sense of herself. Today, the lone giant is a museum piece. Children pay to do bungee jumps from the top. Below her, a sprawl of housing, retirement homes and commercial development is slowly emerging. It's perfectly nice housing. There will be trees and, no doubt, waterfront coffee shops. But where there was once clanging, smoke, pride and vaulting ambition, there is today only the noise of seagulls and the occasional beep of a reversing van. Great ships are still being built in America, Japan, across the continent of Europe, but not here, not in Britain. What happened? What went so wrong?

August 1971 was hot. On the 8th of the month, on the streets of central Glasgow, the scents of petrol, cigarettes and fried food hung in the dusty air and the thud and drone of pipe bands throbbed through it as nearly 100,000 people marched on the city's George Square. They had come out on strike for an inspirational and unusual cause. Celebrities had sent messages of support, and even money. They included Billy Connolly, the Glasgow comedian, and John Lennon, recently of the Beatles. But on this day everyone's attention was focused on someone else, a tousled Communist Party activist and shipyard worker with more than a passing resemblance to Elvis Presley.

Jimmy Reid was determined to save shipbuilding in Scotland, not by leading his comrades out on strike but by persuading them to keep working in a disciplined way without their wages. The Conservative government thought that Upper Clyde Shipbuilders was a basket case. The world believed the Scottish industrial worker no longer had what it took. Really? Well, the men of UCS would show them.

At a mass meeting nine days earlier on 30 July, responding to the company being placed in receivership, shop stewards representing workers from the five shipbuilding yards in the merged group had seized control of the entire operation – the gates, the management offices, the half-built ships and the engineering workshops, the lot. Across most of Britain, the cultural changes of the 1960s meant that people, particularly in midsummer, were informally dressed – hatless, T-shirted, bejeaned. Not in industrial Govan. The sea of men who put their hands up for the work-in were dressed in tweed jackets, dark serge coats and neatly buttoned shirts. Not a few were wearing flat caps.

Glasgow had, however, a fearsome reputation for drinking ('bevvying') and gang violence. Knowing this, Reid addressed the men:

> We are *not* going to strike. We are not even going to have a sit-in strike. Nobody and nothing will come in and nothing will go out without our permission. And there will be no hooliganism. There will be no vandalism. There will be no bevvying – because the world is watching us and it is our responsibility to conduct ourselves with responsibility and with dignity and with maturity.

And so they did. Over seven months, the workforce of the five yards turned up every day and completed their usual tasks, so that half-built ships were finished and (not without debate) finished vessels were released to their new owners. So much for all the higher-paid managers: the workers were doing it all for themselves. Jimmy Reid and his co-leader Jimmy Airlie had decided to keep the yard open not just for the workers' morale but to make a political point for the world's media. They needed everyone to see that discipline held, that the smears about idle Clydesiders were just that, and that this communist-run, worker-run experiment actually worked.

The government was providing no new money. Unbeknown to the shop stewards, both sides were heading straight into an economic argument that would dominate British politics for more than a decade to come. The previous October, the new Prime Minister Edward Heath had unveiled his modernizing economic programme to the Tory conference: spending cuts, and the determination that companies must stand on their own feet. He promised a break with the old consensus, a change 'so radical, a revolution so quiet and yet so total, that it will go far beyond the programme for this Parliament . . . and way into the 1980s'. Heath's Trade and Industry Secretary John Davies, a former boss of the CBI, then promised the House of Commons that 'lame ducks' in industry would no longer be supported by the taxpayer. Heath was also committed to reining in the power of the trade unions, wooing their leaders even as he prepared a tough Industrial Relations Bill for Parliament. On the face of it, this was Thatcherism almost a decade before Margaret Thatcher arrived in Downing Street.

But Heath was no Thatcher, and he never wanted to be. Older than her, he remembered the high unemployment of the 1930s and was determined that Britain under the Tories would never make the same mistake again. Despite his public image at the time as a harsh and uncaring ideologue, Heath was almost obsessed with unemployment, keeping a private running total week in, week out.

Even as the crisis of the early 1970s grew in the Clydeside ship-yards, the Prime Minister had been forced to respond to another industrial flashpoint when the flagship of British engineering, Rolls-Royce, was threatened with bankruptcy. It had been charging too little for new aircraft engines for the American company Lockheed. After much agonizing Heath saved Rolls-Royce by intervening, earning the dislike of the Tory right. UCS would be a bigger challenge still to his hands-off approach. And in Reid he was facing a new kind of political opponent, one who understood the public mood.

Cash to support the UCS workers came from donations from other unions, benefit concerts and foreign – including Soviet – trade unions, but also from tens of thousands of ordinary members of the public. This was, in large part, a battle of public relations. Jimmy Reid was determined to show that the shipyard workers were not workshy. By and large he won that argument.

Even the Glasgow police were quietly on the shipyard workers' side. Reid toured the UK and became a celebrity himself, firing up crowds everywhere. It was a challenge that the unemployment-sensitive Heath couldn't ignore, and he eventually folded. In February 1972, the government pledged £17 million to cover the losses to the shipyards and a further £18 million for new capital development – as near as it comes to complete victory in an industrial dispute.

Jimmy Reid is, rightly, one of Scotland's twentieth-century heroes. He was born in an appallingly impoverished household in Govan and lost two of his sisters early on. Later he would say that, whatever the doctor's death certificates actually stated, the cause of death was social deprivation. A ferociously clever child and an early reader, he had an unlikely career opportunity working on the Glasgow stock exchange. His boss very much wanted him to stay on but, already an opponent of capitalism, Reid chose to leave to become an engineering apprentice. He immediately joined the union, and helped lead a strike of apprentices, becoming an enthusiastic member of the Communist Party. He was eventually chosen as one of its full-time officials, moving to London before returning to Glasgow ahead of the UCS dispute.

Reid's great gift was that he didn't express himself in stale Marxist platitudes but deployed his wide reading and strong sense of morality (as well as his easy charm) to win over people who would in other circumstances run a mile from socialist ideology. The best example of this is his victory in the 1971 Glasgow University Rectorial election. One of Britain's oldest universities, Glasgow was in those days also one of its more conservative ones. Electing the titular head, or rector, is an ancient tradition. Political activists of different stripes had used it as a platform before. In the grand, Gothic setting of the university's Bute Hall, decked out in full academic regalia, Reid gave his inauguration lecture on the fashionable subject of alienation.

This, he said, was an old phenomenon:

What I believe to be true is that today it is more widespread, more pervasive than ever before. Let me right at the outset define what I mean by alienation. It is the cry of the men who feel themselves the victims of blind economic forces beyond their control. It is the frustration of ordinary people excluded from the processes of decision-making. The feeling of despair and hopelessness that pervades people who feel with justification that they have no say in shaping or determining their own destinies.

Going on to quote Christ, Kurt Vonnegut and recent TV adverts, he then appealed to students to look out for more than number one:

Reject the values and false morality that underlies these attitudes. A rat race is for rats. We're not rats. We are human beings. Reject the insidious pressures in society that would blunt your critical faculties to all that is happening around you, that would caution silence in the face of injustice lest you jeopardise your chances of promotion and self-advancement. This is how it starts, and before you know where you are, you're a fully paid up member of the rat-pack. The price is too high. It entails the loss of your dignity and human spirit . . .

The *New York Times* reprinted the speech in full and declared it to be as important as any since Abraham Lincoln's Gettysburg address.

The Communist Party, never the largest organization in Britain, was delighted that it at last had a popular and charismatic leading member. Despite his doubts about the behaviour of the Soviet Union in Hungary and Czechoslovakia, Reid remained a loyal communist for most of his life. Eventually disgusted by the authoritarianism of the party, he left to support Labour during the Neil Kinnock years. But he couldn't stomach Tony Blair, or the Iraq War, and eventually moved again, to the Scottish National Party. He tried to become an MP, standing variously for the communists and Labour but was never elected. A successful newspaper writer and broadcaster in his later years, his death in 2010 was greeted with widespread and genuine sadness in Scotland. In the words of his biographer Kenny MacAskill, he had led the Scottish working class 'through times of fire and fury . . . he most certainly was "the best MP Scotland never had".' All of this depends heavily on those heroic days in 1971 and the work-in he had led.

But there is an unavoidable coda to this story. Heath and Davies did indeed buckle before Reid and his comrades. The UCS work-in, by upending old stories about lazy strikers, blew a hole through Heath's economic and industrial strategy. Tory hardliners like Nicholas Ridley, who had helped devise the 'no bailouts' position, drew the lesson that Heath, rejected by the voters in 1974, was fundamentally weak and they looked for a different kind of leader. Margaret Thatcher recorded it as a 'small but memorably inglorious episode . . . I was deeply troubled.' There is a visible dotted line, if not an absolutely obvious one, between the events of that summer in Glasgow and the arrival of Margaret Thatcher as Tory leader.

Despite that bailout, with the managers back, UCS did not prosper. Closures continued up and down the Clyde. There were further mergers and many more mass redundancies under the Thatcher governments. Privatizations and break-ups came next. Today there are two yards, at Govan and Scotstoun, working on British naval contracts for modern destroyers, but with a perpetual political struggle over their future always in the background. Further down the river, Ferguson Marine, with a long history spanning the twentieth century, was rescued in 2014 and went on to construct car ferries and hovercraft in an atmosphere of local exhilaration and optimism before, tragically, it went bust again in 2019, owing £50 million to the taxpayer.

Looking back up the Clyde, there's little sign now of the sprawling industrial region that used to supply so much of the world's shipping. Near the centre of Glasgow, most of the space where the work-ins took place is semi-derelict or redeveloped for luxury flats, hotels and a conference centre; the grand Finnieston Crane, another relic from the 1930s, stands like a lonely monument and is photographed by tourists. Not much industrial smoke wafts over the river.

During the wild days of 1970 and 1971, British workers and British managers confronted each other – but working harder, even working for months with no pay, was sadly beside the point. You can argue that the big global forces were by then so powerful that the end was inevitable. Sterling was too strong and new, eager competitors, without the burden of industrial history and union pride, hungrier for new markets, were simply impossible to beat. In a way, that is a comforting thought. It allows everyone to escape the blame. But it's too comforting. Below the surface of the Clydeside story, there is a wider point to be made about British industrial decline, relevant to the West Midlands of England, Wales and the Black Country too.

51

WHEN WE MADE GREAT SHIPS

Clyde shipbuilding properly began between the Napoleonic Wars and the arrival of Queen Victoria. Like so many other British industries, it was begun by scientifically minded, hard-headed men who had risen from working-class backgrounds with a limitless sense of possibility. Robert Napier, the son of a blacksmith, evaded the Royal Navy press gangs by becoming an apprentice engineer. He was a practical man who lived for the smoke and noise of workshops and had a great head for numbers. His breakthrough invention was a specialist steam engine for paddle steamers. He borrowed and built and hired and hectored. By the 1830s, at his yard in Govan, he was building record-breaking steamships and engines for commercial companies as well as for the Navy he had dodged as a boy. He got together with Samuel Cunard, the Canadian shipping magnate, to make regular Atlantic steamship voyages popular and reliable. Napier, a local man from Dumbarton on the Clyde, was a classic self-made entrepreneur. His example spawned an industry.

Its growth during the nineteenth century is a complex story of practically minded millwrights, mathematicians and engineers working to find new ways to power bigger ships through rough water. None of them started out rich and most of them lived close to the centre of Glasgow and to the men and families on whose labour they would depend. Eventually, apprentices to Napier, the Elder family, co-founded a full-blown shipbuilding company, Fairfield, named after the Clydeside farm on whose land the first sheds and yards were constructed. Their breakthrough was the compound steam engine – bigger, faster, more reliable.

By the 1860s, Fairfield was employing more than 4,000 men and had built fourteen major steamships. John Elder, father of the business, died of liver disease aged just forty-five, but was remembered by his workforce as a considerate man, who fully understood the responsibilities of employers to working-class Glaswegians. He was a boss, but he was a citizen first. His funeral was a huge display of civic distress. All the Clydeside workshops fell silent and his body was carried in the middle of a large crowd of shipyard workers.

Another Napier employee from the early days was the young Glaswegian engineer George Thomson who, with his brother James, founded another of the great shipbuilding companies at Govan, later part of UCS. J. & G. Thomson's ships included many Cunard Atlantic carriers, and indeed a couple of the warships used by the Confederacy during the American Civil War. Forced to move from their Govan base, the brothers moved further down the river. To Clydebank they also brought their steel foundry business and engineering workshops, effectively creating a new industrial town.

Here is another part of the story relevant to modern industrial failure. Not only were these companies founded by practical engineers who were part of the community in which their companies grew, their success attracted other ambitious entrepreneurs to join them. At the end of the nineteenth century a Sheffield steel maker called John Brown took over Thomsons. Brown, the son of a slater, apprenticed as a factor at the age of fourteen, had himself developed new steel processes, and the technology which literally underpinned the Victorian railway boom (the volute spring buffer). His steel business led him to make iron cladding for Victorian warships, and the company (which he had left by then) arrived on the Clyde in 1899. John Brown would long be a famous Clydeside name and that is fitting, for its Sheffield founder had been of the same stamp, a brother under the skin to Napier, Elder and the Thomsons – though, after departing his own company, the man himself died in poverty in Kent.

By the early part of the twentieth century, John Brown & Co. was producing ironclad battleships for the Royal Navy and the flagships of the Cunard line. To achieve this, they had been forced to build a completely new slipway structure and pay to dredge the River Clyde so that their ships could be launched side-on. Another lesson for the twentieth century: when shipbuilding was growing, its owners invested massively and took huge technological risks in their stride.

Brown's was a company which bulldozed its way through obstacles and was characterized by relentless innovation, in steel plate, turbine technology and the manufacturing process itself. During the First World War, it continued to produce a stream of fine warships such as the battlecruiser *Repulse*. Although badly hit by the depression of the 1930s, John Brown & Co. was a key British shipbuilder during the Second World War, building aircraft carriers like HMS *Indefatigable* and battleships such as the *Duke of York*. When military orders collapsed after 1945, the yard turned back to replacing some of the merchant shipping which had gone down to mines and U-boats, as well as taking on special projects such as the Royal Yacht *Britannia*, launched by a delighted young Queen in April 1953. Later, John Brown built the *Queen Elizabeth II*, launched in 1967, again by her namesake.

The energy and gusto of John Brown and Fairfield is just as evident in the origins of Yarrow Shipbuilders, another of the great Clydeside names. In this case, though, the company was a migrant from England. Alfred Yarrow, its founder, was a poor half-Jewish apprentice from the East End of London. Eventually, as his shipbuilding business grew, he was unable to find enough space on the Thames and moved everything, boiler by boiler, machine tool by machine tool, crane by crane, to a new site on the Clyde. Yarrow also built warships for navies around the world – generally fast destroyers and gunboats – but its unique speciality was cruisers and paddle steamers designed for rivers or landlocked lakes, in the Americas and Africa. These 'knockdowns' were built in the yard and then carefully broken into pieces to be transported to whichever lake or river they were designed for, where they were reassembled on the spot. Risk. Technology. Lateral thinking.

A little of this history of Clyde shipbuilding – and similar points could be made about other yards, such as Lithgow's and Scott's – is an important prelude to the dramatic events of the early 1970s. Scottish shipbuilding had been innovative and forward-looking. It had been created by practical, dirty-handed engineers and designers who lived in their communities and risked everything on the next invention.

In theory, 1945 should have gifted them a great new opportunity. RAF and American bombing had demolished the force of much of the German and Japanese competition so that by the end of the 1940s Britain was producing not very far off half the world's tonnage of new ships. Her workforce was as highly skilled as ever. Its companies had long traditions of supplying both the Royal Navy (a picky and difficult customer) and the fast-changing demands of merchant fleets. It is often forgotten that, in the mid-1960s, Britain still had the world's largest merchant fleet by tonnage.

Yet by then something fundamental had gone wrong. British shipbuilding had stopped innovating. The managers of the great companies no longer lived in Govan, or within many smoky miles of where Jimmy Reid was brought up. They occupied grand houses further down the Clyde with beautiful non-industrial sea views. They didn't have lathes and grinders, or desks covered with slide rules and mathematical notes in their garages. Their families were developing interests in music, the arts and politics. The shuffling columns of welders and riveters making the vessels their wealth depended on lived in a different world and spoke a form of earthy Glaswegian the by now privately educated managers and owners could barely understand. As in so many other British industries of the time, a gap had opened between making and organizing, financing and the actual doing.

And this was also a class gap, which partly explains the industrial mood of the 1970s. It's true that Glasgow had been a centre of Marxist thought and militancy from the 1920s onwards. Rent strikes and communist organizations had worried Winston Churchill and other Tory politicians between the wars. But had the managers and owners still been practical, engaged people talking the same language as their employees, then Scottish marine engineering might have been risk-taking and ambitious enough to have grown, rather than shrunk, during the second half of the Queen's reign. Instead, it was making bespoke, hand-crafted vessels rather than mass-produced ones. There are parallels with the Comet jet story.

The great old companies had declined to learn the lessons of prefabrication, and the more organized factory-based systems the Americans had created for the remarkable 'Liberty ships' project of the Second World War. Managers had somehow lost curiosity and begun to ignore growing new markets. They had allowed the new oil supertankers to be forged, riveted and launched in Japan – by 1965, one single Japanese yard, in Nagasaki, was producing a tonnage equivalent to three-fifths of the entire British industry. They had not sent expert delegations (or indeed industrial spies) to the new yards in Scandinavia and Germany which were already stealing their business.

The blame game is too easy. It was 'all the fault of the unions' because of the intense demarcation disputes and the readiness to strike. Or, alternatively, it was all the fault of the management, the lively, local men who had first created those companies having been replaced by less enthusiastic generations, who lived in Ayrshire or Dunbartonshire. Or, again, it was all the fault of successive governments: they should have realized how dependent British shipbuilding (in Newcastle and Portsmouth, not just in Glasgow) was on naval orders, and they should have encouraged modernization, in labour relations and equipment, much earlier.

Certainly, when the crisis first arrived, in 1965, with Fairfield going into receivership, the government answer was unimaginative. Harold Wilson's Labour administration appointed Reay Geddes, a businessman whose career had been in the soft drinks industry, to investigate and come up with suggestions. Geddes, not surprisingly, found that the industry was in a heck of a mess. But his main suggestion was that the individual companies should be amalgamated into two much larger units, Upper Clyde Shipbuilders (UCS), which included the Govan and Clydebank yards such as Fairfield, John Brown and Yarrow, and on the lower Clyde, the Port Glasgow and Greenock yards, which were merged into Scott Lithgow. It was one of the great fallacies of this period that taking a bundle of failing businesses and sticking them together would somehow produce a successful business. Who was to blame? Unions, management, government? In short, yes: all three.

Who was to be given the thankless, indeed nightmarish, task of leading UCS as it took over from the old bosses? The man chosen was Anthony Hepper, a young executive from the board of Thomas Tilling, a one-time bus company now making Pretty Polly tights. (A soft drinks man and then a tights man? Strange but true.) A good manager is a good manager but, even so, the gap between constructing complex modern warships or supertankers and producing sexy hosiery is a big one. Hepper's own account in an oral history of the decline of British shipbuilding is blunt about his own lack of experience. 'When the company was formed the problem arose as to who would be chairman. There were no other candidates so I took the job on the basis that there would be a managing director with shipbuilding experience appointed. Unfortunately, we were unable to find such a person . . .'

Hepper was particularly critical of the men then in charge of Glasgow shipbuilding. 'Financial management was almost non-existent. Marketing management was completely non-existent.' Meanwhile, union negotiators had achieved 400 different rates of pay in the yards. Getting different categories of worker to work together was a virtually impossible task. There were, said Hepper, two main categories of unionized workers. 'There was on the one side, the Boilermakers, who formed roughly one-third of the labour force. They built the hulls of the ships, doing the welding and associated work. There were, on the other hand, the outfitting trades.' (These accounted for thirteen of the relevant fourteen trade unions.) They did 'everything else, like installing the engines, electrical work, plumbing and so on. The Boilermakers thought that they should have a shilling more than others because they had the greater industrial muscle. The others did not agree. So, you could never build a ship effectively because if you went along with one side, the other would go on strike. You would either have one-third on strike or two-thirds. This was a permanent feature.'

As Jimmy Reid was becoming a national celebrity, Anthony Hepper was desperately trying to untangle old madnesses. John Lennon never wrote *him* a cheque. How much responsibility did the communist-dominated shop stewards, who performed so nobly during the work-in, have for those madnesses? The Japanese and German yards had better managers and more modern equipment, but they also had workers who would move flexibly and quickly from one job to another.

Rather than comfortably concluding that international forces, from the Luftwaffe's Clydebank blitz in 1941 to the price of sterling forty years later, were to blame for the destruction of Scottish shipbuilding, we should accept the gloomy truth that obstinate and self-destructive owners and trade unionists doggedly refusing to see the bigger threats to their livelihoods are equally at fault, and that the political bosses of the Wilson and Heath years didn't really help at all.

52

CLIVE SINCLAIR:
MAKE IT SMALL

Of all the physical changes that marked the Queen's reign, none has been as dramatic as the computing revolution. It has transformed daily life in every area from dating to getting around. It has transformed our culture, from the way millions portray themselves to the distribution of music and film. It has changed almost every kind of business and profession. It has upended journalism and politics. It made the experience of lockdown during the 2020 coronavirus crisis tolerable for many for whom the boredom and loneliness would otherwise have been excruciating.

Even for those who know the Ferranti story, it's easy to think of the computing and online revolution as something imported, something essentially American – or perhaps these days something essentially Chinese. Yet this is a story that not only starts in Britain but features an abnormally large number of British pioneers. Unlike the story of shipbuilding, this isn't mostly about industrial relations and lost opportunities. To this day Britain is a global centre for gaming, an industry that now in size rivals filmmaking.

Earlier on we met the Manchester University pioneers. But there's a lot more to this story than them. If you visit Britain's National

Museum of Computing, in Block H at Bletchley Park in Buckinghamshire, where Turing and the team of codebreakers cracked Nazi messages during the Second World War, then the origins of modern computing in Britain are pretty obvious.

'War! What is it good for?' Well, it gave us this. You can see a reconstruction of Turing's 'Bombe' with its whirling disks, which beat the German Enigma machine. Then there is Colossus, huge and hot, with spinning strips of punctured paper. This is the world's first electronic computer, constructed in make-do-and-mend spirit with Post Office parts, which broke encrypted messages between Hitler and his generals. Post-war, there is EDSAC, created by the Cambridge University Mathematical Society in 1947–9, weighing 2 tonnes and using 300 valves, which spewed out Nobel prizes.

Best of all, blinking, clicking and whirring, there is the wonderful Witch, the world's oldest working digital computer, which has been performing calculations since 1951. By today's standards they are all archaic and ridiculously large and slow. But by any standards they represent big jumps forward in human ingenuity. And, for rigid arrays of electronics, valves, disks and lights, they are really rather beautiful. This is a place where the world of now began.

Post-war Britain had a lively mathematical and electronic engin-eering culture which has, perhaps, been too little remembered. At a high level it boasted brilliant minds like that of Andrew Booth, whose Booth multiplier had a pivotal effect on the development of digital computing, and those of the Bletchley teams and pioneering computer enthusiasts at Wolverhampton and Cambridge. But below this there was a world of mathematically and scientifically enthused hobbyists, awkward young men in tweed jackets with outsized spectacles, building their own radios and receivers in attics, bedrooms and sheds all over Britain. And this was the clubby environment joined by one of the most misunderstood, derided and interesting of the Elizabethan era's business pioneers.

Clive Sinclair was the son of an engineer and grandson of a

notable Vickers shipbuilding naval architect, and he was a brilliant designer who would do more than anybody else to usher this country into the computer age. Sinclair was brought up in rural Berkshire in a happy middle-class family, where numeracy and curiosity were taken for granted. As a child he had designed a submarine, using his grandfather's shipbuilding stories and government-surplus fuel tanks. He was a maths prodigy at school. By the time he was ten, his teachers were telling his father there was nothing more they could teach him.

While only a young teenager, Sinclair designed a calculating machine programmed by punch cards and using the digital system of zeros and ones – well known in university departments, of course, but which he appears to have invented completely independently. Shunning university himself, Sinclair started out in amateur electronics magazines. By the age of eighteen he was running *Practical Wireless*, the hobbyists' favourite magazine – even if it was, to the uninitiated, almost unreadably dense.

A few days after his twenty-first birthday, Sinclair registered his first company, Sinclair Radionics Ltd, selling radio kits based on transistors and other semiconductors for hobbyists at home. Mail order was his preferred way of doing business, and miniaturization was his obsession. During the 1960s he built up a company in Cambridge, making and selling tiny radios, amplifiers and hi-fi equipment before he hit the big time with the first proper pocket calculators. By then microchips were becoming available: Sinclair incorporated them into machines designed to be the size of a packet of cigarettes – he was then a very heavy smoker.

They worked, and also looked so elegant that one was even put on show at the Museum of Modern Art in New York. The Sinclair Executive pocket calculator was launched in 1972. With inflation roaring ahead, and the country obsessed by tax bands and floating exchange rates, it was a good moment for fingertip numeracy.

Clive Sinclair, ever the quiet, tinkering obsessive, moved on to produce new scientific calculating machines, miniaturized television sets – with screens not much bigger than a postage stamp – and a sadly unreliable digital watch. But he was never able to repeat the huge success of the early calculators, which had been well ahead in a global market. The company, like other British manufacturers of the 1970s, was plagued by poor quality and late delivery, and by the end of the decade it was first rescued and then quietly killed off by the new National Enterprise Board.

Sinclair's greatest achievement was still ahead of him, however. At the beginning of the Thatcher era, in 1979, modestly sized and relatively cheap computers were coming on to the market made by companies such as Commodore, Olivetti and Apple, but they were still too expensive for most homes. Sinclair thought they were also simply too big. So, at the beginning of 1980, he launched his ZX80, at the time the world's cheapest and most modestly sized computer.

For a generation this was the machine that brought computing into the home. Manufacturing in Dundee, less than a year after it was launched Sinclair's new company was producing 10,000 computers a month, 60 per cent of them for export abroad. They were hardly perfect. Sinclair, used to selling his products to hobbyists who didn't mind tinkering, had a less than obsessive attitude to quality control. Buy it readymade, or buy it in bits, in kit form. Who cared? Computers that didn't work were simply sent back and replaced. Some of the new machines overheated and infuriated their new purchasers. Slick marketing for non-hobbyists this was not.

There was now, however, a much bigger prospective customer, and a really big chance for Britain's growing computer industry. Worried by the country's sluggish attitude to new technology, working with the government, the BBC was planning new TV programmes to encourage computing all over Britain. It wanted to change attitudes in schools – and to promote its own machine. This would be made by somebody else: not even the BBC, at its most imperialistic, wanted to be a computer manufacturer. But the BBC decreed that the new machine must run the popular computer programme of the day, BASIC, in a form made as friendly and easy to use as possible. Who would get this massive order? Even though the ZX80 was by now the most popular computer in the world, the BBC was also impressed by a rival company, Acorn, created by one of Clive Sinclair's former employees, Chris Curry.

Curry's Proton computer was now in direct competition with the latest Sinclair product, the ZX Spectrum, launched in 1982, with a (somewhat dodgy) colour screen, half-decent sound and enough computing power for gripping games. By the following year, Sinclair was selling 15,000 of them every week and had launched the new computer around the world. In 1983 he celebrated the making of the millionth of his computers at the Timex Factory in Dundee. But it was Chris Curry's Acorn team who got the BBC contract to produce what became known as the BBC Micro. It had a much sturdier case and a steady keyboard and was less unreliable than the Spectrum, a fact Acorn gleefully publicized.

In schools across the country, the BBC Micro would introduce an entire generation to computing. For Clive Sinclair, it felt like a personal betrayal and a stitch-up. Just before Christmas 1984 he got physical – uncharacteristic of a geek – and furiously launched himself at his old friend Curry in the Baron of Beef pub in Cambridge. The two men made up shortly afterwards, and Sinclair recovered his good humour. The ZX Spectrum with its rich array of games had caught the imagination of the lounges and bedrooms of the country. Industry honours showered down. He was knighted. He became a very rich man. As the BBC plugged ahead at educating British youth in computing, Sir Clive was the symbol of the nation's ability to make it in this confusing, fast-changing new digital world. And then it all went horribly wrong yet again.

Sinclair had been interested in electric vehicles since boyhood. But by the end of the 1970s the time, at last, seemed propitious. Rodney Dale, Sinclair's biographer and friend, explains: 'as the world became more conscious of the problems of pollution and the need to conserve energy, governments – and government bodies such as the Electricity Council in Britain – made funds available for sponsoring development work on electric vehicles'. In March 1980 the government abolished motor tax for electric vehicles. This wasn't very costly; there were only 45,000 of them on British roads, of which nine-tenths were milk floats. Sinclair threw himself into designing the first electric vehicle, which would challenge both small petrol motor cars and mopeds. He worked with one of the most respected car-design companies in Britain, Lotus.

The Hoover factory in Merthyr Tydfil that produced them used highly innovative processes including the world's largest massproduced injection moulding for the bodies of what was called the Sinclair C5, launched on a snowy day in January 1985 at Alexandra Palace in London. Here, as with his pocket calculators and his best computers, the quiet, poised but determined geek had found a product that seemed to match the zeitgeist and was far ahead of any competitor. Sinclair Vehicles, Sir Clive explained, was 'developing a family of traffic-compatible, quiet, economic and pollution-free vehicles for the end of the 1990s. You're seeing the baby of the family today . . . a completely new form of practical personal transport . . .' Then the baby crashed.

Three things. First, the British press can be, on occasion, just a little unfair. Second, safety watchdogs have a tendency to worry too much and weren't much impressed by the C5. Third, in the purity of its design, the new vehicle was open, and from time to time it rains in Britain.

But the biggest problem was that you looked a bit silly in a C5, like an adult squeezed into a battery-operated pram. All his life Clive Sinclair had made products and sold them to technically minded hobbyists and mathematical types, men like himself. When it came to the general public, he had forgotten the population's distaste for looking silly. We are all silly. We buy many ludicrously extravagant, overpriced and unnecessary gadgets. We will, it seems, pay out for almost anything. But we won't spend good cash to look like a plonker.

Sir Clive was in many ways a great British Genius. He introduced computing into millions of lives and was one of the undoubted change-makers of the new Elizabethan age. In his defence, we should remember that pioneers, almost by definition, can't get everything right. But he is also a case study in why the geeks, despite all their assumptions, may not inherit the earth.

53

THE REST OF CREATION

When it comes to cultural influence – or 'soft capital' – national power can bubble up unexpectedly. During the coronavirus-hit spring of 2020 the ninety-three-year-old broadcaster David Attenborough released a film looking back over his life and warning about the biggest threat facing mankind, global warming. *A Life on Our Planet*, made with the World Wildlife Fund, charted the growth in human population and carbon in the atmosphere, and the dramatic shrinking of the wild, since Attenborough's childhood. It included some terrifying predictions about the state of the planet by the 2030s and beyond if current policies do not change.

But far from being a simple 'we're all doomed' sermon, Attenborough's witness statement went on to explain how it was still possible to change direction and give mankind a more benign future. He introduced what were, in effect, hero countries, including Japan for limiting her population; the Netherlands for her agricultural revolution; and Costa Rica for rewilding rainforest territory that had been destroyed to grow crops.

Attenborough, a confidant of the Queen, hoped the film would be seen by world leaders. He was by then by far the best-known and most charismatic campaigner for new environmental policies.

He had already addressed world political and business leaders at the annual Davos summit in Switzerland and was as close as anyone in Britain to being a non-political and beloved national teacher. Television is often criticized for being a shallow and trivial medium, but when it comes to nature broadcasting, the British during the Queen's reign have had a global and benign impact.

In what might be called the '*Blue Planet* effect', British broadcasting has generated a lot of money and influence from expertly made films about the natural world, and in particular its more extraordinary and appealing living creatures. There is no obvious reason why a production team based in Bristol should achieve something close to world dominance in this – children of the 1960s would have associated magical undersea revelations with Jacques Cousteau rather than David Attenborough. Yet specific and intense British interest in the animal world is deep and long-standing; the *Blue Planet* effect is also part of the Elizabethan story. And it goes back long before the current reign.

London Zoo opened in 1828. It is the world's oldest scientific zoo, originally designed as a collection for scientists, not as entertainment. Four years earlier, the world's first organization dedicated to combating human mistreatment of other creatures – the Society for the Prevention of Cruelty to Animals – had been formed at a meeting in a London coffee shop. It attracted the patronage of Queen Victoria and became the RSPCA in 1840.

The brutality of early modern societies towards animals – the beating of horses, the hideous treatment of pit ponies, the routine street torturing of cats and dogs – had produced a humane backlash which preceded Victorian Britain. As early as 1822 the first animal welfare law outlawed 'the cruel and improper treatment of cattle'. In 1835 cruelty against dogs and other domestic animals was banned, and bear-baiting and cock-fighting were forbidden. Foxes would have to wait a little longer.

Later, Edwardian Britain was divided by the extraordinary 'brown dog affair', after the illegal vivisection of a brown terrier by William Bayliss at University College London. The dog, according to smuggled-in witnesses (a group of Swedish feminists), had not been properly sedated and the National Anti-Vivisection Society (founded in 1875 – and, yes, the world's first – and, yes, supported by Queen Victoria) took up the cause. Animal-rights activists clashed with protesting medical students.

After a bitter libel case, in 1906 anti-vivisectionists erected a statue of the deceased dog in London's Battersea Park with an inscription recalling 232 dogs vivisected at University College in 1902 and asking: 'Men and women of England, how long shall these things be?' Supporters of vivisection – medical students and others – started to vandalize the statue and a long battle continued until the council finally removed the dog at dead of night. The conditions of animals have always excited strong emotions among the British.

All of this is a long way from the work of the BBC Natural History Unit more than a century later; but there are eloquent connecting stories, which take us well into the reign of Queen Elizabeth II. Legislative battles in the second half of the twentieth century included animal testing of everything from cosmetics to cigarettes, fox hunting with dogs, the treatment of circus animals, shooting and dog fighting. Most of these were politically contro-versial and seemed to pit the liberal urban middle classes against 'authentic' rural people. But a lively fascination with wild animals spread across every group. And this was a lot to do with the influ-ence of television, well-written books and a small group of inspirational pioneers.

Gerald Durrell was a child of the Empire, not a child in Britain. His parents had spent most of their lives in India where the young Gerald, part of a large family which included the famous novelist Lawrence Durrell, was introduced to birds, bears and beetles by his Indian nurse, or ayah. After his father, an engineer, died of a brain haemorrhage, the family returned to Britain in the 1930s. Gerald managed to avoid almost all schooling, but continued his fascination with the animal world.

This deepened and flowered when his depressed and alcoholic widowed mother removed the whole family to the Greek island of Corfu. His adventures there, including lessons from a Greek biologist, eventually became *My Family and Other Animals*, one of the most loved non-fiction books printed in Britain in the early years of the Queen's reign: it appeared in 1956 and has never been out of print since.

One man who loathed the book, however, was George Cansdale, head of the London Zoo, where Durrell had been working. Cansdale, who appeared in front of TV cameras regularly himself, was an outspoken figure in the British zoo world, a man of great influence. The feud between him and Durrell seems to have started with simple jealousy. Jacqui, Durrell's first wife, recalled:

> Cansdale hated Gerry's guts and did everything in his power to thwart him. Cansdale was extremely jealous of Gerry because he regarded himself as 'the only' authority on West African fauna and he deeply resented anyone who intruded into his private domain. The thing that really sealed Gerry's fate was when he brought back an extremely rare mammal that had eluded Cansdale . . .

But there was more to it than that. The argument was also a fundamental one about the purpose of zoos and, by extension, the proper relationship between advanced human societies and wildlife. Durrell believed that the fundamental purpose of zoos ought to be the preservation of endangered species through breeding programmes, and the well-being of the animals themselves – which meant a lot of space and properly designed habitats. It was a long way from how zoos had evolved since Victorian times, as a branch of the entertainment industry, even if their elephants and tigers were kept in better conditions than those of travelling circuses.

Durrell regarded London Zoo itself as a 'commercial sideshow'. Attenborough, a friend and contemporary of Gerald Durrell, put it like this:

> A great proportion of the animals were not bred in the zoo, so specimens had continually to be taken from the wild; and the zoo still had the Victorian idea that a scientific zoo had to exhibit the maximum number of species, like a stamp collection. George Cansdale could be very overbearing and was not really a popular man at the zoo . . . So to have an ex-junior trainee from Whipsnade [Gerald Durrell] pipe up and say this was all nonsense would not have pleased him at all.

The two fell out very badly and Durrell was effectively blackballed by the British zoo establishment. Like so many attempts to freeze out critics, it backfired. Gerald Durrell realized that he needed his own zoo. In 1958, he was filming in South America and met David Attenborough once more, explaining to him that he intended to open a new British zoo. Attenborough couldn't see how anyone other than a millionaire could manage that; but Durrell already had a clear plan worked out. As his biographer Douglas Botting explained, it would be different from typical zoos.

> Most cages and enclosures, he complained, were designed more for the convenience of the public than the comfort and needs of the animals. And most zoos kept the wrong kinds of animals – big, dramatic creatures such as lions and tigers, rhinos and hippos, which cost a lot of money to keep and took up a lot of space . . . 'Most of all,' Attenborough recalled, 'he was critical of zoos which made no attempt to breed their inmates. Sometimes they did not even bother to keep them together in pairs. When one died, the

zoo simply sent somebody to catch another . . . He was going to change all that.'

And he did. After another collecting journey to Africa, the Durrells brought back their collection of wild creatures to Bournemouth, where they tried very hard to persuade the local council to help them create this new kind of zoo. But eventually, despite Gerald Durrell's growing celebrity as an author, the bureaucrats of Bournemouth made it impossible. A chance contact of his publishers led Durrell to the island of Jersey, where he was introduced to a beautiful old manor house, Les Augrès, where with the help of local volunteers he opened his zoo in 1959. For a man still in his early thirties it was an extraordinary achievement, but Durrell was already thinking on a much wider scale as he reflected on the devastating effect mankind was having on the world's natural habitats and wild creatures.

A broadcast he wrote for the BBC's German service in 1956 reads like a manifesto for the conservation movement that would follow in the 1960s and 1970s:

> All over the world there is springing up a new awareness of nature and a desire to preserve rather than destroy, for by helping nature preserve her capital man can be rewarded by the interest. Laws have been passed to check the pollution of rivers and lakes. Reforestation programmes are under way to try and check erosion and recreate the great forests that were destroyed. The protection and reintroduction of game and fur-bearing animals is meeting with great success. Other species of animal are also being protected . . . Large areas of the world are being set aside, untouched, as reserves and national parks, where the flora and fauna can exist untouched, a living museum for future generations.

This was more defiant optimism than accomplished achievement. To win over hundreds of millions of urban dwellers to the importance of conservation at this scale, there was only one medium which mattered in the second half of the twentieth century; and it was television.

Championing the cause of endangered species such as the African lowland gorilla, Durrell became a favourite with the young BBC Natural History Unit and an increasingly deft television promoter of his cause: Attenborough, giving the eulogy at his funeral, called him 'simply magic'. Gerald Durrell was a man of large appetites and complex psychology, who endured depression and alcoholism. But he was also a shrewd manipulator of power. Like the founders of the RSPCA and the Anti-Vivisection Society in Victorian times, for instance, he well understood the advantages of royal support.

Most of Queen Elizabeth's family were animal enthusiasts, with Prince Philip an early advocate of conservation, and Princess Anne so passionate about horses that her mother would joke that she expected her children to have four legs. When Gerald Durrell took Princess Anne to see the Jersey Zoo they came across a male mandrill. The world's largest monkeys, their sexual display is famous, attracting the awed admiration of Charles Darwin among others. Durrell introduced Princess Anne to a monkey accurately named Frisky. He takes up the story himself:

> if Frisky's front was impressive, when he swung around he displayed a posterior which almost defied description. Thinly haired in greenish and white hair, he looked as though he had sat down on a newly painted and violently patriotic lavatory seat. The outer rim of his posterior was cornflower blue (as were his genitals) and the inner rim was a virulent sunset scarlet. As we approached the cage, Frisky grunted and then swung round to display his sunset rear.
>
> 'Wonderful animal, ma'm,' I said to the Princess, 'wouldn't you like to have a behind like that?'

The Princess peered closely and replied that no, on balance, she thought she would not. It is greatly to her credit that, despite this, she became the first royal patron to the new, animal-friendly zoo.

Durrell wrote more than thirty books, which were translated all around the world and formed the basis of the numerous TV series and films. But for him the point of all of this was to fund his real work, which was conservation. He once said that the first word he been able to say was 'zoo' and his version of what that word meant has become mostly accepted. The message spread from Jersey that a zoo should be a place where animals at risk of extinction in the wild are protected and enabled to breed, a place where the first purpose of the animal enclosures is to keep them safe, comfortable and with enough space; and that a zoo is first and foremost a centre to educate humans about the natural world, not a place of entertainment. Even George Cansdale's London Zoo eventually appointed pro-Gerald Durrell managers.

For most British children from 1962 onwards, however, the real voice of the natural world wasn't Gerald Durrell, but that of a Welsh working-class former itinerant musician and storyteller, only posing as a zookeeper. Johnny Morris's *Animal Magic*, shot at Bristol Zoo, ran for more than 400 episodes until 1983. Its jaunty theme tune cheered up many bleak early evenings. Morris's greatest talent was as a ventriloquist, attributing a variety of homely thoughts and local accents to the birds, beasts and fish he featured. This was the animal world as anthropomorphic comedy. Morris, a man of considerable personal bravery as well as great skill, recorded without sound and would then dub on many of the voices. He was a natural comic and a wonderful communicator. But what he was not was a serious conservationist or educator about the natural world.

Gerald Durrell wasn't the only one of those rare beasts. During much of this period Sir Peter Scott, a balding and heavily built former war hero, was just as influential as Durrell. A talented artist, prolific author and able broadcaster he was also, with Prince Philip, one of the founders in 1961 of the World Wildlife Fund (now the World Wide Fund for Nature), whose distinctive panda logo he also designed. Peter Scott was the son of the polar explorer Robert Falcon Scott. In his last letter home, the latter told his wife to try to make their son interested in natural history – 'it is better than games'. As a final message from the ice, it lasted well.

Sir Peter was as physically brave as his father, winning the Distinguished Service Cross during the war, when he commanded gunboats and served on destroyers. His work on naval camouflage is thought to have saved many ships and lives during the Battle of the Atlantic. After the war, Scott stood unsuccessfully as a Tory candidate in the 1945 election, then turned to conservation, creating the Severn Wildfowl Trust in 1946 (which later became the Wildfowl and Wetlands Trust, with Prince Charles as its patron). He saved the Hawaiian goose from extinction; but in the late 1950s and 1960s Peter Scott also began to build a big television following through his BBC natural history series *Look*, which made him, like Gerald Durrell, a household name. Although Durrell was always somewhat in awe of him, Scott was an early and persuasive advocate for exactly the same conservation principles, and supported Durrell at crucial moments.

Among Scott's most enduring achievements was his work to change the policy of the International Whaling Commission, which finally accepted a moratorium on the commercial killing of whales in 1982. Knighted by the Queen in 1973 for services to conservation, Sir Peter himself thought that the high point of his career had been the launching of the World Conservation Strategy in 1980 – a programme for national conservation efforts, identifying the most significant environmental issues and proposing government actions.

Sir Peter was not only a passionate conservationist but a man who understood power and lobbying and how to get his way. One of his friends and rivals as a natural history broadcaster in the 1950s was David Attenborough who, visiting the Wildfowl and Wetlands Trust's Slimbridge Centre in 2017, said of him:

> Peter Scott was one of the first naturalists to recognise that if human beings didn't take care, they could actually exterminate most species. He . . . had great skill and great energy in getting people worldwide to recognise the problem, and to give money to it, and get the conservation movement going. So, he was one of the founders of conservation, not just in the UK, but in the world.

Today, much the same could be said of David Attenborough himself. London-born, and the younger brother of the late film actor Richard Attenborough, he was obsessed by nature from an early age, very much like Gerald Durrell. After a short career in publishing, he was picked in 1952 for the new BBC Television's Talks Department and, despite worries about his 'two large teeth' quickly made himself a popular presenter. An eye-popping range of natural history programmes would follow, above all the famous 'Life' series which began in 1979 with *Life on Earth*. Unusually, Attenborough pursued a parallel career as a highly successful BBC administrator, finally as Controller of the new BBC2 from 1965. There he ushered in a golden age in colour television, commissioning programmes as varied as *Monty Python's Flying Circus*, Kenneth Clark's *Civilisation* and Jacob Bronowski's *Ascent of Man*.

By 1972, he had had enough of life in an office and returned for a series of ambitious films charting the behaviour and condition of much of the planet's fauna. *Life on Earth* in 1979 demonstrated that you can bring to the screen vivid and intimate images of wildlife while making serious and scientifically grounded arguments. This series and the many that followed it depended upon breakthroughs in filming technology, as well as the courage, endurance and skill of cameramen and sound recordists; but Attenborough brought a uniquely engaging and yet tough-minded commentary, which won over new generations to the conservationist cause.

Unlike lesser presenters, he was never a camera-hogger, understanding that people were tuning in to see tigers, dolphins, gorillas, dancing forest birds, rather than him. After a five-year gap, he followed with *The Living Planet*, which had a more self-consciously environmental theme as Attenborough became more concerned with the impact of human populations on the planet, species and climate change. There was nothing sugary or sentimental about these films. In the 1990 series *The Trials of Life* British television viewers watched killer whales hunting sea lions, and chimpanzees violently killing a monkey. Sex, family and death were always the key themes.

Attenborough disliked the almost universal handle he was given of 'national treasure'. Partly it was his genial, avuncular style and partly his sharp intelligence, but for whatever reason he drew millions upon millions of people into a deeper appreciation of, and therefore protective awareness of, the fragile and glorious ecosystems of the planet. Although television is often seen as a mildly disgraceful and second-order medium, Attenborough's was a massive achievement, as big in its way as that of any Elizabethans. That said, it's important to remember that he was a mainstream man, part of a broad, fast-flowing current of pro-animal-rights campaigners and other natural-world conservationists, whose story goes back from Queen Elizabeth to the reign of her formidable great-great-grandmother.

Of all the attitudinal changes among the Elizabethans, the growth of understanding about the interconnectedness of nature, and about the autonomy and value of other creatures, may turn out to be more important than anything else. A country which had taken fox hunting and African big-game shooting as normal, uncomplicated practices in the 1950s was becoming disgusted by them sixty years later. There is a direct line from a gathering in an obscure London coffee shop of high-minded Victorians outraged by the way humans treat animals to the gigantic marketing operation of *The Blue Planet*. And this tradition would have a big impact on how Elizabethans ate, and how they thought about their food.

54

ANITA AND THE KINDLY MARKET

People lie. So these things are hard to measure accurately. But survey after survey finds between 3 and 4 per cent of British people reporting themselves as fully vegetarian. Some other studies suggest a higher percentage than that and that around 4 million British people now will not eat meat. A 2011 Canadian study decided that the United Kingdom had the third highest rate of vegetarianism in the EU.

All that can be said for sure is that vegetarianism is on the rise in Britain, as is veganism, that both are more popular among women than among men, and more popular among the young than among the old. Vegetarian and vegan cookbooks and restaurants are doing big business; advertising campaigns proclaim the case for avoiding meat in one particular month – 'Veganuary' – and in some areas restaurants pledge to serve only vegetarian food one day a week, typically 'meat-free Mondays'.

As with animal rights, modern Britain was a pioneer in the vegetarian movement. The poet Shelley was a keen advocate and the unfortunately named Rev. William Cowherd, who founded the Bible Christian Church early in the nineteenth century, was a prominent promoter of a plant-based diet. Partly thanks to him the world's first vegetarian society had its inaugural meeting at Ramsgate in 1847. Today's vegetarian boom seems to be driven as much by the cost to the planet of land-hogging, methane-producing meat production as by animal-cruelty concerns or religious qualms. To say that vegetarianism is a contemporary trend that is only going to grow seems a safe prediction. So in the Queen's reign, who were the pioneers?

One of them was a determined, tousle-haired girl of Italian-immigrant extraction who had learned about hard work and salesmanship from her parents' chips-with-everything café at Littlehampton on the south coast of England. Her father died young, and her feisty mother, when not fighting with local Roman Catholic priests, kept the business going. As the daughter later remembered: 'There were four of us kids and we worked every weekend, every evening and every holiday in the café. There were no family holidays, very few family diversions at all except for the weekly trip to the cinema; and the café was an extension of our home.' After training as a teacher, travelling much of the world and working for the United Nations, she married one of her mother's customers, a farmer and writer called Gordon Roddick.

Anita Roddick had grown up as a child of the 1960s, determined to avoid working for big corporations. With her new husband, she started a restaurant and a hotel, but with two small children faced a financial crisis when Gordon decided that he wanted to ride a horse from Buenos Aires in Argentina to New York, an adventure he thought would take him about two years. Anita responded by deciding to set up her own skin-care company because she was infuriated by the wastefulness and lack of transparency of the cosmetics industry.

In March 1976, she opened the first branch of the Body Shop, down a small lane in Brighton. Unhappily, given its name, it was sandwiched between two funeral parlours. Local people thought, and some hoped, that it was going to be Brighton's first sex shop. With very little money – the whole affair had been started on a £4,000 business loan – Roddick offered to refill empty containers and fill customers' own bottles. This was recycling long before it was fashionable: 'I ran my shop just like my mother ran her house in the Second World War – refilling, reusing and recycling everything – and what we did in that first year was a thumbprint for the differences that would set the company apart.'

But her biggest ethical cause was hostility to the cruel system of animal testing of cosmetics, then ubiquitous in the industry. As she researched and created her own products, Anita Roddick insisted that her suppliers did not animal-test, and advertised the fact to her early customers. Brighton has always had a radical fringe and, during the second half of the twentieth century, a distinctly hippy vibe. For whatever reason, the ethical agenda of this unusual cosmetics shop made it popular there. Producing vegetarian products – although not always vegan, because Roddick used lanolin from sheep wool, and beeswax – she then went on to focus on the politics of where her products were manufactured.

Excellent soap, it turned out, was produced cheaply because her supplier exploited cheap immigrant labour. So Roddick set up her own soap factory in a deprived area of Glasgow, Easterhouse. Concerned about the destruction of forests and the treatment of native peoples, she pioneered the idea of an environmental audit, while recycling became central to the appeal of the Body Shop. Fair trade, no animal testing, an environmental conscience . . . suddenly what had been a commercial enterprise was beginning to sound and feel like a crusade about values – one made by, and aimed squarely at, the counterculture of the 1960s.

Anita Roddick was always, however, a shrewd entrepreneur. She opened a second shop six months after the first and by 1991 had 700 branches. What had begun, she always insisted, as 'a series of brilliant accidents' became a big commercial force. Roddick always emphasized the hippy nature of the business, telling a magazine in 1993: 'It had a great smell, it had a funky name . . . It was incredibly sensuous. It was 1976, the year of the heatwave, so there was a lot of flesh around . . . What was unique about it, with no intent at all, was that it translated across cultures, across geographical barriers and social structures. It wasn't a sophisticated plan, it's just happened like that.' Really?

By 2004 the Body Shop 'just happened' to have 1,980 stores and was serving more than 77 million global customers. In March 2006, it was sold to the global cosmetic giant L'Oréal, even though they did use animal testing, something which Anita Roddick insisted she could persuade them to stop. By then her campaigns were almost as famous as her company. She was an early ally of the environmental charity Greenpeace and of the homelessness project the Big Issue. Among her campaigns were some that took on the whole business of beauty directly, including the so-called body fascism which insisted that women had to look a certain way. In the words of one of her adverts, 'There are 3 billion women who don't look like supermodels and only 8 who do.'

Roddick has a good claim to be one of the most influential new Elizabethans of all. During her working life – she died of a brain haemorrhage in 2007 – she confronted and reshaped the biggest socio-political force of the age, the power of the market. 'The market' during the 1980s had become a quasi-religious metaphor for profit-driven capitalism.

But of course real markets, where people exchanged, then sold, their wares have always existed, in towns and villages across the world. There they were only one part of communities which also revered farmed land, religion, local schooling and ethical argument. Almost every town and village had a market, but that didn't mean they *were* a market. Anita Roddick began to find ways of putting other values back into the market system – concern for workers, animals, environments and waste. She was much mocked for it. But if our plastics-choked, wasteful, unfair and sometimes cruel version of turbo-capitalism is to thrive successfully in the century ahead, it has a lot still to learn from the tousled Italian immigrant girl in her Brighton lane. And to learn fast.

55

RIDLEY SCOTT

Three years before the first Body Shop opened in Brighton, another Sixties rebel was hard at work to the west, in the Dorset town of Shaftesbury. A wiry red-headed man from South Shields, he was filming an advert on the town's winding cobbled street, a short film which begins with a boy cycling laboriously up it. Almost everybody of the right age in Britain can still hear and visualize that TV advert, which has Dvořák's New World Symphony theme being played by a brass band, and – of course – promotes the virtues of a bread baked with wheatgerm called Hovis.

Ridley Scott's Hovis film was voted Britain's all-time favourite advertisement in 2006 and had the ultimate accolade of being spoofed by Ronnie Barker in *The Two Ronnies*. As with Anita Roddick's beauty products, it picked up on the 1970s obsession with health and naturalness, showcased by BBC Television's 1975–8 sitcom *The Good Life*. Hovis had been invented in 1886 in Cheshire; the name came from a shortening of the Latin for 'strength of man', *hominis vis*, and it was an industrially made wholemeal bread with a record of sharp marketing. In a Britain both addicted to white bread and becoming more health conscious, the time was right for another push.

Ridley Scott, who went on to have a massive Hollywood career creating such iconic movie hits as *Thelma and Louise*, *Blade Runner* and *Alien*, lovingly coated the brand (and, indeed, the bran) in a short film lusciously dripping with English nostalgia – a young lad in serge shorts and flat cap; sunlit, backlit cobbles; whitewashed, higgledy-piggledy house fronts; with brass-band music dimly washing over every gleam, shadow and brick. But this was also a film of its moment. Although the late 1960s and early 1970s are remembered today as a time of youth rebellion and militancy, nothing is ever that simple, and these were also years of revived patriotic nostalgia. The Kinks' album *The Village Green Preservation Society*, with its regret-filled pop elegies to a vanishing England, which had come out five years earlier, is virtually the set text for that aspect of the age.

But where Scott really captured the zeitgeist was in the attention he was giving to the comparatively young trade of television advertising itself. Industrial Britain had always been a country interested in advertising and marketing. Modern Britain still is. Figures from 2016–17 show Britain's advertising market to be the fourth most lucrative in the world, behind only America, China and Japan. An industry which some still see as marginal claims to contribute £120 billion to the UK's GDP and, with marketing, supports 190,000 British jobs. British agencies are among the most influential and powerful in the world and British advertising creativity is globally celebrated. Advertising is part of the story of the shift in the British economy: at the time of the country leaving the EU, services were the largest contributor to economic growth. And none of this was inevitable.

In the 1950s, it wasn't even likely. The beating heart of the advertising world was New York's Madison Avenue. The London advertising scene, by contrast, was timid, conventional and run by ex-military men who employed frustrated poets and novelists to write appalling puns and easy-to-remember jingles. Artists contributed line drawings and jolly personifications of food products. The great American advertising agencies, such as J. Walter Thompson, were moving to London to support US global manufacturers and expected to squash the local competition. In the other direction a few British-born pioneers such as David Ogilvy, a former secret agent and misinformation officer during the war, were having an impact in America. But there was no doubt where the sophistication, energy and ruthless business sense came from. The British? No style.

This began to change in the 1960s when something very similar to what was happening in pop music, fashion and art spread to commerce. A generation of frustrated rebels, learning from America and often schooled not at universities but in art colleges, were tearing up the rulebook. The cultural influence of art schools deserves a book all of its own. They were about more than drawing, important though drawing is. At a time of more generous state funding of education all across Britain they scooped up sharp, rebellious kids and widened their horizons.

Ridley Scott, like the artists who had created the *Eagle*, was a great admirer of American comic strips, and had learned to draw at West Hartlepool College of Art. He said: 'While I was at West Hartlepool, I suddenly became very conscious of music, for example, and writing and other topics. I began to see how they all interrelated with art. I'd also started to become aware of how I saw things personally, how I viewed the world. So the whole process opened up.' David Bowie, John Lennon, Ian Dury and David Hockney had very similar experiences at their art colleges.

Scott, as the son of an Army officer, had had a peripatetic childhood. Often on the move, he followed films more than high art. He went to the Royal College of Art in London, where he taught himself filmmaking with a camera nobody else wanted. A scholarship to America followed, where Scott haunted advertising agencies and begged introductions to documentary filmmakers. More important, he imbibed an uninhibitedly commercial attitude to work, less common in contemporary Britain. After working as a set designer and director at the BBC, which he found stiflingly conservative and bureaucratic, he started to make TV commercials in his spare time, working with what would become a legendary, almost manic, attention to detail.

He decided to create television ads that were as well crafted as the movie work of personal heroes such as Orson Welles, Ingmar Bergman and David Lean. Thanks to art college he could map out every frame from drawings he made himself. Thanks to his BBC training, he could design his own sets and dictate his own more natural and dramatic lighting. And if this was all designed to sell banal everyday products, so what? The time was ripe. Scott said that TV advertising:

> was a light bulb that was about to shine a light on the rest of culture and society. I could see that the way society was going, with consumerism and so on, advertising was going to become a driving force. I could see it was the way that the whole world was going. I got that, and that was what got me to decide to take it very seriously. I decided to elevate the medium.

By the early 1970s, the blare of advertising executives enjoying long lunches echoed across central London. By now, few of them were any longer wearing regimental ties. New agencies with complicated names (Collett Dickenson Pearce; Papert, Koenig, Lois; Boase Massimi Pollitt; Saatchi & Saatchi) were challenging the old guard. Their executives played at being rock stars and gleefully flaunted their wealth. The younger agencies were bringing wit, sex and style to the recently introduced colour magazines of newspapers, to hoardings on motorways and – above all – to commercial television.

Now admen had tequila habits and Ferraris, and zipped around London scented with dope: but so long as the new ads worked, selling more cigarettes, booze, washing-up liquid and cars, they got away with it. Above all, they made bored consumers take notice and giggle. From the appealing tinpot Martians roaring with laughter at the idea of Earthlings washing, peeling, dicing and boiling potatoes ('For Mash Get Smash') to the adventures of the Cresta bear and the increasingly surreal set-ups for the mini-comedies of (cue 'Air on a G String') 'Happiness is a cigar called Hamlet' or the actor Leonard Rossiter in the Cinzano adverts, much of Britain came to laugh along with, quote and hum their new television adverts.

The admen used to joke or fantasize about people at home sitting on the sofa and calling out to their tea-making other halves, 'Hurry up, dear, the ads are coming on.' But it wasn't entirely a joke. A generation of talented British men who would go on to make their reputations as advertising moguls, novelists or filmmakers – the likes of Peter Mayle, David Puttnam, Alan Parker, Maurice Saatchi and Ridley Scott himself – began as copywriters or technicians in the British advertising boom of the 1970s, creating products that were actually better than many of the programmes they interrupted. It was a period when high art collided with popular culture and made the ordinary man and woman laugh or cry.

This was the B-side of a period now wrongly remembered as entirely a time of counterculture and political rebellion – the entrepreneurial, commercial side of 1970s Britain which, at least in London, was roaring ahead long before Margaret Thatcher came within dreaming distance of Downing Street. The British advertising boom was unusual, of course – a world in which nothing was quite what it seemed. Hovis appeared to be a very traditional British loaf, lost in the golden mists of time; Dorset's Shaftesbury appeared to be somewhere in the North of England; Hamlet was never particularly mild; and Smash was horrid. Never mind. We took the commercial magicians to our hearts and they brightened many lives.

56

NICE BOYS, REALLY?

It should be no great surprise that the brightest talents from British commercial advertising would end up in Hollywood, making truly popular global films, to the point where at the 1981 Oscars ceremony the screenwriter Colin Welland boasted (quoting Paul Revere), 'The British are coming!' Modern Britain may not have been much good at manufacturing reliable and economical products, but, as I hope has been demonstrated, the British have been good at scientific research, ingenious design and marketing – all aspects of creativity. And in the new global economy, the creative industries can make good money. They might not bash much metal, but they can no longer be patronized. The job of turning out well-crafted entertainment that people actually want to pay for should not be underrated. This was a lesson mid-twentieth-century Britain learned early.

If William Shakespeare was the hot-glowing cultural figure of the first Elizabethan age, then the Beatles – John, Paul, George and Ringo – performed a parallel role in the second. That might seem an outlandish comparison. But, like Shakespeare, the Beatles won hearts and minds around the world, in many cultures profoundly different to that of Britain's. Their language was more banal and their stories were shallower but, like Shakespeare, they spoke to people of all backgrounds and ages about timeless things – love, loss, ageing, the search for the divine . . . and taxation. They too came out of the contemporary experience of the English, and they transfixed British society at every level. When, for instance, they became briefly entranced by the Maharishi Mahesh Yogi, in 1968, the Queen herself commented worriedly during a garden party, 'The Beatles are turning awfully funny, aren't they?'

The Beatles are such a well-known phenomenon that they are oddly easy to pass over. But, since this section is about how we earned our living, let us start with some rough numbers. Exports? The Beatles have sold well over 600 million albums around the world. Even in America, they outsold Elvis Presley. In their 1964 US television debut, on *The Ed Sullivan Show*, they drew in 73 million viewers, then a record. Their earnings were correspondingly huge. David Fiorenza, an economics professor at Villanova University near Philadelphia, who specializes in popular music, believes that their financial impact today 'is bigger than any other artist, living or deceased'. Paul McCartney, after a successful solo career, is today worth well over £1 billion, and topped the *Sunday Times* Rich List in 2015. The four boys from Liverpool deserve their place in any discussion about earning our bread.

Before the Beatles another British act had broken into the American market. Mary Isobel Catherine Bernadette O'Brien did it, however, not by emphasizing her Britishness but by mimicking American singers, particularly black ones. She did it so effectively that some of her US fans didn't realize she was British at all. Born into a devout if mildly chaotic Irish family in West London, 'Dusty Springfield' was the greatest British popular singer of the Queen's reign. Through the TV programme *Ready, Steady Go!*, she introduced her fellow subjects to the new black American music of Motown. But, more than the Beatles, more than the Rolling Stones, Dusty absorbed the luscious sound and haunting spirit of the new American music and made it her own.

Her very name, Springfield, had been chosen because of the sheer number of towns called that across the United States. The most influential experience of her early life was singing in 1964 at Brooklyn's Fox Theatre with the greatest of the African-American acts of the day – Marvin Gaye, Martha Reeves, Smokey Robinson and the Supremes.

Dusty Springfield, unlike the Beatles, had to fight as a woman in a cocky, swaggeringly male world, and with few allies. Bisexual most of her life, and always strongly attracted to women, she was forced to hide her private life and dodge questions to keep her fan base loyal. Despite her huge fame and glamorous image, she was often short of money and struggled with depression, drink and drugs. She should be remembered, however, not as a tragic heroine but as one of the most successful, professional and driven British performers to break into the American market and, in turn, to introduce the British to the best of the new music.

For all the mayhem associated with their lives, the Beatles were much tougher and more organized about money. It never quite came first. They set up their own commercial empire, the Apple Corporation, but it bled and splurged cash in every direction, subsidizing other artists and investing in hopelessly idealistic and short-lived businesses. What makes them a good symbol of British creativity – its genius and its fatal flaws – is that they were constant, restless, impatient, almost crazy reinventors of themselves. From album to album, they disdained repetition, or – you might say – building up the kind of predictable, bankable, long-term 'product' that their great rivals, the Rolling Stones, assembled. The Stones, perhaps unconsciously, limited themselves. They had one overwhelming subject, sex, and an instantly recognizable rock-blues sound. In Keith Richards they had a band member who understood almost as much about black American music as had Dusty Springfield. They toured relentlessly, under their business-minded leader Mick Jagger. At the time of writing they're still at it.

The Beatles, by contrast, ripped up newly successful ideas in the service of constant experimentation. From their first album *Please Please Me*, released in 1963, to the final one, *Let It Be*, in 1970, there are seven years of dazzlingly fast change. From, for instance, 1965's *Help!* to the following year's *Rubber Soul* there is a giant leap of sensibility. Then, in succeeding years, from 1966, come *Revolver*, *Sgt Pepper's Lonely Hearts Club Band* and the *White Album*, each of them unexpected enough to surprise, even to alarm, fans who thought they knew who the Beatles were.

They wrote and sang about almost everything: family life, ageing, loneliness, the absurdity of celebrity, hypocritical politics, the news and the weather, as well as sex and drugs. Each album introduced new sounds, new musical structures and a new idea of what 'pop music' might be and could do. They were driven, first and foremost, not by wanting to make money but by human curiosity. So, although the Beatles did make a huge amount of money and were globally successful, to the extent that they changed outsiders' views of Britain for ever (and for the better), they were never a stable long-term business.

Like so many other creative partnerships – Crick and Watson of DNA fame, or Gilbert and Sullivan, or other rock groups from Pink Floyd to Oasis – the personal tensions that helped keep them creatively exciting would, eventually, drive them apart. It's not too big a stretch to say that the Beatles can be used as a metaphor for modern British creativity – hugely imaginative, fast, unstable and eventually unreliable. They were the songsters of a country which brimmed with inventiveness and won Nobel prizes, but was too butterfly-minded to build long-term, big-employment businesses from the results.

These days, they are the modern musicians whom grandparents enjoy. But the Beatles, like millions of other youngsters who grew up in the shadow of the Second World War, reacted to the desperate tedium and meagreness of working-class life by becoming rebels against everything their parents stood for. Their parents, of course, had themselves grown up through the twin disruptions of the Depression years and then the war itself.

Like so many other British families, these were survivors' families. John Lennon's father Alf was a seaman; after his son had been conceived during the darkest days of the war, he was almost never at home, away on merchant ships (and sometimes in prisons), while his wife 'carried on' with other men at home. John was brought up by his aunt Mimi, not by his wilder mother. Paul McCartney's family was more conventional; but his father was a volunteer fire-fighter, often away from home, and his mother, a midwife, died of an embolism when he was just fourteen. George Harrison was brought up in extreme poverty. His father had been a merchant seaman and then a corporation bus driver. Richie Starkey, who became Ringo Starr, was like John Lennon in that he barely knew his real father – a confectioner, who turned towards the bottle and away from his family. Young Richie suffered two long and very serious bouts of childhood illness before his mother, who had been desperately poor, remarried.

After all that, if the Beatles sounded a tad antagonistic to comfortable, soft, middle-class Britain, it is hardly surprising. They grew up learning to use their fists, sarcastic and bolshie at school, and sceptical of all adult authority.

In this, they mirrored the story of millions of other hard-grafting, less musical, growing, questioning British people who happened to live in the middle of the twentieth century. The boredom and the frustration of the Beatles was the boredom and frustration of half the country. When the Beatles expressed sentimental affection for old tunes, fairground music and British children's stories, they were likewise speaking for millions. The arc of the John–Paul–George–Ringo stories; their background and where they went next; the rasp, the humour, the specific brilliance of the harmonies and the lyrics; and even their coarse disdain for the disabled, foreigners and anyone different – all these things are not just theirs but ours. This is a collective story.

Liverpool is not England, never mind Britain. Salt in its air, and salty of tongue, it stares out to Ireland and east-coast America. Like Bristol, it made plenty of dirty money from slavery; but in more modern times it has been a grimy, seethingly energetic cultural crossroads, where poor Catholic families from Donegal rubbed shoulders with Jewish immigrants from Russia and Poland, on their way to New York or Chicago, but who had stopped after landing on England's east coast and crossing the country. A low-level war between Protestant and Catholic Liverpudlians crackled and popped through the first half of the twentieth century. The city the Beatles were born into had, furthermore, been smashed to pieces by the Luftwaffe and barely rebuilt. It had once had excellent architecture, a proud artistic heritage and a culture of thriving entrepreneurialism. But by the 1950s it was a battered and resentful place, its bony naked back contemptuously turned on the rest of England.

Some of that 'up for it' attitude would feed into the music of the Beatles, and their famously, often hilariously, spiky press conferences. But John, Paul, George and Ringo were also all born into a musical and literary tradition which they shared with working-class communities across other British cities. Even if their parents and grandparents had struggled to make a living, by the late 1950s it was an aspirational culture: from John Lennon's Aunt Mimi, who made it into a semi-detached house with servants' bells, to Paul McCartney's father, Jim, who wanted him to get to university and follow the example of singers and entertainers in America and London who were making real money, they were surrounded by people who pushed and who demanded better.

Near at hand were the popular English and Irish musical traditions of a world before cheap recorded music. Almost everybody seemed to sing songs round a piano. Paul's father had had a successful dance band between the wars – Jim Mac's Syncopated Band – and his grandfather had played the tuba in his local works band. When Richie, later Ringo, fell ill and was taken to hospital with pleurisy, he was visited by a music teacher handing out percussion instruments. His mother, when she remarried a Londoner, had a party at which 'the old songs were sung'. George Harrison's father, when a steward on an Atlantic shipping line, brought home a guitar – though it was quickly pawned. Harrison was a youthful enthusiast for the music and comedy of George Formby, the inter-war ukulele-strumming singer. Most strikingly, perhaps, John Lennon's mother gave impromptu singing recitals in local pubs and was a dab hand on the banjo. His father, absent for most of his life, was a harmonica player and irrepressible entertainer. This was a world of live music and domestic showing-off.

But it wasn't just music as a tradition that would feed into the creativity of the Beatles. This was a band firmly planted in the soil of English surrealism. Both Lennon and McCartney grew up as avid fans of Lewis Carroll and *Alice in Wonderland*; Lennon was also a lover of Kenneth Grahame's *Wind in the Willows* and Richmal Crompton's *Just William*. They soaked up the surreal humour of BBC Radio's *The Goon Show*, the anarchic Spike Milligan a particular favourite.

English surrealism and absurdity, from Edward Lear to post-war comedy, threads through the work of the Beatles ('I am the Walrus', 'Lucy in the Sky with Diamonds') in an unmistakable way. They knew the same sentimental and music-hall songs, and the same books, and the same jokes, as their British audience, of all classes. From this mash-up we get their unique moment: 'Lucy' is simultaneously a song about LSD – though John Lennon always denied that, claiming it derived from a drawing made by his son Sean at school – and about a scene in *Alice Through the Looking Glass*. Only the Kinks from North London played with British nostalgia as expertly.

This was also a time when the British were becoming hypnotized by (entranced by but simultaneously aghast at) the cultural power of America. For all the richness of their musical working-class background, the Beatles are unthinkable without a series of aural shocks echoing from across the Atlantic – Gene Vincent, Little Richard, Bill Haley and the Comets and of course King Elvis himself. Liverpool as an Atlantic port city, with merchant sailors, 'the Cunard Yanks', familiar on its streets, was particularly open to these new influences. John Lennon later said: 'We were like the 59th state in Britain. We had all the Doris Day movies, and Heinz beans. (We all thought they were *English*.) We were brought up on Americana.'

While critics from cabinet ministers through to the vicar who created Dan Dare were appalled by the crudity and lack of sophistication of the new imported culture, to young and rebellious Liverpudlian boys it was fantastic – it smelled like teen spirit. The Beatles, who had barely known a black person as adolescents, created their unique sound from blending the harmonies of traditional English music and the transgressive urgencies of black American rock 'n' roll. But although they were genius-creators, they were hardly alone: by the early 1960s, thanks to pirate radio stations, local record companies and the big film distributors, much of Britain was being soused in American sounds.

'Melting pot' is a frequently abused metaphor. It suggests ingredients dissolving into a smooth, warm goo, lacking distinctiveness. Twentieth-century Liverpool was sharper-edged, less digestible, than that; and the music of the Beatles was specific, instantly recognizable and strongly flavoured. But they were the products of a city and a time abnormally open to outside influence, and it wasn't just America.

In the late 1950s and early 1960s, as they were forming themselves, much of the rest of Britain was engaged in passionate debate about whether or not to try to join 'Europe'. There was some alarm about the danger of a federal system and, in the words of the Labour leader Hugh Gaitskell, the end of a thousand years of independent history. How deeply did we really want to intertwine ourselves with the French and – worse still – the Germans? In short, what did the Europeans do for us?

John, Paul, George and the other pre-Ringo Beatles answered these questions by actually going there, on an extended contract to play in nightclubs in Hamburg. John Lennon had a brutal English dismissiveness about the 'Krauts' or, as he called them to their faces, the 'Nazis'. (In this age of political correctness, by the way, anyone who believes there should be no quarter given to historical abusiveness, and that people should be judged for life on what they say as angry, ignorant adolescents, should now quit humming the music of the Beatles. Lennon, in particular, said disgusting things about Jews, black people and anyone disabled. Talking about 'crips', 'Mongols', 'Yids' and so on was common practice in working-class British communities in the 1950s, and although the Beatles were sometimes seen later as liberal exemplars, by modern standards they really weren't.)

Hamburg was essential to the making of the Beatles. Another salty, wild, trading-port city, it embraced the new music from Liverpool long before London did. The Beatles had to play relentlessly for hours, night after night, to raucous and drunken audiences of local toughs, prostitutes and sailors. It was in Hamburg that they were forced to become professionals. It was there, ordered to 'make show', that they learned to display on-stage theatrics – the exhibitionist leaping, whooping and shouting – that would make them so exciting shortly afterwards in Liverpool's Cavern Club.

And it was in Hamburg that they began to create a new look – German leather jackets, black leather trousers and cowboy boots, topped off with bizarre pink, and accurately named, 'twat hats'. A German fan, Astrid Kirchherr, took the first decent images of the group and, by the time they returned to Liverpool, they were transformed from the eager but amateurish students they had been. A rival rock guitarist, Chris Huston, tried to explain the change: 'When they came back from Germany it was like they knew something we didn't. They had this arrogance. There was a definite difference: they had a cockiness, confidence, a spring in their step, they knew more songs and they had different instruments.'

We think of the Beatles today as defiantly and entirely British. They could have emerged nowhere else and at no other time. But, like the British generally at the beginning of the 1960s, they were being pressed in upon by outside influences – American and European. Without the American rock 'n' roll explosion, and then the Hamburg experience, they could not have been the group they became.

And although the Beatles, who visited an ashram in 1968, were early exponents of Indian sounds in their music, and of Hindu spirituality, they were certainly not the first Britons on the 'hippy trail' to the East. Earnestly searching for alternative forms of enlightenment, and just as earnestly searching for marijuana, 'Beatniks' had been journeying overland to the Indian subcontinent since at least 1957; Swagman Tours and other bus companies had been operating from the early 1960s, by which time Kathmandu already boasted its own 'Freak Street'. Even in their cotton Indian gowns and beads, which puzzled majority British opinion, the Beatles were an example of a wider trend.

As leaders, they suffered the mockery pioneering spirits often do. When John Lennon finally left his wife Cynthia for Yoko Ono, he set off a wave of racist fury among Beatles fans, who could not understand how they had lost 'their' John to a diminutive Japanese – whose country, after all, we had beaten in the war.

Yoko Ono was the child of a wealthy, privileged and artistic Japanese clan who had been reduced to impoverished refugees during the bombing by the Americans in 1945. One of the original conceptual artists, she first came across John Lennon when he visited an exhibition of her work in central London. He saw her *Ladder Piece*, consisting of a white painted ladder that led to a tiny card on the ceiling with the word 'Yes' written on it. Another exhibit simply consisted of a hammer and nails, and a board with the invitation to hammer the nail in. Lennon asked if he could do so. Yoko Ono said no, because the gallery was not opening until the next day: each nail would cost him five shillings. John Lennon paused and responded: 'Well, I will give you an imaginary five shillings, and hammer an imaginary nail in.'

The Liverpudlian surrealist and the Japanese concept artist found they had a similar way of thinking and a similar sense of humour. John Lennon said later, 'And that's when we really met. That's when we locked eyes and she got it and I got it and that was it.' This was when the British public was beginning to be introduced to puzzling and challenging forms of 'anti-art': what Lennon was experiencing in a tiny gallery near St James's Square would become the stuff of newspaper controversies at the Tate Gallery and elsewhere before long. But the public was not ready for a national icon to fall in love with a Japanese woman.

Yoko was abused and mocked and had her hair pulled by angry fans. In the words of John Lennon's biographer Philip Norman, 'The unanimous public response was blank incomprehension. John still lived a life that was the envy of millions. He could have anything in creation that he wanted. With such clothes and cars and mansions and beautiful dolly birds at his disposal, what could he possibly want with a fiercely unglamorous looking Japanese woman from the art world's lunatic fringe?' But throughout their brief flowering, the Beatles were constantly challenging their audience to think again – from the way they dressed to Paul McCartney's later embrace of vegetarianism.

The difference between the Beatles and their fellow countrymen was that they would then go out and change – in turn – American and European culture. Fans around the world became as emotionally engaged with them as British fans had been, something John Lennon paid for with his life when he was shot and murdered by a deranged American follower in New York in December 1980. But this pushing-out to the rest of the world, this imposing of emotions concocted in Liverpool, is almost a definition of successful export productivity. And the Beatles were nothing if not productive. They turned out not just songs, but styles.

In that seven-year torrent of chords, metaphors and images, as soon as they had established something new, something that hadn't been heard before, they smashed it up and moved on. It was a musical version of today's 'creative destruction' revered by Californian internet moguls. They brought in Eastern musical instruments, full orchestras, synthesizers. The uncanny thing is that, as they hungrily lurched forward from one style to the next, they seemed like a running commentary on wider British changes of style and attitude.

In their earliest incarnation, they are visibly the boys of the post-war British world, who had narrowly avoided National Service call-up by months. They had done badly enough at school – all were serial exam-fluffers – to have no prospect of university and little chance of a conventional working-class trade, so where they were going next was unclear. Then, as the music begins to work its magic, the greased quiffs and bomber jackets of American rock 'n' roll appear. Almost Teddy Boys. Then it's into matching floppy haircuts and self-designed suits, a smart, clipped eager quartet who want to please. 'I don't care too much for money,' they would sing, but although money can't buy you love, they had conventional aspirations – for smart cars, their own houses and swimming pools. In that they mimicked the aspirations of millions of working-class people who had, before Wilson's 1964 election victory, turned to the Tories and consumerism.

As the beards appeared, then grew longer, along with the hair, the Beatles represented the counterculture imported from America in the mid-1960s. Military uniforms, which had been commonly seen on the streets of the country, were now worn ironically or even sarcastically – day-glo cod-Victorian tunics dripping with braid. The National Health spectacles everybody (but in particular the shortsighted John Lennon) had been forced to wear were reinvented as sunglasses. Beards and fabrics brought the culture of once colonized peoples to the heart of tabloid-reading British life.

They were never financial geniuses. Philip Norman argues that in 1967, for instance, 'The Beatles knew nothing – literally nothing – about the vast business they had created and continued to generate. [Their manager Brian Epstein] had always taken care of everything, periodically bringing them contracts or agreements, which they always signed without question, often without even reading.' But after Epstein's suicide they went on to create the holding company controlling their record label, a short-lived shop and other interests. Even John Lennon worked hard at being a business executive, at least for a while.

All of the Beatles enjoyed their money and their Rolls-Royces and their large country houses. And they were enough of the working-class children of their time to celebrate success and be proud of it. They were stroppy, not subversive; cocky, not communist. As they sang in 'Revolution', we may all want to change the world, but when it came to destruction, you could count them out.

Like so much of other British working-class opinion, they were delighted to stick one up to the snotty and easily offended establishment. They protested against war and they campaigned for the legalization of cannabis, but they were a long way from actually wanting socialist transformation. It may be unfashionable to say so, but in that as well they had the tempo of the times. The 1960s were a period of cultural challenge and generational conflict; but for the majority of working-class families this was also a period of greater material wealth, new 'stuff' to delight in and hang on to. Like the Labour movement, the Beatles were always less challenging to the status quo than they seemed at first sight.

57

OUTLANDISH FRUIT

So far we have met many creative change-makers and seen great industries go under. Decade by decade, like the medieval wheel of fortune, the business cycle has hoicked us up and flung us down. But overall we have become materially wealthier. As compared to the British of the early 1950s, we are far better fed, better clothed, warmer, better entertained. Nor are we 'Little Britain'. We know more about far-off cultures. Many more of us go out into the world, and more frequently; for every 1950s soldier heading off to Malaya or Oman, for every accountant heading for Bombay or Egypt, hundreds of inquisitive young Britons flood to Vietnam, Cambodia, Colombia and Peru. And they can, if they choose, be much better read than their grandparents. Despite political arguments and fears of environmental disaster ahead, in so many ways these are the best of times.

But today's British are also adrift on fast-moving currents. They have been granted everything, except identity and purpose. The openness of the economy, buffeted by banking crises or viral disasters, means no Britons can really protect themselves from global currents. In that open economy the signs of failure and disintegration are often more visible and moving than the rebuilding and reorganization going on at the same time. We have already discussed the collapse of heavy industry. We have seen the rise of the advertising industry, partly dependent on much easier access to credit. The missing link is the transformation of the City of London.

Big changes began in the 1960s, through to the early years of the new century when the City was complicit in the global crash of 2008. This in turn helped produce the anti-elite anger behind the 2016 referendum. Few of us really understand it, but the City touches every part of public life. The true story of its power today goes back to 1963 and the arrival of the eurodollar and eurobond markets, which opened up new avenues for the dusty, hierarchical old firms that had evolved to service the British Empire. The next big moment was the abolition of exchange controls by Margaret Thatcher's first Chancellor Sir Geoffrey Howe on 23 October 1979 – something Howe himself described as akin to walking off a cliff to see what happened next.

Three years later, American culture arrived properly in financial London, with the opening of the raucous international financial futures market in the old Royal Exchange. (And the Americans taught commercial Britain one very valuable thing: drink less, particularly at lunchtime.) Then, finally, in October 1986, Mrs Thatcher's next Chancellor, Nigel Lawson, oversaw the abolition of a web of old rules governing the Stock Exchange itself. The most visible sign of the 'Big Bang' was the arrival of screen-based computer trading. This increased the volume of trading as compared to the old gentlemanly days of the early 1980s, fifteen times over. London became a pivot for the new supercharged financial system, exporting vastly more in financial services. From now on, Tory and Labour governments found they could only balance the national books thanks to the annual tax bonanzas brought in by bankers and traders.

As with any great economic change, the unleashing of the City brought unexpected and disturbing shifts in power. Cabinet ministers found themselves deferring to the red-braced, flushed young titans from American merchant banks who had bought up old British firms or opened mysterious and fashionable new hedge funds in Mayfair. Political power has always paid tribute to big money. But now something was different. The new algorithm-driven way of thinking about trading currencies and derivatives required expert and aggressive oversight and regulation. Politicians simply didn't have a clue and were drawn into the new game. When they retired, ministers and senior civil servants were given lucrative board positions in the financial sector.

One way or another, politicians had long understood that, to win votes by funding public services, they needed the money gurgling into HM Revenue and Customs accounts from the financial institutions. The new City courted them, paid them and funded their politics. If the new recruits found it hard to understand exactly what was being traded, and how – well, too bad. The proper balance of power between the state and markets operating inside it began to fail. This, rather than the disconcerting transformation in the way the centre of London looked, with the sprouting of increasingly bizarre and enormous glass towers through the maze of a medieval street-plan, outlandish fruit that could be seen from tens of miles away, was the change that mattered.

But the arrival of the new financial world at the heart of London was only the start of the transformation being wrought by the globalization which followed the end of the Cold War. Russian money followed Arab money into the British property market. The giant Californian tech companies changed the way the British discovered the world around them (Google, Twitter), shopped (Amazon), holidayed (Airbnb) and travelled (Uber). Like the giants of the financial world a generation earlier, they both intimidated and from time to time bought up the British political class. They rarely paid their fair share in taxation while, simultaneously, they quietly throttled small and long-established rivals out of business.

Today, for instance, it is unarguable that the British high street is being gutted by online shopping. Once familiar names, such as Woolworths, Marks & Spencer, BHS, Austin Reed, Jaeger, Toys R Us, Carpetright, Mothercare and Maplin, have been forced to announce multiple store closures or have vanished altogether. Online shopping is dominated by the American behemoths, Amazon in particular. They have a muscle and lobbying influence over British politics which is much stronger than that of traditional British retailers. So this reshaping of the familiar high street is likely to be something that continues, and even accelerates.

A 2016 study by the distributor ParcelHero – clearly an interested party – suggested that in Britain by 2030 half of today's shops will have gone. Had a fraction of the passion and energy that was spent on getting Britain out of the EU gone instead into using taxation and regulation to take back control from global commercial power then we would today be a very different country. Sovereignty can be lost to familiar retail names based out of the reach of the British tax authorities just as surely as to Belgian-based Eurocrats.

Although the high street is a handy example of one problem the modern British economy faces, there are plenty of alternatives. Pharmaceuticals, or drugs, are one of Britain's most important industries. employing some 73,000 people and notching up a healthy £4.3 billion trade surplus. In 2007, Britain's research and development pharmaceutical budget was the third highest in the world, and the highest in Europe. But, in a policy blueprint labelled 'American Patients First', in 2018 Donald Trump declared economic war on Britain for using the bargaining leverage of the NHS to keep down the price of drugs for British patients. He said: 'America will not be cheated any longer, and especially will not be cheated by foreign countries. In some cases, medicine that costs a few dollars in a foreign country costs hundreds of dollars in America for the same pill, with the same ingredients, in the same package, made in the same plant. That is unacceptable.'

The US President's Health Secretary Alex Azar later made it clear that America would use post-Brexit trade negotiations to pile on the pressure: 'The reason why they are getting better net prices than we get is their socialized system.' And these pressures are not limited to pharmaceuticals. Coming only after the City, Britain's aerospace industry is the country's most important sector. Here too, the politics of the Trump administration in the United States and of European protectionism pose huge challenges for British engineering.

Cassandras are always popular, but we need to remember that we are also living through the birth-pangs of a new economy. Registrations at Companies House in London show a tenfold increase between 1979 and the teenage years of the new century in new companies being created. There were 645,000 of them in 2016–17 alone. Yes, the rate of company dissolutions, or failures, has risen sharply as well, but the net effect is strongly positive, and has been particularly so since the recovery from the 2008 financial crisis. There is, in short, decent statistical evidence that Britain has become one of the world's more entrepreneurial countries. But we shouldn't get overexcited. The financial writer David Prosser has made the point that 'very significant numbers of Britain's army of the self-employed aren't what we would traditionally think of as small business founders and owners. They're either surviving hand to mouth through a series of paid work gigs, as and when they're needed, or they have found self-employment to be a more lucrative model for work they would have done in any case, courtesy of the tax system.'

That said, the figures include some quite substantial hi-tech companies, often based around 'Silicon Roundabout' in East London, the creations of agile, sharp-elbowed entrepreneurs who find it easier to raise money in modern Britain – and less humiliating to close businesses – than it was in the past. Away from the shutting-up high-street chains, and the struggles in trade deals between giant industries, we can see the beginnings of a Britain of companies created by designers, smaller-scale architects, niche retailers, brewers and caterers. Before going on to give examples of this new economy, however, it is worth asking whether it will reshape the way the country thinks. As we have seen, the age of mass manufacturing created a certain social system and tone. One thing is for certain: a differently shaped British economy will produce a differently shaped social map of Britain.

Thatcherism was based on the conviction that the free market meant freedom, and that the free British would be necessarily distinctive – more themselves than ever. Thatcher herself was pious, hard-working and mildly puritanical. The smashing of old institutions and corporations that was central to her project unleashed a period of unparalleled borrowing and consumerism, in which we still live and which didn't reflect, really, her own personality or preferences. Free! Yes, but free to do what? Free to shop. Free to become just like consumers everywhere – free to be shaped by American and Chinese technologies, Japanese designs and global trends. Free, in fact, to become less distinctively British.

A British economy based much more on younger, smaller businesses, constantly dying back and regrowing, is bound to feel socially different from the Britain of the twentieth century, the land of the tall, old trees, with quiet spaces between them. It puts a higher premium on individuality and risk-taking. The old disciplines of hierarchical offices, many-layered corporations and authoritarian factories are replaced by a less formal society in which experimentation of all kinds – in dress, language, sexuality, living arrangements, diet – is easier to embrace. We may be moving, in this new economic shrubland, towards a Britain of 10,000 cultural tribes, who share far less than they used to. This is alarming. But it is intriguing and exciting as well. Let us, therefore, meet some of the new economic pioneers bringing it about.

58

THE QUEEN OF THE CURVE

There was an Iraq before its nightmarish Islamist takeover, before its invasion by the British and Americans and before its civil war. There was a comparatively tranquil Baghdad before Saddam Hussein seized power. In that city, a very bright young girl was brought up at a Catholic school where, although a Sunni Muslim herself, she mingled with Jewish, Christian and Shi'ite children. Her mother was an artist. Her father was a successful industrialist and a democratic political leader, co-founder of the National Liberal Party.

All around her, Baghdad was being rebuilt, including by Western architects brought in by the then government. It was a time of optimism. At some point in the late 1950s, Zaha Hadid's father took her on a trip to the south of Iraq to visit the ancient civilization of Sumer. It was a formative experience, she told the *Guardian* later: 'we went by boat, and then on a smaller one made of reeds, to visit villages in the marshes. The beauty of the landscape – where sand, water, reeds, birds, buildings and people all somehow flowed together – has never left me.'

If anyone became a British citizen of the modern world, it was Zaha Hadid. She went on to study maths at the American University in Beirut before moving to London in 1972 to study architecture, where her tutors included the visionary Dutch architect Rem Koolhaas. After a long struggle to get her eccentric and challenging (though extremely beautiful) designs built, her work can now be seen across Britain, all across continental Europe and in China, the United States, Korea, Azerbaijan and Japan. 'The Queen of the curve' who always avoided 90° angles and straight lines, Zaha Hadid was made a dame by the Queen in 2012. She was also an honorary member of the American Academy of Arts and Letters, and the first female winner of the prestigious Pritzker Architecture Prize. There were those who loathed her buildings, characterized by audacious sweeps and biological bulges, as if they had grown, rather than being constructed. But for others she was one of the great architectural geniuses of the modern age.

If and when alien beings land on the planet, they will surely be particularly impressed by some of the objects Hadid has left behind. In Beijing they would find the office complex known as Galaxy Soho, four giant egg-like structures linked together by looping passages, so that they seem almost to be moving. Moving south to Guangzhou, they'd gape at the Opera House there, two huge river rocks which appeared to be covered with polished granite and glass. The *Financial Times* writer Edwin Heathcote described it as a building 'that seems to suck the surrounding landscape into a vortex of movement and swirling space . . . an alien object in a landscape of incomprehensible vastness', while others find that walking into it was like entering a huge moist oyster.

In the politically controversial project of the Heydar Aliyev Center in Azerbaijan, Hadid created a conference centre which appears like a vast white wave erupting from the land around it, less a conventional building than a dream of the ocean in the centre of Asia. It is very much the creation of the young girl who took her sketching pad to the marshy reed beds and villages of southern Iraq. And she kept her interest in ecology: in Seoul, South Korea, her Dongdaemun Design Plaza, while looking like a giant floating mushroom is double skinned and solar panelled and contains its own system for recycling water. When we ask about the British influence in the world of the twenty-first century, then in terms of actual physical evidence the work of Zaha Hadid is unignorable.

But then, if we ask whether this is British influence at all, we have to deal with the slippery, porous internationalism of modern London. For most of the past century, this has been a place where people of power and talent – artists, collectors, entrepreneurs, financiers – have wanted to settle, learn, start businesses and work. The traffic has slightly but noticeably eroded traditional British ideas, but it has given Britain more influence overseas. Even if we restrict ourselves to the categories of Iraq and of architecture, the moral is pretty clear. Along with Zaha Hadid, Iraqis who settled in London included Charles and Maurice Saatchi, who created one of the most globally famous advertising companies of the 1980s; Alan Yentob, the BBC broadcaster and arts promoter; and the creator of the Mothercare chain, Selim Zilkha.

Among the most dominant British architects, Norman Foster is British-born, though his work is also known around the world and he himself lives between the UK, continental Europe and the United States. But his great friend and rival Richard Rogers came, like Hadid, as a migrant to London. Rogers's parents were Italians, Jewish by origin and liberal by instinct. His Florentine father Nino, a doctor, fled Mussolini's fascists and settled in England. His son reflects on what that meant:

> Nino loved England as only a foreigner can. He prized classic English brands – Burberry raincoats, Dents gloves and Lotus shoes – and dressed as the epitome of the saying, 'To be truly English, you have to be a foreigner'. For him, it seemed an oasis of democracy and liberal values in an unstable world. English newspapers, Dickens and G. K. Chesterton's Father Brown stories were his favourite reading . . .

Nino's son, who sounds like a gleeful Englishman and dresses like an Italian fashion designer, would go on to transform parts of London. Like Hadid and Foster, his iconic buildings can be seen all around the world. If modern Paris is marked by his still shockingly modern, trumpeting Pompidou Centre, then contemporary London's skyline is punctuated, almost stabbed, by the so-called Shard, created by Rogers's long-time friend and collaborator Renzo Piano. Buildings like these focus a sharp Anglepoise light on the modern Anglo-Saxons. Our influence around the world is in part driven by recent migrants, and our openness to the world has meant that we are open – vulnerable if you like – to global fashions, in architecture, art and much else. It's a bargain.

Some people, probably including the Prince of Wales, regard it as a rotten bargain. This writer looks up at the Shard almost every day of his life with a shiver of pleasure. A loaded and hostile word for the international class is 'rootless'. Nothing could be further from the truth when it comes to Rogers or Hadid. Rogers is rooted in the traditions of Tuscan living and architecture, and has spent much of his life campaigning to bring a more compact, continental style of living to Britain – terraces and trees, bridges and gardens, rather than high-rise blocks. Hadid's early exposure to the natural swamps of southern Iraq and the huge swooping monuments of the Sumerians has likewise left its mark on modern Britain – the Aquatics Centre built for the 2012 London Olympics being a good example.

Both these architects, and other influential contemporary Britons, were always rooted – just not, originally, here. But they were able to graft ideas from abroad on to native British lives and so produce some interesting flowered hybrids. British? Not British? That is one for philosophers, not writers of history books.

59

STRONG SUCKERS AND RASPBERRIES: MAKING IT HERE

I s it still possible to move on from design and to grow manufacturing from a standing start in Britain? Or has the making-stuff
spirit gurgled away? One retort can be found by driving a short
distance from the ancient town of Malmesbury in Wiltshire. To call
Malmesbury sleepy would be an understatement. One of the ancient
burhs created by Alfred the Great to defend early England against
the Vikings, it boasts its abbey, a rare survivor of the dissolution
of the monasteries, and what is said to be the oldest hotel in Britain.
As you pass its butterscotch-coloured Cotswold houses, you can
almost hear the contented snoring.

And yet, just a few miles outside the town, lies Britain's youngest
university, created by the inventor Sir James Dyson as part of his
manufacturing centre. Ready-built student accommodation, brought
down by truck from Scotland, has been winched into place: engineering students are being encouraged to apply for grants, in return
for which they will agree to work extremely hard and drink very
little beer. Just around the corner is the headquarters of the Dyson
Group, manufacturers of vacuum cleaners, hand dryers, hairdryers

and much else. There is a useful, optimistic buzz about the place, with the workforce both less male than one might expect and clearly international in origin.

Sir James Dyson, a tall, wiry, energetic and opinionated man, seems a typically establishment figure. He is a winner of the Prince Philip Designers Prize, a member of the Order of Merit, a knight, a Fellow of the Royal Society and a former Provost of the Royal College – as well as being a multi-billionaire with a famously funky yacht. His headquarters is festooned with previous examples of great British engineering, from Sir Frank Whittle's original jet engine to Alec Issigonis's Mini and an entire English Electric Lightning jet fighter. Yet this product of art school also has the doggedness, determination and anti-establishment radicalism of so many successful inventors.

He started with the simple concept of replacing the wheel of a wheelbarrow with the ball, to give it greater manoeuvrability, but his real breakthrough came after developing cyclonic separation (the use of cyclones to pick up and discard particles) to replace traditional household vacuum cleaners, which become clogged and depend upon bags of dust being replaced. Surviving on his wife's salary as an art teacher, Dyson produced more than 5,000 prototypes before launching his first cleaner in 1983. Fiercely opposed by traditional manufacturers, he had a long struggle before, a decade later, he was able to launch properly in the UK.

Since his idea was rejected by the major companies, he was obliged to start his own manufacturing centre at Malmesbury in 1993. His first major line became the fastest-selling vacuum cleaner ever made in the UK, outselling popular brands whose owners had turned up their noses at him. Once he was successful, he had to fight legal cases to stop his technology being stolen by competitors, as well as moving on to other products, including a novel kind of hand dryer.

Having created a major engineering centre in rural Wiltshire,

Dyson is now spending about £7–£8 million a week on research and development and employing more than 3,500 engineers and scientists. Deeply disturbed by the lack of well-trained engineers in Britain, he is using his private wealth to create his own educational hub – a Dyson university – alongside the factory. He has also acquired an enormous former RAF airbase, Hullavington, whose giant hangars, once the home of wartime bombers, can be adapted as research and manufacturing centres, and whose long, sprawling runways can be used to test electric cars.

For several years he was determined to build his own electric car before deciding it was simply too expensive and giving up in 2019. This is hardly surprising. The modestly sized and entirely privately funded Dyson team was, after all, taking on Elon Musk's Californian electric car giant Tesla and Japanese global firms such as Toyota and Honda, which are moving ahead quickly on electric technology, as well as the slower-moving but always formidable German automobile industry. But part of the personality of an entrepreneur must be a willingness to oppose conventional wisdom, and an impatience with constraints. And these include the constraint of where you choose to manufacture.

Dyson once campaigned for Britain to join the euro, but since then, having faced innumerable obstacles and legal challenges inside the EU, has become a firm opponent of Britain's continuing membership of what he sees as an anti-competitive cartel. He was an outspoken supporter of Brexit and, after the referendum, of an abrupt British break with the rest of the EU. In the autumn of 2017, speaking as the boss of one of the fastest-growing companies in Europe, he pointed out that the EU is one of the slower-growth areas in the world; that 86 per cent of his company's growth was outside the EU; and that he was already paying World Trade Organization tariffs into Europe but doing fine.

Business, he said, was about uncertainty: 'There's always uncertainty in business, about exchange rates, conditions in markets, natural disasters . . . I think uncertainty is an opportunity, and the opportunity here is actually that the rest of the world is growing at a far greater rate than Europe, so the opportunity is to export to the rest of the world and to capitalize on that.'

But despite his own best efforts in Wiltshire, Britain still has a desperate shortage of trained engineers. Nor has the British government been terribly keen to help him: he was one of those tasked to produce new ventilator designs during the coronavirus crisis, but having commissioned fresh designs from British companies, ministers went cold on the idea. Even with all that, and acknowledging that his most important task is first to survive and then to thrive in a cut-throat global market, Dyson's decision on cars is a deep disappointment.

Clearly, a Britain with a few score energetic, optimistic and determined entrepreneurs on the Dyson model, who were confident enough actually to manufacture here, would be in a much stronger position for the century ahead. So is this story an idiosyncratic one-off on which we shouldn't depend too much? Or are there examples of manufacturing returning, despite all the predictions, to the UK?

Pencoed in South Wales is less than an hour and a half's drive almost due west of Malmesbury. It is a heavily industrialized little town which includes a major Sony factory, and there the best-selling British computer is manufactured. But it isn't a household consumer name, coming in a big silver box or with pre-programmed scenic screens of sunlit mountains. It is, frankly, a rather ugly little beast, albeit with a cute name. But it's another good example of a British industrial initiative going against the grain and succeeding.

Raspberry Pi was conceived at Cambridge University in 2006 by a young and frustrated academic called Eben Upton and some friends. They designed it on a hunch in response to a problem that was beginning to perplex the university's Computer Science Department. University departments, if they are ambitious, depend upon a high proportion of applicants for every student accepted. Academics like to be able to choose the best, which means having a real choice. Back at the time of the dot-com boom in the very late twentieth century to around 2001, when hundreds of thousands thought of computing and saw pound signs appearing in front of their eyes, Cambridge had no problem with computer science. Some 600 people were applying every year for only around 100 places. Eben Upton was of that first generation – young people who had got their first BBC Micro (launched in 1981) or something similar – early computers which more or less forced their users to start to play around and learn programming.

But when he became director of studies at St John's College, Cambridge, in 2004–5, Upton began to notice something worrying. The number of applicants for computer science was dropping sharply, falling to barely 300 a year. This halving of enthusiasm for computer science was potentially very serious for the university. Not enough bright people were coming through. Why?

Upton speculated that it was because computers had become too sophisticated. Later cohorts of young computer games enthusiasts were buying sealed, powerful machines that could not be, and did not need to be, programmed by amateurs – the kind of people the young Sinclair had appealed to. Just as the development of highly computerized and plastic-sealed engines in cars made it far harder for their owners to play around in the engines in their garages at weekends, so the new computers, box-fresh and self-starting, were actually putting off kids who might otherwise have become programmers.

If this was true, what Cambridge needed was a new kind of computer – very cheap, very basic but also very easy to program. Something, in short, that would attract the curiosity of teenagers and lead to an uptick in people applying to read computer science. Upton found many of his friends agreed. Nearly half a century later, their commitment to programming was as enthusiastic and, in its way, as idealistic as the first generation of young computer pioneers at Manchester University in the 1950s. After working with the US chipmaker Broadcom, by 2011 Upton was beginning to put together the tiny, no-frills computer he would call Raspberry Pi. (It has become a mildly bizarre tradition to name computers after fruit.)

When the new computer was at last rolled out on 29 February 2012, the number of order requests vastly outnumbered the tiny company's ability to produce them. The first computers had been built in Shenzhen in China, arriving in cardboard boxes at Upton's garage, after he had mortgaged his house, spent half the proceeds on computer chips and sent them to a friend's flat in Hong Kong with a desperate request to pass them on to the right Chinese factory. Even so, when they came back, he was relieved to find that the new computers actually worked; modern globalization is an extraordinarily effective system.

A few months later, Upton discovered that Sony in South Wales, with a sophisticated engineering manufacturing operation of its own, was prepared to work as a subcontractor to assemble the new British computer nearer to its Cambridge home. Labour costs in the industrialized West – even in Wales – are a lot higher than in China. But, for Upton, being able to deal with people who spoke English fluently and were manufacturing only four hours' drive from his own house was a major attraction.

Today, all of the Raspberry Pi family of computers is entirely manufactured in Britain, with Japanese technology and Welsh workers. By the summer of 2017, some 15 million computers had been sold. The company had realized that its original ambition – to boost the number of computer science graduates at Cambridge University – was pitifully unambitious. The Raspberry Pi is now selling around the world and is used in a vast range of other hi-tech projects, including robotics, as well as introducing children and teenagers to the joys of computer programming.

So, at one level, this is a great modern British success story, as significant in its way as the Dyson operation across the English border to its east. But we have to remember that, having found a genuine and substantial market niche, and with the technical ability to produce the computers, this team still needed Japanese manufacturing expertise and the financial support of larger partner companies to prosper. Their components are manufactured, like so much these days, in the Far East. To compensate for higher British labour costs, which are not wiped out by the lower transport costs, the company has had to invest substantially in higher levels of technology.

Yet, despite all this, it has added substantial value, found a way of employing British workers and is educating the next generation of computer programmers around the world. If James Dyson is the spiritual son of Frank Whittle and Christopher Cockerell, then Eben Upton and his team are surely the spiritual children of the original Manchester and Ferranti computer pioneers of the 1950s. Manufacturing can be brought back 'onshore' to Britain, but these days it requires global partnerships, high levels of manufacturing investment, particularly in robotics . . . and a certain amount of inspiration.

60

A NETWORKED NATION?

For Justine Roberts, the last year of the twentieth century did not feature the greatest family holiday of all time. With her husband, the then newspaper executive Ian Katz, and their one-year-old twins, they had chosen a heavily advertised 'family friendly' resort in Florida. It was, she says, a terrible decision: 'the wrong destination, the wrong time zone, the wrong resort'. The children were up all night, and the resort was a deep disappointment. Roberts ended up more exhausted and stressed, as well as quite a bit poorer, than before she had started. More to the point, all the other British families who had made the flight over seemed to feel the same way. If *only* they had known about this particular resort in advance. But, of course, there was no way of sharing that kind of information with strangers.

Except, of course, there was. These were the early years of the internet. Roberts, who had worked for an investment bank as an economist, stock-market trader and company adviser before giving it all up when she became pregnant to be a freelance cricket and football reporter for *The Times* and *Daily Telegraph* newspapers, realized that this new technology would allow strangers sharing the same experiences to talk together. Since parenting was the most important job she could imagine, and her children hadn't arrived with an instruction handbook, Justine Roberts decided that 'a place about parents' stuff was the most important thing' she could create. By 2018 her company, Mumsnet, was attracting 12.5 million monthly users and was in the top ten of all social network sites in the UK – and extremely unusual in being British-created.

1999 was a big year for the internet in Britain. A poll for the *Guardian* newspaper found that almost half of the adult population (21 million people) expected to be online by the end of the following year. Growth of free internet services was expanding fast and broadband-game stars, such as Lara Croft, were becoming household names. But most internet access was slow, using telephone dial-ups, and it wasn't until the following year, in March 2000, that Gillingham, Kent, became the first town in Britain to get (some) broadband home access. So when Justine Roberts suffered the disappointments of her holiday, the innovative and invasive possibilities of this world-changing technology had not yet been properly imagined.

An era in which almost every child and adolescent would be swapping pictures and comparing the details of their lives, and in which much political argument would take place on mobile phone apps, was still in the future. Writing in *The Times* in September 2000, the commentator Simon Jenkins predicted that the internet would be a flash in the pan: 'I recall someone saying, 10 years ago, that the only groups to make money from the internet would be pornographers and lawyers. He was right.' Others thought it inevitable that democratizing the new media would be bad for the country generally.

John Birt, then Director General of the BBC, said in June 1999, 'Our culture may be degraded by the instant availability in new media of the raucous, the vulgar and the sensationalist.' Some were more sanguine. One observer in that year felt that the internet:

is likely to flatten old hierarchies, link groups of people who could never speak before, and may make many of the basic weapons of the nation-state, such as censorship, reliable taxation of consumers and the restriction of visual information, almost impossible to maintain . . . Commodities of all kinds, from music and film, to tickets, drugs rationed by the state, property and investment, can be bought and sold electronically, in some cases easily bypassing national value-added or purchase tax regimes.

But, above all, at the turn of the millennium, the internet seemed a very boys-and-men space, in which pallid nerds played fantasy games about swords and dragons, and political campaigning was macho and idealistic, led by anti-state, self-described 'cyber-gypsies'. Justine Roberts felt that 'it was just very male, it was niche, for games, played by men'. When she tried to raise money for her new idea, the young male venture capitalists could not get their heads around the idea of a woman running a start-up company. One twenty-three-year-old man said he thought that Mumsnet was a good idea, but not run by her: he would run it himself. Which was a little odd, when you think about it: he was many things, but he was not a mum.

In conventional politics, Mumsnet quickly convinced the parties that it mattered. It had corralled large numbers of politically fluid female voters. That persuaded party leaders to take part in the streamed web-chat conversations with users of the service. As Prime Minister, Gordon Brown faced the mums; so, after him, did David Cameron; and the Mumsnet gig became a staple of the electoral circuit, during which mostly male politicians were bombarded by questions on child care, schooling and equal pay. The apparently innocent 'biscuit question' – politicians were asked about their favourite biscuit – proved surprisingly effective: Brown's refusal to answer was seen as a classic example of his indecisiveness, while Jeremy Corbyn's diatribe against the sugar industry seemed unappealingly ideological. All this may be simple political fun; but in modern Britain, there are not many forums dominated by female voters, and Mumsnet made a difference to the campaigns.

For the macho nature of the internet has evolved, but it hasn't fundamentally changed. Whether they use male or female disguises, the aggressive trolls on Twitter and Facebook sound suspiciously like jeering adolescent boys. For every prominent feminist blogger, such as Laurie Penny or Caroline Criado Perez, there seem to be hundreds of angry men bombarding them with rape and death threats. During a controversy inside the Labour Party about anti-Semitism, prominent Jewish female MPs received vile abuse from people who consider themselves progressive left-wingers.

Elsewhere on the political spectrum, the Channel 4 News presenter Cathy Newman got a flurry of verbal vomit directed at her after interviewing Jordan Peterson, the Canadian psychologist adored by many on the American right. In a later interview with the *Guardian*, she said:

> The internet is being written by men with an agenda. Look at a woman's Wikipedia page and you can't believe a word of it . . . I wasn't prepared for the torrent of abuse after [the interview]. People say: 'Why don't you just block them?' But there were literally thousands of abusive tweets – it was a semi-organised campaign. It ranged from the usual 'cunt, bitch, dumb blonde' to 'I'm going to find out where you live and execute you.'

It is fairly obvious that the anonymity of social media sites, perhaps Twitter in particular, has uncaged a bitter, envious and angry part of the modern psyche which, no doubt, has always existed, but previously in private. Today's heavy and serial users of social media are exposed to a human world that is, frankly, nastier than the three-dimensional world of the streets, the shopping centres and the coffee shops. And this is in part a gender agenda. Today, one of the biggest advantages of Mumsnet is that it is at least slightly more civilized than most other forums.

Its most aggressive problem has been the ongoing battle between transgender-rights activists and feminists, particularly lesbian feminists, who assert that people born biologically male cannot self-describe as female. It is a struggle about identity at the deepest level, which returns us to the very first story that began this book. But Jan Morris was, it should be said, a rather more sophisticated user of prose than most of those fighting Terfs and other dragons. On social media, the loudest and crudest voices are heard most clearly and they tend to be male voices. Mumsnet has a majority of women in charge – three of the five-strong management team. Roberts says: 'Our users really value space dominated by women – it allows them to speak honestly about things they would not discuss elsewhere.' So perhaps the real achievement of Mumsnet is to be measured not by market share or unique users, but by its subtle reshaping of online rhetoric generally.

61

POSH AND HIM

In these tales of Elizabethans, I am very aware that the name itself may cause many readers to flinch. History inclines us all to be sentimentally nostalgic, and to assume that we here today must by definition be lesser people than our forebears. The original Elizabethans were swashbuckling, profound, pious, courageous and properly patriotic. We, whatever we call ourselves, are by comparison trivial, self-indulgent and simply lesser people than they were. Compared to their grandees, with their ropes of pearls, their coloured hosiery, capes and ruffs, we are an inelegant crowd of shabby scruffs.

Yet that last thought, even though it rhymes, is clearly wrong. Modern Elizabethans may be less warlike and less religious, but they can be just as stylish and glamorous as Queen Bess's finest courtiers. And one upwardly mobile couple, who prove the point, are a fitting place to end the story.

And this is because the true tale of Posh and Becks isn't about flashy glamour, style or mere good luck: it's a morality story about hard work. Victoria Beckham was the daughter of an electric components wholesaler, Tony Adams, who had been born into poverty, picking up fag-ends in pubs so that his father could smoke and never seeing a toy in his childhood. One of Victoria's earliest memories was of the whole family sitting around on the floor of the house assembling packages of electrical fittings to be sent out by her father: 'We were the Von Trapps of the light fittings and electrical components world. We did this for years.'

She seems to have got a lot of her drive from him:

> Like me, Dad is a complete workaholic. He never stops; if he's not in the office, he's out delivering. If he's not out delivering, he is in the garden in his wellingtons getting weeds out of the pond, or taking flies off the swimming pool, or mending locks, or a squeaky door . . . My dad had a difficult childhood and he was determined to do better for himself . . .

Victoria was born and brought up on the border between Hertfordshire and Essex, north of London, in a striving, respectable, better-yourself atmosphere of the kind Margaret Thatcher hoped for everywhere across Britain. Ferociously ambitious and single-minded from a young age, it was exposure to the American film and stage show *Fame* that persuaded her she wanted to be a dancer and/or singer herself. She went for it, just like hundreds of thousands of other little girls of her age, except that she worked harder than most. But she also got an early lesson in British snobbery, and the many pitfalls of style all around her.

As his business began to succeed, her father Tony bought himself a second-hand, brownish Rolls-Royce Silver Shadow, which quickly led to the family being mocked and abused. In her autobiography, she wrote:

> I hated that Rolls-Royce right from the word go. The people around us might be quite wealthy compared to other parts of the country, but that didn't mean they had Rolls-Royces. We had the mickey taken out of us so much. Me and my brother and

436

sister used to beg my dad to please take us in the van but it was like talking to a fridge . . .

David Beckham came from a not dissimilar background, a working-class North London family. His father was a kitchen fitter, and Victoria's passion for dancing and the stage was more than matched by David's for football. Like her, he came from a close and supportive family which believed in hard work and helped push him up through the endless rungs of youth football training camps and teams until he finally landed a signing with his parents' favourite, Manchester United. Although the family had some Jewish blood, David attended church every week, and with two sisters was inculcated early on into girl power.

In the Britain of the 1980s, Victoria's and David's ambition and talent would quickly pull them away from any real sense of being working class. David left his local school for extra training in Manchester, in Barcelona and in London with Tottenham Hotspur. Victoria was sent to a non-academic local secondary school where many of the children came from much poorer homes: she was bullied, never fitted in and became a self-reliant loner. Later, when both were globally famous and being pursued by a jeering media, their unease about a jealous and endlessly inquisitive proletarian Britain was obvious – and natural.

The Spice Girls phenomenon was not the cynical production of PR men and producer-Svengalis it was sometimes mocked as at the time. The girls came together in response to an advert, true; and they were auditioned by men who wanted to produce them. But, like Diana Dors, they had been grafting, struggling for opportunities and banging on doors for a long time before opportunity knocked. Victoria promoted perfumes in shops, handed out leaflets in open-air markets and went around newsagents checking on adverts for *Daily Mirror* promotions, while she wrote hundreds of letters to agencies.

When the band were brought together, almost their first act was to ditch the greedy and controlling producers who had auditioned them; and later, at the height of their global fame as the Spice Girls, they famously sacked their manager, Simon Fuller. Before the money-making machine roared upwards, there had been a period of insanely hard work and high risk. And if 'girl power' means anything, it is this. Before their fame came, the Spice Girls worked long, long hours developing songs and dance routines in dingy studios and grubby hired houses. The image might have been glamorous and fluffy, but, as Diana Dors could have told them half a century before, the way to the top smelt only of sweat.

Meanwhile, although David Beckham was a young footballer of eerie natural ability, he too was famous as a grafter. Alex Ferguson, Manchester United's great manager, who brought on the young Beckham as part of his nest of 'Fergie's Fledglings' and who would go on to have arguments with him about the bad effect of celebrity and his union with Victoria, nevertheless acknowledged: 'He was never a problem until he got married. He used to go into work with the academy coaches at night time, he was a fantastic young lad. Getting married into that entertainment scene was a difficult thing – from that moment, his life was never going to be the same. He is such a big celebrity, football is only a small part.'

The hostility 'Posh and Becks' faced by the end of the twentieth century was the possessiveness of fans who didn't want to share – the soccer fans who felt that the golden boy Beckham had gone off and was somehow being sucked dry by his unsmiling wife; and the Spice Girls' fans who felt that Victoria's pregnancy, marriage and family life were not the kick-ass, Team Girl fantasy they'd hoped for. John Lennon and Yoko Ono would sympathize.

But this is also a story about class. Early on, Posh and Becks were roundly mocked for their Norah Docker-ish lack of true style – their addiction to designer labels, foppish fashions, vastly expensive sports cars, golden thrones at their wedding in an Irish castle and the extravagance of their country house, 'Beckingham Palace', which came complete with its own ruins, private chapel, maze, barbecue area, professionally tended football pitch, recording studio, indoor swimming pool, snooker room and gym. Upper- and upper-middle-class Britain could sneer at them for designer sunglasses being worn inside, for the sarong and for the proliferating tattoos. Furious fans could abuse them for accelerating off into the never-never-land of the super-rich. There was something for everyone.

There is, and probably always has been, a strange club of very wealthy celebrities, brought together by their shared hatred of the popular press and its intrusive lenses, by their equally strongly felt distaste for the British taxman and by the proximity of their refuges – the Côte d'Azur villas, the discreet Mayfair clubs, the private Caribbean islands. But the Beckhams evolved away from such regrettable vulgarities. Family first: in many ways they have been a traditionalist couple, lavishing as much attention on their children as on their global brands, as they move smoothly up the still-existing class hierarchy. David Beckham can be seen sporting tweeds, a gun dog at his knee, and giving every sign of enjoying country pursuits. Victoria, now running her own fashion label, can be seen steering Arab mares round paddocks, as well as BMWs round the Home Counties.

Any red carpet is under-dressed without them. They mingle with the royal family and were among the small number of the instantly recognizable guests when Prince Harry married Meghan Markle at Windsor Castle in spring 2018. 'Posh' might once have been a sarcastic insult thrown at the girl from the borders of Essex. It's now a frank and fair monicker, and shows that we cannot exactly say class obsessions have died during the reign of Queen Elizabeth II. If, some four centuries in the future, a second Elizabethan age is remembered in some later version of the National Portrait Gallery, it is easy to imagine Posh and Becks as exquisite, enamelled portraits like the pearl-lassoed, ruffed, coiffed courtiers of the original Elizabeth.

62

BEYOND THE MARKET

There has been something wistful in the story of this book. It tells of the changing attitudes of the British, during a reign in which their country lost its swollen status in the world and struggled to come to terms with dramatic social change. Had Britain been much more economically successful, then all that would have been easier to deal with. The social changes, the economics and the international politics are intimately related. Had Britain not claimed vast international territories as an imperial power, then she would not have seen anything like the scale of immigration which, in itself, changed the notion of the British about who they were. Had the authority and status of the British ruling classes not been so badly shaken by imperial withdrawal and economic failure, then the rebellions against the old order might not have been so determined and successful.

But we can turn all of this round and look at it from the other side. During the mid-1950s, much British opinion seems to have been myopic. We patted ourselves on the back, endlessly, for winning a war which had in fact mostly been won by Russian communist conscripts on the one side and the awesome industrial machine of the United States on the other. British children were brought up to be proud of the British Empire and discouraged from studying the slavery, the famines in India, the horrendous human cost of Partition or the arrogance of British administrators and soldiers in the Near East and large parts of Africa. Like many, I was brought up to look the other way. We lived more easily by sugar-coating our past. This could never have been sustained, any more than the old Royal Navy could have sustained the power of its battleships and cruisers in the age of the atom bomb. There was always going to be a reckoning. We may not be happier. But at least, perhaps, we are a little more honest.

Having lost our industrial lead long since, it also turned out that we had lost much of our ruthless social organization and our readiness to work incredibly hard in bad conditions to win overseas markets. Other nations, more devastated or humiliated by defeat, were hungrier and harder. They took what we had come to think of as our rightful lunch.

During the Queen's reign, while her consort spotted very clearly what was going on, British decline was hidden by British success in cultural and creative areas, and by British ingenuity in computing and engineering. These are things we can still celebrate, without guilt or embarrassment. The Sinclair home computers, the songs of Dusty Springfield and Dyson cyclonic technology are as much part of our story as the collapse of shipbuilding on the Clyde or mutual recrimination after the vote to leave the European Union.

In terms of the big social and economic picture, there are only two obvious roads ahead for modern Britain. Brexit makes logical sense if we use it to take a rougher, chillier economic path – if we cut taxes and welfare, reduce environmental and labour regulations and, in short, try to behave much more like some of our Asian competitors. What is the point of leaving the EU if we then behave as if we hadn't?

But it is likely that, if Britain pursues a deregulated and tax-cutting agenda, the UK will break apart. Scots feel very differently about the EU and so do many in Northern Ireland. The English may end up going it alone. I don't think I am making an overly political point if I say that I hope the Queen does not live to see that. The alternative road ahead is to try to maintain the broadly social-democratic society and economy that we have followed for the forty-five years of our EU membership. This could be done alongside the EU, inside its economic orbit but without taking part in its political decision making – although to many this seems to be giving up control, or at least a voice, in return for very little.

Many will argue that we can begin to diverge from an economically slow-growth bloc without losing our underlying values. Let's hope so. But let us reflect on those values as well. In earlier parts of this book I have made much of the underrated influence of the Church and Christian values. Even as we evolve as one of the most secular societies on earth, these values underpin much of our common notions of fairness, decency and mutual respect. *Why* should those of us in work care about those on the breadline? *Why* should any of us in relatively safe and well-ordered Britain concern ourselves with the plight of refugees? The market, our dominant economic order, has no answer to these questions and no way of even beginning to think about them.

That is a problem because we have become an increasingly market-saturated society. Relentless consumers, we are schooled to see most of our human exchanges in terms of price and profit. We measure success by wealth. We confuse happiness with cool stuff. Of course, this is a caricature and an unfair one. Most of us gain nourishment from warm families, glimpses of the numinous and conscience-driven living which requires that we think about what we consume, its environmental cost and our duties to our neighbours.

When Britain was obliged to lock down and retire to behind front doors during the coronavirus outbreak of 2020, there was a distinctive upsurge of community feeling and empathy. People looked out for and shopped for their more vulnerable or elderly neighbours. They stood to applaud the NHS on their doorsteps. Some remarkable individuals, from the ninety-nine-year-old Captain Tom Moore to a boy with spina bifida, undertook extraordinary exertions to raise money. Despite the economic horrors ahead, many Elizabethans felt proud of themselves in a new way. Was this a premonition of a better future? Wasn't it, candidly, how things were always supposed to be?

63

A FUTURE

On 25 May 2020, in Minneapolis, Minnesota, a forty-six-year-old black man called George Floyd was arrested and handcuffed by American police for using a fake banknote. As he was held on the ground, his neck was knelt on by one of the officers, while for nearly nine minutes he complained that he could not breathe and begged the officer, Derek Chauvin, for his life. But Chauvin's knee did not move and Floyd died beneath it. The episode, which was filmed, ignited protests across the US. Under the banner 'Black Lives Matter' the demonstrations spread around the world, including to Britain.

On 6 June, 15,000 protesters gathered in Parliament Square in London. There were confrontations with the police. The statue of Churchill outside the Commons was attacked and later daubed with 'was a racist'.

On the following day, in Bristol, the statue of a seventeenth-century slave trader, Edward Colston, who had given much money to the town, was hauled down by protesters. To cheers, he was rolled along the streets and thrown into the river. Other statues were then attacked. Scotland's medieval hero monarch, Robert the Bruce, was attacked for racism – somewhat prevalent in the 1300s.

Oxford students reignited the campaign to tear down the statue of the South African imperialist Cecil Rhodes.

Colleges, schools and other institutions promised to change the names they had been given in honour of racist Britons. The statues of Lord Baden-Powell, founder of the Scouting movement, in Poole, and in Whitby of Captain Cook the explorer were given round-the-clock protection by their admirers. This was not a UK phenomenon only. Across much of the world, images of colonists, imperialists and racist leaders were being toppled. But it was clear that Elizabethan Britain was being obliged once more to confront her history.

Throughout the reign, the British had tended to gloss over the extent to which the nation's historic wealth had been built on the Atlantic slave trade. Children had been taught more about William Wilberforce's virtuous and ground-breaking campaign to abolish slavery, and the Royal Navy's role in eradicating the trade, than about how the wealth it produced had reshaped the country. The profits of slavery built many grand country houses and the centres of great cities such as Bristol and Glasgow, and founded many schools, hospitals and other institutions. Now that Britain has become a multiracial society, it has become frankly impossible to ignore this.

At first, the argument seemed inevitably bitter and divisive, perhaps irreconcilably so. For the majority of British people, Churchill, to take an obvious example, remains a hero. Without his decisive intervention in 1940 there is little doubt that this country would have sued for peace with Nazi Germany. Hitler would have had the whole of Europe, and later the British Commonwealth, to do with as he pleased. As one online commentator put it, referring to the 'racist' graffito on Churchill's statue, 'Just wait until they find out about the other guy.'

How do you balance that historic achievement against Churchill's determination to keep control of the Indian Raj, or his attitude to the famine in Bengal? Statues, by their nature, are rarely nuanced. To compound the ironies, a later protest by right-wing football supporters saw Churchill's image and the nearby Cenotaph war memorial being 'protected' by men wearing German coal-scuttle helmets and swastika tattoos.

But before we shudder at what must come, we should remember the actions of two black British men who in very different ways offered an alternative way ahead. During the right-wing protests in early June, Patrick Hutchinson, a personal trainer and grandfather, rescued one of the anti-Black Lives Matter protesters who had been involved in confrontations outside Victoria Station. Hutchinson lifted him on to his shoulders and carried him to safety. The picture was shared across Britain and Hutchinson was widely applauded as a British hero, including by the Prime Minister. He later said: 'You just do what you've got to do . . . I just want equality, equality for all of us. At the moment, the scales are unfairly balanced and I just want things to be fair for my children and my grandchildren.'

A younger man who also felt the scales were unfairly balanced, at around the same time, was Marcus Rashford, the Manchester United and England footballer. With millions of children unable to go to school during the coronavirus crisis, he had himself already raised around £20 million to supply 3 million meals to vulnerable people. Now, in early June 2020, Rashford wrote an emotional open letter to Britain's MPs, calling on them to reverse a decision not to provide free school-meal vouchers during the summer.

The twenty-two-year-old striker explained: 'My mum worked full-time, earning minimum wage, to make sure we always had a good evening meal on the table, but it was not enough. The system was not built for families like mine to succeed, regardless of how hard my mum worked.' Altering the decision he said was 'not about politics but about humanity'. Although the Prime Minister Boris Johnson initially rejected his plea, many Tory MPs disagreed and sided with Rashford. Within hours, the Prime Minister capitulated.

His U-turn meant that 1.3 million children who were eligible for free meals during term time would get them for the whole summer holidays of 2020, in the form of vouchers which can be spent in supermarkets. Rashford responded by tweeting: 'I don't even know what to say. Just look at what we can do when we come together. *This* is England in 2020.'

These two men, Hutchinson and Rashford, teach us that as this story ends we have no reliable way of guessing where the next important British attitude-changers are going to come from. They show us that the instinct for human solidarity is at least as strong as the rancid debates across both the traditional and the new media. Rashford reminds us too that fundamentally old-fashioned political choices about wealth, nutrition and fairness are likely to be more important to the next generation of British people than cultural debates about statues and history.

All of that said, there are hard choices which cannot be dodged. It is frankly impossible for post-Brexit Britain to be a genuine global force if it does not confront, think about and try to redeem some of the darker phases of its history. We can tightly hug a comforting, partial story of who we are and turn our backs on a changed and challenging world. Or we can look rather more toughly and harder at ourselves and re-emerge, a little battered, but more confident and clear-eyed. Perhaps it's no longer a choice. As the Floyd and Hutchinson episodes showed, we live in a world where almost everything can be instantly shared – images and films which punch through gently accumulated, long-woven philosophies.

As I have argued throughout this book, we tend to overestimate the influence on our lives of the EU and underestimate the influence of America. The 'culture wars' have been imported, but not from Brussels or Paris, rather from New York and Los Angeles. If there is one lesson from the troubled spring of 2020 as Britain staggered out of the coronavirus lockdown, it is that hearts and minds change not because of large and aggressive public protests, but through listening intently, watching carefully and – but I would say this – by reading.

And listening, watching and reading will also enable us to make the most of our history as we look to the future. If a society comes to judge success by personal wealth, how can it deal with the large majority who will feel forever bruised and excluded? If we judge our happiness by what we consume – holidays, consumer goods, large houses – how can we deal with the inevitable and necessary constraints of a planet groaning under too many people who want to live a 'good' middle-class life? Isn't everything by that definition simply going to get worse?

Here, I believe, is where we can learn from our past selves – from that more consciously moral, frugal, hard-working and optimistic Britain that is also part of our common history. Yes, it was in many ways bigoted and rigidly hierarchical; but we know better now. The royal family itself has learned harsh lessons as attitudes have shifted: Prince Andrew, the Duke of York, saw his public reputation shredded because of his relationship with Jeffrey Epstein, the American billion-aire sex-trafficker. Our attitudes to powerful men exploiting vulnerable young women have changed dramatically, and much for the better. Meanwhile Harry and Meghan made it clear they no longer wanted to be part of the royal circle and to create new lives for themselves abroad. American observers and supporters of Meghan felt that she was the victim of racism and snobbery, with the implication that snooty old Britannia hadn't changed her spots. I think that this is a harsh and mistaken judgement about modern Britain, but it demonstrates that many of the themes discussed in this book remain as potent as ever.

History requires that we learn lessons, not that we submerge ourselves in reverie. Today, we have to learn to work harder, while being more generous in our global outlook, kinder to neighbours who look and sound different to ourselves, and more restrained in our personal tastes. Does that sound impossibly pious? Or simply impossible? Then we should remember the struggles and achievements of our grandparents and parents. They were there first. They can teach us still. A decent future means taking the best of the past, ditching the mistakes and starting again.

Acknowledgements

A book like this is a long and laborious process and I'd first like to thank my wife Jackie Ashley and my children, Harry, Isabel and Emily for putting up with my distracted air and long hours during it. I would like to thank my friend and loyal agent Mary Greenham; my editor Arabella Pike at HarperCollins and the superbly professional team there, not least the brilliant copy editor Peter James, but also Jo Thompson and Marigold Atkey, and to Jo Thomson for the jacket design. They pumiced, burnished, polished and oiled my creaking text, pulling out some terrible mistakes cleverly inserted by the dictation system I now have to use.

In writing books, I tend to do my own research. But this emerged from a television project at the BBC, inevitably a collaborative process, where I benefited enormously from the hard work and insight of my director Alex Leith and his team, Jonathan Parker, Nick Tanner, Kathryn Ellinger and Alec Webb. Needless to say neither they nor anyone else except for the author should be held responsible for any mistakes in the text or opinions that the reader may dislike.

Plate Section Image Credits

Queen Elizabeth II on her coronation (Hulton Deutsch/Getty)
Queen Elizabeth and Prince Philip on the balcony (Keystone/Getty)
The streets of London on coronation day (Mirrorpix/Getty)
Edmund Hillary and Tenzing Norday (Royal Geographic Society/
  Getty)
Jan Morris (Fairfax Media Archives/Getty)
Shirley Williams (Central Press/Getty)
U and Non-U
Helen John (Lynn Hilton/Mail on Sunday/Shutterstock)
Diana Dors (Interfoto/Alamy)
Ruth Ellis (Hulton Archive/Getty)
Quentin Crisp (United News/Popperfoto/Getty)
Frank Critchlow and owners of the Mangrove restaurant (Keystone/
  Getty)
The Mangrove restaurant (Evening Standard/Getty)
Dan Dare comic (Universal History Archive/Getty)
Lara Croft (Simon Robinson/Easy on the Eye/Alamy)
Enoch Powell (Wesley/Getty)
Tony Benn (Evening Standard/Getty)
Monty Python actors (Hulton Archive/Getty)
Mary Whitehouse (Central Press/Getty)
Tony Crosland (Associated Newspapers/Shutterstock)
Roy Jenkins (PA Archive/PA Images)
Plath and Hughes (Everett Collection Inc/Alamy)
Dusty Springfield (Popperfoto/Getty)

Tracy Emin and her bed (Sean Dempsey/EPA/Shutterstock)

Lord Mountbatten (Fox Photos/Getty)

A. K. Chesterton (Mirrorpix/Getty)

The Aden Emergency (Tony Prime/Associated Newspapers/ Shutterstock)

Clive Sinclair (Dick Barnatt/Getty)

The Comet (Central Press/Getty)

Gerald Durrell (Loomis Dean/Getty)

David Attenborough (Mirrorpix/Getty)

Anita Roddick (Larry Ellis/Getty)

John Lennon and Yoko Ono with Paul McCartney (Hulton Deutsch/ Getty)

Bob Geldof and Live Aid (Georges De Keerle/Getty)

Jayaben Desai (Keystone Press/Alamy)

Grunwick protests (M.Fresco/Getty)

Elizabeth David (Picture Kitchen/Alamy)

Elizabeth David's book *French Country Cooking* (Neil Setchfield – Vintage/Alamy)

David Lammy launching Khadija Saye's photography (Charlie J Ercilla/Alamy)

James Dyson (Geoff Wilkinson/Shutterstock)

Zaha Hadid (Jeff J Mitchell/Getty)

Ridley Scott (Stanley Bielecki Movie Collection/Getty)

Patrick Hutchinson and the Black Lives Matter London protests (Luke Dray/Getty)

Clapping for Carers (John Keeble/Getty)

Captain Thomas Moore (Justin Tallis/Getty)

Jacket Image Credits

Index

INDEX

West Hartlepool College of Art 397
West Indies 24–5, 221, 222, 223, 245, 246
The West Wing (TV series) 34
Westminster, Hugh, 2nd Duke of 126
Wevill, Assia 143, 145
Whitaker's Almanack 51, 52–3
White Bears, Calvi 273
Whitehouse, Mary 108, 111–20, 121, 122, 147
Whitlam, Gough 177
Whittle, Sir Frank 349, 424, 429
The Who 204
Wigmore, Andy 174
Wikipedia 433
Wilberforce, William 445
Wildfowl and Wetlands Trust 386, 387
Wilkinson, Ellen 96–7
William, Prince 206
Williams, Freddie 333–4
Williams, Shirley 22, 29–31
Willmott, Peter 50
Wilson, Harold 17, 67, 92, 96, 114, 134
  bans pirate radio 148
  and the Beatles 166
  educational reform 106
  and former colonies 220
  and newspapers 151
  plots against 187, 191
  religion 21
  and shipbuilding 369, 370
Wimpy Bars 267
Windrush scandal 311, 314–15
Windscale 335–6
Wise, Damon 73–4
Wolsey 331
Wolverhampton 245
Woman's Hour 111
women xviii
  abortion 47, 108
  artists 155–60
  and computer gaming 168–70
  contraception 45–6, 47, 49, 108
  Greenham Common protest 208–10

Grunwick strike 234–40
Mumsnet 431, 432–3, 434
single mothers 45–9
working class 68–78
Women for Life on Earth 207
Wooldridge, Adrian 32
Woolworths 416
working class
  in the 1950s 16, 342
  in the 1970s 353
  changes in family life 49–50
  education 99, 103
  elocution lessons 56–7
  Labour Party and 96
  Profumo affair 82–3
  trade unions 354–5
  upper-class attraction to 166
  women 68–78
World Conservation Strategy 386
World Health Organization 176
World Trade Organization 425
World Wildlife Fund 378, 386
Worsley, T. C. 99

Yarrow, Alfred 366–7
Yarrow Shipbuilders 366–7, 369
Yates, Paula 201–3, 205
Yentob, Alan 421
Yield to the Night (film) 74
Young, Hugo 32
Young, Michelle 50
Young British Artists (YBAs) 158
youth culture 163–7
Yugoslavia 200, 219

Zanzibar 230, 231
Ziegler, Philip 290, 291
Zilkha, Selim 421
Zimbabwe 249, 283
zoos 379, 381–5
Zoroastrianism 230, 231
Zurich University 285
Zweig, Ferdynand, *The Worker in an Affluent Society* 50

483